EARLY TRADE UNIONISM

Malcolm Chase

Early Trade Unionism
Fraternity, Skill and the Politics of Labour

BREVIARY STUFF PUBLICATIONS
2012

Published by Breviary Stuff Publications,
BCM Breviary Stuff, London WC1N 3XX
www.breviarystuff.org.uk
First published in 2000 by Ashgate Publishing Limited
First paperback edition
Copyright © Malcolm Chase, 2000, 2012
This new edition copyright © Breviary Stuff Publications, 2012
The centipede device copyright © Breviary Stuff Publications
All rights reserved

A CIP record for this book is available from
The British Library

ISBN: 978-0-9570005-1-3

Contents

Abbreviations	*vi*
Introduction	*vii*
1 Covins and Fraternities: A 'Prehistory' of Trade Unionism	1
2 Trade Associations in the Age of Manufactures	23
3 'No Strangers to the *Rights of Man*'?	55
4 'A Young and Rising Commonwealth'	83
5 Across the Frontier of Skill: General Unionism	109
6 Trade Unionism and the Early Chartist Movement	143
7 Out of Chartism	167
8 Conclusion: Trade Unions in the Early 1860s	187
Bibliography	203
Index	225

Abbreviations

ASE	Amalgamated Society of Engineers
BL Add. Mss	British Library Additional Manuscripts
BSSLH	*Bulletin of the Society for the Study of Labour History*
DLB	*Dictionary of Labour Biography*, eds J. Bellamy and J. Saville
GNCTU	Grand National Consolidated Trades' Union
HO	Public Record Office, Home Office Papers
LHR	*Labour History Review*
LWMA	London Working Men's Association
MAGBI	Miners' Association of Great Britain and Ireland
NAOT	National Association of Organized Trades
NAPL	National Association for the Protection of Labour
NAPSS	National Association for the Promotion of Social Science
NAUT	National Association of United Trades
NCA	National Charter Association
NUWC	National Union of the Working Classes
PP	*Parliamentary Papers*

Introduction

In its 1861 edition, the *British Almanac* commented with some exasperation on the character of 'trade societies': 'they are organized for objects other than the merely provident; and at times they make their existence known in a very threatening way'. Many operated a sick or burial fund and therefore sought registration under the 1855 Friendly Societies Act by sending their rules to the government officer responsible for certification: 'but in most cases this is impossible. Some of the rules are very extraordinary ... and may be stretched very widely in the direction of tyranny'. Several examples were given. The rules of 'a Ribbon Weavers' Society at Macclesfield' prescribed that when an 'outsider' enters a shop,

> he shall be solicited to enter the society. Immediately after such request by the shop's committee, if such person shall refuse to comply, such committee shall forthwith inform the officers of the trade, who shall wait upon such person in order to induce him to comply with the wishes of the society; and in the event of him refusing to comply, the officers shall submit the case to the next delegate meeting of the society, whose decision shall be final.

The *Almanac* added: 'this decision usually is that the poor fellow shall be worried until he either enters the society or leaves the town'. 'This society will not recognize', declared the Millstone Builders of Southwark, 'any person, not being a millstone builder ... employed by any master to build stone, or to use the hammer and pritchell for the purposes of facing the stone ... members *may strike against them*'. The Manchester and Salford brickmakers bound themselves not to accept work on anything but the traditional pattern of production, or from any master who had turned away a worker 'for reasons unsatisfactory to the society', and not to allow any woman to engage in brickmaking, 'in consequence of the same being an injury to any trade wherein women are employed to do men's work'. The account concluded by quoting the Registrar of Friendly Societies, sharing his incredulity at 'the unseen power' exerted by trade societies over their members.[1]

These remarks had been made in the wake of the 1859-60 lock-out of trade unionists in the London building trade, in which donations from other trade and friendly societies had been an important factor in resisting employers' hostility. There was, however, nothing new in the patterns of behaviour about which the article complained. The blurring of friendly and trade societies had been endemic to these popular associations since their inception and a matter of concern since the late eighteenth century in the minds of officialdom. The workplace was an opaque world to outside observers and the solidarity generated there frequently seemed incomprehensible or threatening. A place within it was not won without sacrifice and the loyalty even of new arrivals able and qualified to work there was often keenly tested. For skilled artisans especially the workplace was a masculine sphere and attitudes to women could veer sharply to misogyny if female participation in the trade concerned threatened to displace men.

This study explores when and why these attitudes evolved and looks in particular at how they came to be expressed in the formation of trade societies and trade unions. The distinction between the

---

1 *Companion to the Almanac; or, Year-Book of General Information for 1861*, London: Knight, 1860, 116-17. First published by the middle-class reformers of the Society for the Diffusion of Useful Knowledge in the 1820s, the *British Almanac* is a useful barometer of progressive middle-class opinion.

trade *society* and trade *union* is not straightforward. As in the *British Almanac* article just quoted, 'trade society' was the prevalent term even at the time this study terminates. The first parliamentary legislation to use the term 'trade union' did not appear until 1871. In the eighteenth century the use of 'union' in connection with associations of workers' was very infrequent. When Tiverton woolcombers used it in 1750 they did do so in a generalized sense, advising 'manufacturers in general' (by which they meant skilled workers) 'to enter into still stricter engagements of BROTHERLY LOVE and MUTUAL ASSISTANCE for it is their UNION alone that can preserve them'.[2] The word was occasionally used to denote the coming together of otherwise separate trade societies for the purpose of mutual assistance, such as the Woolstaplers' Society, described as a union by its Exeter adherents in 1784.[3] However, 'trade union' only achieved wide currency from the late 1820s when, as we shall see in Chapter 5, its use conveyed something rather more portentous than simply a federation.

For most of the period considered in this book even 'trade society' was apt to be eclipsed by the term 'combination'. As late as 1859 influential trade union circles used it in discussing recent legislation on the right to strike.[4] Yet combination itself was relatively recent in a succession of legal terms used to describe workers' associations, its main precursors being 'covin' and 'conspiracy' (see Chapter 1). The use of the latter term as a noun denoting workers' associations endured because their legal status was bound up with the common law of conspiracy. However, the combinations and conspiracies prosecuted under a variety of legislation in the eighteenth and nineteenth centuries were sometimes little other than momentary truculence. Combination was used interchangeably with 'strike', 'riot', and 'confederacy', and less damningly with 'club', 'association' or 'society'.

Though the terms 'trade union' and 'trade unionism' appear in the present study mainly in reference to the post-1815 period, they do not do so exclusively. This is because its concern is as much with the trade unionist *mentality* as it is with trade unions as institutions. The historical roots of that mentality, it will be argued, were very deep. 'Mentality' denotes more than simple ideas. The concept has been widely adopted by historians from social theory to denote collective attitudes which rest on largely unspoken assumptions rather than explicit theory, existing as '"common sense" or what appears to be common sense in a particular culture'.[5] This book is especially concerned with the collective 'common sense' of skilled workers about their place in the world and with striking continuities within it. In his recent study of 'labour, leisure and economic thought before the nineteenth century', John Hatcher concludes:

> During the half-millennium and more between the Middle Ages and the onset of industrialization the structure of economy and society underwent profound change, but the priorities of those who laboured and those who did not changed far less. The portfolio of ideas, attitudes and policies regarding wages, work, workers, subsistence, consumption, leisure and charity proved exceptionally durable, as did the behaviour of the labouring poor.[6]

---

2   Quoted in Robert Malcolmsom, 'Workers' combinations in eighteenth-century England', in Jacob and Jacob (eds.), *The Origins of Anglo-American Radicalism* (1984), p. 158.

3   John Rule, 'Labour consciousness and industrial conflict in eighteenth-century Exeter', in Barry Stapleton (ed.), *Conflict and Community in Southern England: Essays in the Social History of Rural and Urban Labour From Medieval to Modern Times* (1992), p. 100.

4   *Report of the Executive Committee of the National Association of United Trades on the Proceedings Connected with the Combination of Workmen Bill, 1859* (1859). The NAUT defined itself as a 'general confederation or union of trades' (and see below Chapter 7).

5   Peter Burke, *History and Social Theory* (1992), p. 92.

6   John Hatcher, 'Labour, leisure and economic thought before the nineteenth century', *Past and Present*, 160 (August, 1998), p. 66.

INTRODUCTION

Skilled workers, even in 1860, still shared much of the mentality of their predecessors a century and more before. Nor can the label of skill be confined to those trades in which a place was secured by formal apprenticeship. As will be argued particularly in Chapter 2, apprenticeship was a crucial issue in shaping the mentality of trade unionism; but the outlook of other occupations wherein status derived from length of service was not essentially different. Indeed, in one of these seniority sectors, flint glass making, trade unionism achieved tighter control than perhaps anywhere in Victorian industry.[7] Furthermore, in Victorian Britain personal status for the vast majority of the population derived from being a producer, in contrast to our own society where consumption is seemingly all. We should not therefore be surprised at the extent to which status and the demarcation of skill preoccupied organized labour. Indeed, this remained a central element of continuity in British trade unionism. 'Economists unenlightened by history', Henry Phelps Brown reminds us, 'have fallen into the trap of supposing that trade unionists conducted their bargaining as a way of maximizing their gains'.[8]

One of the themes explored in this book is the convergence and subsequent divergence of trade unionism and popular politics. It will be suggested in Chapter 6 that convergence was potentially powerful as long as radical politics focused to a significant extent on control of productive processes. Once this receded as a political objective the common ground between radicalism and labour organization fell away, leaving trade unions in their political life concerned primarily to consolidate and protect their own freedom of operation. This is as evident in the National Association of United Trades (1845-60) a Chartist body at its inception, as it is in the far-better known history of labour representation in the late nineteenth and early twentieth centuries. It must be stressed, though, that the central issue was very much one of control rather than ownership. There is a revealing parallel here in popular attitudes to the land around the same time. These similarly hinged on issues of access and control as much as, and often more than, public ownership.[9] Like agrarian radicals, skilled labour drew upon a lively popular concept of communally regulated use-rights. For industrial workers the community in question was their trade and use-right was acquired through apprenticeship or seniority. Occasionally, especially in free mining communities, it might also derive explicitly from birth. Even where it did not, patrimony was by no means a negligible factor at the workplace: in mid-nineteenth century England a staggering 44 per cent of all sons followed an occupation identical to their fathers'.[10]

As will be seen repeatedly in the chapters that follow, the language, hierarchy and inner life of workers' associations reflected their perception of themselves as self-regulating communities, bound in an allegiance to 'the trade' as strong as any they might also have felt to place. Where communities of trade and place closely overlapped, as in the east midland and Pennine textiles regions, particularly forceful resistance to encroachment on what were perceived as communal rights was often evident. Even where occupational and residential communities were not homogeneous a significant degree of overlap was usual in this period. Most workers continued to live in the vicinity of their work. Even in London, this pattern had not begun significantly to break down before 1860.[11] The extent to which it did so thereafter, especially for higher-paid workers in the larger cities, offers a clue to differentials

---

7   Takao Matsumura, *The Labour Aristocracy Revisited: The Victorian Flint Glass Makers* (1983).
8   Henry Phelps Brown, *The Origins of Trade Union Power* (1986), p. 19.
9   Malcolm Chase, 'The People's Farm': English Radical Agrarianism, 1775-1840 (2010), pp. 156-7.
10 Mike Savage and Andrew Miles, *The Remaking of the British Working Class, 1840-1940* (1994), p. 45.
11 David R. Green, 'Distance to work in Victorian London: a case study of Henry Poole, bespoke tailors', *Business History*, 30, (1988)

in trade union activism and militancy, especially when the combined effect of suburban migration, increased leisure time and diminishing hours of work are taken into account.

Until the mid-nineteenth century, however, trade societies and unions arguably occupied a more central place in the associational life of those who belonged to them. Paradoxically, they were also likely to be more amorphous, shading off into the other self-help initiatives, the pubs where they met, the local communities in which they were situated and the inner life of the workplace itself

The chapters that follow trace the origins and early development of trade unionism from these roots. Throughout, I have tried to take account not just of England but also Wales, Scotland and Ireland. This is done with some trepidation for the contrasting labour histories of the four nations each deserve detailed treatment.[12] Aggregation is hazardous and for failure to avoid the pitfalls I apologize. I hope, though, that this broader focus has some compensations. The first chapter explores aspects of workers' associations in the medieval and early modern period that in some ways anticipated trade unionism. Chapter 2 relates the continuing development of labour association to accelerating economic and social change in the eighteenth century. Ideas concerning apprenticeship, skill and gender are particularly discussed in this chapter. Chapter 3 is framed by the years of the French Revolution and the Napoleonic wars, 1789-1815, a momentous period for Britain in which the history of trade unionism needs to be related to broader themes of radical politics and popular unrest. This theme recurs in the fourth chapter which explores the changing character of trade unionism in the decade which culminated in 1824 with the Combination Laws Repeal Act. Chapter 5 focuses upon the period 1829-34, perhaps the best-known years in the history of British trade unionism and, arguably, among the least-understood. The surge of interest in general unionism during these years, and its rapid decline, was a key factor behind the convergence of organized labour and the Chartist movement. This is considered in detail in Chapter 6, culminating in the 1842 strike wave. After 1842 trade unionism and Chartism diverged. The consequences of this are a central theme of Chapter 7. In the Conclusion an assessment is made of the overall strength and character of trade unionism in the early 1860s.

---

[12] The following are useful starting points for a more detailed investigation of their respective labour histories: Scotland – W. H. Fraser, *Conflict and Class: Scottish Workers, 1700-1838* (1988) and the *Journal of the Scottish Labour History Society*; Ireland – Emmett O'connor, 'A historiography of Irish labour', *Labour History Review*, 60/1, (1995) and *Saothar* (the Journal of the Irish Labour History Society); Wales – D. J. V. Jones, *Before Rebecca: Popular Protest in Wales, 1793-1835* (1973) and *Llafur: Journal of Welsh Labour History*.

1

Covins and Fraternities: A 'Prehistory' of Trade Unionism

THE BROAD CONTEXT[1]

Evidence for post-Roman urban centres in Britain is effectively confined to London and York. However, new settlements for trade and industry were established in southern and eastern England during the eighth century. If sources permitted, a continuous history of wage labour could be written from this point. Urban development in the rest of the British Isles was slower, but there was a network of urban centres elsewhere in England by the tenth century. By the twelfth century the Scottish burghs were well established as market and trading centres, and the coasts of Wales and southern and eastern Ireland punctuated with significant urban settlements. It was from this base that the urban economy of medieval Britain grew, so that by the sixteenth century there were between 600 and 800 market towns in England alone.

Population growth was vigorous, if slight by modern standards, and around 1300 the population of England and Wales reached a figure of perhaps six million, a level that was not exceeded again until the eighteenth century. However, in the mid-fourteenth century Britain suffered a demographic setback of seismic proportions. Between 1348 and 1375 the Black Death carried off perhaps half of the population. There was a further decline in population in the later fourteenth and fifteenth centuries, with food prices also falling. Initially, urban craftsmen benefited from these trends. However, there was far from a simple rural/urban division in economic fortunes. Much industrial activity, notably in textiles, had been penetrating the countryside since at least the fourteenth century. By the 1420s a combination of diminishing urban-generated demand and high wages was rendering many products uneconomic compared to those produced in rural areas (and also abroad). London weathered this upheaval better than almost any provincial centre. Its merchants enjoyed significantly better access to capital, essential as commerce and manufacturing restructured. Merchants from York and Bristol, for example, even moved to London, further depleting provincial urban trade. One consequence of the capital's commercial ascendency was that increasingly the experience of its

---

1   The following account is necessarily compressed. The following introductory texts also all contain pointers for further reading: J. D. Chambers, *Population, Economy and Society in Pre-Industrial England* (1972); R. A. Dodgshon and R.A. Butlin (eds), *An Historical Geography of England and Wales*, second edition (1980); J. Hatcher, *Plague, Population and the English Economy, 1348-1530* (1977); E. Miller and J. Hatcher, *Medieval England: Towns, Commerce and Crafts, 1086-1348* (1995). On Scotland see Ian D. Whyte, *Scotland before the Industrial Revolution: An Economic and Social History c. 1050-1750* (1995). L. T. Clarkson, 'Introduction: wage-labour, 1500-1800', in K. D. Brown, *The English Labour Movement, 1700-1951* (1982), is a very valuable survey of variations in the supply of, and demand for, wage labour in the early modern period. Though weak on social relations, J. Blair and N. Ramsay (eds), *English Medieval Industries* (1991) is an excellent survey of industrial activity.

growing workforce would be out of step with that of provincial urban labour.

The reversal of demographic decline from the late fifteenth century laid the foundations for a more general expansion in the numbers of those partly or wholly dependent upon waged work. The subdivision of land holdings in upland and forest areas of England (where manorial control of land distribution was weak) encouraged the emergence of a dual economy as small cultivators supplemented the modest returns on their efforts by manufacturing work. In lowland areas, where manorial controls were stronger and arable farming predominated, there was both a high demand for labour and a stimulus to enclosure. Hence there emerged significant numbers of landless labourers whose economic choice (apart from beggary) was waged labour either on the land or in the town. Levels of pay were almost invariably higher in towns. However, by the end of the seventeenth century, manufacturers were recruiting shoemakers and knitters in these lowland areas to produce goods for export and the lower end of the domestic market.

State intervention in the urban labour market and in the regulation of beggars and vagrancy, is a prominent feature of the late-sixteenth and seventeenth centuries. Although the 1563 Statute of Artificers remained a benchmark in labour affairs, such legislation might affect the symptoms of change in urban economies but it could do little to influence the sources. With a growth in the supply of labour relative to that of land and capital, real wages fell: by 1611 the purchasing power of the wages received by skilled tradesmen in the building industry of southern England was less than half that of a century before.[2] Since labour costs, in a technologically unsophisticated economy, are the largest ingredient in the final price of manufactured goods, the long-term consequences for waged labour were largely negative. Increasing demand for goods and services, and a consequent stimulus to the growth of urban communities, were not matched by any increase in the wages craft workers received, the secular trend of which was downwards. The wages of labourers, roughly two-thirds of those enjoyed by craftsmen, followed the same trend.

Of course the pace of these changes varied between regions and across occupational groups. Regions without a significant urban dimension to their economies (notably non-coastal Ireland and the Scottish Highlands) were barely touched by them. There were sub-regional economies based on mineral industries, such as north-west Derbyshire (lead), Tyneside (coal), and the iron-making areas of Wealden Kent and Sussex and later the West Midlands and South Yorkshire, which exhibited distinctive patterns of growth and employment. The development of textiles industries, in what were essentially rural areas such as Ulster and the Lancashire and Yorkshire Pennines, gave rise to special forms of social and economic organization. These, along with parallel rural-based activities in metals, are frequently characterized as *proto-industrialization* — though historians' acceptance of the concept is far from universal. There has been a tendency for the most enthusiastic proponents of proto-industrialization to underestimate the social and economic significance of the town-based handicrafts sector. This both exaggerates the 'backwardness' of artisan-based production and the extent to which an integrated industrial economy had emerged by 1700. There were, however, significant differences in the ethos and associational lives of waged workers in urban and rural industry. Rural industrial workers were frequently too dispersed to engage in sustained collective action, while the 'relationship of employer to employee was more often that of creditor to debtor than one expressed in payment of wages'.[3] Hence the roots of trade unionism in Britain derive from the

---

2   E. A. Wrigley and R. S. Schofield, *The Population History of England, 1541-1871: A Reconstruction* (1989, paperback edition with new introduction; first published 1981), p. 642.

3   Christopher Hill, *Reformation to Industrial Revolution* (1969), p. 91.

traditions of urban craftsmen rather than from rural industrial workers. And thus this survey of the 'prehistory' of trade unions takes as its starting point associations of workers in the medieval town.

THE GUILDS, CRAFTS AND WORK

Any account of working life in the medieval town must necessarily start with the guilds. As Sylvia Thrupp has observed:

> The occupational gilds of the west are one of the best-known forms of medieval association, familiar both on account of their long post-medieval career, and because they had early lent themselves to the ordering of economic and political life in urban society. Their traditions of corporate charity and piety further attest that they were once genuine communities within the larger community, with a social and religious character transcending mere economic interest and the struggle for power.[4]

Some care is needed in using the term 'guild' ('gild' is a common alternative spelling) and a recurrent feature of recent studies of the subject is the issue of definition. As Swanson observes 'it is as vague as the word association', covering a range of organizations from 'a handful of people who clubbed together to pay for a light to burn on the altar of their parish church' upwards.[5] It is generally used to denote an official organization of master craftsmen, but frequently occurs in historical studies as 'craft guild', a hybrid term of dubious provenance implying an association embracing or governing the whole of an occupational group. This, as we shall see, is misleading: a guild's authority over its craft was seldom total.

There are no exact equivalents of the guilds today, though direct linear descendants can be found in the Livery Companies of London and in vestigial survivals in a few other cities (for example the Sheffield Cutlers' Guild, now a modern trade association, or the Shoreporters' Society of Aberdeen, originally the Pynours' Society but now a removals and haulage company run as a mutual partnership). Membership of such associations may (but not invariably) be restricted to a particular occupational group. None of them, however, replicates the functions of their medieval forebears beyond perhaps the promotion of conviviality and fraternal spirit: the religious context and content of a medieval guild's work is irretrievably absent.

Until very recently historians took little interest in the guilds. Effectively they were consigned to history's scrap heap, seen as having little relevance to the modern world. Historians in general are apt to concentrate upon new forms of organization or behaviour to the exclusion of continuities amongst old ones. This is particularly the case in Britain. Here guilds have been seen as ceasing to play any meaningful part in economy or society by the early eighteenth century at the latest — in contrast to continental Europe where they survived to the French Revolution and even beyond, for example in Austria and some German states where they were abolished in 1859 and the 1860s respectively. It has also been argued that the particular trajectory taken by Protestant England, towards a market society based on a philosophy of possessive individualism, negated the influence of guilds from an early date: 'it was in England that the doctrine of freedom of trade and production — the antithesis of guild doctrine — developed earliest and, compared with the rest of Europe, remained strongest in modern times'.[6] However, there are good grounds for casting doubt upon much conventional wisdom

---
4   Sylvia Thrupp, 'The gilds', in M. Postan, E. E. Rich and E. Miller (eds.), *The Cambridge Economic History of Europe*, vol. 3 (1963), p. 230.
5   Heather Swanson, *Medieval Artisans: An Urban Class in Late Medieval England* (1989), p. 5.
6   Antony Black, *Guilds and Civil Society in European Political Thought from the Twelfth Century to the Present* (1984), p. 159.

concerning the English guilds. Several recent historians have been impressed by the flexibility of the guilds and have seen their decline after the Reformation as uneven and episodic, with many guilds enjoying a renaissance after 1660.

The medieval guild was primarily an employers' organization, but with extensive responsibilities for what would now be termed vocational training and consumer protection. In addition, and these were by no means supplementary roles, each guild was closely involved in the civic life and governance of the community of which it was part and, until the upheavals of the Reformation in the sixteenth century, played an integral part in local religious life. Finally, and this is a supplementary aspect, *some* guild organizations can be seen as anticipating *some* of the activities of what since the mid-nineteenth century have been called trade unions. Usually, but not invariably, these activities are most evident in organizations which were ancillary and occasionally opposed to the guilds proper. In Eric Hobsbawm's words:

> Social differentiation within or between crafts produced organizations modelled on the pattern of the older gilds or fraternities, but expressing the specific interests of particular sections, notably the journeymen, and a good deal of the traditional pattern was subsequently taken over into the early trade unions of skilled wage-workers in the industrial period.[7]

However, a note of caution is needed here. The association of workers in a fraternity separate from the guild which regulated their occupation is not necessarily evidence of polarization between employers and employed, still less of any 'class-conscious' thinking. A relatively high degree of mobility, especially in the labour shortages of the late fourteenth and fifteenth centuries, predisposed town dwellers (especially immigrants and their children) to form credit and fraternal networks to replace the support systems of the more intimate rural world. Credit and mutual trust were necessary for economic survival, for workers generally neither owned the materials with which they worked nor received immediate payment for the goods they produced. To be of good standing in the community was therefore vital: it promoted trust, accessed credit and was likely to ameliorate the problems of ill-health and old-age. 'The most frequently employed means of claiming such status in local society was participation in one or more of the voluntary clubs, generally known as guilds, confraternities or fraternities.' Gervase Rosser suggests that most urban dwellers beyond the permanently indigent belonged to some form of association, usually occupationally based; and that distinguishing oneself from the indigent was a key motive for association: 'The many thousands of medieval fraternities defy generalization, but common to them all was an aspiration to respectability'.[8]

This perception that association powerfully enhanced respectability applied with equal force to later trade unionism. However, it is not an aspect of medieval life to which early historians of guilds were particularly attentive. Working within a mind-set dominated by the emergence of industrial capitalism, they were apt to view associations of journeymen as evidence of modernizing processes. Ironically, although the reluctance of the Webbs to examine guilds and fraternities as part of the history of trade unionism erected unhelpful fences around 'labour history', they were right to emphasize the profound 'otherness' of work in the medieval world. At the same time, it is difficult to share the prevailing view of most of the twentieth century that the modern history of labour can be neatly fenced off by the 'Industrial Revolution'.

---

7   Eric J. Hobsbawm, *Primitive Rebels: Studies in Archaic Forms of Social Movement in the 19th and 20th Centuries* (1971), p. 109.

8   See especially Gervase Rosser 'Crafts, guilds and the negotiation of work in the medieval town', *Past and Present*, 154, (1997) and other work cited there, to which this discussion is indebted.

Among labour historians the power of this convention has been strengthened by an understandable preoccupation with trade unions, a social formation seen as replacing guilds chronologically and fulfilling the function of protecting workers' interests that guilds performed at best accidentally and imperfectly. In addition, British historians, taking their cue from the Webbs, have long sought to demarcate trade unions off from guilds: 'We assert, indeed, with confidence, that in no case did any Trade Union in the United Kingdom arise, either directly or indirectly, by descent, from a Craft Guild'.[9] The Webbs were horrified by cheerfully uncritical antiquarians in the labour movement, notably the bricklayers' leader and MP George Howell, who evinced an almost romantic interest in supposed connections between guilds and trade unions.[10] In doing so, and also in seeking to trace the origins of guilds to Anglo-Saxon England, Howell was subscribing to a refinement of the old popular radical notion of the Norman Yoke. The latter hinged on the notion that a wide range of fundamental liberties were established under the Anglo-Saxons, only to be suppressed or curtailed by the 'alien' Norman invasion of 1066, to which could also be traced the origins of the aristocracy. The Norman Yoke, though politically most potent in the seventeenth century, was a long time dying. It remained a notable ingredient in the politics of early nineteenth-century radicalism and Chartism and it occasionally resurfaced thereafter, for example in the Clarion movement, contemporary with the early Fabian socialist movement in which the Webbs were very prominent. By the time of the revised 1920 edition of their *History of Trade Unionism*, the Webbs' views on the origins of trade unionism had doubtless also been reinforced by an antipathy to contemporary 'Guild Socialism', an alternative to Fabianism which proposed the restoration of a guilds system to facilitate workers' control in industry.

The literature on the labour force of the pre-industrial period is now extensive and its relationship to the later evolution of trade unionism can be considered with some confidence. Such consideration here can only be brief and unlikely to satisfy specialists in the medieval or early modern periods. It is also important to realize that in focusing backwards in this way there is a risk of distortion bordering on violence to the sources.[11] It is both futile and fallacious to comb through the twelfth to seventeenth centuries with a view to identifying 'the first trade union': but by the seventeenth century there is ample evidence of what one of the very few historians interested in the field has termed 'partially organized labor groups'.[12] Though their organization was certainly partial compared to modern trade unions, such groups are recognizable as labour organizations: the broad objectives that brought them together were not only economic but related to their members' social function as producers rather than as consumers. Furthermore, they were preconceived rather than spontaneous in character. Their aims were variously to discuss grievances and to identify possible solutions to them, to draw up

---

9 Sidney and Beatrice Webb, *The History of Trade Unionism*, revised edition (1920, first published 1894), p. 14.

10 Ibid., p. 13; George Howell, *Conflicts of Capital and Labour, Historically and Economically considered. Being a History and Review of the Trade Unions of Great Britain* (1878), pp. 1-81.

11 By way of damage limitation, the reader requiring more detailed information on the European guilds should consult Antony Black, *Guilds and Civil Society*, Steven A. Epstein, *Wage Labor and Guilds in Medieval Europe* (1991), Steven A. Epstein, 'Craft guilds, apprenticeship, and technological change in preindustrial Europe', *Journal of Economic History*, vol. 58, no. 3, (1998) and Sylvia Thrupp, 'The gilds'. Gervase Rosser 'Crafts, guilds and the negotiation of work' is an important revisionist account. Particularly recommended English case-studies are Ian W. Archer, *The Pursuit of Stability: Social Relations in Elizabethan London* (1991), D. M. Palliser, 'The trade gilds of Tudor York', in Peter Clark and Paul Slack (eds.), *Crisis and Order in English Towns, 1500-1700* (1972), Charles Phythian-Adams, *Desolation of a City: Coventry and the Urban Crisis of the Late Middle Ages* (1979) and Heather Swanson, *Medieval Artisans*. Unfortunately, the best study of the later English guilds remains unpublished: M. J. Walker, 'The extent of guild control of trades in England, circa 1660-1820: a study based on a sample of provincial towns and London companies', unpublished Ph.D thesis, (University of Cambridge, 1985)

12 Mary Roys Baker, 'Anglo-Massachusetts trade union roots, 1130-1790', *Labor History*, vol. 14, part 3, (1973), p. 382.

petitions, to select representatives to advance their case, to reach mutually binding agreements aimed at strengthening their economic position, and — though usually only in the last resort — to organize strike action.

The emergence of these kinds of activities alerts us to the development of a mentality in which the formation of separate trade-based organizations for waged labour came to seem both natural and, for the workers anyway, desirable. The historian does need, however, to be cautious. First, as we have seen, occupational-based associations at sub-guild level were common in medieval Britain and are by themselves no reliable indicator of polarizing workplace relations. Second, as Archer observes, 'The polemics into which men are drawn in the heat of a particular conflict are not necessarily typical of their normal positions. It is easy to string together isolated instances of conflict to create an impression of polarization.'[13] However, this is not to suggest that trade and manufacture were pursued in a climate of unalloyed social harmony, which is arguably the cumulative picture in Rappaport's 1989 study of London artisans, for example.[14] It is over-reliant upon official guild records, documents which naturally tended to be written by those most inclined to conjure up a picture of social composure.

Most early historians of the medieval guilds claimed to identify notable continuities with Roman *collegia*, a word applied to organized groups of people in a particular trade or line of business, and particularly to occupationally — specific burial societies that existed — notably in the Roman armies — to ensure a decent burial for their subscribing members. Evidence for *collegia* is to be found in almost every corner of the Roman Empire, Britain included. Given the importance of funeral provision in so many early British trade associations, it is interesting to note how frequently people wished to be buried with their 'brothers' — the term is a common one — from the same *collegium*.[15] Recent historical accounts have argued against such connections, stressing that the essentially coercive nature of the Roman labour system contrasts sharply with the situation of urban workers in the medieval period. The real Roman legacy rested in the law of contract, and in the acceptance of the state's right to intervene in economic matters. Steven Epstein suggests that the guilds emerged across western Christendom effectively in parallel with waged labour, as a means to recruit, train, retain and control the labour of landless workers.[16] Though the survival of source material is very patchy for the earliest period, these functions are evident in a handful of European towns, London included, in the twelfth century, and become more refined and widespread in the thirteenth. Their durability and efficiency is evident in their having survived the stern test of the Black Death in the fourteenth century. In Scotland, however, occupational guilds — commonly termed incorporations — largely date from the fifteenth and sixteenth centuries, though there were earlier merchant guilds.

Epstein's wide-ranging synthesis can be criticized on a number of grounds. It is narrowly economistic and oblivious to the breadth and richness of medieval associational life. It largely overlooks the extensive religious functions of the guilds, which as solemn confraternities upheld key features in the religious life of the early towns. It was they, for example, who were charged with the responsibility of performing the Corpus Christi or Mystery Plays of York and other medieval cities

---

13 Ian W. Archer, *The Pursuit of Stability*, p. 102.

14 Steve Rappaport, *Worlds within Worlds: Structures of Life in Sixteenth Century London* (1989).

15 The bulk of the evidence for the Roman *collegia* derives from tombstone inscriptions. There is no accessible history in English: the standard work remains J.P. Waltzing, (1895-1900), *Etude historique sur les corporations professionnelles chez les romains*, 4 volumes, Louvain; see also F. M. Ausbuettel, *Untersuchungen zu den Vereinen im Westen des Moemischen Reiches*, (1982). (I am indebted to various contributors to a discussion about *collegia* on the H-LABOR electronic list in 1997.)

16 Steven A. Epstein, *Wage Labor and Guilds*.

and towns.[17] Religious functions were not incompatible with the economic ones which medieval guilds fulfilled; and acts of collective worship or recreation (there was seldom a firm dividing line) by masters, men and apprentices would have served to diminish any tensions generated in the workplace. Another deficiency of Epstein's argument, especially in the British context, is that the emergence of waged labour and the guilds was not mono-causal. In many towns regulation of apprenticeship and wages was directly undertaken by civic authority. In some centres guilds developed late (for example Hull, Grimsby and Leeds in the late-fifteenth, sixteenth and seventeenth centuries respectively). Yet waged labour existed in urban communities where there were insufficient masters to justify a guild system; and it existed alongside guilds in other trades which did not seek such public status (but which, by the late-fourteenth century probably boasted a fraternity). As already pointed out, the existence of waged labour is therefore not necessarily indicative of hardening social divisions: 'it was far from unusual for craftsmen, for a variety of reasons, to move to and fro across the line between wage-labour and independence'.[18]

Even so, guilds were an effective means by which the majority of larger urban communities came to manage labour. As late as the 1750s, this was the motive in Bath for establishing a range of guilds for the first time.[19] Guilds did this as the licensed agents of the state, being established by royal charter, or by civic authorities to whom the state had conceded extensive governmental powers. Whatever the circumstances of their foundation (and more than a few simply asserted their independence and claimed the authority of custom, for example the London Watermen and Newcastle upon Tyne Keelmen), guild control over waged labour rested on several powers. The first of these was to regulate entry to the trade. Guilds decreed who could become apprentices and who might offer apprenticeships. Senior officers, usually titled 'searchers' in England, were empowered to investigate the effectiveness of the training apprentices received and to check that regulations were obeyed by them and masters alike. The second was to examine apprentices at the end of their 'time' (typically seven years), after which the satisfactory apprentice became a journeyman — a waged worker in the employ of a master. Journeymen were usually then admitted to the guild in some form of associate membership, or to an ancillary fellowship over which the guild proper exercised some control or at least influence. The usual term in both cases describing such workers was the 'yeomanry'. The Statute of Artificers of 1563 formalized the seven years' duration of apprenticeships, extended guild regulations governing them and gave these the force of national legislation. Full guild membership was confined to the masters. It conferred not only power within the organization, but also status in the wider community and a right to participate in its political processes. For much of the medieval and early modern periods many journeymen had realistic opportunities to become a master on their own account and enter into full membership of their guild which, in the meanwhile, represented the interests of both them and their masters. But theirs was a kind of second-class existence, elusive to the historian. Occasionally, glimpses of their participation in guild business can be obtained, for example at Beverley where changes to the ordinances of the weavers' guild in 1500 gave journeymen an equal share with masters in the election of the two aldermen (though they could not themselves serve in this office). Most of the town's guilds provided for their subscriptions to be made at a lower rate than masters' with, interestingly, the weavers explicitly providing for a separate payment to be made by the journeymen to the searchers, suggesting that the guild existed to protect

---

17 M. James, 'Ritual, drama and the social body in the late medieval town', *Past and Present*, 98, (1983).
18 Gervase Rosser, 'Crafts, guilds and the negotiation of work'.
19 R. S. Neale, *Bath: A Social History or; A Valley of Pleasure, yet a Sink of Iniquity* (1981), p. 65-8.

their interests as well as those of their employers.[20]

The above, somewhat condensed account does not encompass the full breadth of guilds' activities: they existed to advance the interests of the masters and to protect the consumer by regulating the quality of work, as well as to incorporate and regulate waged labour. They were partners with the church in the observation of the religious calendar and they were a powerful means through which town and city corporations sought to ensure the stability of the local community. Thus, when the Coventry Carpenters', Millwrights' and Wheelwrights' Company received a new set of regulations in 1686, these were summarized as being

> for the better advancement of Trade and encouragement of able Artists in the several Misteries aforesaid and for the discountenancinge [of] Foreigners and other unskilful persons pretending themselves to be workmen without having been Apprentices to the great prejudice of settled freemen of this City [and] for better binding of Apprentices and imploying of Journeymen of known skill and Integrity at moderate rates without enhancing of wages.[21]

This example is consistent with other locations where a revivified guild structure was an important element in restoring stability in the wake of the dislocations caused by the English Revolution. It is also mirrored to some extent in attempts by authority in the American colonies to encourage guilds as a means towards regulating the conduct of business.[22]

It is important to bear in mind that the system summarized here varied over time and place. It could not apply to rural areas and much industry at this time was located in the countryside. Large villages and newly emerging urban communities, which by certain criteria might be regarded as towns, were without guilds, though possibly not craft fraternities of some other kind. Some particularly vibrant urban economies seem to have outgrown the capacity of their guilds to regulate them at an early date, though it is very far from being the case that guilds only survived in stagnant or declining local economies. Whatever the state of the local economy, opportunities for elevation to a mastership in the English guilds declined from the seventeenth century. It is noticeable that when the Exeter Weavers', Tuckers' and Shearmen's Company took action in 1655 against those who had 'mutually agreed and promised each to the other not to work henceforward in this Citty or County for less than 4s a weeke in all for their wages', the offenders were all journeymen who had been admitted to the Company since 1650, suggesting the emergence of a group who had come to regard themselves as wage-earners rather than as potential masters of their craft.[23] The intake of apprentices levelled off in the second half of the seventeenth century and was then curtailed sharply in the early eighteenth.[24] By the 1740s masters were seeking to break, not uphold, apprenticeship, for example by permitting

---

20 East Yorkshire Archive Office, Beverley, BC/II/3 f. 84 and BC/II/5/I (part I) f. 37. I am grateful to David Lamburn for both these references.

21 Preamble to charter ordinances, 20 January 1686, Coventry Carpenters', Millwrights' and Wheelwrights' Company Order Book, Coventry Record Office, quoted in M. J. Walker, 'The extent of guild control of trades in England, circa 1660-1820: a study based on a sample of provincial towns and London companies', unpublished Ph.D thesis, (University of Cambridge, 1985), p. 362. Note, though, that Coventry Corporation, like others, would sometimes overrule a guild's privileges if the public interest was judged to require it. When the price of candles soared in 1641 non-free chandlers were allowed to work within the city, one of several examples of corporate barriers being lowered in the face of labour shortages, Ronald M. Berger, *The Most Necessary Luxuries: the Mercers' Company of Coventry 1550-1680* (1993), pp. 164-5.

22 Mary Roys Baker, 'Anglo-Massachusetts trade union roots'.

23 Joyce Youings, *Tuckers Hall, Exeter: The History of a Provincial City Company Through Five Centuries* (1968), pp. 60-1.

24 Christopher Brooks, 'Apprenticeship, social mobility and the middling sort, 1550-1800', in Johnathan Barry and Christopher Brooks (eds.), *The Middling Sort of People: Culture, Society and Politics in England 1550-1800* (1994); Ian D. Whyte, *Scotland before the Industrial Revolution*, pp. 197-8.

the recruitment of 'foreigners' (that is, workers from outside the community) who had not served a recognized apprenticeship — the very thing opposed in Coventry in 1676. Another strategy was to permit an increase in the number of apprentices each master could train. Both courses of action, taken in response to a shortage of labour, tended to depress the wages, expectations and status of the journeyman. However, this is to anticipate subject matter relating to the next chapter.

EARLY ASSOCIATIONS OF JOURNEYMEN

There is no shortage of evidence from the seventeenth century for organization and behaviour anticipating in some way the later development of trade unions, though much of it relates to London and is unlikely to be typical of the rest of England, still less the rest of the British Isles. Even before the seventeenth century, there were real social tensions between commercial and manufacturing capital and between large and small masters. In these journeymen tended to be allied with small masters, whose ranks they might realistically hope in time to join. However, in certain trades — notably shoemaking and tailoring — separate journeymen's organizations are apparent by the late medieval period. Official recognition of a fraternity of Coventry's lesser craftsmen ('laborarios et artifices mediocres') was given in 1384 but quickly withdrawn on suspicion that it was in some way subversive. In 1407 'the servants of tailors and other artificers' formed a new fraternity that endured some seven years despite being likewise condemned. It then metamorphosed into another body, 'the fullers and tailors of the Nativity of Christ'.[25] The York Cordwainers' Guild, in an edict of 1430, forbade waged workers ('servientes stipendarii') to form a confederacy, but the continued existence of a journeymen cordwainers' association has been inferred and, as the Guild of St Augustine, was mentioned in 1506.[26]

The earliest, and also most extensive, evidence for journeymen's combinations is to be found in London, reflecting its particular economic trajectory. As early as 1299 journeymen carpenters and smiths were accused of forming illegal associations described as 'parliaments'.[27] Early historians exaggerated the extent to which the yeomanry of the late-medieval London guilds were 'invariably' journeymen, or even 'a real working-class'.[28] In some cases tension between journeymen and masters may simply have been the consequence of age difference and therefore of the contrasting concerns of successive stages in the life cycle. In the 1470s, for example, ten ringleaders of unrest within the London goldsmiths were imprisoned. All were in their late twenties: four of them went on to become office holders in the company, one of them warden, and all the rest appear to have become masters.[29]

However, from the mid-fourteenth century London found it increasingly difficult to contain associations of journeymen.[30] The pious tone of these fraternities was beginning to cloak expressly economic objectives. The shearmen (who cut the nap of woollen cloth) were

> wont to go to all the vadletts within the City of the same trade, and then, by covin and conspiracy between them made, they would order that no one among them should work, or serve his own master, until the said master and his servant, or vadlett, had come to an

---

25 Gervase Rosser, 'Crafts, guilds and the negotiation of work', p. 292.
26 D. M. Palliser, 'The trade gilds of Tudor York', p. 104; Gervase Rosser, 'Crafts, guilds and the negotiation of work', p. 298.
27 R. H. Hilton, *English and French Towns in Feudal Society: a Comparative Study* (1992), p. 146.
28 George Unwin, *The Guilds and Companies of London* (1908), p. 224; Luigi Brentano, *On the History and Development of Gilds, and the Origin of Trade-Unions* (1870), p. 76.
29 T. F. Reddaway and L. E. M. Walker, *The Early History of the Goldsmiths' Company 1327-1509* (1975), pp. 24-9.
30 R. H. Hilton, *English and French Towns in Feudal Society*, pp. 146-8.

agreement.[31]

An Act of 1361 prohibited all 'alliances & covignes des Maceons & Carpenters'. At the end of the century London's master sadlers complained 'that under a certain feigned colour of sanctity' a fraternity of journeymen saddle-makers had succeeded in more than doubling wages in a little over a decade. Questioned by the City Sergeant, the 'governors' of the fraternity claimed it had existed since 'time out of mind' and they described their ceremonial religious procedures which were similar to those of a guild. 'But the said masters of the trade asserted to the contrary of all this, and said that the fraternity ... dated from only thirteen years back.' It is possible that this was a long-standing fraternity that had ceased to be amenable to the guild's influence; or it may have been, as the employers claimed, the result of recent 'covins ... with the object of raising their wages greatly in excess'.[32] Either way, the consequence was clearly an association whose members shared a definite awareness of their social function as wage-earners. Similarly the journeymen bakers, organized from their own 'revelling hall', struck for higher wages in 1441, agreeing to black master craftsmen who dismissed any of their number. Rosser points out that journeymen's fraternities generally preferred to attach themselves to churches on the outskirts of their city or to the jurisdictionally marginal friaries.[33] It is noticeable in late-medieval London that four of them held their principal festival on the same day, evidence of inter-trades awareness that probably also contributed to the reduction in waged workers' hours agreed in six London trades between 1321 and 1389.[34]

The form taken by combinations of wage-earners need not have been highly formalized. The religious reformer John Wycliffe, writing in the fourteenth century, believed it almost axiomatic that stonemasons,

> conspire together that no man of their craft shall take less on a day than they set, though he should by good conscience take much less; and that none of them shall make steady, true work which might hinder other men's earnings from the craft; and that none of them shall do ought but hew Stone, though he might profit his master twenty pounds by one day's work laying a wall, without harm or paining himself. See how these wicked people conspire against truth and charity.[35]

As Woodward has observed of the building trades in northern England, strikes, or the threat of them, particularly by waged workers, played a crucial role in determining wages.[36] However, we need to be cautious in ascribing such actions to sustained pre-existing organizations.

Journeymen's combinations occasionally exercised considerable influence upon their trade. For example the London Clothworkers' Company suppressed a labour-saving device for rowing cloth (raising its nap) in 1560, apparently because of a combination between journeymen in their company

---

31 L. F. Salzman, *English Industries in the Middle Ages* (1923), pp. 342-3.

32 H.T. Riley, *Memorials of London and London Life in the Thirteenth, Fourteenth and Fifteenth Centuries*, (1868), pp. 542-4. See also Gervase Rosser, 'Crafts, guilds and the negotiation of work'. The word 'covin', here and in two previous quotations in this paragraph, was the common precursor of 'combination' as a collective noun for workers in a context opposed to their employers. Even more than combination it carries unfavourable connotations, especially of conspiracy and intent to defraud or injure: see the Oxford English Dictionary from which the quotation of 1361 is taken.

33 Gervase Rosser, 'Workers' associations in English medieval towns', in Pascale Lambrechts and Jean-Pierre Sosson (eds.), *Les métiers au moyen age: aspects économiques et sociaux* (1994), p. 299.

34 Mary Roys Baker, 'Anglo-Massachusetts trade union roots', p. 359.

35 Adapted from G. C. Coulton, *Social Life in Britain from the Conquest to the Reformation* (1919), p. 491.

36 Donald Woodward, *Men at Work: Labourers and Building Craftsmen in the Towns of Northern England 1450-1750* (1995), p. 194.

and that of the Merchant Tailors. Conceivably journeymen were even weakening some guilds financially by diverting subscriptions to their own immediate ends, for by the later sixteenth century there was a noticeable decline in all London trades in the number of journeymen making quarterage payments to their guilds.[37] This may have been linked to the re-emergence of separate associations for waged workers, bereft, unlike their pre-Reformation counterparts, of religious connotations but focused upon strengthening the economic position of their members. Such associations need have been little more than a regular gathering at a particular alehouse, to 'talk shop'.

In London something like a democratic movement had emerged among the lower ranks of the manufacturing guilds by the time of the Revolution as yeomanries pressed guild officers to enforce customary regulations. In the first decade of the century artisan skinners observed of their guild that it was 'a matter disputable whether we be members of the said company or not'.[38] In 1619 the leathersellers, an entrepreneurs' guild, stoutly resisted attempts by the lowly glovers to establish their own company, calling it 'playne Monopoly and a Confederacy' and a precedent 'to all the Mechanick trades about London'. In 1630, having first met in a pub, yeoman of the Weavers' Company sent a delegation to the Lord Mayor to protest at the abuse of apprenticeship regulations; in 1648 the 'commonalty' of the same guild asserted a right to collect quarterage from journeymen because, they claimed, the masters of the Weavers' Company had consistently failed to protect the interests of the trade as a whole.[39] The 'Free Journeymen Printers in and about London' petitioned Parliament, describing themselves as 'oppressed and kept in bondage all their lives' and 'made perpetual bondmen to serve some few of the rich ... upon such conditions and for such hire, and at such times as the Masters think fit'. They were particularly concerned at growing abuse of apprenticeship regulations.[40] After the Restoration, the authorities (largely composed, of course, of guild officers) rejected requests from trades such as sawyers, paviors, coal porters and basket makers to be allowed to form their own guilds. The tone of the case made in 1670 by the sawyers suggests that they were already effectively organized into a combination. The members of the carpenters', joiners' and shipwrights' companies who employed them complained that in four incremental stages during the last twenty-five years the sawyers had raised their prices from five to nine shillings a load. They were described as labourers, to whom the concession of guild status would be an encouragement to further strike action and 'an evill president [sic], [to] all other Labourers, to Masons, Bricklayers, Plaisterers, &c. having the same reason to alledge incorporation'.[41]

However, one London trade, the Hatters, was granted guild status by Royal Charter in 1667. Here the articles of incorporation interestingly contain explicit reference to potential combination by journeymen. In order to pre-empt it the articles provided for an annual negotiation of piece-work rates to be presented to the City of London's Court of Aldermen. The following year the journeymen subscribed towards the costs of securing legal confirmation of the regulations of the guild. This suggests they were accustomed to organizing independently of their masters, since the latter were clearly reluctant to cramp the development of the trade with an excess of regulation. For the first decade of its life the journeymen hatters were prompt in reporting to the guild's court masters who employed foreigners, or who failed to give proper notice of redundancy. In 1681, however, they

---

37 Ian W. Archer, *The Pursuit of Stability*, pp. 102. 115.
38 Ibid. p. 100.
39 Joseph P. Ward, *Metropolitan Communities: Trade Guilds, Identity and Change in Early Modern London* (1997), pp. 130-1.
40 George Unwin, *Industrial Organization in the Sixteenth and Seventeenth Centuries* (1904), p. 210; A. E. Musson, *The Typographical Association: Origins and History up to 1949* (1954), p. 8.
41 George Unwin, *Industrial Organization*, p. 213.

sought legal redress to enforce regulations against masters who employed more than one 'sindging boy' (in the workshop an apprentice's basic task was to heat the fabric to remove surplus fibres). The costs of this action were apparently met by the journeymen diverting their quarterage payments from the guild to their own funds. By the end of the century, they were locked in a dispute with the masters over the employment of 'country journeymen' (hatters who had not served an apprenticeship according to the regulations of the guild): this involved a lengthy strike. More than forty strikers were indicted for conspiracy. The journeymen were sufficiently legally astute and well-funded to get their case transferred from the Lord Mayor's court (where they could expect little sympathy) to the Surrey assizes. From there the case was referred to the arbitration of Surrey magistrates whose compromise decision nonetheless represented significant gains for the journeymen.

The behaviour of the London hatters sufficiently impressed their first historian for him to tag them 'a seventeenth-century trade union'. As very few workers' associations before the 1820s ever described themselves as a trade union, like Unwin we should not worry unduly that this is an anachronistic title. It does after all encapsulate a great deal of the character of what the post-Restoration hatters were about. However, the absorbing interest of the hatters' history for anyone curious about the antecedents of trade unionism should not lead us to suppose it to be typical. These were London journeymen. The metamorphosis of the capital's guilds into powerful corporations of commercial capitalists took place in a local economic and political context that was not immediately repeated elsewhere. In terms of our survey of the 'prehistory' of industrial relations, it is the extent to which guilds continued to *defend* the interests of their journeymen that must be stressed. They did so well into the eighteenth century, for the rapid demise of their religious significance at the Reformation was not inevitably paralleled in the economic sphere. In both London and provincial England they tended to experience a growth in membership in the post-Restoration period, as corporations and guilds sought to rebuild stability and also resist the incursion of large numbers of 'foreign' workers. The latter was partly a product of the revolutionary years; but short-term fluctuations were also stimulated by good harvests, which by depressing food prices and thus enhancing the demand for non-food products, rendered trades attractive to incursion by strangers. Joseph Ward points out how officers of the London Weavers' Company were preoccupied by aliens and women entering the trade after the Restoration: they dealt with the latter rather more effectively than the former, but also treated anti-engine loom rioters with discretion, even offering financial support to several imprisoned members despite the destruction of officers' property during the unrest.[42]

The situation was similar in Scotland. Craft-based (as opposed to merchant) guilds did not emerge north of the border until the fifteenth and sixteenth centuries. Once established, these craft 'incorporations' benefited from Scottish law which was favourably disposed to exclusive corporate privileges. Fraser suggests that Scottish incorporations prospered for significantly longer than their English counterparts.[43] The decline of guilds in England is usually exaggerated; however, it is clear that Scottish incorporations, operating in urban economies that were more self-sustaining and contained than those of England, generally represented the interests of both masters and journeymen to the broad satisfaction of both until towards the end of the eighteenth century. Indeed, as late as 1803 the Incorporation of Bakers in Glasgow was obtaining Court of Session decisions in its favour

---

42 Joseph P. Ward, *Metropolitan Communities*, pp. 136-8.
43 W. H. Fraser, *Conflict and Class: Scottish Workers, 1700-1838* (1988), p. 19.

against the incursion of 'outentowners'.⁴⁴

Where Scottish journeymen nursed grievances against their incorporations, this was most likely before the 1780s because wage regulation was seen as acting in the interests of employers rather than (as in England) employees.⁴⁵ It is possible, however, to exaggerate the extent to which English journeymen functioned as independent entities, for example entering into collective bargaining. To expect that they would naturally have done so is ahistorical: for much of the period collective bargaining was undertaken by the guild on the behalf of the trade as a whole. In 1552, the Corporation of York imprisoned a number of craftsmen who had struck, claiming that wage rates laid down in an agreement of 1514 were inadequate. Their guilds petitioned the mayor: masters in their trades had been paying above the 1514 rates because 'all thynges ar so dear and outte of the waye'. The city authorities promptly responded by gaoling the guild officers who presented the petition; but wage rates sanctioned by the Corporation shortly after suggest that, ultimately, this protest was successful.⁴⁶ In trades enjoying a near-monopoly in the supply of essential goods or services, the tactics deployed in such bargaining extended on occasion to all-out strikes. Chester's bakers struck in 1577 and again in 1578, the same year that the entire butchers' guild was imprisoned, having organized a strike when the mayor 'admitted forren butchers'.⁴⁷ The Tyneside keelmen struck in 1654 and again in 1659 when they blockaded the river.⁴⁸

Where a guild's claim to protect the interests of its craft as a whole was not an empty one, it functioned to the advantage of masters, journeymen and apprentices alike. The journeymen's lack of independent bargaining power, and acceptance of uniform wage rates, was compensated by stability of employment and the guild's enforcement of a form of 'closed shop'. If a guild could not guarantee a monopoly for its members, such as the Chester butchers sought, there were still a number of strategies it could employ to control competition from foreigners. It could use its influence to secure the best trading pitches and prosecute the most flagrant incursions, thus ensuring that foreign competition was low quality and/or inaccessibly placed out in the suburbs. Outside London, there were few examples before the 1720s of a guild behaving exclusively in the interests of masters and in Scotland this situation seems to have prevailed until the 1780s.

ASSOCIATIONS OF LABOURERS

A survey of workers' associations in the medieval and early modern periods would be incomplete without some consideration of organizations of unskilled labour. York provides an example of systemized labour relations in what Woodward describes as a 'Free Labourers' Guild'. Here elements of the guild format were extended to an area of work — quayside portering — which was not a trade, where apprenticeship did not apply and wherein there were no masters. Yet the authorities seem to have encouraged the formation of a guild, periodically reviewing the wage rates it had agreed with the labourers to allow for inflation. The labourers were not allowed to appoint their own officials (but instead had to nominate a panel from which the Corporation chose), and had to forswear drink and playing at cards as long as there was work to be done on the quays; but they enjoyed the protection of the Corporation. For example, in 1593 the latter prevented shipowners from employing labourers

---

44 Ibid., p. 21.
45 Ibid., p. 64.
46 D. M. Palliser, *Tudor York* (1979), p. 224.
47 R. H. Morris, *Chester in the Plantagenet and Tudor Reigns* (1893), pp. 421, 438-41.
48 David Levine and Keith Wrightson, *The Making of an Industrial Society: Whickham, 1560-1765* (1991), p. 391.

whom the guild had blacked. Porters and creelers in Beverley were possibly grouped in a similar way.[49] Two centuries later, in Bristol (where a booming economy saw most guilds in decline) a Porters' Company was approved by the Corporation in 1670, at the request of the quayside labourers and with the agreement of the large capitalist Merchant Venturers. In return for accepting a degree of discipline (a uniform coat and badge and decrees against heavy drinking and swearing), guild members enjoyed privileged access to employment on the quays and an official forum for collective bargaining.[50] At Aberdeen the society of the Pynours, Warkmen and Warkwomen, dating from 1498, lay outside the conventional craft framework but membership was obligatory for those distributing goods from vessels in the harbour round the town.

London provides the most extensive example of incorporation of labourers — specifically porters and carters — as 'fellowships' governed by Act of the Corporation's Common Council. A series of such fellowships, each governed by one or more Aldermen nominated by the Corporation without reference to the members, were instituted between 1579 and 1584. (The Billingsgate fishporters' fellowship was not dissolved until 1894.) The motives governing their formation derived principally from employers' need to ensure a constant and disciplined workforce. Guaranteed rates of wages paid to the latter were a premium for security in the transit of goods which were often of high value and to avoid the extortions of gangs. In this the fellowships proved ineffective and there was a further prohibition forbidding labourers 'to refractorily associate themselves in gangs' in 1668.[51] A further consideration was that labouring and carting work should be readily available to the 'poor decayed freemen of this City (whereof there is a competent and sufficient number to perform the labours of all manner of porters without any help of foreigners at all)'.[52] Eventually the Corporation, despairing of suppressing them, effectively took to licensing gangs through the fellowship system.

Labourers' associations were not incipient trade unions: they were neither spontaneous nor independent movements towards self-help on the part of their members. Their relevance to the history of trade unionism, however, lies in their being a recognition of the positive functions of collectivity in wage bargaining. It is unlikely that the York, Bristol and London labourers' associations were unique. Other towns without this type of guild seem to have sanctioned some form of collective organization for labourers. Ports often eschewed casualism and instead maintained groups of labourers on a quasi-permanent basis. Hull corporation's accounts contain regular references to employment of 'the mayor's men', 'our own men' or 'our labourers'. The gang operated as a quasi-collective and, though paid no more than casual labourers, was able to negotiate regular employment and access to extra earnings: every week it emptied 'the tubs of office' at the Town Hall, and each quarter dug-out the latrines in the dungeon. Members were also employed to keep watch on the freshwater dyke to prevent nuisances — contamination by dead dogs and the like. These were not, readers may feel, plum jobs; but this was not a world that could afford to be as squeamish as our own. 'It seems highly likely that the system was used elsewhere'.[53] The labourers of the early modern town may well have been accustomed to a greater degree of collective control over their working lives than is customarily credited to them.

In general we remain profoundly ignorant about the landless labourers of medieval and early-

---

49 D. M. Palliser, 'The trade gilds of Tudor York', p. 95; D. M. Palliser, *Tudor York*, p. 161; Donald Woodward, *Men at Work*, p. 95.
50 M. J. Walker, 'The extent of guild control of trades', p. 173.
51 Walter M. Stern, *The Porters of London* (1960), p. 95.
52 Joseph P. Ward, *Metropolitan Communities*, p.58.
53 Donald Woodward, *Men at Work*, p. 105.

modern Britain, situated near the very bottom of the hierarchies of skill and civic status. Of their rural counterparts our ignorance is still more profound, whether they were agricultural labourers or workers in 'proto-industry'. Unless they blundered onto the wider stage of the criminal courts, 'from this disparate, marginal and illiterate mass there is only silence'.[54] Not only were they least-satisfactorily situated (in terms of income, wage contract or relation to sources of employment) to form associations of their own, they also lacked that awareness of the guild and fraternal tradition that underlay collectivities of their urban counterparts.

THE SIGNIFICANCE OF THE GUILD AND FRATERNAL TRADITION FOR INDUSTRIAL LABOUR

The medieval workers' fraternal tradition, even though attenuated, powerfully informed the trade unions of the eighteenth and nineteenth centuries. The most basic evidence for this is to be found in the longevity of guilds in certain centres. English guilds recovered after the Restoration to reach a renewed peak of membership in the first two decades of the eighteenth century. Thereafter they entered a phase of gradual and uneven decline, retailers' guilds (e.g. mercers and drapers) first, followed in the second quarter of the century by the manufacturing trades (tailors, cordwainers, smiths). A broad spectrum of trades in the service sector (e.g. barbers, porters) and construction industries (house and ship-building) survived with their capacity to influence trade more or less intact until the last quarter of the century.[55] In Bath, guilds in construction and services were only established in the 1750s, though the experiment was short-lived.[56] Guilds' fortunes, then, varied widely across trades and localities, as they either became defunct or transformed themselves into social and philanthropic institutions with little or no pretence to exert influence on the trade whose name they retained. (In itself this process illustrates a growing social divide in eighteenth-century urban society, as well as a widening cleavage of polite and popular cultures.) In the nineteenth century the survival of guilds was usually in vestigial and largely ceremonial forms. The huge 'snapdragon', once the emblem of the Guild of St George, appeared in Norwich civic ceremonial until 1835. The Hammermen (an aggregation of various metals and construction trades) of Ludlow, Shropshire, last carried their elaborate banners in a civic procession in 1824. A putative city company for Newcastle's boilermakers, mentioned in the 1830s, was presumably scuppered by the local government reforms of that decade which removed guilds' remaining political influence in the city.[57] But as long as ritual and ceremony derived from the guilds was a recurring feature on the streets, so the memory of the 'pre-industrial' world of work remained green.

The sense embodied in the guilds of belonging to 'genuine communities within the larger community', as Sylvia Thrupp termed it, was a powerful one. It can be identified across time and cultures and could, and often did, cut across the boundaries of employment status — apprentice, journeyman, small master, large employer — even after highly capitalized markets had emerged. This ethos has perhaps best been summarized by William Sewell in his history of the language of labour in France. 'The term *communauté* did not describe the tone of relations within a trade so much

---

54 Andy Wood, 'Social conflict and change in the mining communities of north-west Derbyshire, c.1600-1700', *International Review of Social History*, vol. 38, part 1 (April, 1993), p. 49.

55 M. J. Walker, 'The extent of guild control of trades'.

56 R. S. Neale, *Bath*, pp. 65-8.

57 See displays in the Ludlow and Norwich Castle museums; for Newcastle see M. J. Walker, 'The extent of guild control of trades', p. 164. More research is needed into the social and political 'work' of ritual and ceremonial in the modern period, in which guilds, friendly and trade societies played an important part. Gervase Rosser, 'Myth, image and social process in the English medieval town', *Urban History*, 23/1 (1996), pp. 19-25, makes some pertinent observations about post-Reformation urban ceremonial.

as the assumption that whatever their differences, members of a trade community belonged together and owed their art a certain loyalty against other categories of the population'.[58]

The concept of a trade as a moral community was not exclusively the product of the guild tradition. It can be seen powerfully at work in those mining areas where 'free miners' to some extent controlled (or had once controlled) the circumstances in which production took place. Like guilds, the miners' courts of Stannary and Barmote (in Cornwall and north-west Derbyshire respectively) upheld a structured world-view in which the credentials of those qualified to belong were confirmed and defended, from which 'foreign' workers were excluded and in which customary law regulated production. Like the guilds, the power of such courts positively to influence workers' lives was ebbing away by the beginning of the eighteenth century. Yet even in the early nineteenth century there remained 'a language and mentality conditioned as much by the memory of lost liberties and independence as by the new realities of a wholly industrial age'.[59] In the previous century, an age not wholly industrial still, this mentality was all the stronger.

Perhaps the most important legacy of the guilds lay in their investing the world of work with a profound solemnity. 'Mystery' is perhaps the most appropriate word, being part of the guilds' own vocabulary. Guilds infused dignity and a broader moral purpose into the mundane and often numbing routine of earning one's living. In so doing they can be seen as crucially shaping the artisan ethic, which in turn shaped the culture of early trade unions. 'This sense that work was much more than a physical act, but also a social and moral statement as well, was of course embodied in the "customary" attitudes and practices which so enraged the late-eighteenth-century improvers and their successors'.[60] For example, the inner life of the guilds anticipated the character of craft unionism in emphasizing the hierarchy of the trade, underpinned by a fundamental common bond of fellowship. Both of these were powerfully informed by rites of initiation and ritual. The place of ritual in guild life may well have been stronger in the early eighteenth century than at any time since the Reformation, as guilds sought to preserve and consolidate a corporate ethos (by, for example, the ostentatious observance of members' funerals) in the face of encroaching commercial considerations which eroded traditional fraternal links. Ritual, as we shall see, was an important and enduring element in craft unionism, in some cases as late as the 1960s. Surveying voluntary organizations in the early-modern period, Barry suggests that through an elaborate social vocabulary of antiquity, honour and precedence, the 'middling sort' vested 'their associations with precisely those qualities, associated with continuity, that the gentry claimed, as individuals, from their relationship to land and family'.[61] We have also seen, though, that the quest for respectability was a prime objective of medieval fraternities too. At the heart of the artisan experience there was an increasingly sharp tension between independence and dependency. The completion of apprenticeship made one a free man. It did so not merely in the sense of casting of the tutelage and guardianship of the master one had served, or in the acquisition of certain civic rights, but also because one acquired property in a skill and with it a capacity to become one's own master. It was comparable with the ownership of land and, unlike mere common labouring, it offered (at least potentially) freedom from the vagaries of the market in waged labour and the whim of employers. Yet increasingly this was no more than a latent capacity. Journeymen's dependency on larger employers was increasing and so too their use of

---

58 William H. Sewell, *Work and Revolution in France: The Language of Labor from the Old Regime to 1848* (1980), p. 33.
59 Andy Wood, 'Social conflict and change', p. 50.
60 Michael Roberts, 'The empty ladder: work and its meanings in early modern Cardiganshire', *Llafur*, vol. 6, no. 4, (1995), p. 21.
61 Johnathan Barry, 'Bourgeois collectivism? Urban Association and the Middling Sort', in Johnathan Barry and Christopher Brooks (eds.), *The Middling Sort*, p. 102.

collective action to assert their fundamental freedoms. When the extensive journeymen fraternities of late-medieval Coventry were dissolved in 1549, it was a sign not of a renaissance of the guilds as an *integrating* force, but rather of an emerging *polarization* within society, a process which was both downgrading the status of the journeymen and marginalizing them from the focal points of power in the local community. This process was already evident in 1517 when the city authorities suppressed the Rough Masons' and Daubers' fellowship, decreeing that its members should revert to the status of 'comen laborers as they were afore', and again in 1527 when the journeymen dyers suffered a similar fate.[62]

The artisanry's sense of status was critically defined by the frontier of skill that separated it from the labouring poor. Elaborate ritual, hierarchy and the language of brotherhood was one means by which the frontier of skill was defended. For example, the fullers and weavers of fifteenth-century Ruthin in north Wales, sub-divided their guild into 'maistres', 'brethren', 'felawes' and 'werkemen' (plus, presumably, apprentices). This masculine terminology is all the more striking in a craft dedicated to 'Our Lady'.[63] The rungs scaled by the trade unionist as he ascended the hierarchy of his society can be seen as mimicking the hierarchies of the guilds. Early craft societies were probably more hierarchical than was subsequently the case in British trade unionism. For example, like many of the *compagnonnages* of France, the Benevolent Society of Coachmakers, founded 1816, had three levels of membership — citizens, subjects and people.[64] The trade societies that placed most emphasis upon ritual, however, were those of the masons. Their highly ritualized procedures — with secret passwords, signs, grips and ceremonies — were well established by the last quarter of the sixteenth century, having developed partly to facilitate the administration of a craft in which tramping had long been an unusually important element.[65] The masons' ritual also helped fill something of the vacuum resulting from an abnormal, or non-existent, family life. London's journeymen masons finally and irrevocably split from their employers when the latters' Company was granted a royal charter in 1677.[66] We have already noted the incorporation of the London hatters ten years before. This journeymen stonemason's combination, however, was less successful than the hatters' and soon afterwards London lodges were opened to non-masons, thus ensuring continuity of income. Precedent for augmenting operatives' lodges with 'accepted masons' in this manner can be found as far back as the first half of the sixteenth century. There are also later parallels elsewhere, in an Edinburgh porters' society and a Newcastle upon Tyne tailors' body, both of whom opened their doors to non-members of the trades concerned. Obviously the admission of other occupational categories severely dilutes the claim such societies have on the attention of the historian of trade unionism. However, when the London masonic lodges formed the United Grand Lodge in 1717 (the birth of modern freemasonry) its senior officers still included carpenters and a stone cutter.[67] Considerable time elapsed before freemasonry completely shed its plebeian character, especially in

---

[62] Charles Phythian-Adams, *Desolation of a City*, pp. 129, 116-17, 270-1.

[63] Michael Roberts, 'The empty ladder', p. 97.

[64] Iorwerth J. Prothero, *Artisans and Politics in Early Nineteenth-Century London: John Gast and His Times* (1979), p. 36; cf. Eric J. Hobsbawm, *Primitive Rebels: Studies in Archaic Forms of Social Movement in the 19th and 20th Centuries* (1971), p. 161.

[65] Douglas Knoop and G. P. Jones, *The Medieval Mason: an Economic History of English Stone Building in the Later Middle Ages and Early Modern Times* (1933), pp. 56-62, 273-5.

[66] J. R. Kellett, 'The breakdown of guild and corporation control over the handicraft and retail trade in London', *Economic History Review*, 10, (1958), p. 388; Andy Durr, 'Ritual of association and the organizations of the common people', *Ars Quatuor Coronatorum* (Transactions of the Quatuor Coronati Lodge, No. 2076, London, 1987), vol. 100 (publ. 1988), p. 90.

[67] Andy Durr, 'Ritual of association', p. 90.

Scotland[68] and it is notable that as late as 1834 masonic authorities had to order the 'putting down [of] all spurious lodges, whether of Trades Unions or Secret Societies'.[69]

The ritual life of freemasonry was attractive to the middling sort precisely because of the qualities identified by Jonathan Barry in the passage quoted earlier. It can also be argued, though, that the retention or development of ritual in freemasonry and trade societies alike was in part a reaction to changing power and gender relations. Early trade societies (and even more so the French *compagnonnages*) affirmed patriarchal values through the creation of a 'fictive family situation' and a hierarchy of membership grades, through which journeymen were able to rise 'as compensation for their inability to become masters'.[70] The ideology of the guilds was likewise emphatically gendered. Whatever the economic significance of women workers outside the domain of the home, by the late seventeenth century the guilds largely upheld a masculine world view to which women were admitted only in exceptional circumstances, such as widows who took over the business of guild-member husbands. Though mitigated to some extent by women's membership of non-guild fraternities, the antipathy of guild ideology to female participation increased over time, a consequence of the stresses economic development placed upon traditional working patterns. Shortages of labour in some late-medieval English towns had provided opportunities for women to assert a considerable degree of economic independence. In some instances married women were permitted to trade as if they were males and in London women engaged in different crafts to their husbands were allowed to take apprentices. There are even references to designated women's guilds in Beverley (brewsters) and Southampton (woolpackers); but generally women who were guild members were not allowed to participate in the selection of officials.

As labour shortages abated in the long term, the tendency within guild-controlled trades was for women increasingly to be marginalized. This was true of Europe as a whole,[71] but it was particularly so in Britain. For example 'warkwomen' appear for the last time in records relating to the Aberdeen shoreporters in 1636.[72] A century later the tailors' and bakers' guilds of the same city introduced punitive measures to exclude female participation in their trades.[73] The consequences of such processes are likely to have been particularly profound at wage-earner level. In a study of German guilds in the early modern period, Merry Weisner argues that journeymen guilds cultivated a male solidarity that became a substitute for — and consolation for the loss of — the prestige of mastership.[74] Guild ordinances, which had once spoken of decorum and discipline as *Zucht*, now qualified it as *Manns-Zucht*. The guild tradition, at least as it was perceived in the period of industrialization, did nothing to soften trade unions' defensiveness on gender issues. As Anna Clark has argued, the masculine solidarities of early British trade unionism operated in a similar way to the journeymen associations in the guild context: 'Traditionally, apprenticeship had been linked to adolescence, whereas journeymen were rowdy young men who settled down only when they became masters and married. When journeymen could no longer hope to run their own workshops, they

---

68   Douglas Knoop and G. P. Jones, *The Medieval Mason*, p.94; Chapter 4 below.
69   *Poor Man's Guardian*, 24 May 1834
70   Mary Ann Clawson, 'Early modern fraternalism and the patriarchal family', *Feminist Studies*, 6/2, (1980), p. 385.
71   James R. Farr, 'Cultural analysis and early modern artisans', in Geoffrey Crossick (ed.), *The Artisan and the European Town, 1500-1900* (1997), p. 68.
72   George Gordon, *The Shore Porters' Society of Aberdeen, 1498-1969* (1969), p. 26.
73   Ebenezer Bain, *Merchant and Craft Guilds: A History of the Aberdeen Incorporated Trades* (1887), pp. 228, 256-60.
74   Merry E. Weisner, 'Guilds, male bonding and women's work in early modern Germany', *Gender and History*, 1, 2 (Summer, 1989).

remained stuck in the bachelor stage of the trade's life cycle.'[75]

The memory of the guilds also validated collective action at the workplace. We need to be cautious here: it is certainly not the case that without the guilds there would have been no trade unionism. However, trade union history in the eighteenth and early nineteenth centuries was often marked by the tension between authority's suspicion of workers' combinations in any form and a grudging recognition that such association was natural and in some respects even desirable. This heightened the appeal of the guild tradition to trade unionists seeking to legitimize what they were about. In an era of explicit anti-trade union legislation, there was often merit in claiming that one's trade society was the linear descendent of a guild, or even that guild in substance and fact. Such claims were reflected in the titles of several early Irish trade unions: for example, the United Brothers of St Joseph (later the Regular Carpenters of Dublin), formed in 1764 in the wake of the Irish anti-combination acts in 1757 and 1763, and the Ancient Corporation of the Carpenters of the City of Cork (another mid-eighteenth-century formation).[76]

Similar considerations probably influenced London shipwrights in their choice of a title for an association formed towards the end of the century. The St Helena Society, though registered under the 1793 Friendly Societies Act, carried out trade union activities, including the attempted enforcement of closed shops in Thameside shipyards and representing striking shipwrights in negotiations with employers.[77] Meanwhile the caulkers who worked alongside them, reacting to the employment of non-indentured labour in the Royal Dockyards, actually sought to have their trade incorporated as a London company.[78] Sheffield trade societies firmly believed they were the rightful heirs of the Cutlers' Company. As late as 1844 the spring knife cutlers adopted a nomenclature and structure of office-holding to reflect this.[79] More commonly, early trade unions simply mimicked guilds. This was particularly the case in the cloth trade, where many of the earliest English trade societies were formed, strongly resonant with the associational life of the guilds which, in many cases, they overlapped. In Essex, weavers at Bocking were electing 'wardens' as early as 1689 (and along with their colleagues at nearby Braintree continued to do so as late as 1796). Braintree combers, 'under the wardens of their fraternity' organized parades and dinners.[80] As the postscript to this chapter shows, the combers of another Essex town, Coggeshall, provide an especially well-documented and informative example of trade indebtedness to the guild tradition. In the West Country the weavers of Taunton were joined in an association which had 'a common seal, tipstaff and Colours' prominently displayed during their meetings at a local inn. The woolcombers of Alton, Hampshire, were said 'to act as Body corporate, by electing two Supervisors and a Book keeper, using a common Seal, and making By Laws or Orders, by which they pretend to determine who hath a Right to the Woolcombers' Trade'.[81] Almost identically-worded complaints were made of the Devon woollen workers. Much of the tone, trappings and vocabulary of the guilds were carried over

---

75 Anna Clark, *The Struggle for the Breeches: Gender and the Making of the British Working Class* (1995), p. 33.

76 Sidney and Beatrice Webb, *The History of Trade Unionism*, pp. 721-4.

77 *PP* 1825 (437) IV, The Effect of the Act of 5 Geo IV c. 95, Select Committee Report, pp. 300, 312.

78 Iorwerth J. Prothero, *Artisans and Politics*, pp. 33, 37.

79 Sidney Pollard, *A History of Labour in Sheffield* (1959), pp. 66-7.

80 A. F. J. Brown, *Essex at Work, 1700-1815* (1969), pp. 24-5.

81 *Journals of the House of Commons*, vol. 15 (1705-08), p. 312 (26 February 1707); *Ipswich Journal*, 7 August 1725, cited in Robert Malcolmson, 'Workers' combinations in eighteenth-century England', in Jacob and Jacob (eds.), *The Origins of Anglo-American Radicalism* (1984), p. 157. See also E. P. Thompson, *Customs in Common: Studies in Traditional Popular Culture* (1991), pp. 59-60, in which is reproduced a membership certificate of the Alton combers.

into waged workers' associations. It is difficult to see how this could be otherwise, for the guilds, in continuing fact or idealized memory, provided almost the only model for what these early combinations aimed to do, as well as what was held to be legal precedent for workers' organizations. 'Let it be remembered', members of the Manchester smallware weavers' trade society were told in 1756, that 'a great many worshipful Companies, now held by charter in this Nation, had once no better a Beginning, and acted as much contrary to the Law'.[82] Where they retained significant plebeian memberships, lodges of the freemasons would have exercised a similar influence.

Labour's sense of the guild tradition contributed towards the validation of collective action and helped legitimize its aims. The 1563 Statute of Artificers remained a benchmark, even after its final repeal in 1814, partly because it embodied a central element of the guild ethic: the institution of apprenticeship. So central was apprenticeship to the concerns of the early trade unions that their emergence corresponded closely to the decline in effectiveness of the Statute in enforcing it. The emergence of trade unionism was necessitated as the erosion of communal and guild-based norms was paralleled by the diminishing authority of statute law regarding apprenticeship. Without this enduring knowledge of the guilds and what they had stood for, the possessive individualism that came to characterize British economic and political discourse might have been yet stronger.

POSTSCRIPT: COGGESHALL, 1687

This chapter has emphasized the relevance of the guilds and other medieval fraternities to our understanding of the origins of trade unions. We shall see in the following chapter that, even in the midst of industrialization, agreement upon what constitutes a 'trade union' can still be problematic. It is better to relax the understandable aspiration for definitional neatness in order to be more attentive to the evolution of trade unionist mentalities. This is not to suggest that connections between guilds and trade unions were always direct. Sometimes, however, a genetic lineage can be traced. This is particularly the case in the long-established textiles industries of Essex and the West Country. In the case of Coggeshall the connection is explicit; E. P. Thompson drew attention on several occasions to the apparent continuity between the Coggeshall clothiers' company and a workers' organization there calling itself the Combers' Purse.[83] This is readily apparent in a document relating to the 'Company of the Occupation, Trade and Misterie of the Clothiers, Fullers, Baymakers, and New Drapers in the Town of Coggeshall' in the last quarter of the seventeenth century.[84] The division revealed between masters and journeymen is consistent with what is known of the woollen textile industry elsewhere at this time. What is unique for this early date is clear evidence for the journeymen's action having been translated into an associational form completely independent of the guild.

North-east Essex was a long-established centre of the woollen textile industry and Coggeshall one of its principal towns. The area shared in the economic downturn of the mid-1670s and, as in London, weavers were involved in riots in Colchester in 1675. But generally the region's textile industry prospered. This, however, was not without its problems, as the Coggeshall trade's

---

82 'Shuttle' 1756, p. 27.

83 E. P. Thompson, 'English trade unionism and other labour movements before 1790', *BSSLH*, 17 (Autumn, 1968); 'The moral economy of the English crowd in the eighteenth century', *Past and Present*, no. 50 (1971), reprinted in E. P. Thompson, *Customs in Common*, pp. 58-63.

84 University of Leeds, Brotherton Library, Special Collections, MS/8-10: diaries of Joseph Bufton (b. 1651) of Coggeshall. References in the diaries (actually notes made on the blank pages of printed almanacs) extend up to 1709. The diary (MS/10) relating to this episode appears to have been compiled in 1703. In the quotations that follow most of the author's contractions and spellings have been modernized. An extensive transcription of MS/10 in modern English can be found in the Historical Manuscripts Commission's *Report on Manuscripts in Various Collections, Volume VIII* (1913), pp. 569-92.

remembrancer, Joseph Bufton, recorded:

> Notwithstanding the great care of our forefathers for the well managing of our trade & keeping out Intruders, it hath of late years, whilst most Combers had full Employment, bin much neglected. And many men of other occupations did Intrude themselves into this art, & many boys came to learn it without being bound & serving seven years according to law, thereby offending against the orders in our Warden's book. Insomuch that at length some that had served as apprentices to the trade were in great want of work & forced to go out of the town for employment to get a livelihood, whilst at the meantime Intruders into the trade were set at work in town.

Those most afflicted by these problems, and therefore presumably journeymen rather than masters, assembled to discuss the state of the trade and thereafter 'agreed to meet once a month for the better looking after it'. A subscription of sixpence was levied and a memorial drawn up 'to the fulling trade'. Its aim was clear: the enforcement of entry to the trade by apprenticeship, as set out in the Elizabethan Statute of Artificers (1563).

> From such as would our rights invade
> Or would intrude into our Trade
> Or Break the law Queen Betty made
>   Libera nos Domine

In an interesting gesture that perhaps indicates a widening social consciousness, intruders who had no other trade were accepted provided they agreed to be bound for seven years and 'pay their freedom according to the custom'; but intruders who had 'left the trade they were brought up to' would not be tolerated. Members pledged to 'be more constant in frequenting and upholding the Guild, and there and then to be careful to choose such Wardens as may of right be chosen, and men likely to stand up for the good of the trade'.

As a result of this pressure group's exertions the company underwent something of a renaissance. The festival of Bishop Blaize, patron saint of the textile industry, seems to have been celebrated with a new vigour and in 1687 representations were made to local magistrates who granted 'a new warrant', requiring the Company's Wardens and Coggeshall's parish constables jointly to apprehend intruders and bring them before the justices. Thus far, the picture that emerges in Coggeshall fits what is known from elsewhere about tensions over the relaxation of trade regulation within guilds. However, 'after these things', Bufton recorded, the combers 'still continued their meeting as before, where having succeeded thus far in their design a proposal was made amongst themselves about raising of a purse for the maintaining of those among them that fell into want'. Articles, based on those of 'their fellow brethren the pursers in Colchester' were drawn up in 1688 for a new body, the Coggeshall Combers' Purse.

Having written out the articles in full, Bufton added a postscript: 'In April 1690 the combers broke up their purse. It was occasioned by Jonathan Cable being so unreasonable. It was thought if he might he would have had all their money belonging to the purse.' The Weavers of Coggeshall subsequently formed a society, with elected wardens and trustees, the rules of which were ratified by local magistrates in 1709. Shortly afterwards it prosecuted a clothier for employing non-apprenticed labour.[85] Perhaps this body, rather than the Combers' Purse, might reasonably be regarded as a form

---

85 A. F. J. Brown, *Essex at Work*, pp. 24-5.

of trade union. There is nothing in the articles of the Purse that refers to any matter other than the collection and administration of a fund that 'we may show that love we have to our trade, & one to another for our trade sake'. However, the correlation of trade unionist behaviour with the constitutional format of a sick or 'box club' became so commonplace in eighteenth-century Britain it would be surprising if the Combers' Purse had not to some extent involved itself in broader trade matters. 'Trade Union' and 'Sick Club' represented the two ends of an organizational continuum which cannot be neatly divided.

As Thompson suspected, the Coggeshall Combers' Purse (to which should probably be added Colchester's) constitutes something of a breach in 'the Webbian walling-off of trade unionism proper from guild traditions'.[86] What is particularly striking is the generalized assumption that the Purse represented the interests of 'the Trade'. The one consistent feature of both the Company's articles and the documentation of the Purse is this argot of 'the trade', 'the love of the trade', 'our trade'. With it went a profound sense of the status in his local community a time-served craftsmen ought to enjoy. The interests of the latter were always to be preferred to those of the intruder, as the Company's ordinances decreed: 'it shall be lawful to displace the said stranger and in his work to place the said poor townsman, so as he be reputed a true man, of honest life and conversation, and so esteemed'. The same concern about status and good standing is evident in the articles of the Combers' Purse:

> It is our intent that when any man or his charge be afflicted, he shall not sell, pawn or embezzle any of his goods or wearing clothes, nor run himself into debt; but to be in as good a condition, when it shall please God to restore him, as he was when he was first taken.

Neither the pressure group within the Clothiers' Company nor the self-help club that emerged from it was ephemeral. Both were preconceived associations structured round written terms of reference and regular meetings. (Unfortunately, like many subsequent self-help organizations, the Purse was also not immune against unscrupulous office-holders.) Both associations are built upon notions of masculine solidarity and responsibility: not only are fellow-workers 'brethren' but there is an emphasis upon the male family breadwinner having to provide for '*his charge*'. The ethics of 'the trade' and those of the local community are mutually reinforcing: strangers and intruders are 'not to be tolerated' whilst 'townsman' and workman are virtually synonymous. Yet there are also indications of a wider consciousness that differentiates workers from those employing them: tolerance is extended to intruders who, having no other trade, agree to comply with the combers' regulations and there are references to 'our fellow brethren the pursers in Colchester'. Above all the status and good standing of those who follow the craft are paramount. The time-served craftsman has, in effect, a *property* in his skill which carries with it a *right* to work.

---

86 E. P. Thompson, 'English trade unionism', p. 20.

2

Trade Associations in the Age of Manufactures

THE BROAD CONTEXT

'Eighteenth century economic history is not the subject for those who wish for certainty', it has recently been suggested.[1] The causes and course of industrialization in Britain are very much a contested area.[2] Old certitudes, based on an heroic notion of *the* Industrial Revolution, have come under attack. In their place a picture has emerged in which the emphasis is upon evolution rather than revolution, where continuities are as important as discontinuities and which stresses the huge differences that existed between regions and between industries.

The diminution of the industrial revolution's stature has been closely bound up with widening and more sophisticated statistical analysis. It has also mirrored modern preoccupations with economic growth — or the lack of it. The concept of industrial revolution was most pervasive when the British economy seemed at its most unassailable. Just as historical interest in trade unions has declined with shifts in the fortunes of contemporary trade unionism, so too has the industrial revolution languished — though vigorous revisionism rather than neglect has been responsible for this.[3]

What is left of the industrial revolution, familiar from generations of school textbooks? Taking the broadest view, the transition to a predominantly industrial workforce, with the corollary of an increasingly urbanized population, remains the single most striking feature of modern British history. This is all the more so because Britain was the first country to undergo the most epoch-forming change since farming replaced hunting and gathering as the means of human subsistence in the neolithic age. We might cavil about how this was achieved and also point to the minority status of the developed world's population when seen from a global perspective. Increasingly we may beg to question whether the change was an unqualified good; but it was, surely, revolutionary. More locally and precisely, historical demographers point to a sustained increase in population levels, sufficient to

---

1 N. F. R. Crafts, 'The industrial revolution', in Roderick Floud and Donald McCloskey, (eds.), *The Economic History of Britain Since 1700: Volume I — 1700-1860* (1994), p. 59.

2 The most recent survey is Roderick Floud and Donald McCloskey, (eds.), *The Economic History of Britain*, but those interested in work and labour are likely to find this disappointing. Pat Hudson, *The Industrial Revolution* (1992) looks set to remain the best single introductory text for some time to come. See also Peter Mathias, *The First Industrial Nation* (1983), and M. J. Daunton, *Progress and Poverty: An Economic and Social History of Britain, 1700-1850* (1995). For the eighteenth century the work of Maxine Berg, *The Age of Manufactures, 1700-1820* (1985), and her chapter in Floud and McCloskey, is indispensable.

3 On the interaction of contemporary economic preoccupations with historical perspectives see D. Cannadine, 'The present and the past in the English industrial revolution, 1880-1980', *Past and Present*, 103, (1984), pp. 131-72; J. Raven, 'British history and the enterprise culture', *Past and Present*, 123, and Hudson, *The Industrial Revolution*, ch. 1.

provide both cheap labour and a growing domestic market for industry, but sufficiently constrained not to swamp the capacity of the economy to feed it. Quite why this should have occurred when it did — from the 1740s — is still a matter of some controversy and beyond the scope of this book to consider.[4]

Accounts of Britain's industrial performance in the eighteenth century still affirm the crucial role of overseas markets, particularly the colonies, an advantage enjoyed to only a lesser extent by Britain's competitors. Cheap coal is still seen as important and so too are the contributions of the cotton and iron industries to the economy as a whole; increases in the productive capacities of agriculture and improvements in transport continue to be recognized. However, rather less emphasis is now placed on factory production, steam power and mechanization than was once the norm. Britain was the *workshop*, not the factory, of the world. Epochal as the central transition may have been, many economic historians have worried that the use of the word 'revolution' — which is, after all, only a metaphor — misleads us into supposing that changes were more sudden and all-embracing than was actually the case. And they point to relatively modest rates of economic growth, measured in terms like real output and gross domestic product, to suggest that change was evolutionary rather than revolutionary.[5]

Cynically, the outsider may feel that the debate has been reduced to a controversy about the aptness of 'revolution' as a metaphor in the face of increasingly sophisticated statistical indicators. Given the high degree of regional specialization within the British economy, stable or modestly-increasing rates of growth might obscure fundamental dislocation at 'lower' levels, along with enduring changes in particular sectors. We must also always be mindful of the experiences of those who lived at the time. Although contemporaries' appreciation of the long-term significance of economic change was attenuated before the nineteenth century, the eighteenth presents abundant evidence to the effect that the pace of economic change was gathering, in a way that caused contemporaries both excitement and disquiet and to an extent that was unparalleled and unprecedented elsewhere in Europe.[6]

Yet economic growth in the eighteenth century was steady rather than dramatic. There was an acceleration after 1760, but nothing so sudden as historians supposed even as recently as the 1970s. Consequently, the concept of one particular decade representing a 'take-off' ('into self-sustained growth' as the economist W. W. Rostow put it, referring to the 1780s) is now rejected. Along with this has gone a radical re-evaluation of the textiles industries: historians have not discounted the innovations that characterized this sector — especially cotton — but relative to the economy as a whole they are now seen as quite small. (This is a particular factor in the downsizing of later eighteenth-century growth rates.) There is a greater recognition of the British economy's diversity and of its corollary, namely that the scale of industrial enterprises has tended to be exaggerated in uncritical accounts of the industrial revolution. 'There was no linear development of organizational

---

4   The central work is E. A. Wrigley and R. S. Schofield, *The Population History of England, 1541-1871: A Reconstruction* (1989), which includes an introduction reviewing the responses to the original 1981 edition. Readers without a grounding in historical demography, though, are best advised to start with Pat Hudson, *The Industrial Revolution*, ch. 5.

5   Roderick Floud and Donald McCloskey, (eds.), *The Economic History of Britain*, and Pat Hudson, *The Industrial Revolution*, both detail the arguments surrounding growth rates. The key text, however is N. F. R. Crafts, *British Economic Growth during the Industrial Revolution* (1985), helpfully abridged in N. F. R. Crafts,'The industrial revolution: economic growth in Britain, 1700-1860', in Anne Digby and Charles H. Feinstein, *New Directions in Economic and Social History* (1989).

6   D. C. Coleman, *Myth, History and the Industrial Revolution* (1992); Patrick O'Brien, 'Introduction: modern conceptions of the industrial revolution', in Patrick O'Brien and Roland Quinault, *The Industrial Revolution and British Society* (1994).

structure from small-scale to large-scale, proprietorial to managerial, or dispersed to centralized systems'.[7] Even very large enterprises sometimes disguised the continuation of smaller units of production. For example, Sir Ambrose Crowley's massive iron undertaking founded at Winlaton, County Durham, in 1691, used a system of internal contracting in which master manufacturers drew materials from the works' stores and employed their own hammermen, journeymen and apprentices. They were then credited with the selling price of the goods their team made, less the costs of materials and Crowley's overheads and profit margin. The concentration of production on this site might tempt the unwary to describe the operation as a factory: but the way in which production was structured was effectively that of a putting-out system. Spatially, the work was not 'put-out' very far, but the overheads Crowley charged his craftsmen were akin to the frame rents hosiery manufacturers charged their knitters and also to loom rents in the domestic cotton industry. Similar procedures can be identified in the metal trades of the Midlands. Elsewhere the practice of sub-contracting labour recruitment through senior hands — to whom were given the tasks of finding, directing and paying their helpers — was commonplace throughout the eighteenth and nineteenth centuries and continued in some sectors, for example mining, well into the twentieth century.

With steady economic growth went the continued vitality of 'pre-industrial' institutions and structures. Guilds were one such survival, not as incompatible with technological innovation as has usually been supposed,[8] though after the 1730s, the degree (in intensity or duration) to which their influence endured varied widely. Apprenticeship was another. Although the recruitment of apprentices never matched the rates of the early seventeenth century, it remained relatively stable up until the 1730s. In the 1740s shortages of labour (a consequence of incremental economic growth not being matched by that of population) initiated its erosion in many trades and centres; but the decline was a slow one, sufficiently so — as we shall see in the next chapter — for the repeal of traditional apprenticeship legislation in 1814 to be considerably more than an academic issue.

However, the most significant 'pre-industrial survivor' was domestic outwork. In the introduction to the previous chapter reference was made to proto-industrialization: the growth of rural domestic manufacturing which has been seen by many historians as the pivotal phase linking medieval and modern industrial societies. How pivotal depends upon the extent to which one subscribes to one or other of the models of proto-industrialization. At the very least the concept has stimulated historians to investigate and conceptualize the processes of transition to industrial society with far greater detail and sophistication than was hitherto the case. One of the consequences of the debate which has surrounded proto-industrialization has been a growing appreciation of how much there still remains to understand about the nature of industrialization.[9] At the other extreme, however, the idea of proto-industrialization can obscure more than it illuminates. Why 'proto-industry' evolved in certain regions and not others cannot be reduced to a simple equation concerning upland or pastoral agriculture — to which it is usually linked. The East Anglian heartland of the early English textile industry was certainly not a hill-farming area. Plebeian access to land was more important than topography — not necessarily to a market in land but perhaps to cheaply rented holdings or squatting opportunities. Nor was there a straightforward transition from proto-industrialization to modern industry. Labour and the intellectual and finance capital for industrialization were not mainly derived

---

7   Maxine Berg, 'Factories, workshops and industrial organisation', in Roderick Floud and Donald McCloskey, (eds.), *The Economic History of Britain*, p. 129.

8   Steven A. Epstein, 'Craft guilds, apprenticeship, and technological change in preindustrial Europe', *Journal of Economic History*, vol. 58, no. 3, (1998).

9   Pat Hudson, 'Proto-industrialization in England', in S. C. O'Gilvie and M. Cerman (eds.), *European Proto-Industrialization* (1996).

from proto-industries, as a slavish adoption of the model suggests they should have been. The East Anglian and West Country textile heartlands declined rather than grew in economic importance. There was enormous variation in the structures 'proto-industries' took: entrepreneurs putting out work to family-centred production units was the most common; but the woollen industry of west Yorkshire rested upon independent masters, whilst artisan workshops typified arrangements in Birmingham and the London suburbs. As we have just seen, Crowley's works might plausibly be characterized as proto-industrial. *Proto-industrialization*, no less than *industrial revolution*, is a metaphor. However, it does throw light upon certain economic and social relationships that can help explain the forms taken by, and the timing of trade unionism.

Revisionist interpretations of the industrial revolution carry interesting implications for our understanding of trade unions. The emphasis upon continuity rather than discontinuity across the threshold of industrialization reinforces the case for treating 'pre-industrial' workers' associational life seriously as part of the history of trade unionism, as outlined in the previous chapter. It helps explain why trade societies, when they were formed, emerged in the artisanal sector with its profoundly historicized sense of property in skill and the interests of 'the trade'. And it fortifies the case against the walling-off of a 'modern' labour history from what had gone before. If, as Crafts has argued, 'the main feature of British industrialization involved getting a lot of workers into the industrial sector, not getting a high level of output per worker from them once they were there',[10] then the circumstances were every bit as propitious for the growth of workers' intra-trade awareness as those premised by the old heroic model of industrial revolution — maybe even more so, for they predicate the possibility of drawing out organizational forms and ethos from previous experience rather than inventing them from scratch. Thus the historically deep-rooted character of waged labour, explored in the previous chapter, assumes particular significance as the growing numbers of waged workers during the eighteenth century drew upon the strands of custom, experience and association in shaping their own response to industrialization.

There was no simple correlation between industrialization and the growth of labour organization. There could not be, for industrialization was not a uniform process even within England, still less the rest of the British Isles and Ireland. Nonetheless, evidence for industrial unrest can be documented across the whole century. Its climax in the 1790s will be examined in the next chapter. However, two earlier periods of unrest also stand out: the early decades of the century and the late 1750s and 1760s.

The evolution of trade societies also has to be considered against the background of changes in the rewards to labour. Real incomes of English labouring and artisan households had been rising since the mid-seventeenth century. By the mid-eighteenth century, datal (daily paid) labour in the building industries enjoyed money wages that were perhaps 50 per cent higher than a century before.[11] It is difficult to present such a crisp summary of real wages, but the emerging consensus is that these too rose over roughly the same period: 'Regional and occupational variations could clearly be very wide ... but there can be little doubt that the gains were substantial in many places and significant almost everywhere'.[12] Many household incomes were boosted by the incorporation of growing numbers of children and women into the market for waged labour.

This had a paradoxical effect. 'Rewards to labour' were more than just pecuniary. Before the early

---

10 N. F. R. Crafts, 'The industrial revolution', p. 72.
11 D. C. Coleman, *Myth, History*, pp. 99-105; Donald Woodward, *Men at Work: Labourers and Building Craftsmen in the Towns of Northern England 1450-1750* (1995), pp. 169-287.
12 John Hatcher, 'Labour, leisure and economic thought before the nineteenth century', *Past and Present*, 160 (August, 1998), p. 75.

nineteenth century, and in some industries well beyond it, leisure preferences were as powerful a determinant of working patterns as wages. A situation in which rising real wages for men were accompanied by increased wage-earning capacities among women and children strengthened the hand of male labour wishing to adhere to 'pre-industrial' patterns of a short, concentrated working week in preference to longer hours and greater earning potential. 'Every Body knows that there is a vast number of Journey-men ... who, if by Four Days Labour in a Week they can maintain themselves, will hardly be persuaded to work the fifth.'[13] Restrictions on entry to the skilled trades facilitated the same objective. Yet a growth in female waged workers potentially undermined the exclusiveness of the trades, as did the admission of more (and/or more-youthful) apprentices. Artisans' concern to regulate apprenticeship therefore grew almost in parallel with increases to real wages: this may help explain the high incidence of labour disputes in the first three decades of the century. Then, the sustained upward trend in real wages was halted around the middle of the century and subsequently reversed in many regions as a result of inflating food prices. Though early calculations of the impact of industrialization on earnings exaggerated this effect, more recent revisions still suggest that nationally real wages fell from the mid-eighteenth to the early nineteenth century.[14] The century's second cluster of industrial disputes, in the late-1750s and 1760s, has to be seen in this context. Interestingly, it overlapped with a significant change of mood among writers on economic issues, in which widespread belief that low wages were a necessary stimulus to labour productivity gave way in the 1760s and 1770s before a growing concern that wages might sink too low .[15]

We saw in the previous chapter how a widening cultural gap between employers and employed became more evident during the seventeenth century. The extent to which masters, through their guilds or companies, had the interests of their trade as a whole at heart was increasingly questioned by journeymen. The first decades of the new century saw social divisions begin to harden around this concern, especially in the textiles trades, a process linked in part to the decline of guilds in the manufacturing sector. The earliest premeditated combinations with evident aspirations to permanence appeared around this time in the textile industries of Essex, Devon and Somerset and in the tailoring and hatting trades of the capital: curriers, smiths, farriers, sail- and coach makers were not far behind. Probably the earliest Irish labour associations, of Cork tailors and Dublin woolcombers, were formed in the 1720s. In Scotland, the Aberdeen wrights and coopers were 'entering into signed associations among themselves whereby they become bound to one another under a penalty' by 1732.[16] Though the evidence is imperfect, labour disputes appear to have increased in number in each of the first three decades of the century.[17] In particular there were extensive riots among Wiltshire textile workers in 1726-7 whilst a strike across the Durham coalfield in 1731 revealed an unprecedented degree of collective identity and self-assurance on the part of the miners.[18]

The handling of industrial disputes at law also underwent something of a sea change at this time,

---

13 Bernard Mandeville, *The Fable of the Bees*, (1697), quoted in John Hatcher, 'Labour, leisure and economic thought', p. 69. On the evolution of leisure and work patterns see ibid, E. P. Thompson, 'Time, work-discipline and industrial capitalism', *Past and Present*, 38 (December), (which is reprinted in E. P. Thompson, *Customs in Common: Studies in Traditional Popular Culture*, (1991)), and Douglas Reid, 'The decline of Saint Monday', *Past and Present*, 71 (May, 1976).
14 E. A. Wrigley and R. S. Schofield, *The Population History of England, 1541-1871*, pp. 407-9 and appendix 9.
15 John Hatcher, 'Labour, leisure and economic thought'.
16 Ebenezer Bain, *Merchant and Craft Guilds: A History of the Aberdeen Incorporated Trades* (1887), p. 246.
17 C. R. Dobson, *Masters and Journeymen: A Pre-history of Industrial Relations* (1980), pp. 154-7.
18 David Levine and Keith Wrightson, *The Making of an Industrial Society: Whickham, 1560-1765* (1991), pp. 399-409.

first with the 'Tailors' Combination Act' of 1721 (the first statute to use the term 'combination') and second a landmark decision in the case of the Cambridge journeymen tailors (1721). This extended the common law of conspiracy to collective actions by workers if taken in pursuit of trade claims. It thus rendered criminal actions that, taken by an individual alone, were legal.[19] Thereafter conspiracy proceedings against trade combinations, and doubtless even more so their threatened use, were a persistent feature of industrial disputes.[20] A parallel development saw the early expression of classic liberal arguments about wages: 'labour as to its price, is like everything else, it rises or falls according to the proportion that there is between the demand and the quantity then in the market, all restraints are unjust, let them be upon what side they will'. Daniel Defoe observed in 1724 that 'the common people had gone through a "kind of general revolution, or change in their disposition, temper and manners … such as I believe no nation has undergone but themselves"'.[21] Contemporaries spoke of a decline in deference even on the part of servants and it was alleged that some

> are arriv'd to that Height of Insolence as to have enter'd into a Society together, and made Laws by which they oblige themselves not to serve for less than such a Sum, nor carry Burdens or any Bundle or Parcel above a certain Weight, not exceeding Two or Three Pounds, with other Regulations directly opposite of those they Serve.[22]

This may be satirical, or an exaggerated view of a simple friendly society, but it is one of several similar comments around this time.

Recorded labour militancy increased in the late-1750s and 1760s, exacerbated by a subsistence crisis in 1763. However, not all unrest was linked to food prices. The years 1759-61 saw unprecedented levels of labour unrest in the West Midlands metal trades, consequent upon sudden rises in the prices of raw materials: spontaneous combinations emerged across the region in the firearms, needlemaking and Birmingham metals trades.[23] The years 1767-8 saw a marked acceleration of labour militancy in Scottish cities.[24] There was a major dispute in the London tailoring trade in 1768.[25] There were two other notable disputes in 1768: first the Port of London was brought to a complete standstill by striking mariners and coalheavers;[26] second, concerted action in Lancashire destroyed machinery and other millowners' property.[27] There was to be a further and far more serious series of disorders there in 1779.

By the 1760s formal associations of workers, at least in London, appear to have shed any remaining air of novelty and to have become broadly accepted as a part of routine daily life: Horace Walpole, author and arbiter of taste (and a prime minister's son), for example, wrote of them in

---

19 J. V. Orth, *Combination and Conspiracy: A Legal History of Trade Unionism, 1721-1906* (1991), pp. 29-32.
20 C. R. Dobson, *Masters and Journeymen*, pp.127-30.
21 Both quotations in John Rule, 'Against innovation? Custom and resistance in the workplace, 1700-1850', in Tim Harris (ed.), *Popular Culture in England c. 1500-1850* (1995), pp. 294 and 289.
22 Jean Hecht, *The Domestic Servant in Eighteenth-Century England* (1980), p. 286.
23 Marie B. Rowlands, *Masters and Men in the West Midland Metalware Trades before the Industrial Revolution* (1975), p. 162.
24 W. H. Fraser, *Conflict and Class: Scottish Workers, 1700-1838* (1988).
25 John Rule, *The Experience of Labour in Eighteenth Century Industry* (1981), p. 153ff.
26 Peter Linebaugh and Marcus Rediker, 'The many-headed hydra: sailors, slaves and the Atlantic working class in the eighteenth century', *Journal of Historical Sociology*, 3/3 (September, 1990), pp. 236-400; Andrew Charlesworth et al., *An Atlas of Industrial Protest in Britain, 1750-1990* (1996), pp. 12-17.
27 Arthur G. Rose, 'Early cotton riots in Lancashire, 1769-79', *Transactions of the Lancashire and Cheshire Antiquarian Society*, vols 73 and 74, (1963-4).

approving terms.²⁸ The existence of trade unions should not, however, be taken as a general indicator of a more 'mature' or 'modern' response to the exigencies of waged labour. Organization through a trade society was far from the most common means to effect wage increases (and any concerted move in this period by workers to do so was likely to be described as a combination). Furthermore, whilst the evolution of trade unionism comfortably pre-dated the onset of wide-scale mechanization, workers' responses to the latter were more likely to involve the use of spontaneous or calculated violence. Workers used a repertory of tactics to improve the quality of their lives, of which trade societies were just one. During the eighteenth century unions were to be found chiefly in those occupational groups which were able to maintain or strengthen workers' security of employment through mutual association by controlling entry to the trade and maintaining employment opportunities within it. The formative context of early trade unionism was accelerating urbanization which expanded the numbers of waged workers in craft-based industries. Furthermore, with urbanization there emerged a vibrant culture of voluntary association. Historians, following Habermas's influential notion of the growth of the 'public sphere' in the eighteenth century, have generally viewed this culture as essentially bourgeois in character, but the growth of friendly societies and trade associations in the lower social strata indicate it was a wider phenomenon.

THE URBAN DYNAMIC

Urbanization was the dynamic that carried Britain, and in particular England, into forms of society and economic activity hitherto unknown. Towards the end of the seventeenth century the proportion (around 10 per cent) of England's population living in towns of 10,000 inhabitants or more was not markedly different to the rest of north-west Europe. The early decades of the following century saw England overhaul her neighbours in this respect: the 'great manufacturing towns of Manchester, Warrington, Macclesfield, Hallifax, Leeds, Wakefield, Sheffield, Birmingham, Froome, Taunton, Tiverton and others', wrote Daniel Defoe in 1728, 'are full of Wealth, and full of People, and daily increasing in both; all of which is occasioned by the meer Strength of Trade, and the growing Manufactures establish'd in them'.²⁹ The process continued relentlessly until by the end of the century around a quarter of the English lived in towns of 10,000 people and above. Yet the proportion elsewhere in Europe had barely altered.³⁰

In these early stages of industrialization workshops rather than factories predominated. 'No sooner do we enter the Town of Sheffield than the voice of industry is heard in the Streets and every house is a manufactury [sic] where the hammers strike Unison with our horses feet', wrote an American visitor to Yorkshire in 1776.³¹ Needing 'green field' sites adjacent to plentiful running water, early mills and factories such as Cromford and New Lanark *de-urbanized* industry. They attracted attention for their novelty and size, but also the extent to which they confined their workforce. Trying to describe them in terms contemporaries might readily understand, a visitor to Derbyshire wrote in 1790: 'these cotton mills, seven stories high, and fill'd with inhabitants, remind me of a first rate man

---

28 'The journeymen carpenters, like the cabinetmakers, have entered into an association not to work unless their wages are raised; and how can one complain? The poor fellows, whose all the labour is, see their masters advance the prices every day, and think it reasonable to touch their share', letter to Sir Horace Mann (British envoy at Florence), 1 July 1762, quoted in E. F. Carritt, *A Calendar of British Taste*, (1948), p. 303.

29 Quoted in John Stevenson, 'Social aspects of the industrial revolution', in P. K. O'Brien and R. Quinault (eds.), *The Industrial Revolution*, p. 238.

30 E. A. Wrigley, 'Urban growth and agricultural change: England and the continent in the early modern period', in Peter Borsay (ed.), *The Eighteenth-century Town: A Reader in English Urban History* (1990), pp. 62-7.

31 Kenneth Morgan (ed.), *An American Quaker in the British Isles: The Travel Journals of Jabez Maud Fisher 1775-79* (1992), p. 155.

of war; and when they are lighted up, on a dark night, look most luminously beautiful'.[32]

The new factories were not fertile ground for labour association. Expanding manufacturing towns were. Urban economies at the turn of the seventeenth century were gently buoyant, stimulated by the growth of new industries and services and sustained by a considerable degree of 'localised and basically circular' migration, upon which the 'pull' factors of urban life and wages were the main influence.[33] Long-distance migration, though not unknown — especially in London — did not underpin the earliest phases of industrialization; even after it emerged in the mid-eighteenth century it was still accompanied by more localized and circular currents. It was itself characterized by a ripple-effect, most long-distance migrants moving in a series of step-like movements, often pausing for years at a time in smaller urban centres before arriving at their eventual destination.[34] These patterns softened the personal dislocation of moving and meant that, even in the teeth of unprecedented industrial expansion, workplaces remained 'knowable communities'. New arrivals were likely to be known to at least one established worker; even if unknown their accent was likely to be familiar and so too the character and range of their conversation. Such a situation encouraged mutual trust and the emergence of friendly societies and localized forms of trade unionism. The enforcement of closed shops was often realizable even in trades where formal apprenticeship seldom applied.

In many towns guilds continued to provide a framework for industrial relations. Guilds' continued existence could to a great extent depend upon their functioning as an electoral college for local government, or upon the less formal — but no less vital — contribution they could make to local political life. The survival of a guild in itself should never be taken as indicating that it continued to control trade. On the other hand, the extent to which guild control of trades and manufactures survived in the eighteenth century has often been underestimated. Through close regulation of hiring, surviving guilds continued to have an impact upon the labour market. Some provided an administrative base for tramping. A related innovation was to operate a rudimentary labour exchange, which the Newcastle house carpenters did from 1767.[35] New ordinances were granted to the Bristol carpenters in 1730, to help exclude 'foreign' labour whilst other crafts in the city continued, with local magistrates' support, to seize and burn goods well into the eighteenth century.[36] Guilds established in Bath during the 1750s aimed to control wage rates.[37] Similarly, guilds in several Irish cities continued as effective employers' organizations and were even revived in Cork in 1787 precisely to counter the power of journeymen's combinations there.[38]

Restrictive aspects of continuing guild control of the labour market were often ameliorated by ancillary journeymen's clubs. Over time the connection of the latter to the parent company or guild

---

32 John Byng, *The Torrington Diaries: Containing the Tours through England and Wales of the Hon. John Byng (later fifth Viscount Torrington)*, edited by C. B. Andrews, vol. 3 (1935), p. 196.

33 Peter Clark, 'Migration in England during the late seventeenth and early eighteenth centuries', in Peter Clark and David Souden, *Migration and Society in Early Modern England* (1987), p. 243.

34 Arthur Redford, *Labour Migration in England 1800-1850* (second edition, revised and edited by W. H. Chaloner, 1964); Peter Clark, 'Migration in England'.

35 M. J. Walker, 'The extent of guild control of trades in England, *circa* 1660-1820: a study based on a sample of provincial towns and London companies', unpublished Ph.D thesis (University of Cambridge, 1985), p. 354.

36 John Latimer, *The Annals of Bristol in the Eighteenth Century* (1893), pp. 154-5 and 181.

37 R. S. Neale, *Bath: A Social History or; A Valley of Pleasure, yet a Sink of Iniquity* (1981), pp. 65-8.

38 Andrew Boyd, *The Rise of the Irish Trade Unions*, second edition (1985), pp. 19-21; Sean Daly, *Cork: A City in Crisis — A History of Labour Conflict and Social Misery 1870-72* (1978), pp. 263-4.

tended to become tenuous, as was seen in the previous chapter apropos of the hatters in the mid-seventeenth century. Dobson[39] provides the fullest account of the eighteenth-century guilds and their journeymen sections, though since it is confined to London its general applicability is questionable. However, the capital's experience is noteworthy, not least because of London's size and its importance as a manufacturing centre. Furthermore, metropolitan issues were paralleled elsewhere, for example Aberdeen. According to the evidence of a journeyman flesher recorded in 1785, it was 'usual for Servants of different corporations of Aberdeen in imitation of their Masters to Hold Meetings and Elect Nominal Deacons and Boxmasters and from these Nominal Office-bearers they also form a Nominal Convener Court and Elect a Convener and Master of Hospital'. The latter title, though probably not that of Boxmaster, was likely to have been honorific. As Kenneth Logue comments, 'although mimicking the officials and methods of the old guild, in practice they operated like a rudimentary trade union by controlling entry to the trade'.[40]

Early trade societies such as the Aberdeen fleshers' were not, however, merely self-help initiatives. They were imitative of the official and social life of employers but this was more than a matter of pretension or of claiming pedigree or precedent for their actions. These associations were also part of the flourishing social life of the urban renaissance of the eighteenth century and of a burgeoning culture of homosociality. Socializing with the same sex in this period has been studied mainly with reference to the aristocracy and 'middling sort';[41] but the obvious convivial function of most, if indeed not all, permanent trade societies shows them to be part of the same phenomenon. (Nor perhaps can their memberships be readily excluded from the notion of a middling sort.) To give just one example, Manchester's 'Tradesociety of Worsted Small-ware Weavers', founded 1747, was concerned to shake off the tag of 'The Weavers Committee' which, in the words of an early chairman, 'is a name I abominably hate'. They were emphatic that this was a society, united in 'Unity, Concord and brotherly love', and they published both articles for the conduct of business in their 'Club-Room' and a chairman's 'discourse' on the model of a masonic charge.[42]

Deteriorating relations between masters and men were the product of associational forms as well as economic change. A marked increase in disciplinary offences committed by journeymen appears in guild proceedings during the early eighteenth century. Continued attempts by larger employers to control, for example, wages or the length of the working day met with increased resistance from journeymen for whom the benefits of guild membership were diminishing. With declining oversight of the routine of their trade, the benefits of active participation in a guild were increasingly confined to those already holding senior office. By definition the holders of such posts were larger employers and this doubtless influenced their attitude to their journeymen and vice versa. Many eighteenth-century trade combinations, therefore, grew out of workers' resistance to a guild in a manner similar to that, noted in Chapter 1, of the London hatters towards the end of the previous century. For example, an exodus of smaller masters from the Oxford Tailors' Company in the 1740s was followed very soon after by 'an unlawful combination or confederacy' by the 'journeytailors' to shorten the working day from fourteen to thirteen hours.[43] Coggeshall combers, as we saw in the previous

---

39 C. R. Dobson, *Masters and Journeymen*.
40 Kenneth Logue, *Popular Disturbances in Scotland 1780-1815* (1979), p. 162.
41 Marie M. Roberts, 'Pleasures engendered by gender: homosociality and the club', in Roy Porter and Marie M. Roberts (eds.), *Pleasure in the Eighteenth Century* (1996)
42 H___ M___, *Articles to be observed by the SOCIETY (when met) of Worsted Small-Ware Weavers* [1756], p. 27; *A DISCOURSE Made to the Worsted Small-Ware WEAVERS OF MANCHESTER* [1756], p. 32. See note 11 for full details of these items.
43 M. J. Walker, 'The extent of guild control of trades', p. 342.

chapter, established a pressure group to remind their guild officers of the interests of the whole trade and the weavers' society founded there in 1709 probably owed its origins to the same process. The weavers of Colchester were in dispute with the Weavers' Company in the city from around the beginning of the century, when they formed a friendly society which generated sick pay and unemployment benefits. In 1715 their demand for the right to elect wardens to the Company was refused and in 1745 they took the case of a wage reduction to the Quarter Sessions: they were promptly accused by the Company of being an illegal combination.[44]

Among London's incorporated trades, industrial disputes emerged between the masters and recognized journeymen's clubs among the curriers, blacksmiths, wheelwrights, painter-stainers, masons, wiredrawers and again the hatters. There were at least twelve strikes between 1720 and 1750 arising from such disputes and the general picture is one of polarization between masters and men. The blacksmiths' Court of Assistants failed to resolve a dispute regarding working hours in 1717 (the journeymen were demanding a thirteen-hour day in place of the customary fourteen) and in 1724 the Wheelwrights' Company expelled members of the journeymen's club from its Court of Assistants. The employment of foreigners (i.e. non-freemen) was a major source of grievance. The Common Council had sought to resolve this in 1712 in the journeymen's favour by streamlining the procedure by which they could enter complaints against employers of foreign labour. In a celebrated case in December 1749, 'the Club of Journeymen Painters' successfully prosecuted a liveryman of the Painter-Stainers' Company for employing a foreign workman, a precedent which if upheld would, in the words of one newspaper, have made the 'Leaders in Combinations (many of them with low Minds and worse Hearts) ... MASTERS OF THE LIBERTIES OF LONDON'.[45] Employers' attempts to overturn the verdict met with a concerted campaign by London journeymen, among other things stimulating the printers to organize themselves for the first time since the Restoration, using as a base the Hole in the Wall public house in Fleet Street (which remained a location for print union activity well into the Victorian period). The united trades argued that union was their only feasible action in the face of moves to increase the employment of those who had not served a recognized apprenticeship: 'It is a task above the strength of a few individuals, nor can it be accomplished without our uniting into great bodies, and unanimously joining to seek redress'.[46] A resulting Act of Common Council the following November sought to reconcile masters and employers by closely regulating the employment of non-freemen.

This episode was but one flurry in a gradual process in which the traditions of apprenticeship were eroded. This, together with wages, was the most common cause of industrial action in eighteenth-century London. In their concern to uphold the concept of apprenticeship, as defined in guild practice and the Statute of Artificers, trade unions exhibited one of their most significant continuities with earlier traditions of workplace collectivity. It also pitched them into the midst of evolving tensions surrounding the gender division of labour.

WOMEN AND THE EIGHTEENTH-CENTURY TRADES

> We all know that women in pre-industrial society worked ... Sense tells us that in the proto-industrial phase their role was crucial. They were the more numerous sector of the cheap labour force. Yet we have very little detailed modern research bearing on the nature and importance of

---

44 A. F. J. Brown, *Essex at Work, 1700-1815* (1969), pp. 24-5.

45 *General Advertiser*, 13 December 1749, quoted in C. R. Dobson, *Masters and Journeymen*, p. 52.

46 Cited in C. R. Dobson, *Masters and Journeymen*, p. 54.

their labour.[47]

During the eighteenth century the dramatic expansion of some sectors of the industrial economy dramatically increased female employment opportunities. Textiles industries, especially spinning processes, provide the most obvious example of this phenomenon, but it was true of other industries in which the employment of women has been less-readily appreciated, for example the West Midlands metalware trades.[48] When population growth was low, celibacy and late marriage were maintained and as a consequence there were high numbers of single women. Significant numbers were apprenticed to a wide range of occupations and seem not to have been resented by male workers. This was true not only of the luxury and lighter trades such as tailoring (where guilds were admitting both female apprentices and journeymen 'free sisters' in the early 1700s), but also of trades that to 'modern' sensibilities seem unambiguously masculine, such as shipbuilding and blacksmithing. The London Shipwrights' Company bound numerous women, particularly from 1690 to 1720, presumably to secure cheap labour for its members. Both within and outwith guild control, significant numbers of women were apprenticed by their families and even greater numbers (otherwise dependent upon poor relief) by their parishes.[49] In some trades, females accounted for around a third of those bound apprentice. The travel-writer William Hutton wrote of the journey into Birmingham from Walsall, in 1741:

> I was surprised at the prodigious number of blacksmiths' shops along the road; and could not conceive how a county, though populous, could support so many of the same occupation. In some of these shops I observed one or more females, stripped of their upper garments, and not overcharged with the lower, wielding the hammer with all the grace of the sex. The beauties of their faces were rather eclipsed by the smut of the anvil; or, in poetical phrase, the tincture of the forge had taken possession of those lips, which might have been taken by a kiss. Struck with the novelty, I enquired, 'whether the ladies of this country shod horses?' but was answered, with a smile, 'they are nailers'.[50]

The voyeuristic tone of Hutton's remarks, written nearly forty years later, should alert us to changes that were taking place in the second half of the century (though female employment remained a norm in the Birmingham trades and Black Country nail and chain manufacture, until at least the late-nineteenth century). A sampling of parish apprenticeship details in the southern counties reveals that the overall female percentage of apprentices fell over time and, furthermore, that the range of occupations to which parishes bound females diminished, the emerging norm being household and

---

[47] O. Hufton, 'Women in history 1: early modern Europe, *Past and Present* 101, p. 132, (1983). Important studies since this survey article was written include Maxine Berg, 'Women's work, mechanisation and the early phases of industrialisation in England', in Patrick Joyce, (ed.), *The Historical Meanings of Work* (1987), Angela V. John, *Unequal Opportunities: Women's Employment in England 1800-1918* (1986), Lindsay Charles and Lorna Duffin, *Women and Work in Pre-Industrial England* (1985), Jane Rendall, *Women in an Industrialising Society* (1990) and K. D. M. Snell, *Annals of the Labouring Poor: Social Change and Agrarian England 1660-1900* (1985). Snell's sixth chapter is also the most substantial study of female apprenticeship in the eighteenth and nineteenth centuries available, though its emphasis is predominantly on southern counties of England. On the female apprentices of the London shipwrights see M. J. Walker, 'The extent of guild control of trades', pp. 202-7. Among older studies Ivy Pinchbeck, *Women Workers and the Industrial Revolution, 1750-1850*, (1981, first published 1930), still stands out.

[48] Marie B. Rowlands, *Masters and Men*, p. 160.

[49] K. D. M. Snell, *Annals of the Labouring Poor*.

[50] William Hutton, *History of Birmingham* (1781), quoted in Maxine Berg, 'Women's work', p. 86.

needlecraft occupations.[51] The seismic shift in the labour market occurred in the wake of population increase from the mid-eighteenth century. The London shipwrights, for example, bound their last female apprentices in the 1760s. This was also the point from which female participation in southern English agriculture sharply diminished. There was no increase in agricultural employment to offset the effects of demographic growth in the second half of the eighteenth century and in consequence both male employment and real wages were depressed. As opportunities of realistic economic independence diminished, women married — and therefore gave birth — earlier, factors which in themselves further limited women's participation in the labour market while reinforcing demographic growth. 'The late eighteenth and early nineteenth centuries saw a narrowing of the possibilities for female artisan activity, and the trades to which they were apprenticed became more limited to needlework occupations'.[52] Women more than men tended to be the victims of mechanization. Although there were exceptions (pre-eminently the Lancashire cotton trade), industrialization led to a contraction in the range of opportunities for women's employment in industry.[53] Increasingly their contribution to the industrial economy was in the form of poorly paid, specifically 'female' work, much of it 'sweated' and undertaken in the home.

This restructuring of the labour market was neither swift nor uniform: but it was unrelenting. While it lasted, shortage of labour provided opportunities for many women to assert their economic independence; but demography stacked the odds against continued female participation in the market for industrial labour at a time when growing capitalization was both removing work from out of the framework of the family economy and glutting the market for male labour.

The evolving pattern of sexual segregation of labour reinforced an air of 'otherness' about women as industrial workers, which in turn was used to legitimize the aggressive defence by men of what was increasingly seen as a masculine territory. We saw in the previous chapter that guild control of trade was an integral part of this pattern. The attitudes of organized labour help trace this process, though the picture of female participation in trade unions is far from as clear as some historians have supposed. For example, Manchester's worsted smallware weavers set up a trade society in 1747 apparently comprising workers of both sexes; certainly the fourth of the *Articles* of the Society, approved 1754, contains the terminology 'Journeyman or Journeywoman'. However, another article added the following year provides for 'undertakers' (i.e. master weavers) to apprentice their daughters to the trade, suggesting that entry for other females might well have been blocked. Furthermore, it is clear from the language of the standing orders governing its meetings that the formal business of this self-styled 'trade society' was a masculine affair. This is even clearer in the commentary accompanying them ('give me leave, Gentlemen, before I conclude, to recommend to you once more, Unity, Concord, and brotherly Love') and in a formal charge by the chairman in January 1756: 'let me beg of you, that when you send Members to this Society, you would choose Men of good and reputable Characters, and that will act upon just and honourable Principles, betwixt Man and Man'. The insistent refrain of masculinity in an organization formed less than a decade earlier suggests that the exclusion of women from the trade was fundamental to the society's function. This is reinforced by its founding principle that 'no Undertakers should take an Apprentice for less than Seven Years, except the Lad or Man be full fifteen Years of Age; then the Master is allowed to take him for Six Years'. Obviously the language here precludes female participation, but to a great extent so also

---

51 K. D. M. Snell, *Annals of the Labouring Poor*, pp. 278-85.

52 Ibid, p. 309.

53 Maxine Berg, 'Women's work'.

would the institution of a six or seven years' term in a trade hitherto without regular apprenticeship.[54]

A putative trade society exclusively of Leicester female woolspinners in the 1780s has been widely cited as evidence of women's involvement in trade unionism in this period. However, this rests on a single reference to a spinner: she 'having more spirit than discretion, stirred up the sisterhood, and they stirred up all the men they could influence (not a few) to go and destroy the mills lately erected in and near Leicester'.[55] This is an interesting instance of community-sanctioned protest against mechanization but it is by no means evidence of a trade union. Neff[56] and more recently Lewenhak[57] misdated the incident to 1788 instead of 1780 but more critically gave the protesters an unwarranted formality as 'the Sisterhood of Leicester women woolspinners', a misnomer that has in turn misled other historians.[58]

Examining the evidence in detail, it is hard to avoid the conclusion that female trade unionism in the eighteenth century was very sparse indeed. Once trades became formally organized they tended to exclude women as members and sought to restrict their entry to the occupation concerned. In a formal agreement drawn up with their masters in 1769, Spitalfields silk weavers barred women from better-paid jobs in the trade, even though women and child workers constituted the great majority of the labour force in the silk industry as a whole. Ten years later the newly formed London bookbinders' trade society excluded women. Early the following century brushmakers and the Stockport Hatmakers' Society struck to eliminate women from the trade and the Cotton Spinners' Union reversed an earlier policy of accepting women members. When the United Framework Knitters petitioned parliament in 1812 to regulate their trade it issued an unambiguous instruction: 'All the Males in the Trade may sign but no Women'.[59] Early trade unionism was inherently antipathetic to women and thus became a particular and institutionalized expression of that frequent male antagonism to women workers in trades that men regarded as their own. This antagonism was mainly manifested in prejudice but occasionally also in violence. In mid-eighteenth- century Colchester, for example, sporadic violence was directed at weaving couples following the breakdown of corporate regulation of the trade; and as late as 1791, when weavers' wages had fallen to the point when only poor women would accept them, female weavers might still be roundly abused and find their 'goin geers' destroyed.[60]

---

54 *Articles to be observed by the Worsted Small-Ware WEAVERS of MANCHESTER*, 11-12, 14 and 15; H___ M___, *Articles to be observed by the SOCIETY (when met) of Worsted Small-Ware Weavers, Together with the ARGUMENTS for the Use of Such ARTICLES. As they was delivered and read to the Society*, June 6 1755, p. 27; *A DISCOURSE Made to the Worsted Small-Ware WEAVERS OF MANCHESTER, AT THEIR SOCIETY-MEETING, and published at the Request*, January 12, 1756, p. 32. All these items, continuously paginated and apparently published in 1756 are in the reference collection of Manchester Central Library, catalogued under the title of a fourth, 'Timothy Shuttle', *The Worsted Small-Ware Weavers APOLOGY*.

55 *To the NOBILITY, GENTRY, MAGISTRATES and REPRESENTATIVES IN PARLIAMENT of every County and Town in Great Britain; more especially those of the Town and County of LEICESTER. The HUMBLE PETITION of the POOR SPINNERS*, [Leicester], 1788, p. 5.

56 Wanda Neff, *Victorian Working Women: An Historical and Literary Study of Women in British Industries and Professions, 1832-50* (1929), p. 32.

57 Sheila Lewenhak, *Women and Trade Unions: An Outline History of Women in the British Trade Union Movement* (1977), pp. 16-17, and *Women and Work* (1980), p. 172.

58 For example Maxine Berg, *The Age of Manufactures, 1700-1820* (1985), p. 160 and 'Women's work', p. 73; K. D. Brown, *The English Labour Movement, 1700-1951* (1982), p. 34; Robert B. Shoemaker, *Gender in English Society 1650-1850* (1998), p. 243; Malcolm Thomis and Jennifer Grimmett, *Women in Protest, 1800-1850* (1982), p. 72.

59 *Records* 1952, 140.

60 Pamela Sharpe, 'De-industrialization and re-industrialization: women's employment and the changing character of Colchester, 1700-1850', *Urban History*, 21, 1 (April, 1994), pp. 81 and 82-3.

Misogynistic violence and the masculine solidarity engendered on a trade club night were just two facets of a burgeoning culture of male worker solidarity in the later eighteenth and early nineteenth century. At its simplest and ostensibly most innocuous it was manifest in the special solaces (fines in the form of rounds of drink) paid by a bridegroom-to-be to his fellow workers and, yet more symbolically, on the first occasion his wife appeared at the workplace and temporarily infringed upon its masculine territory. A groom might also be treated to a coarse workshop travesty of the wedding ceremony, with a fellow worker acting as his 'bride'. It is important, however, to sound a note of caution at this point. Misogyny alone does not explain the origins and functions of trade societies. Unions were far from simply being an expression of new solidarities engendered by industrialization. Rather, they reflected and perhaps intensified, behaviours that were commonplace in the communities beyond them. Modern historians are more mindful than their predecessors that trade unionists were a minority of almost every occupational group and that there were many groups where formal organization was non-existent. But this does not mean that such groups were unorganized. The communities in which they lived and worked had their own networks, structures and therefore capacities to organize (for example in times of dearth and in defence of customary rights). Trade consciousness and community consciousness were virtually coterminous in the handicraft textile trades[61] and there is no reason to suppose that this was not the case across a wide range of industries.[62] What needs more attention than it has so far received is why certain workers, in certain places, so strongly inclined to formal organization as a trade *per se*. Part of the answer to this lies in the extent to which each trade was affected by variations in the customary and legal observation of apprenticeship.

APPRENTICESHIP AND PROPERTY IN SKILL

For much of the eighteenth century the usual route through which to acquire a skilled trade in England, Wales and Ireland was a formal contract to be taught at the workplace by a designated master. Not to do so would be to risk going through one's working life stigmatized as 'dishonourable', 'illegal', 'foul', a 'scab', or, if a hatter a 'cork' or a tailor a 'dung'. Apprenticeship was more than an education: it made men of boys and it was intended to define status as surely as did the possession of land elsewhere on the social scale. From 1662, completed apprenticeship in a particular parish secured the right of settlement there, that is an entitlement to poor relief in sickness or old age, not to have which might entail the humiliation of eviction. In urban communities apprenticeship might confer the status of 'freeman', access to local privileges such as grazing rights on town commons, or the right to vote. It might, as in Coventry, confer all three of these or, as in Newcastle, only the first two yet still with enhanced access to local political processes.

Although, as we shall shortly see, legal enforcement of apprenticeship varied widely, the act governing it remained on the statute book until 1814: the 1563 Statute of Artificers — 5 Eliz. c. iv, to give it its legal reference, or 'the law Queen Betty made' as we have seen Coggeshall combers describe it. Enforcement depended upon voluntary agency (where they existed, the guilds), there being no national or local governmental mechanism to bring those breaching the law before local

---

61   J. Bohstedt, *Riots and Community Politics in England and Wales, 1790-1810* (1983); Adrian Randall, 'The industrial moral economy of the Gloucestershire Weavers in the eighteenth century', in John Rule (ed.), *British Trade Unionism, 1750-1850: The Formative Years* (1988), and *Before the Luddites: Custom, Community and Machinery in the English Woollen Industry 1776-1809* (1991); David Rollison, *The Local Origins of Modern Society: Gloucestershire. 1500-1800* (1992).

62   Maxine Berg, 'Women's work', pp. 88-92.

magistrates. The statute affected a number of areas of working life — hours of labour, security of contract, negotiation of wages — but its essential stipulations as to apprenticeship were that no master could take more than three apprentices at one time, that apprentices were to serve a term of seven years and that a written legal indenture was required between the master and a parent of the youth concerned (or, in the case of pauper children the parish overseer of the poor); only a magistrate's decision could break an indenture.[63]

The trades in general and early unions in particular were insistent upon the proper regulation of apprenticeship. Though the law allowed for apprenticeship in husbandry and housewifery, a majority even of male workers lay outside the Statute's reach and in general were regarded as unskilled. The key issue for the skilled artisans of the eighteenth century was the corrosive effect of economic change upon the line separating them from the unskilled. It is not fanciful to see trade unionism as emerging primarily to police and defend that line and uphold the entitlement to work that completed apprenticeship was held to confer. Adam Smith, in his seminal study of *The Wealth of Nations*, endorsed this interpretation, though decrying the practice, and linked it explicitly to the guild tradition:

> The inhabitants of a town, being collected into one place, can easily combine together. The most insignificant trades carried on in towns have accordingly, in some place or other, been incorporated, and even when they have never been incorporated, yet the corporation spirit, the jealousy of strangers, the aversion to take apprentices, or to communicate the secrets of their trade generally prevail in them, and often teach them, by voluntary associations and agreements, to prevent that free competition which they cannot prohibit by bye-laws. The trades which employ but a small number of hands run most easily into such combinations. Half a dozen woolcombers, perhaps, are necessary to keep a thousand spinners and weavers at work. By combining not to take apprentices they can not only engross the employment, but reduce the whole manufacture into a sort of slavery to themselves, and raise the price of their labour much above what is due to the nature of their work.[64]

'Over stocking' a trade was a frequent source of complaint. The focus might be the incursion of 'foreign' journeymen, but the practice of unscrupulous masters using cheap apprentice labour to do journeymen's work was equally a cause of grievance. As early as 1700 the weavers of Taunton in Somerset attributed their 'most unhappy circumstances' to masters taking as many as five apprentices for the 'luere of a little money'.[65] Manchester's smallware weavers similarly complained in 1756 'that this beautiful and beneficial Branch of Business hath been mangled, abused, and with Regard to the poor Workmen, almost ruined, by a few self-designing Men, who payed no Regard, but for the present Lucre, either to the Trade, or their own Posterity, much less to their poor Neighbours'.[66]

However, skilled Workers' desire to enforce apprenticeship rested on more than simply the promotion of the relative scarcity of their labour. A completed apprenticeship was a form of property.

---

63 The curious paucity of recent historical literature on apprenticeship has to some extent been remedied by Margaret Lane, *Apprenticeship in England 1600-1914* (1996), which summarizes the relevant legal framework and considers apprenticeship as an economic and social institution in some detail. However, its analysis of the changing extent and nature of apprenticeship is weak. Though its focus is on the late-nineteenth and early-twentieth centuries, Charles More, *Skill and the English Working Class, 1870-1914* (1980), contains useful material on earlier apprenticeship.

64 Adam Smith, *The Wealth of Nations, Books I-III*, (1776), edited by Andrew Skinner (1970), pp. 229-30.

65 Margaret Lane, *Apprenticeship in England*, p. 8.

66 'Timothy Shuttle', *The Worsted Small-Ware Weavers APOLOGY &c*, (Manchester: n.p., 1756?), p. 6.

It would usually have been bought, often at some sacrifice, by the apprentice's parents through a premium paid at indenture. Premiums varied over time and between towns and trades, but in the first half of the century a parent would usually pay £10 (sometimes £5, occasionally £20 or more) to indenture a son to a carpenter or joiner; binding to the textiles trade could usually be secured for less.[67] The apprentice paid a huge contribution themselves over seven years of labour which, typically in the early stages, was often menial. For this they were generally paid in kind (board, bed and annually a suit of clothes). If they were paid cash then the rate would be a fraction of that for a journeyman. Occasional indentures stipulating holidays suggest by their very rarity that such time-off was unusual. Furthermore, an apprentice was subject to significant restrictions upon their personal freedom. Their master stood in *loco parentis*, permitted even to beat them so long as life and limb were preserved. Indentures routinely stipulated 'he shall not commit Fornication', 'he shall not play at Cards, Dice, Tables' and 'he shall not haunt Taverns or Playhouses, nor absent himself from his said masters service day or night unlawfully'.[68] Nor could an apprentice marry (a female apprentice might, thereby cancelling her indenture, but a male was likely to be dismissed and forbidden to work at the trade). Local regulations might from time to time deny them the enjoyment of playing tennis (as in London) or even football (as in Carlisle and Manchester). And in an age when the master slept 'over the shop' his apprentices might very well sleep *in* it, as the thirteen-year old Francis Place discovered when indentured to learn 'the art and mistery of Leather Breeches making'.[69] Small wonder that, on occasional customary holidays such as Shrove Tuesday, apprentices acquired a reputation for boisterous, bellicose recreation.

Of course not all was drudgery. Furthermore the worst excesses were probably visited upon paupers bound by parish authorities to the lowest trades (Oliver Twist being a famous fictional example) rather than those indentured to a skilled craft. Yet most apprentices must have ended their time not only with feelings of relief and achievement but also a profound sense of having earned a right to follow their trade through personal privation as well as their parents' investment. In the words of a London trades' paper early in the nineteenth century: 'Every Workman who has served an apprenticeship of seven years, and who, of course during that time, has never received the full remuneration for his labour, has acquired a property in his trade, for which he has paid the full price'.[70]

Completion of apprenticeship was a major rite of passage, especially for males for whom it was comparable to marriage. Seven years before each newly arrived apprentice would have been the butt of jokes and subject to initiation rights: Aberdeen wrights ceremoniously washed the heads of new apprentices, each of whom then took an oath 'to keep their word secret'[71] and in Glasgow print works incoming apprentices were 'fined', the money being spent on drink for the consumption of all members of the union, 'the employer taking his seat at the head of the table, and no work being done by anyone until the fund was exhausted'.[72] Rituals concerning the completion of apprenticeship in various trades underline the importance of the occasion. Only now might a worker be said to have arrived at man's estate: 'I became a *full blown man*' as a Nottingham cabinetmaker recalled.[73] Newly

---

67 Margaret Lane, *Apprenticeship in England*, pp. 142 and 170-1.
68 Ibid, p. 251.
69 Mary Thale (ed.), *The Autobiography of Francis Place (1771-1854)*, (1972), p. 71.
70 *Gorgon*, 28 November 1818.
71 Kenneth Logue, *Popular Disturbances in Scotland*, p. 162.
72 Sidney and Beatrice Webb, *The History of Trade Unionism*, revised edition (1920), p. 75.
73 Jodelyne B. Goodman, *Victorian Cabinet Maker: The Memoirs of James Hopkinson, 1819-1894* (1968), p. 57.

qualified journeymen would stand their workmates copious drinks and often an 'outcome supper'; they might be chaired or even crowned. Scottish colliers underwent a 'brothering' ceremony on attaining the status of 'a full man'. Birmingham gunmakers drank from a loving-cup as 'a welcome to their new associate in manhood' and sang to 'him that's now set free, / Who once was prentice bound'.[74] 'Thus I became absolutely free', recollected Thomas Gent, a printer who completed his time in 1717, 'which made me give thanks to the Almighty from the inward recesses of my soul'.[75] Gent's perception that apprenticeship had made him would have been common to all skilled craftsmen. 'By *that and that alone* he must abide: he is, in the one case, as irretrievably fixed in that trade, as if he belonged to one of the Castes of India; in the other he has no alternative; he *must starve!*'.[76]

For most of the eighteenth century, however, the situation was far from being as set in stone as the anonymous author from 1814 just quoted suggests. Two immediate exceptions need stressing. First, the alternative of learning a craft within one's own family was generally seen as equivalent to formal apprenticeship. Second, in Scotland apprenticeship was regulated by local customs only: these tended to be flexible, a three-year term being typical. On both sides of the border, the imposition from 1709 of stamp duty on formal indenture encouraged evasion. Though the centrality of apprenticeship within artisan psychology was undiminished, an increasing proportion of the labour force arrived at their adult occupation by routes other than formal indenture. How early this process began is a matter of some complexity. As Keith Snell observes there are 'few other English historiographical issues in which such a wide variety of contradictory views prevails simply over the basic facts of change'.[77] Historians of the seventeenth century are apt to date the decline from then, and those of the eighteenth in the early decades of that century. Labour historians from Thompson onwards tend to locate 'a general erosion of apprenticeship restrictions, both in practice and at law'[78] from the later years of the Napoleonic wars, culminating in the repeal of the Elizabethan apprenticeship laws in 1814.

As we shall see in Chapter 3, apprenticeship was certainly a live issue at this late date; but it had come to be important as much for the general ethos it represented as for its practical continuation. It may be nearest the truth to say that apprenticeship was always in decline. Widespread evasion, for example, is evident in extensive early-Stuart prosecutions for non-observance. During the eighteenth century the extent and detail of regulation varied widely between trades and regions. Some occupations — notably cotton manufacture, papermaking and many metals trades — were exempted by legal rulings that they did not exist at the time the original statute was passed. Furthermore, the application of the Act diminished over time. A period of five or seven years' regular work in an occupation was a widely accepted alternative to formal apprenticeship, even within trade unions themselves. The septennial ideal itself came to be just that — an ideal and not an enforced norm. Using a large sample of data from southern England relating to journeymen's right of settlement, Snell[79] shows that the seven-year norm for apprenticeship was clearly eroded in the second half of the century, the mean length falling to under four years by the 1790s. The fall was sharpest from the 1780s. These findings can be linked both to diminishing guild regulation of trade and to the likelihood that buoyant agriculture and population growth from the 1740s encouraged industry to

---

74 Margaret Lane, *Apprenticeship in England*, p. 115.
75 Thomas Gent, *The Life of Mr Thomas Gent, Printer; of York; Written by Himself* (1832), p. 67.
76 Anon, *The Origin, Object and Operation of the Apprentice Laws* (1814), cited by Margaret Lane, *Apprenticeship in England*, p. 1.
77 K. D. M. Snell, *Annals of the Labouring Poor*, p. 230.
78 E. P. Thompson, *The Making of the English Working Class* (1968), p. 279.
79 K. D. M. Snell, *Annals of the Labouring Poor*, ch. 5.

increase its workforce. Cheap, plentiful, biddable apprentice labour was a tempting alternative to time-served craftsmen. During the preceding period of relative agricultural stagnation, the fall in the price of foodstuffs may also have stimulated urban demand, encouraging an expansion in apprentice numbers: for example Manchester's weavers dated the decline in their fortunes to the late 1720s when, 'determined *To make Hay while the Sun shin'd*', both journeymen and masters 'took Apprentices how, or where they could, upon any Terms, or for any Time'.[80]

Legal challenges to the Statute of Artificers from around mid-century eased restrictions on the numbers of apprentices that could be taken by master hosiers, framework knitters, woollen weavers, shoemakers and wheelwrights. In 1751, a parliamentary committee, calling for the abolition of the seven-year rule, remarked on the scarcity of prosecutions for flouting it, suggesting evasion had become commonplace. By 1756 the Lord Chancellor himself was condemning the apprenticeship clauses of the 1563 Act as contrary to natural justice. In 1777 both dyers and hatters were specifically exempted from legislation regulating apprenticeship and in 1779 new legislation to control framework knitting was refused.[81] The legislative trend towards liberalizing labour law is unmistakable. It received cogent expression in a charge to a Dublin Grand Jury in 1763:

> I believe, no Principle is truer in Trade, than, that every Commodity, and the Labour attending it, will find its own true Value: That there should be one set Rate both for the one and the other, seems to me unreasonable, as well as unpracticable; as it gives no Encouragement to, nor makes any Allowance for superior Skill, Strength, Diligence and Honesty. … The greatest Discouragement to virtuous Industry, as well as the most unreasonable Restraint on the natural Rights of Mankind; [is] I mean that Sort of Combination amongst Journeymen, that no Man should work in his Trade without a Ticket, or Certificate from those Confederates, denoting that it was free and lawful for him to do so. … they are all equally illegal and void, and require the most immediate Interposition of the Law to punish and suppress.[82]

The only move in the opposite direction was the Spitalfields' Act of 1773 (which endorsed apprenticeship, wage-fixing and magistrates' direction of labour relations). However, 'it was coerced out of parliament by widespread riot and sabotage by the London silk weavers', the danger of disorder in the capital always being a consideration that weighed heavily upon Westminster.[83]

The Spitalfields' Act, which lasted until 1823, none the less influenced the expectations of other trades, both within and beyond London. Almost as soon as it was passed the silk weavers of Manchester announced their intention to prosecute abuse of the apprenticeship laws and soon after the London masons advertised nationally a similar intention.[84] In 1785 Essex shoemakers publicized the formation of a society to prevent abuse of 5 Elizabeth.[85] The Spitalfields' Act can also be seen as

---

80 'Timothy Shuttle', *The Worsted Small-Ware Weavers APOLOGY*, p. 4.

81 K. D. M. Snell, *Annals of the Labouring Poor*, p. 242; C. R. Dobson, *Masters and Journeymen*, p. 49; M. D. George, *London Life in the Eighteenth Century* (1966), pp. 182, 197, and 233-4; David Levine, *Family Formation in an Age of Nascent Capitalism* (1977), pp. 20-2; John Rule, *The Experience of Labour in Eighteenth Century Industry* (1981), pp. 113-14.

82 Richard Aston, *A Charge given to the Grand Juries of the County of the City of Dublin, and the County of Dublin*, (1763), reprinted in Georges Lamoine, (ed.), *Charges to the Grand Jury 1689-1803* (Royal Historical Society, Camden Society Fourth Series, vol. 43, 1992), pp. 405-6. Judges' opening remarks (charges) at Quarter Sessions often took the form of strongly political statements as well as legal explanation. For other charges condemning labour combination in the same volume see pp. 219, 425-6 and 469.

83 Douglas Hay and Nicholas Rogers, *Eighteenth-Century English Society: Shuttles and Swords* (1997), p. 105.

84 John Rule, *The Experience of Labour* (1981), p. 111.

85 A. F. J. Brown, *Essex at Work*, p. 116.

reinforcing expectations that the Statute of Artificers, in spite of its gradual erosion, still provided the overarching structure within which labour relations should be regulated: 'it was understood (and indeed most law is like this) as a set of guide posts to acceptable behaviour'.[86] Even in the West Riding woollen trade, where indentured apprenticeship had lapsed by the middle of the century, a customary notion of apprenticeship remained 'woven into the fabric of the domestic industry'.[87] Rule[88] adds that, 'the equivalence of seven years' working to a fully indentured apprenticeship' became well established in custom and case law during the eighteenth century, while 5 Elizabeth itself continued to give 'an important sustaining sense of legitimacy' even in trades where it was no longer enforced at law.

The Statute of Artificers was not, though, the only basis for the sense of legitimacy that sustained the organized trades in their dealings with the market. The concept of a trade as a moral community was not solely the product of a tradition of apprenticeship and the guild tradition. The outlook of Philadelphia artisans, as summarised by Nash, applied to Britain too:

> The notion of belonging to a 'Trade' carried with it a sense of cooperative workshop labour where master craftsman, journeyman and apprentice were bound together in service to themselves, each other and the community. A man was not simply a carpenter or cooper in Philadelphia, striving independently to make a living; he was also a member of a collective body.[89]

Nor was this exclusively an urban phenomenon. Workers in rural industries could also adhere to a concrete sense of property in their skills and thus a collective right to participate in and regulate their trade. This mentality is most readily identified among free miners,[90] but it is evident too in the associational behaviour of rural-industrial outworkers. Here, as Margaret Somers has argued, 'regulative solidarity was contingent upon community institutions and practices of association which promoted the power of sanction and the conferring of collective rights. Like urban skilled artisans, rural-industrial textile workers negotiated with market forces through cohesive political association. Association *preceded* organization; indeed, it was its foundation.'[91] It would be a mistake to picture such workers as perpetually degraded, in a position similar to that of the handloom weavers in the 1830s and 1840s. For much of the eighteenth century outworkers enjoyed relatively high standards of living, particularly so relative to farm labourers. Though the secular trend in their real wage rates was downwards this was for some time offset by a superior quality of life derived from the control they enjoyed over the pace of their work. This enhanced rather than diminished awareness of their own status as wealth producers. Their capacity for association also derived from the degree of spatial and political independence from authority enjoyed by rural-industrial villages (another manifestation of this was the frequent strength there of religious non-conformity) and a tradition of self-regulated co-operation, born of mutual economic interests and tightly regulated kinship networks. But at its root

---

86 Douglas Hay and Nicholas Rogers, *Eighteenth-Century English Society*, p. 103.
87 Herbert Heaton, *The Yorkshire Woollen and Worsted Industries, From the Earliest Times up to the Industrial Revolution* (1965), p. 308.
88 John Rule, *The Experience of Labour* (1981), pp. 109-10.
89 Gary B. Nash, 'Artisans and politics in eighteenth-century Philadelphia', in M. Jacob and J. Jacob, (eds.), *The Origins of Anglo-American Radicalism* (1984), p. 166.
90 Andy Wood, 'Custom, identity and resistance: English freeminers and their law, c.1550-1800', in Paul Griffiths *et al.*, *The Experience Of Authority in Early Modern England* (1996).
91 Margaret R. Somers, 'The "misteries" of property: relationality, rural-industrialization, and community in Chartist narratives of political rights', in John Brewer and Susan Staves (eds.), *Early Modern Conceptions of Property* (1995), pp. 75-6.

was a belief in skill as a property to which rights were attached. As a Lancashire Weavers' committee expressed it in 1813 (and in the cotton industry the Statute of Artificers had never applied):

> The Weavers' Qualifications may be considered as his property and support. It is as real property to him, as Buildings and Land are to others. Like them his Qualification cost time, application and Money. There is no point of view (except visible and tangible) wherein they differ. And when Buildings are removed, or Land engrossed for Roads, Streets and Canals, the proprietors are paid for them. Then, if two dependencies, of exactly equal value to the proprietors are sacrificed for convenience, does not equity require, that while one is remunerated, the other ought not to be totally neglected?[92]

It is a well-established conclusion of historical studies of early industrial workers that the riots that peppered early modern Britain contained a strong element of negotiation. 'Riot was less a form of self-help than a way of demanding that certain legitimate rights of the common people be respected and that the authorities live up to the standard of their own paternalistic rhetoric'.[93] Destructive behaviour on the part of work collectivities was not simply tolerated, it was often licensed. The power to search premises and even destroy tools and materials had long been vested in the guilds, awareness of which helped legitimate machine-breaking and the occasionally violent actions of trade unionists. For example in 1707, journeymen in the Bristol cloth trade destroyed goods belonging to masters who employed non-members of the men's combination: at the same time, Bristol corporation was actively supporting the masters' trading companies in the destruction or confiscation of substandard and 'foreign' goods. As late as 1751, shoes imported into the city from Scotland were ceremoniously burnt in the market place having been 'judged by a jury of six worthy men to be made of unlawful leather'.[94]

This study has already argued that trade unions inherited, sometimes consciously so, certain aspects of the mentality of the guilds. They should also be seen as occupying the space that had once been filled through negotiation by riot. Far from representing a new kind of industrial organization, early trade unions were heirs to the means by which the seventeenth and eighteenth century crowd sought to uphold a moral economy (and which impresses as much by its lack of violence as its propensity to it). Beneath the vocabulary and structures of bureaucracy (and sometimes barely concealed) there lingered a language and mentality conditioned by memories of lost rights and independence. It is ahistorical to 'compartmentalize' trade unionism from riot. Victorian labour leaders, operating in a culture that was highly tentative in its recognition of trade unions, naturally stressed that theirs were modern organizations that eschewed the use of violence. Indeed, this was at the crux of the mainstream trade-unionist response to the parliamentary enquiries of 1867-8, which succeeded in diverting virtually all attention away from the furore caused by the Sheffield outrages.[95] Subsequent historiography has largely been shaped by this compartmentalization. But the reality of lived experience for many Victorian workers, and still more so their predecessors, was that no such

---

92 H0 40/18, fo. 3, March 1813, quoted in J. L. and Barbara Hammond, *The Town Labourer 1760-1832: The New Civilization* (1917), p. 300.
93 Keith Wrightson, *English Society 1580-1680* (1982), p. 179.
94 John Latimer, *The Annals of Bristol*, pp. 70 and 154-5.
95 Following the abolition of the regulatory powers of the Cutlers' Company in 1814, Sheffield trades had not infrequently resorted to physical action to enforce compliance with 'the feelings of the trade' about apprenticeship and union membership. As a symbolic minimum, drive bands might be removed from grinding equipment but in a few extreme cases attempts were made on the lives of 'offenders'. See Sidney Pollard, *A History of Labour in Sheffield* (1959), pp. 71-4 and 152ff. and his introduction to *The Sheffield Outrages: Report presented to the Trades Unions Commissioners in 1867* (1971).

ready dividing lines existed. The assumption that they did formerly hobbled historical understanding of Luddism (for which see Chapter 4).[96] However, much of the historiography of the labour movement has used a contrast between 'modern' trade unionism and pre-industrial violence as an organizational device.

The interweaving of 'new-style' trade unionism with 'old-style' moral economy has been skilfully revealed by Adrian Randall in his ground-breaking research on the eighteenth-century woollen industry. 'Historians', he writes, have 'often chosen to see industrial violence as symptomatic of organisational immaturity, as a "pre-industrial" method of resisting change utilised by labour groups insufficiently sophisticated to organise more orderly forms of protest'.[97] Cloth dressers, organized upon the basis of federated local trade societies and box clubs, used violence against machines when pre-emptive action was needed and formal combination would have been inappropriate and ineffective. Informed contemporary opinion recognized this two-pronged approach to the prosecution of labour's interests. As Spencer Perceval commented on the destruction of gig-mills by Wiltshire shearmen in 1802: 'it is most probable that they are too cunning to keep any papers but such as would be referable to little more than a friendly society'.[98] As we shall see in the next chapter, after 1799 the Combination Acts were a firm incentive for organized trades themselves to screen off the use of violence from day-to-day associational activities. Nor was the disposition to violence confined to those areas where cloth manufacture was contracting in the face of competition from the West Riding. Randall[99] cites numerous examples from the latter — where the croppers (the equivalent Yorkshire term to shearmen) were among the best-organized trades — including this letter to the directors of an insurance company, postmarked Huddersfield, 25 September 1805:

> Gentlemen Directors,
>
> At a general but private meeting of the Chairmen of all the committees of cloth workers in this county, it was ordered to desire you (for your own profit), not to insure any factory where machinery was in belonging to the cloth workers. For it was ordered again to petition Parliament for our rights; and if they will not grant us them by stopping the machinery belong us, we are determined to grant them ourselves but does not wish you to be any loser thereby. By order of the cloth workers.

This letter makes clear the federal nature of organization in the trade concerned. But what exactly were the associational forms at 'grassroots' level from which such federations were formed? Trade unions did not spring up, small but perfectly formed, with industrialism. They were the consequences of a wide range of antecedent organizations and looser structures. It is anachronistic to think in terms

---

96 The most powerful contradictory statement is of course that of E. P. Thompson, *The Making of the English Working Class*, but much subsequent work has tended in the same direction, for example D. Bythell, *The Handloom Weavers: a Study in the English Cotton Industry during the Industrial Revolution* (1969), pp. 180-1, Malcolm Thomis, *The Luddites: Machine Breaking in Regency England* (1970), p. 132, John Stevenson, 'Food riots in England, 1772-1818', in R. Quinault and J. Stevenson (eds.), *Popular Protest and Public Order: Six Studies in British History 1790-1920* (1974) pp. 62-3, 67 and E. H. Hunt, *British Labour History 1815-1914* (1981), p. 196. It is dissected by F. K. Donnelly, 'Ideology and early English working-class history: Edward Thompson and his critics', *Social History*, 2, (1976), John Rule, *The Labouring Classes in Early Industrial England 1750-1850* (1986), pp. 369-75 and Adrian Randall, *Before the Luddites*, esp. pp. 123-3, 149-51 and 288-9.

97 Adrian Randall, *Before the Luddites*, p. 149.

98 HO 48/11, 22 July 1802. For the detail of these outrages see Adrian Randall, 'The shearmen and the Wiltshire outrages of 1802: trade unionism and industrial violence', *Social History*, vol. 7, no. 3, (1982) and Adrian Randall, *Before the Luddites*, ch. 5.

99 Adrian Randall, *Before the Luddites*, p. 176.

of branches. Rather the picture is of local clustering of workers, round the focus of pub, sick club or the workplace itself.

UNIONS AND ALEHOUSES

'The rise of the British trade union movement is intimately linked with that of the public house'.[100] Quite simply, alehouses were the most obvious locations for workers to gather: few had homes large enough to accommodate such meetings, which would of course be neither tolerated nor tactically sensible if held at the workplace. The strategic importance of the alehouse as a place of resort for talking shop and planning collective action is clear from the earliest times. In 1677 William Brewer, a Trowbridge clothier

> saw a great company of men ffolowing a ffidler and one of them made a kind of Proclamacon that 'whosoever was of their side should ffolow them'. Afterwards, hearing that they were att an Alehouse neere the bridge he went thither with the Constables where he heard Aaron Atkins say he was the man who made the Proclamacon and that the intention thereof was to engage as many as he could for the raising of their wages sixpence per weeke and that Samuel Bowden (and others) affirmed the same and were with him in the streete upon the same designe, and Atkins said he had a sword and wished he had had it with him.[101]

From such simple beginnings there evolved more complex relationships between workers and the public houses they frequented. At their heart was the box club. By the 1750s these 'great and numerous societies' were a well-established feature of London life:

> These clubs, erected by mutual consent, are supported by an amicable contribution of two, three or more pence per week by each member; who weekly met at a certain alehouse, where they spend two or three pence each; and wherein they have orders for their better regulation, and a strong box or chest, with divers locks, for the conservation of their books, cash, &c. The advantages arising to the several members of the respective clubs are that every member, when sick or lame, whereby he's rendered incapable of working during his sickness or incapacity, receives a certain sum of money per week, provided his indisposition does not proceed from a venereal cause, in which case he is not entitled to any benefit from the society. And when any of the members die, there is not only a sum of money allowed by the society for the burying of such members but likewise the widows or nominees of such deceased members receive from the society the sum of five, ten or more pounds.[102]

There was nothing new about such clubs. A 'Saileris box' was set up by seamen from Bo'ness on the Firth of Forth in Scotland as early as 1634, on the model of similar associations in north-west Germany and the Dutch Republic.[103] In a calling as precarious as the sea there were obvious advantages in systematic mutual aid, but by the 1660s the practice had spread to the tailors of nearby Queensferry. We saw in the previous chapter how the Coggeshall Combers' Purse of 1687, modelled itself upon a similar society at Colchester. The Edinburgh 'Charitable Concert of Journeymen Tailors'

---

100 C. R. Dobson, *Masters and Journeymen*, p. 25.
101 Journal of William Brewer, a Trowbridge clothier, quoted in B.H. Cunnington (ed), *Records of the County of Wiltshire*, (1932), pp. 259-60.
102 William Maitland, *History and Survey of London*, vol. 2, London, (1756), p. 1326, cited in C. R. Dobson, *Masters and Journeymen*, pp. 38-9.
103 Karel Davids, 'Seamen's organisations and popular protest in Europe, c.1300-1825', in Catharina Lis, Jan Lucassen and Hugo Solly, 'Before the Unions: Wage Earners and Collective Action in Europe, 1300-1850', *International Review of Social History*, 39, Supplement 2, (1994).

was established, amidst the suspicions of masters, in 1714, closely followed by the shoemakers, skinners and other crafts.[104] London trades and workers in the woollen industry of the West Country were forming societies around the same time. According to an account of 1725, the weavers of Taunton, whose mimicry of guild life was also described in Chapter 1, displayed their tipstaff and colours 'as often as they think fit, at their Club-house, being an Inn'.[105] This association almost certainly dated from the beginning of the century and like many box clubs it had assumed trade unionist characteristics, enforcing apprenticeship rules and playing a key part in the disturbances in the woollen trade in 1707, along with similar societies in Tiverton and Bristol.[106] Less dramatically, Sheffield's tailors combined in the early 1720s through their sick club in order 'not to work for an unreasonable time for their employers'.[107] The conviviality of club night was also an opportunity to talk shop: societies that held back from collective action would none the less have enhanced work place solidarity in this way. We should therefore beware of drawing a rigid boundary between types of friendly societies when it comes to examining their relationship to the emergence of trade unionism: 'many of the early one-trade [friendly] societies might well have called themselves trade unions had circumstances been different'.[108]

This was recognized by contemporary employers and authorities who often saw little to distinguish a workers' box club from a combination and were apt to use the latter term for both. Occasionally, as in the case of the Liverpool journeymen tailors in 1756, a society would stress 'we have entered into no unlawful Combination, but united ourselves into a common Box-Club', in terms suggesting this was a departure from the norm.[109] In the textile trades especially the intersection of friendly society and trade unionism was considerable. Combinations among the Wiltshire and Somerset shearmen in 1769, 1787-8 and 1791 rested on the federation of parochial box clubs.[110] Employers in the West Riding worsted trade in the 1770s opposed any extension of freedoms to friendly societies because of their 'prejudiciall Tendency, by enabling the members thereof to form illegal Combinations'.[111] This tendency was most pronounced in the early 1800s, when numerous trade societies sought protection from the Combination Acts by registering under the Friendly Societies Act of 1793. Some, like the London shipwrights' St Helena Society, did so successfully; others were refused, for example the 'Subscription Societies of Carpenters and Joiners' rejected by Essex Quarter Sessions.[112] Societies in the Manchester area were credited with sustaining the Weavers' strike of 1808, while Macclesfield was described in 1812 as 'a nest of illicit association ... full of sick and burial societies which are the germ of revolution'.[113]

Perhaps the most dramatic example of box clubs being mobilized to pursue the interests of their members' trade was the Brief Institution of 1796-1802, which brought together West Country shearmen and Yorkshire croppers. It was essentially a confederacy of pre-existing trade clubs,

---

104 W. H. Fraser, *Conflict and Class*, p. 41.
105 Robert Malcolmson, 'Workers' combinations in eighteenth-century England', in M. Jacob and J. Jacob (eds.), *The Origins of Anglo-American Radicalism*, p. 156.
106 John Latimer, *The Annals of Bristol*, p. 70.
107 F. W. Galton, *Select documents illustrating the History of Trade Unionism I: The Tailoring Trade* (1896), p. xiv.
108 P. H. J. H. Gosden, *Friendly Societies in England 1815-75* (1961), p. 71.
109 Alfred P. Wadsworth and Julia Mann, *The Cotton Trade and Industrial Lancashire* (1931), pp. 376-7.
110 Adrian Randall, *Before the Luddites*, p. 116.
111 Quoted in Herbert Heaton, *The Yorkshire Woollen and Worsted Industries*, p. 320.
112 A. F. J. Brown, *Essex at Work*, p. 135.
113 Robert Glen, *Urban Workers and the Industrial Revolution* (1984), p. 111; See also Chapter 3 below.

combining to brief each other on the state of the trade with the specific objective of protecting labour.[114] Chameleon-like, box clubs functioned as simple initiatives in self-help but could quickly be turned to pursue a more assertive, even aggressive, defence of members' wages, pulling back into a routine of conviviality and sick-fund collection when the crisis had passed. In provincial towns, unlike London, a trade was likely to need only a single meeting place and if a club sought to influence conditions of employment it could do so clandestinely, confederation usually being unnecessary; but the Brief Institution demonstrates the potency of federation in particular circumstances.

Skilled workers' box clubs were frequently well-resourced: in 1753 a box belonging to the Gloucester plush weavers' society was stolen, containing £40. Fourteen years before *The Gloucester Journal* observed: 'The *Manufacturers* have stocks raised by their *Clubbing*, sufficient to carry on Prosecutions of any kind, being several hundred pounds capital'.[115] In 1758 check-weavers' box clubs around Manchester combined, seeking to control entry to the trade and to raise a strike fund. This they deployed during a four-month strike the same year.[116] According to the Lord Lieutenant of the West Riding, the power of the croppers, 'the tyrants of the country', had 'grown out of their high wages, which enable them to make deposits that puts them beyond all fear of inconvenience from misconduct'.[117]

With documentation so sparse and the activity — when it occurred — so secretive, it is impossible to assess the correlation that may have existed between box clubs and trade unions. The ultimate significance of the clubs for the nascent trade union movement lay more in their sheer ubiquity. Reported figures of 9,672 benefit societies with nearly 750,000 members in 1803 were very likely underestimates. In 1794 an Oldham handloom weaver described in his diary over 1,200 members of fifteen friendly societies of the town attending church as part of a sick club feast — a ratio of about one in two of the adult male population.[118] In 1804 membership in Lancaster peaked at over one-third of the city's population.[119] In 1813, according to the Society for Bettering the Condition of the Poor in the Welsh-border town of Oswestry, the town's six clubs had 841 members, an average of one per household.[120] Such a level of participation familiarized a significant swathe of the workforce not only with the values of thrift and self-reliance, but with practical management experience. Participation also reinforced social solidarities; one historian — remarking on the neglect friendly societies have suffered, at the hands of labour historians particularly — has even suggested that they 'should be seen as a continuous tradition based on gilds, with their active cultural life, participation in civic ritual, and sense of group solidarity'.[121] Whatever their origins (and the history of local societies, as opposed to the later national affiliated orders still remains to be written), box clubs and friendly societies were important to their members for more than just directly economic reasons. They were part of the burgeoning associational culture of the times. Furthermore, club night was a free space to talk shop beyond the workplace. In trying to explain both the rise of trade unions

---

114 Adrian Randall, *Before the Luddites*, pp. 137-45.
115 Quoted in David Rollison, *The Local Origins*, p. 233.
116 Alfred P. Wadsworth and Julia Mann, *The Cotton Trade*, pp. 342-3 and 362.
117 HO 42/66, Fitzwilliam to Pelham, 27 September 1802.
118 John Foster, *Class Struggle and the Industrial Revolution*, (London: Methuen, 1974), p. 217.
119 Shani D'Cruze and Jean Turnbull, 'Fellowship and family: oddfellows' lodges in Preston and Lancaster, c.1830-c.1890', *Urban History*, 22/1, (1995), p. 26.
120 Peter Clark, *The English Alehouse: A Social History 1200-1830* (1983), pp. 320 and 330.
121 M. J. Daunton, *Progress and Poverty*, p. 10.

and the great political mobilizations of the early nineteenth century, it is to the bedrock provided by the early friendly societies, as much as any other single factor that we should look. They were the cornerstone of the natural affiliation of workers that renders the 'continuous association' so emphasized by the Webbs in their history of trade unionism redundant. It was to their clubs and pubs that the skilled trades looked when they organized regional and national networks for communication and labour exchange.

THE TRAMPING ARTISAN

Even for a club that eschewed workplace action, it was clearly beneficial to maintain full employment among its members in order to maximize income and minimize expenditure. London clubs especially (operating as they did in a metropolis whose sprawl limited the effectiveness of local gossip networks), increasingly matched news of job vacancies to lists of members wanting work. Usually this was done on their behalf by the landlord and indeed the provision of this service often preceded the formation of a box club. Some observers believed that a 'house of call' tended to force up wages, as workers exerted pressure on employers when the labour market operated in their favour. Employers, though, seem generally to have tolerated this as a premium paid to ensure a ready supply of appropriately skilled labour. 'Instead of serving as an alternative to the gild system, the alehouse was beginning to operate as its replacement'.[122] Other critics attacked the association of employment exchange with the consumption of alcohol, arguing that unemployed workers — obliged to visit the alehouse in seeking work — drank when they could not afford to do so: 'The house of call runs away with all their earnings, and keeps them constantly in debt and want'.[123] We should be cautious of accepting at face value the criticisms of polite outsiders. It is not unlikely that these conflated the entirely separate practice of employers paying their workers on licensed premises and the existence of publican undertakers (recruiters and paymasters) for certain areas of casual labouring. On balance the benefits of the house of call to workers outweighed the drawbacks. Some contemporaries pointed how houses of call operated in the interests of employers and the economy generally:

> I could not resist sending for some of the most Intelligent amongst the *Journeymen Taylors* and on a very strict Enquiry, I found it plainly to stand as follows, *viz.* THAT the Business of a *Master Taylor* being very precarious; sometimes very full of work, at others nothing at all to do; the *Master Taylors*, in order to be secure of having a sufficient Number of *Journeymen* always ready to answer their Occasions, did long ago, amongst themselves, contrive to encourage the *Journeymen* to assemble daily at certain publick Houses of Call. from whence they could, at a Minute's Warning, be supply'd by the Master of the House with any Number of *Journeymen* they wanted.[124]

Confederacies of box clubs, to increase the bargaining power of the tradesmen who belonged to them, date from the beginning of the eighteenth century, the journeymen tailors' being the earliest documented. By 1721, the master tailors of the capital, applying to Parliament for legislation to control 'this combination', spoke of confederated 'houses of call or resort' being imitated by curriers,

---

122 Peter Clark, *The English Alehouse*, p. 230.
123 R. Campbell (1747), *The London Tradesman*, 193, cited in C. R. Dobson, *Masters and Journeymen*, p. 39.
124 *A Letter to a Member of Parliament. on the Importance of Liberty; towards Enjoying the National Benefit of any Useful Branch of the Manufactures &c.* (1745), pp. 18-19, reprinted in Kenneth E. Carpenter, *Labour Problems before the Industrial Revolution: Four Pamphlets, 1727-1745* (1972).

smiths, farriers, sailmakers, coachmakers 'and artificers of divers other arts and mysteries ... and the Journeymen Carpenters, Bricklayers, and Joyners have taken some steps for that purpose, and only wait to see the event of others'.[125] By 1764 complaints from the same source spoke of 'a Kind of Republick ... illegal Meetings at 42 different Public Houses commonly called Houses of Call and appointed from each of those Houses Two Persons to Represent the Body and fform the Grand Committee for the Management of the Town'.[126] By this time the effective unionisation of London trades through houses of call had spread to printers, peruke [wig] makers, bakers and very probably others, for most London trades by this date were operating box clubs and there were complaints to the Middlesex Quarter Sessions that 'divers unlawful combinations, confederacies and conspiracies' among journeymen were planned from the capital's alehouses. A similar correlation between industrial militancy and an effective house of call seems to have prevailed among tailors in the Scottish capital, who established their premises in 1742.[127]

In his pioneering essay 'The Tramping Artisan', Hobsbawm[128] speculated that tramping as a specifically trade union activity originated in the West Country textiles industry. The obvious influence of the woolcombers' internal procedures on those of other trade societies perhaps supports this. However, neither box clubs nor trade unions were the first to introduce tramping as a means towards managing the labour market. Masons had a well-regulated system for supporting 'strange felaus' from the 1580s at the latest,[129] while the Coventry silkweavers' guild was paying relief to travelling journeymen immediately after the Interregnum to help meet increased demand for silks accompanying changes in fashion at the Restoration.[130] This was as much a function, however, of the itinerant nature of their craft as a means of ironing out variations in local markets for labour. The Coventry silkweavers, as other guilds that may have supported travellers, accepted this as 'quid pro quo' for an ensured supply of labour. Tramping relief paid by the Society of Freemasons was increasingly incidental to the real function of the organization as, during the early eighteenth century, it slipped from artisan control under the influence of the gentlemen masons whose interests in it were essentially antiquarian or sociable. Genuine trade societies encouraged tramping as a means of minimizing charges on the unemployment relief funds that they operated and of removing surplus labour from those locations where it might undermine wage rates:

> [Wool]combers have for a number of years past erected themselves into a sort of Corporation (tho' without a charter) ... When they become a little formidable, they give laws to their Masters, as also to themselves ... And that they may keep up their price ... if any of their club is out of work, they give him a ticket and money to seek work in the next town ... by which means he can travel the Kingdom round, be caressed at each club, and spend not one farthing, nor strike one stroke of work.[131]

---

[125] Quoted in F. W. Galton, *Select documents illustrating the History of Trade Unionism I*, pp. 1-3.
[126] Quoted in Charles Tilly, *Popular Contention in Great Britain, 1758-1834* (1995), p. 187.
[127] W. H. Fraser, *Conflict and Class*, p. 45.
[128] Eric J. Hobsbawm, *Labouring Men: Studies in the History of Labour* (1964), p. 37.
[129] Douglas Knoop and G. P. Jones, *The Medieval Mason: an Economic History of English Stone Building in the Later Middle Ages and Early Modern Times* (1933), pp. 273-5.
[130] M. J. Walker, 'The extent of guild control of trades in England, *circa* 1660-1820', pp. 147-8 and 332-7. The author also makes the point that even the tailors tramped in the eighteenth century, which Hobsbawm's pioneering study, *Labouring Men*, thought improbable. See also R. A. Leeson, *Travelling Brothers: The Six Centuries' Road From Craft Fellowship to Trade Unionism* (1980).
[131] *A Short Essay upon Trade in General* (1741), quoted in R. A. Leeson, *Travelling Brothers*, p. 79.

The 'number of years past' noted in this comment of 1741 extended back at least to the beginning the century, for by 1707 the Tiverton woolcombers' society was issuing members with 'a certificate under their hands and common seal, and money out of their common stock, to travel from their families'. A parliamentary committee of 1725 noted 'the weavers have many clubs in several places in the West of *England*, particularly at *Exeter*; where they make bye-laws ... to appoint places of meetings, fix their officers, make allowances to travelling workmen, and to ascertan their wages.'[132] Thomas Gent described how printers from Ireland and London 'received assistance from ... the fraternity' in Scotland and York as early as 1715.[133] The existence of 'houses of call', such as those already noted among London tailors from the 1720s, facilitated tramping, though like travelling relief earlier paid by guilds it operated in the interests of masters as much as, if not more than, men. Beyond the textile trades, curriers and hatters seem to have been the next to adopt tramping systems, but only in the 1750s and 1770s respectively.

Shoemakers established an extensive network for tramping in 1784, when the Friendly Society of Cordwainers of England brought together numerous local bodies, issuing the members of each with a membership card: 'Jas. Yeates is a Legal Man and a member of the old Rainbow Society Salisbury. Age 24 years, Height 5ft.2½ in., complexion Brown, Woman's Man'.[134] The Rainbow Society itself appeared alongside the city's guilds in Salisbury civic processions, underlining how interconnected these associations often were in local communities. In 1791 Londoner Thomas Preston fled the shoemaker to whom he was apprenticed and initially obtained work in Gravesend. He then commenced a tramp that took him from Kent into Essex and thence to Birmingham, Nottingham, Sheffield, Warrington, Manchester and Liverpool. Crossing the Irish Sea he then worked in Dublin and Cork, returning via Milfordhaven and Bristol to further stints in workshops in Bath, Oxford and Maidenhead. Three years later he returned to London. 'To those who are totally unacquainted with the shoemaking trade, it will not be amiss', he later wrote, 'to state that these sort of peregrinations are by no means unusual with such as have insufficient employment at *home*'. Preston's itinerary is interesting not only for covering both Britain and Ireland, but also for his involvement in a strike by Cork journeymen shoemakers. Tramping had a powerful ancillary benefit in the dissemination of news and the creation of a broader trade culture. Preston saw his time on the tramp as a political apprenticeship: he had never been involved in trade issues before arriving in Cork and at all places along his route he became increasingly aware of the social and political issues of the day.[135] How far his journey was relieved by trade societies rather than by the craft more generally it is impossible to say: but in any case the distinction is a somewhat artificial one to make.

The great age of the tramping artisan, however, was the first two-thirds of the nineteenth century. Thereafter tramping went steeply into decline. In this later period examples of trade societies directly administering 'travelling systems' are frequently encountered.[136] An 1860 report on trade unionism detailed such arrangements in more than a dozen trades: printers and lithographers;[137] calico printers, boot and shoemakers, tailors (limited to those on strike), coachmakers, bookbinders, smiths, flint

---

132 Dunsford, *History of Tiverton*, (1790), quoted in Alfred P. Wadsworth and Julia Mann, *The Cotton Trade and Industrial Lancashire* (1931), p. 341; *Journals of the House of Commons* vol. 20 (1722-7), pp. 598-9, 3 March 1725.
133 Thomas Gent, *The Life of Mr Thomas Gent, Printer*, p. 21.
134 Charles Haskins, *The Ancient Trade Guilds and Companies of Salisbury* (1912), p. 228.
135 Thomas Preston, *The Life and Opinions of Thomas Preston, Patriot and Shoemaker* (1817), p. 7.
136 Eric J. Hobsbawm, *Labouring Men*; R. A. Leeson, *Travelling Brothers*.
137 cf. A. E. Musson, *The Typographical Association: Origins and History up to 1949* (1954).

glass makers,[138] steam enginemakers,[139] stonemasons, morocco leather finishers, carpenters and joiners, coopers (though 'systematic tramping is discouraged') and ironfounders.[140] Other trade unions known to have provided for tramping in the nineteenth century included boilermakers, brushmakers, shoemakers, tin-plate workers and hatters.

Finally, in view of the extensive overlap of friendly society and trade union identities and functions, it is worth pointing out that the larger affiliated orders such as the Oddfellows, Foresters and Free Gardeners also operated travelling systems for their unemployed members.[141] 'In fact', claimed a Bolton printer and Oddfellow in 1844, 'the travelling system is the one grand principle contemplated by the constitution and laws of oddfellowship ... the distinctive feature between these orders and the more unpretending societies formed solely to afford relief in cases of sickness and death.' Much of the symbolism, ritual and secrecy of these friendly societies was reinforced by practical considerations in administering travelling, though it drew the wrath of the Registrar of Friendly Societies.[142] The Manchester Unity of Oddfellows dispensed nearly £5,200 to tramping members in 1842 but, as in the trade unions, the number of 'clearances' (travelling cards) issued diminished from the 1860s: 'the demand for this mode of relief is becoming less every year'.[143]

WORKPLACE CULTURE

Tramping and box clubs closely bound early trade societies to the public house. No less important, though, was the contribution of alcoholic refreshment generally to the routine and culture of the workplace. The seemingly prodigious quantities of beer consumed there need to be understood in a broader context of workers' consumption of foodstuffs. First, the average working day was long — fourteen hours was typical — so it was only logical for it to be interspersed with refreshment. Second, in diets where good quality food, meat especially, was a rarity beer accounted for a significant portion of calorific intake. Two pints of strong ale constituted perhaps one-quarter of adult nutritional needs, and this in communities with no running water (and such water that was available frequently contaminated). The noisome atmosphere of many workplaces needs also to be borne in mind. Many workers sought partial escape from its effects by observing 'Saint Monday' (Monday Offday in Calvinist Scotland), during which alcohol consumption was conspicuous. As no less than the father of political economy, Adam Smith, himself, observed 'excessive application during four days of the week is frequently the real cause of the idleness of the other three'.[144]

That alcohol consumption was routinely part of life both at and after work, should not then surprise us. Workers valued drink for both its nutritional and narcotic effects; furthermore it was often available on credit. Many tradesmen and women, especially those whose working environment

---

138 cf. Takao Matsumura, *The Labour Aristocracy Revisited: The Victorian Flint Glass Makers* (1983).

139 cf. Humphrey Southall, 'Towards a geography of unionization: the spatial organization and distribution of early British trade unions', *Transactions of the Institute of British Geographers*, new series vol. 13, (1988).

140 NAPSS 1860, pp. 141-5.

141 P. H. J. H. Gosden, *Friendly Societies in England 1815-75*, pp. 76-7 and 221-3.

142 'Affiliated orders' were national or semi-national societies with a wide network of branches and, increasingly from the 1850s, a full-time executive. The standard history of the affiliated orders only glances at tramping provision (ibid).

143 James Spry, *The History of Oddfellowship* (1867), pp. 180-1.

144 Adam Smith, *The Wealth of Nations, Books I-III*, p. 185. See also Douglas Reid, 'The decline of Saint Monday'. Mark Harrison, 'The ordering of the urban environment: time, work and the occurrence of crowds, 1790-1835', *Past and Present*, 110, (1986), p. 140, argues that from the mid-eighteenth century Saint Monday was more typically the second day of the weekend, with the emergence of a formalized Tuesday to Saturday working week.

was hot, dusty or foul-smelling, drank at work as a matter of course. Virtually all workers drank at moments of celebration, to lubricate new workplace relationships and to foster solidarity, the completion of apprenticeship being only one example. Arriving in London from Cornwall in 1821, William Lovett sought work as a carpenter. Whilst working at a furniture repairers he was advised by a Scottish journeyman,

> to offer myself as a member of the Cabinet-Makers' Society, he having kindly pointed out to me the extreme difficulty I should have of ever obtaining employment in any respectable shop unless I belonged to them. But as I had not 'worked or served five or seven years to the business' (as their rules required), and as a jealous countryman of mine had informed them that I had served my time to a ropemaker and not a cabinet-maker, they refused to admit me. Failing in this object, my kind friend got me a situation at Messrs. _____ cabinet manufactory ... this was a not a Society [i.e. unionised] shop, and a number of persons were employed there of very drunken and dissipated habits. When I first went among them they talked of 'setting Mother Shorney' at me; this is a cant term in the trade, and meant the putting away of your tools, the injuring of your work, and annoying you in such a way as to drive you out of the shop. This feeling against me was occasioned by my coming there to work without having served an apprenticeship to the business ... I thought it best to call a shop-meeting, and lay my case before them. To call a meeting of this description the first requisite was to send for a quantity of drink (generally a gallon of ale), and then to strike your hammer and holdfast [vice] together, which, making a bell-like sound, is a summons causing all the shop to assemble around your bench.

Lovett successfully argued his case, 'but the demands made upon me for drink by individuals among them, for being shown the manner of doing any particular kind of work, together with fines and shop scores, often amounted to seven or eight shillings a week out of my guinea'.[145] Lovett's account, written in old age, is doubtless coloured by its author's consciousness of his subsequent reputation — the very archetype of the respectable radical. It is, though, consistent with many other accounts: for example, a century before, Benjamin Franklin found his printers' shop retained a potboy in constant attendance. Franklin, too, had to treat his way to acceptance and his work was constantly disrupted by 'the chapel ghost' until he did so.[146] Nor would Lovett's expenditure on alcohol have notably diminished if he had been accepted into the Cabinet-Makers' Society. Not only was the completion of an apprenticeship an occasion for extensive celebration, it was customary to extract a 'maiden garnish' from even a time-served craftsman upon his entering employment in a new shop. The consumption of beer at union meetings was effectively compulsory in many instances. In this way a trade society reimbursed the landlord for his hospitality and could also reward its members' attendance. Article VI of London's Society of Journeymen Brushmakers, instituted in 1806 at the Craven Head, Drury Lane, stipulated 'That on every meeting night each member shall receive a pot ticket at eight o'clock, a pint at ten, and no more'.[147]

Feasting and drinking, both real and symbolic (as in churches and chapels), had long been — as it remains — a staple feature of associational life. For workers, whether formally in union or not, drinking both symbolized and reinforced collective solidarity. In tracing the evolution of trade

---

[145] William Lovett, *Life and Struggles of William Lovett in His Pursuit of Bread Knowledge, and Freedom* (1920), vol 1, pp. 31-3.

[146] Ellic Howe (ed.), *The London Compositor: Documents relating to Wages, Working Conditions and Customs of the London Printing Trade, 1785-1900* (1947), p. 28.

[147] Cited in William Kiddier, *The Old Trade Unions, From Unprinted Records of the Brushmakers* (1930), p. 37.

unionism the importance of pre-existing workplace solidarities is an important factor. This is perhaps difficult to appreciate in a modern world where people are attuned to think of themselves primarily as consumers rather than as producers, and in which that proportion of life which is spent at work is significantly smaller than was the case in the eighteenth or nineteenth centuries. In some jobs, notably mining and the iron industry, a worker's life literally depended on workmates' vigilance and efficiency. Everywhere, the widening social gulf between employers and employed would have strengthened solidarities among the latter. Solidarity was a means towards holding back exploitation, but also of guaranteeing standards of workmanship; and it eased the rigours of the working day. The nineteenth-century radical William Hone, himself a printer, collected details of printers' culture that stretched back two centuries:

> Every printing-house is called a *chappel*, in which there are laws and customs, for the well and good government of the chappel, and for the orderly deportment of all its members while in the chappel. Every workman belonging to it are *members of the chappel*, and the eldest freemen is *father of the chappel*; and the penalty for the breach of any law or custom is in printers' language called a *solace*.

Hone went on to enumerate eighteen laws, many of them governing standards of workmanship, along with regulations appertaining to apprenticeship, maiden tributes ('benvenue' in printers' parlance) and the observance of rites of passage. For example a journeyman paid half-a-crown upon marrying and his wife sixpence when first she visited his workplace, 'and then all the journeymen joyn their 2d a piece to make her drink, and to welcome her'.[148] The conviviality and solidarity developed in a chapel would have laid firm grounds for trade union activity (and of course the 'chapel' and its 'father' remain standard terms within print unions, denoting institutions that emerged out of an unbroken evolutionary process). Equally, though, the chapel and its culture might be seen as an *alternative* to trade unionism, able to fulfil the functions of collective bargaining and policing entry and wage settlements, while appealing to no authority other than custom and the force of its existence. We have seen how Lovett's shop, though non-Society, none the less exercised considerable discretion over entry. A less articulate and forceful personality than Lovett might well have been driven out. As Iorwerth Prothero has observed:

> We must, first, not take too institutional a view of trades or too bureaucratic a definition of 'membership'. Too often trade union studies focus narrowly on the institutional structure, especially leadership, to the exclusion of the much more important substructure of workshop practice. Yet here was an infinite number of usages and practices that were generally known and adhered to, and were therefore enforced within the shop without any recourse to a supra-workshop organisation'.[149]

The historian of early trade unions is therefore presented with a continuum of activities, through which it is impossible to draw a meaningful distinction between that which was a trade union and that which was not. Box clubs, journeymen's associations within or in opposition to guilds, masonic lodges and workplace cultures might all shade off into the activities of what would later be termed trade unionism. This is true, too, of community politics, especially if we are conscious of the varying parameters of the concept 'community' embodies. 'The miners' community was less that of the parish

---

148 William Hone, *The Every-Day Book*, (1824), columns 1133-43.
149 Iorwerth J. Prothero, *Artisans and Politics in Early Nineteenth-Century London: John Gast and His Times* (1979), p. 33.

than of the coalfield across which they moved in the course of their working lives', Levine and Wrightson have written of eighteenth-century Durham.[150] They are impressed by 'the capacity of the pitmen to organize themselves to present their grievances and further their cause almost a century before the emergence of the first formal trade unions in the coalfield', a view which is supported in the standard history of the British coal industry in this period.[151] Annual hiring and the cohesion and compactness of British coalfield communities meant that long before the emergence of trade unionism there, miners' negotiations with their employers were collective ones.

Trade unionism, then, had deep and resilient roots, in the ethos of guild organization and control of the trades, in the politics of gender, in apprenticeship and 'the law Queen Betty made' and in the culture of workers' mutual help, leisure patterns and communities. A 'modern' perspective shaped by deference to institutional bureaucracy and continuity makes it difficult to grasp the full extent and character of early trade unionism's roots. This did not trouble contemporaries who used 'combination' to describe independent collectivities of workers without regard to whether these were spontaneous or premeditated, ephemeral or permanent. There is no reason why they should have done otherwise: sustained formal organization was not a prerequisite for effective collective action, nor was the latter being supplanted by trade unionism in any simple, linear progression. Once this is realized it becomes signally easier to understand the wide-scale mobilization of labour in the final years of the eighteenth century.

---

[150] David Levine and Keith Wrightson, *The Making of an Industrial Society*, p. 399.
[151] Michael W. Flinn, *The History of the British Coal Industry Volume 2: 1700-1830: The Industrial Revolution* (1984), pp. 396-411.

3

'No Strangers to the *Rights of Man*'?

THE BROADER CONTEXT

Economic historians are now far less inclined than was once the case to frame the idea of the industrial revolution around a single, pivotal decade. Hobsbawm and Rostow, writing from very different perspectives in the early 1960s, both focused on the 1780s.[1] As the introductory section to the previous chapter discussed, the tendency now is to view British industrialization as a much flatter, evolutionary process. Rumours of the death of the industrial revolution have been an exaggeration, but it is unlikely that the old heroic model will ever be reinstated. This being the case, the acceleration of trade union activity in the late 1780s and 1790s is all the more remarkable, for it can no longer be explained in any simplistic way as linked to the 'take-off' of the industrial economy. Economic history's recent emphasis upon continuities and evolution requires a re-evaluation of the evolution of labour movements. A period once seen as little more than a curtain raiser to the history of trade unionism proper, now demands a more rounded and detailed evaluation. Fortunately, for obvious reasons there never has been any shortage of interest in the history of Britain in the era of the French Revolution. More recently, an appreciation of the central importance of the last British subsistence crises — arguably deserving the description of 'famine' — has opened up the 1790s to historical scrutiny on a scale never seen before.

For virtually all historians of trade unionism, this period is chiefly notable for the Combination Acts, the anti-trade union legislation passed in 1799 and 1800. These have fulfilled a convenient function of demarcating a prehistory, in which putative trade unions were at best tolerated, from a 'modern' era in which they emerged from the twilight of repression into the light of quasi-legality. However, before considering these Acts and their impact, it is essential first to look at the dimensions of labour unrest in the preceding years.

TRADE UNIONISTS IN EMBRYO? AGRICULTURAL WORKERS IN THE 1790s

In November 1790 a Norwich newspaper noted that labourers in several north Norfolk villages had struck work and gathered 'for several days … In order to have their wages raised; but by the vigilance of the neighbouring justices, we hear they were dispersed quietly, and several of the most active committed to the Aylesham Bridewell'.[2] This incident has several noteworthy features: strike tactics

---

[1] See E. J. Hobsbawm, *The Age of Revolution: Europe, 1789-1848* (1962), ch. 2, and W. W. Rostow, *The Stages of Economic Growth: A Non-Communist Manifesto* (1960), esp. ch. 4.

[2] *Norwich Mercury*, 13 November 1790, quoted in E. A. Goodwyn, *Selections from Norwich Newspapers, 1760-1790*, (Ipswich: East Anglian

are being employed not by skilled artisans or urban workers but by agricultural labourers; the local establishment acts quickly to suppress it; and significantly the dispute is not localized to a single employer or village. Indeed it is among the earliest concerted efforts by farmworkers to strike. Earlier documented examples[3] all occurred at haymaking or harvest, when demand for labour was at its peak. The timing and character of the Norfolk incident are suggestive of a more considered and less overtly opportunist approach to collective bargaining.

This incident was by no means isolated, for during the 1790s reports of combinations and strikes among 'unskilled' labourers like these became increasingly common, especially in East Anglia. This was the region where the capitalization of agriculture and the transition to cash wages was most complete. It was also one where rural friendly societies were particularly strong and in whose industries, as we have seen, there was a long tradition of trade organization. In 1793 Isaac Seer of Thaxted 'became the first known farmworkers' leader' in Essex when he was arrested having headed a party that toured farms in an attempt to spread a strike.[4] The same year, 'hinds and bound men' in the Alnwick area of Northumberland held meetings to demand enhanced payments in kind, equivalent to an increase of 25 per cent in market values.[5] Norfolk farm labourers co-ordinated claims for increased wages in the autumn of 1795, the same year that twenty-seven labourers from Burgh-le-Marsh, Lincolnshire, successfully 'entered into and signed a league under the pretence of wages'.[6] Four west Sussex labourers were imprisoned for a similar action. There were also strikes in Berkshire, Kent and Hertfordshire, where agricultural labourers at Hoddesdon withdrew their deposits in the village friendly society 'for the express purpose of standing out against their employers'. The containment of this incident was followed almost immediately by several incidents of arson.[7]

In 1800 labourers struck in Hampshire, Essex and Berkshire, where troops from volunteer regiments had to be used to disperse rioting strikers. In the Essex marshlands of the Dengie peninsula, the leaders of an 'illegal insurrection' were indicted to appear at the next assize. At a time of abnormally high prices, they had sought to bring labourers out on strike throughout Dengie for a rise in wages. They were tried before none other than the Lord Chief Justice who 'expatiated largely upon the heinousness of the offence, and declared that it bordered upon High Treason'. Sentencing the farm-hands to twelve months' imprisonment, he also bound them over for seven years on recognizances of £100 each. The severity of the sentence and the threat of further imprisonment for any subsequent misdemeanour suggests the incident had struck a raw nerve in the establishment. *The Times* reporter at the trial urged that the sentences be widely publicized to show agricultural labourers 'what would be the consequences of combining to distress their employers'.[8] Despite this there were further farmworkers' strikes in Kent the following year. However, reactions to the Essex strike can be seen as part of a developing pattern, the ferocity of which impelled agricultural labourers away from overt trade unionist and strike activity and towards tactics of arson and machine-breaking.

    Magazine, 1972), p. 80.
3   C. R. Dobson, *Masters and Journeymen: A Pre-history of Industrial Relations* (1980), appendix 1.
4   A. F. J. Brown, *Essex at Work, 1700-1815* (1969), pp. 131-2.
5   J. Bohstedt, *Riots and Community Politics in England and Wales, 1790-1810* (1983), p. 186.
6   J. W. F. Hill, *Georgian Lincoln* (1966), pp. 167-8.
7   J. Bohstedt, *Riots and Community Politics*, p. 192.
8   A. F. J. Brown, *Essex at Work*, p. 132; C. R. Dobson, *Masters and Journeymen*, pp. 145-5; Roger A. E. Wells, 'The development of the English rural proletariat and social protest, 1700-1850', *Journal of Peasant Studies*, vol. 6, no. 2, (1979), p. 41, and *Wretched Faces: Famine in Wartime England 1793-1803* (2011), p. 166.

The use of these tactics reached a dramatic and tragic climax in the Captain Swing movement of 1830. It would be simplistic to argue that oppression of agricultural trade unionism was the sole reason for Swing. However, farmworkers were more sophisticated than has often been allowed: connections with radical politics were among the factors that shaped the Swing rising. It was the disturbing novelty of farm labourers' combinations in the 1790s, one suspects, that gave rise to their particularly forceful suppression. The eighteenth-century establishment was familiar with combinations of skilled artisans, weavers and miners. It may not have liked what it saw, but at least the spectacle was a familiar one. However, combinations of agricultural labourers were different. We have to remember, too, the wider context in which these episodes occurred. Peasant uprisings were a crucially destabilizing element in revolutionary France. Of course, French rural society was profoundly different from that of England: but it is doubtful whether local authority in rural England in the 1790s was so discriminating. It is impossible for us fully to comprehend either the thrill or the horror of apprehension with which news of events unfolding in France were received at this time, or the extent to which they coloured all aspects of British and Irish life: 'Everything rung, and was connected, with the Revolution in France; which, for above 20 years, was, or was made, the all in all. Everything, not this thing or that thing, but literally everything, was soaked in this one event.'[9]

In seeking an answer to the question why a parliament overwhelmingly composed of landowners — conservative by tradition and paternalist by nature — readily acceded to the calls of middle-class employers and passed anti-trade union legislation at the end of the decade, we need do little more than look to the emerging evidence of labour militancy in rural England during the years before. Furthermore, besides the European dimension, actions like these of the farmworkers were also located within more immediate, domestic crises — a sharp acceleration of British radical political activity (itself much stimulated by the French Revolution), and an economy racked by inflation and food shortages. To the implications of these for trade unionism in Britain generally we now turn.

THE ACCELERATION OF TRADE UNION ACTIVITIES IN THE 1790s

The convergence of continued industrialization, dearth and distress, revolution abroad and radicalism at home was a powerful impulse behind the acceleration of trade unionism during the 1790s. Historians have failed to agree, however, on the relative importance of each of these factors.[10] Some would deny radical politics played any part at all, whilst until recently there was little appreciation of the full dimensions of food shortages in this decade. The Webbs, arbiters of trade union historiography for much of the twentieth century, paid little heed to the period before the Combination Acts of 1799-1800. It was only after the historical landscape had been redefined by Edward Thompson in *The Making of the English Working Class* (first published in 1963), that the trade unions and their place in British society in the 1790s were reassessed. Thompson argued that an acceleration of trade union activity in the 1790s was radically fused with 'Jacobin' politics. This was particularly so after the Combination Acts which 'served only to bring illegal Jacobin and trade union strands closer together', the activities of political organizations like the Corresponding Societies

---

9   Henry Cockburn (1856), *Memorials of His Time*, Edinburgh, p. 80. Cockburn added that 'Jacobin' quickly became the common nickname given 'to those who were known to have any taste for any internal reforms of our own'.

10 The literature on French Revolutionary Wars and the potential for insurrection in Britain is considerable, with particularly weighty contributions from *The Making of the English Working Class*, (Harmondsworth: Penguin, 1968) and Roger A. E Wells, *Insurrection: The British Experience, 1795-1803* (1983). The wide-ranging collection of essays edited by Mark Philip, *The French Revolution and British Popular Politics*, (Cambridge University Press, 1991), is both the best introduction to, and summary of the debate.

having been suppressed by legislation in 1795. This process was further strengthened by 'the simultaneous default of the middle-class reformers and the rapid "leftwards" movement of the plebeian radicals',[11] and by working people's reaction to what was not uncommonly referred to afterwards as 'the English Reign of Terror'. Thompson was not suggesting that radicalism and trade unionism fused to form a single common movement, though *The Making* has sometimes been read in this way. Rather, two movements, hitherto largely separate, were henceforward increasingly thrown together and acting in response to common stimuli. The result, readily apparent by the time of the Luddites, was an invigorated popular radicalism and newly militant trade unionism. The emergence of a Jacobin dimension to trade unionism was therefore a building block in the making of working-class consciousness.

At least one contemporary believed 'Infidel-propagandists' had already 'made use of ... Benefit Societies' to spread radical political ideas 'in which they were but too successful',[12] but Thompson suggested that trade unionism and Paineite radicalism were only occasionally connecting strands before 1799. It took the Combination Acts to fuse Jacobinism and trade unionism. This was especially the case in the Pennine textile districts where, in Thompson's view, the two were 'jolted ... into a widespread secret combination, half political, half industrial in emphasis'. We will return to this secret combination later: but first it is necessary to explore the situation of organized labour in the years immediately preceding the Combination Acts.

Two sharply conflicting interpretations of trade unionism in the 1790s have been advanced in recent years. The first, opposing Thompson, has denied the validity of any connection between trade unionism and the quickening political temper of the times. The second, extending the thesis of *The Making of the English Working Class*, has traced and emphasized such connections. Whichever of these essentially incompatible interpretations one favours, it is clear that the 1790s marked a prodigious increase in the incidence of strikes. In Dobson's 'prehistory of industrial relations',[13] the acceleration of workplace militancy in the decade is self-evident. Of the 383 labour disputes identified by him in the years 1717 to 1800, 106 date from 1790-9, substantially more than his next most 'militant' decade, the 1760s. According to Dobson's data, recorded disputes per decade actually diminished in both the 1770s and 1780s, a decline which if correct serves further to emphasize the importance of the events in the closing years of the century. The unevenness of industrial disputes during the 1790s, however, is significant. Three years, 1791-3, account for nearly two-thirds of the disputes traced by Dobson during the decade. They represent years of relative prosperity for skilled workers. In the downturn that followed, accompanied by a major subsistence crisis in 1794-6, the occurrence of industrial disputes was below the average for the decade.

Dobson's data is open to criticism. It is based almost entirely on newspaper reports, mainly from the metropolitan rather than provincial press, and is thus profoundly biased towards London. It is particularly weak on Scotland and Ireland and Wales does not feature at all. However, a series of provincial data collated by Steve Poole provides a useful test of the general contours Dobson outlined. A total of 90 incidents were traced in Bristol, Somerset and Wiltshire during the period 1717-1800. Recorded disputes similarly diminish in the 1770s and 1780s, though the sample is too small for confident generalization. However, the 1790s account for 42 reported incidents, an even higher proportion than Dobson found nationally. As in the latter series, the peak year for reported

---

11 E. P. Thompson, *The Making of the English Working Class*, pp. 199-200.
12 William Reid (1800), *The Rise and Dissolution of the Infidel Societies in this Metropolis*, pp. 19-20.
13 C. R. Dobson, *Masters and Journeymen*.

industrial unrest is 1792. However 1795-6, rather than 1791 or 1793, are the other years exhibiting high levels of unrest.[14] On the basis of Dobson's data, Rule suggests that 'the rhythm of disputes, with its peaks when the economy was doing well, suggests strongly that the context for trade union action was industrial rather than political'.[15] However, whilst confirming the strike boom of 1792, the West Country data hints at a more complex chain of connection.

It is also useful to compare Dobson's series of data with labour disputes cited in his study of early Scottish labour history by Fraser,[16] using legal records rather than the press as his source. Dobson identified only fifteen labour disputes in eighteenth-century Scotland, as opposed to at least 50 cited by Fraser (only three of which duplicate events noted by Dobson). Recorded disputes barely diminish in the 1770s and 1780s (again with the caveat that data is too restricted for firm generalization). The 1790s account for sixteen reported incidents (32 per cent of the whole) again a higher proportion than that suggested by Dobson for the British Isles and Ireland as a whole. No clear peak year for industrial unrest emerges from the Scottish legal records examined by Fraser, but consistent with the pattern in Poole's series Fraser cites *no* industrial disputes in either 1791 or 1793.

Imperfect though these aggregate analyses of eighteenth-century trade disputes are, it is unlikely that further research will displace the conclusion that the 1790s saw a marked upturn in workplace militancy compared to anything that had gone before. Slightly more tentatively, it would appear that industrial militancy during the decade was at its greatest in 1792 and then again during the subsistence crisis years of 1795-6.

Given that evidence for increased industrial militancy towards the end of the century is so substantial, how is it that some historians have felt comfortable denying the premise that radical politics and trade unionism converged in the wake of the French Revolution and the British government's reaction to its impact on domestic politics? The answer is to some extent ideological, though it is not often the practice among British historians to confront questions of ideology overtly. Some found the basis of Thompson's historical method in Marxism politically disquieting. Others, recognising its subtlety and emphasis upon empirical research, nonetheless saw in the labour history of the period a clustering (certainly not a coherent movement) of essentially reactionary and conservative responses to industrialization. At their most extreme, epitomized by Thomis,[17] these views denied the possibility of a convergence of political and trade union militancy. This is not in itself irreconcilable with the evidence of mounting workplace disputes discussed above. Indeed it is possible to argue, as Calhoun[18] does in a rather more rigorous study than Thomis, that the events of the 1790s represented a quickening of collective action in response to industrialization, but that the

---

14 'Industrial disputes 1700-1860', unpublished data collected by Dr Steve Poole of the University of the West of England, Bristol. I am very grateful to him for generously making this research available to me. No more than three or four incidents are duplicated in the two series during the crucial decade of the 1790s, the yearly totals for which are as follow (Dobson's totals in brackets): 1791 4 (15); 1792 11 (29); 1793 4(20); 1794 3 (6); 1795 7(9); 1796 8 (3); 1797 2 (3); 1798 1(6); 1799 3 (9). The 1795-6 cluster offers some support for Roger Wells' conclusion that these years constituted the 'seminal period of union activity' (*Insurrection*, p. 48), about which Rule ('Trade unions, the Government and the French Revolution, 1789-1802', in John Rule and Robert Malcolmson (eds.), *Protest and Survival: The Historical Experience — Essays for E. P. Thompson* (1993), pp. 122-3), is doubtful. However, neither Dobson's nor Poole's data permit statistically rigorous analysis and the need for more systematic regional studies is clear. For example a recent analysis for London alone, (David R. Green, 'Lines of conflict: labour disputes in London, 1790-1870', *International Review of Social History*, 43/2, (1998), p. 214), found just 18 disputes in the 1790s, which is two *fewer* than Dobson's total for the capital.

15 John Rule, 'Trade unions, the Government and the French Revolution, 1789-1802', p. 123.

16 W. H. Fraser, *Conflict and Class: Scottish Workers, 1700-1838* (1988).

17 Malcolm Thomis, *The Luddites: Machine Breaking in Regency England* (1970).

18 Craig Calhoun, *The Question of Class Struggle: Social Foundations of Popular Radicalism during the Industrial Revolution* (1982).

social foundations of such action were rooted in a community-based populism rather than any emerging class consciousness.

Perhaps the most plausible account of trade union activity in this period which seeks to refute the fundamental premises of Thompson and his supporters is that provided by Ian Christie in his reflections on Britain's avoidance of revolution.[19] Its plausibility partly rests on its borrowing from the 'stock in trade' of mid-Victorian labour history the notion that trade unionism retarded rather than advanced class consciousness. In Ian Christie's view, eighteenth-century trade unions were a force for social stability, not instability. Their payment of benefits blunted the impact of unemployment, whilst their administration of tramping may actually have helped increase the efficiency of the market for labour. Christie's image of trade unionism also has a theatrical dimension, in which tensions and antagonisms between employers and employed are played out on the stage of union activity. Unions were 'a ritualistic working-out of the element of combativeness in human nature', strikes a safety valve for discontent and trade union membership a social context within which individuals were helped to play out their lives, giving and receiving help and securing status and friendships. Christie believes that this was especially the case in London:

> By the 1780s and 1790s a system of negotiation and pressure, with at least some degree of ritualistic observance, had come into operation among those involved in a number of skilled trades in the capital, through which the aspirations of working men could often be at least partially satisfied, and by which the danger of a really explosive build-up of discontent was averted.[20]

Ian Christie's interpretation of late eighteenth-century trade unionism is an attractive one, not least for its discrete application (in a very English manner) of sociological ideas about the function of ritual in societies, the displacement of tension, and the containment of hostility within a system that permits its regulated expression. Dobson's 'conservative interpretation of labour history' can be read to a similar end.[21] It is important for Christie's interpretation that the Combination Acts be seen as making little difference to the realities of trade union activity, and as we shall shortly see considerable evidence can be adduced to suggest this was in fact the case. However, as in most historical interpretations, some sleight of hand is involved. Christie may be broadly right in his analysis of metropolitan trade unionism: it is certainly germane to the subject of Britain's avoidance of revolution, for even cursory European comparison shows the mobilization of national capitals to be a critical ingredient in a successful revolution. It does not necessarily follow, though, that provincial trade unionism paralleled the situation that may have prevailed in London. It is in Yorkshire and Lancashire that the fusion of Jacobinism and trade unionism has been particularly identified. Christie's reflections on Britain's avoidance of revolution are selective in their use of evidence and largely ignore the substantial body of evidence accumulated by Wells[22] of a very real threat to the security of the British state, especially during and immediately after the grain crises of 1794-5 and 1800-1801.

Historians' handling of the evidence for famine in Britain in the 1790s and 1800s does not,

---

19 Ian Christie, *Stress and Stability in Late Eighteenth-Century Britain: Reflections on the British Avoidance of Revolution* (1984).
20 Ibid, p. 141.
21 C. R. Dobson, *Masters and Journeymen*, pp. 151-3.
22 Roger A. E. Wells, 'The development of the English rural proletariat and social protest, 1700-1850' and *Insurrection*; See also *Wretched Faces*.

however, directly concern this study. It is though central to Thompson's and Wells' case that trade unionist activity was conspicuous among the means through which popular responses to the grain crises were articulated. As a concerted and public statement of discontent trade unionism is a more 'modern' behaviour than, for example, riot (and potentially therefore evidence for a growth in working-class consciousness); it also has an institutional dimension which legitimises speculation about likely overlap with other political arenas, in this case Painite radicalism. What forms did trade union activity in the 1790s take, and what is the evidence for convergence with radicalism?

To a considerable extent the trade unionism of the 1790s replicated forms of action and focuses of concern from the preceding decades. The development of trade unions as a defensive mechanism to protect skill and status, evident throughout the century, continued. So too did strikes to protect or increase wages. It is worth recalling that, until the industrial militancy of the 1790s, the peak decade for trade disputes appears to have been the 1760s, another time of acute food shortage and spiralling inflation. Yet, just as 1763, the year of most privation, does not register the highest extent of trade disputes in the 1760s, so too disputes in the famine years of 1795-6 were exceeded in 1792. Evidence to support Wells' contention that 'the seminal period of unionist activity belongs to the grain crisis between December 1794 and May 1796'[23] can be found in the West Country data discussed above, but is otherwise ambiguous. Indications of agricultural trade unionism have already been noticed during this period, when the price of food doubled after two successive poor harvests, but it would be foolish to use them alone as a measure of militancy in these years. The incidence of industrial action elsewhere is more compelling. Tailors struck in Hull and Newcastle, coalminers in Somerset, Gloucestershire and Yorkshire. The United Journeyman Shoemakers' Society of Edinburgh was formed 'on account of the dearness of the times'.[24] Nottinghamshire miners celebrated a short, successful strike for higher wages by seizing corn from local farms and forcing millers to grind it; there were also strikes in the county's hosiery industry. At Storrington in Sussex delegate meetings of all the building trades in the locality are recorded. Most branches of the Sheffield cutlery trades struck during 1796, along with Stockport hatters. West Yorkshire colliers successfully starved Leeds of coal until they were granted additional binding fees and subsidized coal. Other disputes have been noted among journeymen hotpressers in Norwich, convicted of forming a combination (a notice was issued reminding the city that the penalty for this offence was three months' hard labour) and Sussex blacksmiths and wheelwrights.[25]

The Pennine textile districts saw the greatest level of concerted trade union activity during the food crisis. Here traditions of trade militancy were well developed, whilst mechanization and the factory system were creating new contexts for workplace tensions. Among the flagships of the textile revolution was Benjamin Gott's new factory in Leeds, erected in 1792. The presence of such an enterprise in their midst seems to have sharpened local authority's appreciation of the potentially destabilizing effect of trade unionism, and there was a growing awareness that, in the textile trades at least, there was more than a rudimentary network for the exchange of information beyond the region. Gott's workforce did not strike until 1801, but evidence for effective combination among Yorkshire textile workers, especially croppers, is clear. Similarly, across the Pennines there is evidence of a buoyant trade union movement in the textile trade, though there were important variations in the timing and extent of union implantation within the different sections of the trade, with mule spinners

---

23 Roger A. E. Wells, *Insurrection*, p. 48.
24 Ibid.
25 Roger A. E. Wells, *Wretched Faces*, pp. 164, 175-6.

more completely unionised than weavers, whose Association was itself weaker in Manchester than its satellites, communities whose size facilitated organisation.[26]

The evidence of trade union activity during the grain crisis of 1794-6 is considerable but it never displaced 'pre-industrial' forms of popular mobilization such as riot and *taxation populaire*. The latter term is used to cover a variety of forms of protest, in which crowd action forcibly seizes foodstuffs from producers, wholesalers or vendors, and then distributes it at what it is regarded as a fair price to the purchasers: the Nottingham miners' action in 1795 described above is a good example. In that instance farmers were believed to be forestalling the market, holding back grain at a time of shortage until the price was further inflated. In a highly influential article, Thompson[27] advanced the view that the 1790s marked an ending of the tradition of *taxation populaire*, and its displacement by other forms of action, particularly trade unionism. He was far from mechanistic in the picture of the chronological process he painted and it was another historian who subsequently declared that the 1790s saw the 'convergence of rising union mentality with declining taxation populaire'.[28] Following Wells' exhaustive researches into the events of these years it is impossible to sustain this interpretation. There was no simple transition from a 'moral economy' to a 'unionist mentality' in which bidding up wages, not controlling prices, was the central objective. Workers for whom trade unionism seemed a feasible and relatively safe form of agitation attempted to ameliorate the problems of getting by in 1794-6 through trade union tactics: some, like the farmworkers or the Norwich hotpressers, found it was not safe after all. Most never attempted a unionised response to their condition. In situations of spiralling food prices and occasional real dearth, moral economy provided 'the only rational ideology appropriate'.[29]

TRADE UNIONISM IN THE 1790s: A JACOBIN DIMENSION?

What is the evidence for an explicitly radical political dimension to the trade union activities described here? Historians have to be on their guard against a 'heroic march of labour' viewpoint: there was no ready correlation between political and labour militancy. Revolutionary France itself provides no model: the Le Chapelier Law of 1791 not only anticipated British anti-union legislation, but was considerably more draconian.[30] It is doubtful how far British Jacobins or trade unionists were aware of the Le Chapelier Law. Much more crucially, a culture of industrial militancy was not in itself sufficient grounds for the growth of political radicalism. The separation of labour and capital was a long-established feature of the Gloucestershire woollen trade by the 1790s, as were frequent industrial disputes and trade union activity; but workers looked to authority to uphold their rights in any dispute with employers. Law, bolstered by custom, regulated the trade. Adrian Randall, in his major study *Before the Luddites* comments:

> The radicals needed to be able to offer not just an explanation of current ills which married with the experiences of their audience. They had also to offer a solution which would fit within the cultural heritage of that community. Here the ideas of Paine were always at a disadvantage when presented to a culture, as in the West of England, so rooted in its own view of a traditional

---

26 J. Bohstedt, *Riots and Community Politics*, ch. 6.
27 E. P. Thompson, 'The moral economy of the English crowd in the eighteenth century', *Past and Present*, no. 50 (1971).
28 Elizabeth Fox-Genovese, 'The many faces of moral economy: a contribution to a debate', *Past and Present*, no. 58, (1973), pp. 164-5.
29 Roger A. E. Wells, *Wretched Faces*, p. 158.
30 William H. Sewell, *Work and Revolution in France: The Language of Labor from the Old Regime to 1848* (1980), pp. 88-91.

past.[31]

However, if the radicalization of labour was far from automatic, it was also a long way from being as improbable as Dickinson suggests: 'The radicals of the 1790s, despite their more popular support ... had not yet appreciated the political potential of organised labour'.[32] Well before 1799, some radicals at least clearly saw a political dimension to the activities of organized labour. Paine's *Rights of Man* (1791-2) was strongly critical of the state's incursion upon workers' rights to organize: 'Personal labour is all the property they have. Why is that little, and the little freedom they enjoy to be infringed?' It is worth noting in this context that Paine had 'frequently spoke' at a debating society that met in the hall of the London Coachmakers' Society.[33] John Thelwall, a leading London Corresponding Society activist and indefatigable lecturer in the provinces, believed 'every large workshop and manufactory is a sort of political society which no Act of Parliament can silence and no magistrate disperse' and he developed early the argument that labour was the source of all value, though to what general effect remains unclear.[34]

Yet it does not follow that such views indicate an unequivocally favourable stance on trade combinations. The monopoly of the right to practise a specific trade which most artisan unions, in line with their guild inheritance, sought to uphold sits uneasily alongside Paine's enthusiasm for an unrestrained free market in commerce and manufacturing:

> In all my publications, where the matter would admit, I have been an advocate for commerce, because I am a friend to its effects. It is a pacific system ... Commerce is no other than the traffic of two individuals, multiplied on a scale of numbers; and by the same rule that nature intended the intercourse of two, she intended that of all.[35]

We shall see in the next chapter, in the example of Alexander Galloway, that a commitment to republican politics and admiration for the French revolutionary model could combine with a profound antipathy to labour organization at the workplace. John Rule also points out how Coventry watchmakers associated the ending of statutory apprenticeship in England with those processes which in France had fomented the Revolution.[36]

No radical writer at this time advocated industrial action as a means of obtaining political objectives. The agrarian reformer and revolutionary Thomas Spence came close, though, when he commended the Naval Mutinies of 1797 as 'unions of the People' and exemplars of collective political action. His call for 'Conventions of parochial Delegates' to take the land into public ownership and manage it may also have owed something to the example of trades organization.[37] (Spence and his circle subsequently feature prominently in the intersection of trade unionism and radicalism, as we shall see.) The paucity of radical writing on the subject of trade unionism cannot

---

31 Adrian Randall, *Before the Luddites: Custom, Community and Machinery in the English Woollen Industry 1776-1809* (1991), p. 280.
32 H. T. Dickinson, *The Politics of the People in Eighteenth-Century Britain* (1995), p. 247.
33 *Daily Advertizer* 7 September 1791, cited in Donna T. Andrew (compiler), *London Debating Societies, 1776-99* (1994), vol. 30 for 1993, p. 311.
34 John Thelwall, *The Rights of Nature Against the Usurpations of Establishments*, (1796), p. 19.
35 Thomas Paine, *The Rights of Man*, Part Two quoted in Philip Foner (ed.), *The Complete Writings of Thomas Paine* (1945), vol. 1, 399-401. For Paine's economic views see the cumulative evidence in the conference report, 'Thomas Paine and Popular Radicalism' in *BSSLH* 52/3 (1987), pp. 3-40 and references cited therein.
36 John Rule, 'Trade unions, the Government and the French Revolution, 1789-1802', p. 114.
37 Thomas Spence, *The Restorer of Society to its Natural State*, (1801), pp. 16-17, quoted in Malcolm Chase, *'The People's Farm': English Radical Agrarianism, 1775-1840* (2010), pp. 60-1. For details of Spence's life see the latter and *DLB* vol. 8.

clinch the argument that there was no meaningful connection between them. There has been a tendency for much writing on the radical and revolutionary politics of the 1790s to be located entirely within intellectual history, the dependence of which on largely 'polite' literary sources obscures the realities of lived experience. This is not to argue that the history of ideas is unimportant, but to suggest that a truer understanding of the impact of the French Revolution on British politics will be found only in merging social, political, intellectual and labour histories.

The French Revolution quickened the political temper even of those countries it did not directly touch: it was as natural for people to ponder its example as it was for authority to fear its imitation. Its impact may sometimes have been delayed, and mild when at last apparent, yet it was seldom reversible. The experience of the Colchester tailors, recollected by one of them, provides an instructive example. The war against 'the Great Napoleon' galvanized the city's workshops and 'led them to take some additional interest in public affairs'.

> Until this time I do not remember to have heard them talk much about matters of this description. Now, however, they clubbed their pence to pay for a newspaper and selected the 'Weekly Political Register' of that clever man, the late William Cobbett ... The 'Political Register' was soon thought to be deficient in matters of general interest. It was therefore exchanged for the 'Courier', which in a short time gave place to the 'Independent Whig'. From this time the men were warm politicians — not indeed very well conversant with public affairs, but what they lacked in knowledge they made up by a rather large amount of zealous partisanship.[38]

Soon afterwards the tailors successfully demanded a wage rise, in writing, 'a copy being left with each master for his private consideration, and a time being named when his answer would be looked for. They saw by the simultaneousness of their respective workmen's movements that they were acting in concert, although in respectful manner. They therefore soon proposed a conference.'

The influence of European revolution on Colchester might seem mild, but its widening of the tailors' political awareness and in turn a link between this and their collective confidence as workers is clear. In itself this is not evidence of any revolutionary intent, though by its nature such activity — if it occurred — would not be readily documented. In his charge to a Dublin Grand Jury in 1793 the judge deplored 'the fatal spirit of combination', adding 'it is well known that much pains have been taken to inflame and excite some of the neediest and most desperate among the journeymen, and to *affiliate* them into subordinate Jacobin Clubs, for the blackest and most atrocious purposes'.[39] In Sheffield there was, wrote a government informer, a 'general spirit of disaffection created in every class of artisan and mechanics by the late Bill [the Combinations Act] ... which I am afraid has already caused more to *combine* than would have thought of such a measure but for the Bills'.[40] In 1800, the Merthyr Tydfil ironmaster Samuel Holmfray commented upon the interlocking strikes and food riots in the town, 'I am very apprehensive that this sudden commotion is owing to political principles'.[41] He was possibly aware that John Thelwall was living only 25 miles away, and had been seen near Merthyr on the same day as both a general meeting of ironworkers from all the area's

---

38 [John Carter], *Memoirs of a Working Man* (1845), pp. 89-90, 169-70. For details of the author and further excerpts from his autobiography see A. F. J. Brown, *Essex People, 1750-1900, from their Diaries, Memoirs and Letters* (1972), pp. 104-15.

39 Georges Lamoine (ed.), *Charges to the Grand Jury 1689-1803*, (London: Royal Historical Society, Camden Society Fourth Series, vol. 43, 1992), pp. 469-70.

40 Quoted in E. P. Thompson, *The Making of the English Working Class*, p. 546.

41 Chris Evans, *'The Labyrinth of Flames': Work and Social Conflict in Early Industrial Merthyr Tydfil* (1993), p. 175.

works and the exposure of bad weights in the town's market. There was, though, no automatic merger between Merthyr's political radicals and workers' militancy: on the contrary, whilst evidence is available for some convergence in 1792 — when a local Jacobin publican organized a strike for increased wages in all the local trades — it is largely absent thereafter. The reasons for this may be sought in the desertion of middle-class radicals, or more precisely in their turning away from general agitation to the more specific arena of local politics; but it does not mean that local unions were henceforward left untouched by radicalism.

> In most manufacturing communities the initiation of *any* organized movement is likely to have fallen upon a minority of active spirits; and the men who had the courage to organize an illegal union, the ability to conduct its correspondence and finances, and the knowledge to petition Parliament or consult with attorneys, were likely also to have been no strangers to the *Rights of Man*.[42]

Nor is it the case that radicalism stiffened the sinews of trade unionism without there being any reciprocal benefit. Spence, the most extreme of the radical theoreticians, was developing an idea of collective action which owed something to the example of trade unions. We have also examined the inter-relationship of trade unions, strikes and *taxation populaire*. It is worth noting how the latter often overlapped trade unionist forms: in Exeter 'Men stiling themselves Delegates "selected and appointed" by the Mob, constantly communicate from Town to Town and by this Means carry Intelligence from Place to Place'.[43] Arguably, trade-union initiated action could mobilize working people in a way that the 'Jacobins' could not, whilst the larger unions' delegate and tramping networks opened up an effective means of communication. For example in 1796 a trade unionist from Cupar, East Fife, drafted a petition 'for dismissing the Ministers which he gave to the Convenor of the eight Trades for a purpose of calling a Meeting to see [which] of the Trades would adopt the petition'.[44] London provides the best-known examples of early involvement of radical activists in trade unionism. Francis Place is the most obvious of these, though his involvement in the 'Breeches Makers' Benefit Society' ('intended for the purpose of supporting the members in a strike for wages' he later admitted) pre-dated his joining the London Corresponding Society.[45] Place's important contemporary, the shipwright John Gast, likewise joined his trade society some time before taking up radical politics — but was then associated with the Spencean circle.

The histories of trade unionism and radicalism cannot be disentangled. They were certainly not fused into a single movement (although the situation in early nineteenth-century Lancashire approached fusion) but neither can they be isolated from each other. By 1799 they had certainly become entwined in the mind of the government — a government which maintained extensive and sophisticated intelligence-gathering networks throughout the country, penetrating almost all aspects of society. The Duke of Portland was Home Secretary between 1794 and 1801. This letter from him to a Bolton magistrate, who regularly supplied information gathered from workers in the town, is worth quoting at length:

> Although it should seem ... that the object of the persons styling themselves the Presidents and Secretary of the Associated Weavers is to petition Parliament on the subject of the manufacture

---

42 E. P. Thompson, *The Making of the English Working Class*, p. 546.
43 Quoted in Roger A. E. Wells, *Wretched Faces*, p. 157.
44 Roger A. E. Wells, *Insurrection*, p. 51.
45 Mary Thale (ed.), *The Autobiography of Francis Place (1771-1854)* (1972), p. 112.

in which they are engaged, and that, so far, it is not contrary to the Act of 39 George III, c. 81 [the 1799 Combination Act], or any other laws affecting the same subject, it is manifest that the manner in which this Association is conducted, viz. by delegates, monthly meetings, the election of a Secretary and Presidents, and particularly by the printing [of] an Address to the Public must lead to the conclusion that, if nothing injurious to the safety of the Government is actually in contemplation, Associations so formed contain within themselves the means of being converted at any time into a most dangerous instrument to disturb the public tranquility.

The observation in your letter, that the spirit of association has spread itself into many parts of Lancashire and the neighbouring Counties, has great weight with me; and connecting that circumstance with this case, as it appears from the representations of the persons themselves, I must earnestly recommend it to you to take every measure in your power in order that the proceedings and Progress of these Societies be carefully attended to and watched.[46]

THE COMBINATION ACTS OF 1799 AND 1800

The Government's hostility to trade unions was founded, then, more upon an apprehension of possible political unrest rather than actual insurgency. To quote the Home Secretary again: 'If nothing injurious to the safety of the Government is actually in contemplation, Associations so formed contain within themselves the means of being converted at any time into a most dangerous instrument to disturb the public tranquility'. The Combination Acts were not, however, the product of this line of thought alone. There is a need to separate out the motives that prompted the introduction of the Acts from those which influenced their subsequent application. Much historical fug has been generated around this legislation, some at least of which we must attempt to clear. A small point first: historians almost habitually write of the Combination *Acts*. Consciously or not, there is an implication here that the first act was in some way extended and strengthened, even rendered more draconian, by the second. John and Barbara Hammond, the influential radical historians, in their book *The Skilled Labourer*, failed to mention the second of the Acts at all. However, the general tenor of the first Act (1799) was in key respects softened by the second (1800). The 1799 Act was 'repealed and then reissued in somewhat cleaner form'.[47] On the other hand thirty-two earlier acts (fourteen English, eleven Irish and seven Scottish) remained on the statute book. The new laws did not apply in Scotland and Ireland, for whom separate acts were passed: for Ireland only in 1803 and 1807, and for both countries in 1817.[48] At the time the English Acts were passed Ireland still had its own parliament: trade combination, in any case, was attenuated there compared to England. North of the Tweed, 'because of the basis of the Scottish legal system in Roman law, which recognised associations, there was almost an encouragement to journeymen to organise to present their cases to the courts'.[49] Though Scotland was undoubtedly touched by enthusiasm for the French Revolution, there is less reason to infer the existence of a revolutionary movement there than in England.

---

[46] HO 43/1 1/222-3, 8 August 1799, quoted in Arthur Aspinall, *The Early English Trade Unions: Documents from the Home Office Papers in the Public Record Office* (1949), pp. 26-7.

[47] J. V. Orth, 'The legal status of English trade unions, 1799-1871', in A. Harding (ed.), *Law-Making and Law-Makers in British History* (1980), p. 197.

[48] The number of earlier Combination Acts is usually put at 'at least forty' (e.g. E. H. Hunt, *British Labour History 1815-1914* (1981), p. 198), but see J. V. Orth, *Combination and Conspiracy: A Legal History of Trade Unionism, 1721-1906* (1991) pp. 77-8, who also points out two of the fourteen English acts applied only to employers' combinations. See also J. V. Orth, 'The Combination Laws reconsidered', in Francis Snyder and Douglas Hay (eds.), *Labour; Law and Crime: An Historical Perspective* (1987).

[49] W. H. Fraser, *Conflict and Class*, p. 2.

Furthermore, there is little evidence that much linkage was made between political agitation and economic distress.

The two English Acts marked something of a departure in trade union legislation. The Hammonds[50] described this as 'The War on Trade Unions'. Subsequent scholarship has tended to soften that generalization. The Acts reflected a contemporary tendency to simplify justice by widening the remit of magistrates acting summarily.[51] On the other hand, the first Act reached the statute book the same day as other legislation banning political corresponding societies, an unfortunate coincidence, if coincidence it was; and both Acts broke new ground 'in the inclusive nature of their prohibition of *all* combination; and in the fact that, unlike legislation in the earlier paternalist tradition, they included no compensatory protective clauses'.[52] This legislation applied to *all* categories of workmen in all trades, a compliment hitherto paid only to Irish workers by the Dublin parliament. On the other hand the 1800 Act *did* add provision for arbitration, with power vested in magistrates to make a binding award if the arbitrators (one nominated by each side in a dispute) themselves failed to agree. This attempt to nip industrial disputes in the bud effectively reaffirmed clauses in 5 Elizabeth and it reinforces the evidence of mounting labour unrest in the 1790s. (Another arbitration act specific to the cotton industry was passed the day before the 1800 Act.) Historians from within the trade union movement and of 'the left' generally have also supposed that the Act's prohibition of employers' combinations was purely a technicality and widely ignored. The Webbs made this point, adding 'there is no case on record in which an employer was punished';[53] though it remains the case that the penalties they faced were slight in proportion to those that might apply to employees, it is now suggested that 'a few were prosecuted'.[54] To the extent that it was window-dressing, the prohibition of masters' combinations subsequently embarrassed the government, the Attorney General claiming in 1804 that 'the impartiality of Government would be awkwardly situated, if, after undertaking a prosecution at the instance of the Masters against the Conspiracy of the Journeymen, they were to be applied to on the part of the Journeymen to prosecute the same Masters for a Conspiracy against their Men'.[55]

In the absence of a definitive study of the life of the 1800 Act, it is impossible to be more specific about prosecution of employers, and likewise about a number of other aspects of its application. Perhaps such a study will never be forthcoming, for a striking degree of unanimity has emerged among historians right, left and centre. To the opinion of Dorothy George[56] that they were 'in practice a very negligible instrument of oppression', we can add that they 'in short, were of little significance', that the use made of them was 'slight' while facing 'the paradox that it was in the very years that the Acts were in force that trade unionism registered great advances'.[57] So do the Combination Acts matter?

---

50 J. L. and Barbara Hammond, *The Town Labourer 1760-1832: The New Civilization* (1917).
51 Clive Emsley, 'Repression, "terror" and the rule of law in England during the decade of the French Revolution', *English Historical Review*, vol. 100, no. 397 (October, 1985), p. 820.
52 E. P. Thompson, *The Making of the English Working Class*, p. 551.
53 Sidney and Beatrice Webb, *The History of Trade Unionism*, revised edition (1920), p. 73.
54 E. H. Hunt, *British Labour History 1815-1914*, p. 199.
55 HO 42/79, 5 October 1804.
56 M. D. George, 'The Combination Laws reconsidered', *Economic History*, vol. 1, supplement, (1927) p. 214.
57 E. H. Hunt, *British Labour History 1815-1914*, p. 199; James Moher, 'From suppression to containment: roots of trade union law to 1825', in John Rule (ed.), *British Trade Unionism, 1750-1850: The Formative Years* (1988), pp. 84-90; E. P. Thompson, *The Making of the English Working Class*, p. 550.

Most assuredly, yes. However infrequently the Acts may have been applied (another issue about which we simply cannot be clear), the Acts of 1799 and 1800 had immense psychological and practical impact on the way trade unionism evolved. The typical penalty of two months' gaol and £5 costs was not negligible[58] and it is small wonder the existing habits of secrecy and ritual became more deeply ingrained, shaping the cultural tone of craft trade unionism for more than a century to come. However well-managed a trade union might be, it was cast in the role of an enemy to the establishment until the repeal measure in 1824. The mere presence of such a measure on the statute book underlined the convergence of landed and manufacturing interests in opposition to those of labour, and even its perfunctory application constituted a powerful reminder of the power relations within contemporary society. It was not alone responsible for the increasing affinity between radicalism and trade unionism, but in the earliest years of the nineteenth century it lent significant impetus to that development. Even Scotland was influenced by the legislation as attempts were made to construe it as applying north of the border, as employers demanded an English-style anti-combinations law, and finally, in 1813, when judicial interpretation effectively established a simple crime of combination in Scotland. Subsequently, the agitation to repeal this measure became a defining moment in the evolution of British trade unionism. Once repealed, it assumed a kind of totemic significance for both trade unionists and their historians (though, as we shall see in the next chapter, the legal freedoms enjoyed by trade unionists were considerably qualified by both the law of conspiracy and that regulating master and servant relations).

Although the 1800 Combination Act moderated some of the ferocity of its predecessor, the potential threat to organized labour was very grave indeed. 'The 1799 Act was a straightforwardly repressive one, outlawing all collective agreements concerning wages, hours, quantity of work, apprenticeship, or "for controlling persons carrying on any manufacture, trade or business in the conduct or management thereof".[59] Justice was summary: the decision of a single magistrate sitting informally, at home even, was sufficient. There was to be no appeal beyond the local magistracy sitting in general session. The evidence of a single witness was sufficient to secure a conviction, which could be punished with up to three months in gaol, or two months' hard labour in a house of correction. Picketing, attendance at meetings and the payment of subscriptions were also made illegal. Reaction to the 1799 Act was at first muted, Moher suggests, because the Act was so closely based on a 1796 measure specific to the papermakers that it needed little parliamentary time. Only the following year was there a significant reaction, mainly in the form of petitions from journeymen in the North-west. Liverpool's MPs were then prompted to persuade Parliament to review the measure.

The 1800 Combination Act which resulted tempered its predecessor by requiring at least two magistrates to hear cases, while the procedure for summons was tightened. A record of all decisions was required to be lodged with the Quarter Sessions, to which appeals could be taken. A judicial review of a magistrates' decision was possible. However, the Prime Minister, William Pitt, expressly reaffirmed that the aim of the Act was to ban collective agreements by workers. Pitt had introduced the 1799 bill personally, saying that 'it was his intention to endeavour to provide a remedy to an evil of very considerable magnitude: he meant that of unlawful combinations of workmen in general — a practice that had become too general, and was likely, if left not checked, to produce very serious

---

58 The penalty for example imposed on William Aslin, a journeyman tailor in 1807, see *Records* (1952), p. 66.
59 James Moher, 'From suppression to containment: roots of trade union law to 1825', p. 82, quoting the 1799 Act,

mischief'.[60]

Pitt's remarks on that occasion were consistent with an intention on the government's part to eliminate political as well as industrial unrest, in line with the thinking of the Home Secretary quoted earlier, but in practice the government shrank from a policy of wholesale repression. Pitt's ministry faced two primary problems: the threat of invasion by France, and the threat of insurrection at home. The fact that neither occurred should not be allowed to obscure just how profound a threat both posed at the time in government circles. It was grave enough for the government to see little grounds for optimism that an invasion would be readily resisted, by either the home-based military or the civilian population. To a considerable extent, this explains the somewhat limited terms on which peace was agreed with France in 1801. That peace, lasting until 1803, was a crucial 'breathing space' during which both the food and domestic political situation became less serious. Though the threat of invasion was arguably greatest after the resumption of the war in 1803, by then popular unrest and radical mobilization had diminished. So, while the Combination Act was retained on the statute book there was no need for it to be systematically applied.

The Combination Acts were effectively enabling legislation: they made possible the criminal prosecution of workers for combination, for those masters who wished to initiate it; but no requirement was placed on any public authority to enforce them. Even during the life of the 1799 Act the Government declined to assist or encourage prosecutions and, in a letter to Bolton subsequent to that quoted earlier, the Home Secretary expressed relief that no prosecution of the Weavers' Association under the Combination Act would take place.[61] In 1804 a new Home Secretary sought the advice of the Attorney General (Spencer Perceval, Prime Minister 1809-12) about a proposed prosecution of the London shoemakers. Perceval replied that 'Upon the point of Law I have no difficulty in stating to your Lordship that the Combination is illegal'. However, he firmly advised against the Government instituting a prosecution:

> As it will be viewed as precedent of what the Masters in this trade and in others will expect Government to do in the future, it seems to me to deserve very serious consideration — for it is not only to be collected from these papers, but it is otherwise too notorious that similar Combinations exist in almost every trade in the Kingdom. And if Government attends to this application on the part of the Boot and Shoemakers, similar applications must be expected from every other trade, and it will lead to an opinion that it is not the business of the Masters of the trade who feel the injury to prosecute, but that it is the business of Government. ... Such prosecutions had better be in the hands of the Masters than of Government It must be admitted indeed that the offence has grown to such a height and such an extent as to make it very discouraging for any individual to institute a prosecution — as the persons whom he would prosecute would be supported at their trial and during their imprisonment by the contributions of their confederates, and his own Shop would probably be deserted by his Workmen. But then it is clear that it is owing to the inertness and timidity of the Masters that the Conspiracy has reached this height.[62]

The means existed for the Government to initiate prosecution under the Combination Act, should it believe that there was sufficient evidence, or risk, of serious social or political disturbance. 'He quite agrees with the magistrates of Nottingham that it is not fit for them to interfere until there is a danger

---

60 Ibid, p. 95.
61 HO 43/11/234.
62 HO 42/79, 5 October 1804.

of the peace being broken', the Home Secretary wrote in 1821 in connection with a stockingers' strike.[63] However, almost every case considered by the Government fell short of these criteria. Was it therefore consciously protecting organized labour? There is no evidence to this effect. It is impossible to reconcile Christie's contention that the 'acts did not forbid workmen from associating to improve wages and conditions of work'[64] with a detailed reading of the 1800, and still less the 1799, Act. But it seems to have been the case that a combination was likely to be unscathed as long as it held back from strike action. Alan Fox, in a detailed review of the state's attitude to the application of the 1800 Act, summarizes the situation thus:

> The objection was not to class bias — manifested in the fact that the government had no intention whatsoever of prosecuting masters for combination — but to its being made public and overt in a way which would greatly weaken the government's assertion of even-handedness. Employers were to be left to their own uncertain and often somewhat nervous courses, and it became clear that, deprived of whole-hearted state support backed by full effective coercive forces, they lacked the stomach, the resources and the unity for any attempt at the total destruction of worker combinations. These stances taken up by the state and by the general run of employers were to remain constants of Britain's industrial relations system.[65]

Why did employers 'lack the stomach' to apply the Combination Act? Fearful of more damaging consequences if they pursued a trade society through the courts, some employers grudgingly accepted combinations as an unavoidable evil. However, there were trades in which workers' combinations functioned within something approaching a balanced system of industrial relations, and others where the economic and social distance between master and employee was not so great that combinations were anathema. London's master tailors routinely applied to the journeymen's combination, 'the most perfect of any', when seeking labour, since unemployed tailors entered their names at one of the union's thirty houses of call as a condition of receiving relief. Any journeyman who was three-times subject of complaint by employers for unworkmanlike performance was expelled by the union. In most trades a strong stigma was attached to slacking. Trade union sanctions might be directed as much against negligent workmen as employers, typically so in those societies for whom control of entry and high wages was balanced by acceptance of a substantial workload. John Carter, an Essex tailor, arrived at a London house of call in 1810. He later related:

> I was called to work the very day on which I had my name entered on the call-book. ... It required my utmost efforts to get through the allotted amount of a day's work within the appointed time — for the time as well as the amount of work was strictly regulated. The daily task was considerably too much for anyone but a clever and very quick hand, but then, as it was fixed by the workmen themselves, there was neither room for complaining of the masters, nor any good end to be answered by grumbling to the men. This task was, in shop-board phrase, called 'the log' and a very appropriate name it truly was, for the task was indeed a heavy one. Yet, as it showed the equitable principles upon which our trade unions were founded, — in providing that the largest possible amount of labour should be given in exchange for the good wages demanded, — it was generally approved of even by such as, like myself, were not fully equal to the labour it imposed.

---

63 Arthur Aspinall, *The Early English Trade Unions*, pp. 348-9.
64 Ian Christie, *Stress and Stability in Late Eighteenth-Century Britain*, p. 147.
65 Alan Fox, *History and Heritage: The Social Origins of the British Industrial Relations System* (1985), pp. 77-8.

> When I received my first week's wages, amounting to thirty-three shillings, I was not a little pleased. I felt that I had fairly performed the part of a man.[66]

In some trades earnings could only be maximized by effective team work. Here again workplace solidarity and trade unionist ethics stigmatized the deficient workman. Printers' chapels exemplify this approach to work.[67] Consequent high productivity meant that union organization was easily assimilated into the industry. The London printing trade provides a good example of the emergence of a systematized approach to industrial relations incorporating a trade union. The Compositors' Union Society, founded in 1801 but derived from the earlier Phoenix Society of Compositors of 1792, sent delegates in equal number to the masters, to form the committee that drew up the 'the scale of 1805'. This followed a request from the Union that a single list of prices be established in place of a multiplicity of customary practices in the capital's workshops. Four years later the compositors requested substantial amendments to the list in order to restore earnings lost through wartime inflation. This time the masters were less accommodating, and nine months of negotiation were accompanied by selective strikes. By making judicious concessions the Union Society prevailed and on average wages were increased by 12.5 per cent. With further adjustments in 1816, 1866 and 1872, the clauses of the London Scale of Prices of 1810 remained unchanged until 1891.[68]

Other societies paralleling the compositors included the London Philanthropic Society of Coopers and the brushmakers. *Articles of the Society of Journeymen Brush-Makers, Held at the Craven Head Drury Lane* were openly published in 1805, followed ten years later by a *List of Prices Agreed Upon Between the Masters and Journeyman Brush Manufacturers*.[69] The 1824 Parliamentary Select Committee on Artisans and Machinery gathered extensive evidence of trades beyond London maintaining combinations, often in discourse with employers, though few were probably so situated as the 90-strong cabinetmakers of Dublin:

> The Society was not a benefit society, though called the Samaritan Society. It was simply for trade purposes, but though illegal, the employers do not seem to have looked upon it with any great aversion; and when on one occasion the chief constable had the men attending a meeting arrested, the employers came forward to bail them. Indeed they professed that their object, though primarily to defend their own interests against the masters, was also to defend the interests of the masters against unprincipled journeymen. Many of the masters on receiving the bill of a journeyman were in the habit of sending it to the trades' society committee to be taxed, after which the word committee was stamped upon it.[70]

Trade societies that operated in a climate of greater distance from employers were often at greater risk from prosecution. Yet it is noticeable that the number of permanent combinations increased throughout the first two decades of the nineteenth century, frequently characterized by a degree of sophistication and geographical extensiveness not previously evident. The year after the 1800 Combination Act, for example, the papermakers circulated 'sick, and secret articles of our trade,

---

66 [John Carter], *Memoirs of a Working Man*, pp. 123-4.

67 Jan Materné, 'Chapel members in the workplace: tension and teamwork in the printing trades in the seventeenth and eighteenth centuries', in Catharina Lis, Jan Lucassen and Hugo Solly, 'Before the Unions: Wage Earners and Collective Action in Europe, 1300-1850', *International Review of Social History*, 39, Supplement 2 (1994).

68 Ellic Howe (ed.), *The London Compositor: Documents relating to Wages, Working Conditions and Customs of the London Printing Trade, 1785-1900* (1947), pp. 84-90, 134-87.

69 William Kiddier, *The Old Trade Unions, From Unprinted Records of the Brushmakers* (1930).

70 NAPSS 1860, p. 370.

which ... will establish it in every mill from Berwick to Lands End'.[71] In this they excelled, for by 1808 their society was linked to similar associations in Ireland and Scotland, each receiving or remitting money as needed 'for the purpose of maintaining and forwarding the object of the general combination'.[72]

The growth of tramping meant that the routine bureaucracy of union was light. For example, in 1803 the officers of a newly established shoemakers' society in Bath wrote 'to the secretary of the Shops Meetings in London' about arrangements for tramp relief, concluding: 'we hope that we are going to do something for the Good of the Trade in General. Gentlemen, we Sincerely hope and wish to keep a Regular Correspondence with you, And to be in Unity with you, and hope that you will send us the Best Advice for the good of our Cause.' Striking shoemakers' societies would be helped financially by others. Liverpool shoemakers, writing 'in defence of the traide' to their 'Loving Shopmaites' in London, promised

> at aney time should aneything of the kind happen to you, you lose no time to inform us of your sittuashion that we may shew our selfs as much in your intrest and wellfaire as lyes in our power, and we still and allways shall think our indeted to you for the suploys we received from you without which we must have suffered.[73]

Federations such as these were responding to economic pressures, but tramping also facilitated the exchange of political information. The policies of the wartime governments were undoubtedly a formative influence here: the very fact of there being a general Combination Act made workers more alert to the existence and preservation of their legal rights under other legislation. Trades offset the risks of possible prosecution against the need — as they saw it — to establish or maintain a wide correspondence that might strengthen their resolve in uncertain times and increase their effectiveness in lobbying for political change. Britain's avoidance of revolution cannot be taken as an indicator that working people were unchanged by the events of these decades. An incident on the eve of the Luddite rising in Lancashire provides a telling example. On 8 April 1812, a public meeting at the Manchester Exchange to adopt a loyal address was cancelled for fear it would be swamped by radical opponents. The building was broken into and windows and furniture smashed. This was something of a watershed, breaking down 'the inhibitions which had hitherto checked disorder in the surrounding region'. When the meeting reconvened in St Ann's Square it adopted a set of reform resolutions previously moved by the London radical Robert Waithman at a meeting in the capital the previous month. 'The occurrences of that day', recalled one who was there, 'indicated a turn in the current of popular opinion, Previously to that time "Church and King" was the favourite cry, and hunting "Jacobins" great sport' 'We had no Church-and-King mobs after that!' observed another.[74]

To help withstand the impact of the Combination Acts, workers turned with renewed vigour to their legal rights under other laws. 'Is it not time', asked Bolton Weavers in June 1808, 'to drag the British Constitution from its lurking hole, and to expose it in its original and naked purity, to show

---

71 HO 42/62, 2 September 1801.
72 Quoted in W. H. Fraser, *Conflict and Class*, p. 82.
73 HO 42/79, 9 August 1804.
74 An anonymous witness and Thomas Kershaw, both quoted in Archibald Prentice, *Historical Sketches and Personal Recollections of Manchester* (1851), pp. 51-2. For the reconvened meeting see John R. Dinwiddy, *Radicalism and Reform in Britain, 1780-1850* (1992), p. 381; also E. P. Thompson, *The Making of the English Working Class*, p. 644, for evidence that popular indignation on the same occasion (the failure of the Regent to form a peace reform ministry) helped trigger Luddism in Yorkshire.

each individual *the law of his forefathers?*'.[75] To ensure that these were effective they petitioned Parliament. The rejection of their petitions was a plain enough example of class bias and they drew conclusions accordingly about the need for parliamentary reform. But the economic imperatives of declining real wages and overstocking would not wait on reform to the House of Commons. So workers switched tactics, selecting forms of expression suited to the moment and the purpose. For example the failure to secure legislation to guarantee minimum wages in handloom weaving in 1806 led to widespread machine breaking two years later. The containment of this in turn strengthened the process of federalization between Lancashire, Carlisle, Scottish and Belfast cotton weavers in 1809. 'This association', noted one of its officers, 'required a great exertion to mature; and the organization was almost perfect at the close of 1812, when it was finally broken up, by the interference of government'.[76] However, there were other strains at work in this federation. Operating in the very different context of Scottish law, the General Association of Operative Weavers in Scotland pushed hard for regulation of apprenticeship and enjoyed some success in securing wage rates. They also toyed with plans to employ members who were out of work. A strike to enforce a table of wage rates that had recently been approved by Glasgow magistrates failed in 1813, but only after the arrest and imprisonment of its leaders. It is understandable, then, that Scottish weavers were (in the words of an English observer, cited by Fraser,[77] 'particularly cautious to avoid Luddism' while there seemed a realistic chance of securing their objectives by other means. Conceivably, had this outcome happened in 1811 or 1812, Luddite-style agitation might have been more in evidence in Scotland.

THE LUDDITES AND TRADE UNIONISM

It is hard not to become absorbed by Luddism. The Luddites' story, as told by the Hammonds,[78] E. P. Thompson[79] or more recently Robert Reid[80] has the qualities of an epic novel, as Charlotte Bronte recognized in making Yorkshire Luddism the backdrop to her 1849 novel *Shirley*. Yet Luddism is, to use the vocabulary of post-modernist historiographical analysis, a *construction*. A succession of disturbances during the economic slump of 1811-12 somewhat haphazardly acquired the title, which implies a greater degree of coherence and unity of purpose than the events perhaps warrant. Coherence in any case is not necessarily indicative of a hidden guiding hand. This was partly because establishment and middle-class opinion saw in its worse fears a distinct pattern; and partly because protesters saw in the idea of General Ludd a potent focus for protest as well as a useful cloak to anonymity. As a result 'Luddite' has passed into the English language as a word to describe the short-sighted and naïve assumption that progress can be stopped by the rejection of new technologies. Yet machine breaking was only part, perhaps not even the most important part, of Luddism. The disturbances lumped together under this title consisted of three interlocking, yet distinct, movements. In the East Midlands, especially Nottinghamshire, it is the name given to a brief physical force phase (November 1811-February 1812) in the evolving history of trade unionism among the framework knitters. In West Yorkshire's Colne, Calder and Spen valleys it is applied to the combers' protest movement of February to May 1812, with a pitched battle at Rawfolds Mill (between Bradford and

---

75 Quoted in Arthur Aspinall, *The Early English Trade Unions*, p. 101.
76 Alexander B. Richmond, *Narrative of the Condition of the Manufacturing Population and the Proceedings of Government which Led to the State Trials in Scotland* (1824), p. 14.
77 W. H. Fraser, *Conflict and Class*, p. 94.
78 J. L. and Barbara Hammond, *The Skilled Labourer 1760-1832* (1919).
79 E. P. Thompson, *The Making of the English Working Class*.
80 Robert Reid, *The Land of Lost Content: the Luddite Revolt* (1986).

Dewsbury) on 11 April pushed to the forefront of all narratives. Finally events in Lancashire are conventionally subsumed under the same heading though, as Thompson observed, 'it is difficult to know how far the unrest in Lancashire may be described as authentic Luddism'.[81] Lancashire exhibited the most overt political thrust, yet even there the revolutionary reflex was not sustained and we must be cautious of reading back from Lancashire an insurrectionary intent on the part of Yorkshire and, especially, midland Luddism.

What all three Luddite locales did have in common, however, was a pattern of concerted trades action to extend or restore parliamentary regulation of their particular industry. The framework knitters were heavily committed to constitutional reform and regulation of their trade. The Stocking Makers' Association for Mutual Protection, the earliest sustained trade society in the industry, had been founded as far back as 1776, 'to enforce the bye-laws of the [Framework Knitters'] Company by inducing the workmen to take-up their freedom, and oppose persons working at the trade who had not served a regular apprenticeship'.[82] There were further revivals of trade unionism along with repeated expressions of the regulative ideal in 1787, the 1790s, 1805 and 1811.[83] The Yorkshire croppers were still smarting at Parliament's repeal in 1809 of statutory regulation of the woollen industry, a move which had been made in response to Wiltshire shearmen (the West Country term for cropper) petitioning for the renewal of a long-standing ban on gig mills. The classic understanding of what Luddism entailed is perhaps most applicable in Yorkshire; but we should note there was extensive connection between West Country shearmen and Yorkshire croppers in the form of the Brief Institution (see also Chapter 2) founded in the West Riding in 1796 but which around 1800 extended over both areas. In 1803 it had achieved a notable victory, nominally against infringements of statutory apprenticeship at the mills of Leeds' largest employer, but in reality against the incursion of machinery onto workers' control of the trade as a whole.[84] In Lancashire cotton workers had petitioned energetically for a minimum wage and, failing to obtain it, turned some of their energies towards steam-driven weaving. Workers in all three regions were confronted by a government in which sympathy for *laissez-faire* economics was increasing and there were growing numbers of 'Dr A Smiths Disciples to contend with', as Gravener Henson, the framework knitters' leader, ruefully observed.[85]

A considerable degree of planning and management by elected trade delegates, representing a structure of committees, was evident in Luddism in its midland, Yorkshire and Lancashire phases. This does not mean that Luddism was simply a form of trade unionism, rather that the two overlapped in terms of who participated in them, how they were organized and their objectives. Journeymen, many of them members of trade clubs and societies, turned to 'Luddite' tactics as it became apparent that peaceable combination alone would not suffice to defend their interests. 'Is it an act of policy on the part of a Magistrate', the United Committee of Framework Knitters asked the Mayor of Tewkesbury in 1812, to prevent 'them from venting their plaints in a constitutional way[?] — they may be driven to the commission of crimes, for the purpose of exercising their *vengeance*, when they cannot exercise their *rights*'.[86] At the funerals of Luddite casualties appropriate trade obsequies were observed. In the cortège of a stockinger killed in fighting at Bulwell, Nottingham, in

---

81 E. P. Thompson, *The Making of the English Working Class*, p. 618.
82 Gravener Henson, *The Civil, Political, and Mechanical History of the Framework-Knitters, in Europe and America* (1831), p. 338.
83 Richard Gurnham, *200 Years: The Hosiery Unions, 1776-1976* (1976), pp. 6-7, 1042.
84 Adrian Randall, *Before the Luddites*, pp. 131-48.
85 *Records* 1952, p. 157.
86 Ibid, p. 139.

November 1811, 'the corpse was preceded by a number of the deceased's former club mates, bearing black wands, decked with knots of crape'.[87] The cause for which he died closely paralleled the objectives of early trade unions. John Rule has argued that machinery in itself was not the issue of the midland Luddite disturbances. 'What was at issue was the use of unskilled labour to manufacture inferior products. It was after attempts to get a parliamentary regulation of the trade had failed that the machines, only of those employers who had used untrained labour ("colts") to produce cheap products ("cut-ups") were smashed.'[88]

> These Engines of mischief were sentenced to die
> By unanimous vote of the Trade
> And Ludd who can all opposition defy
> Was the grand Executioner made.
>
> Let the wise and the great lend their aid and advice
> Nor e'er their assistance withdraw
> Till full fashioned work at the old fashioned price
> Is established by Custom and Law.
> Then the Trade when this ardorous contest is o'er
> Shall rise in full splendour its head,
> And colting and cutting and squaring no more
> Shall deprive honest workmen of bread.[89]

A particularly vivid instance of this ethic at work occurred when two 'inspectors from the Committee' visited Ashover, Derbyshire.

> They summoned all the Stockingers ... to a Publick House with as much consequence as if they had a mandate from the Prince Regent. ... Where they found a frame worked by a person who had not served a regular apprenticeship, or by a woman, they discharged them from working, and if they promised to do so, they stuck a paper upon the frame with these words written upon it — 'Let this frame stand, the colts removed'.[90]

Seen from this perspective, Luddism has clear roots in guild regulation of production, a tradition that can be traced in officially sanctioned destruction of knitting frames as far back as 1710. Technically, the London Framework Knitters' Company still exercised this authority, upheld in an apprenticeship case contested through the courts only a few years before.[91] Thus it was not just custom, rich though the sense of it was, that sustained the Luddites but a very real perception of legal precedent and rectitude.

Of course, Luddism was about a far wider range of grievances than simply apprenticeship: even at Ashover the inspectors were also concerned to establish their committee's price list. However, we should not lose sight of the extent to which unionist forms and mentalities underlay Luddism. The latter was a tactical form adopted when peaceable action through trade unionism was rebuffed. The

---

87 Quoted in E. P. Thompson, *The Making of the English Working Class*, p. 641.
88 John Rule, *The Experience of Labour in Eighteenth Century Industry* (1981), p. 116.
89 'General Ludd's Triumph', quoted in J. L. and Barbara Hammond, *The Skilled Labourer 1760-1832*, p. 260.
90 HO 42/118, 22 December 1811.
91 William Felkin, *A History of the Machine-Wrought Hosiery and Lace Manufacturers* (1967, first published 1867), p. 435; T. K. Derry, 'The repeal of the apprenticeship clauses of the Statute of Apprentices', *Economic History Review*, 3 (1931-2), p. 69.

secret committees of Lancashire Weavers credited with the direction of the Luddite movement there grew out of, or were identical to, those that had organized petitions for a minimum wage in the preceding period. In February 1812, with a Bill before Parliament to make frame-breaking punishable by death, midland Luddism dissolved swiftly into constitutional agitation once more. The Union Society of Framework Knitters agitated for a parliamentary bill to regulate the trade. Gravener Henson (sometimes cast as 'King Ludd' himself) disingenuously claimed before a parliamentary committee that he had then advised the Nottingham Luddites 'in order to prevent the breaking [of] machinery ... to form clubs and combinations'.[92]

E. P. Thompson long ago suggested that 'the Luddites were some of the last guildsmen'.[93] This sounds like a rhetorical flourish until one reads the words of Gravener Henson, 'Deputy' of the United Society of Framework Knitters in a letter of May 1812 when he was managing their campaign for parliamentary regulation: 'We have hopes that the Trade will be incorporated, the same as the Cutlers at Sheffield, or in other Words, the Charter will be ratify'd by Act of Parliament'. The union anticipated the appointment of 'searchers', backed by magistrates' warrants and its petitioners spoke of being 'Professors of the Art and Mystery of Framework knitting'. Henson found to his surprise that membership of the Dublin Company of Hosiers still included operative framework knitters. Indeed the issue of incorporation caused a rift between the English union and Dublin knitters, who complained 'they had no Right to incorporate Great Britain and Ireland we never Sought for this incorporation we are already a Corporate Body'.[94]

Similar emphases are evident in Yorkshire and Lancashire Luddism, in both of which the interweaving of a lively awareness of the interests of 'the trade' with a radical political awareness was more evident than in the midlands. At a night-time meeting on Dean Moor, near Bolton in April 1812 delegates from across Lancashire discussed 'the Act of Queen Elizabeth which empowered the Magistrates to raise Wages to the price of Provisions', (that is the Statute of Artificers). Stockport delegates told the meeting that since 'Government would give them no satisfaction it became necessary to take the means into their own hands'.[95] At Huddersfield around the same time 'the solicitor to general Ludd' wrote that 'the Cloth dressers in the Huddersfield district as spent seven thousand pounds in petition Government to put the laws in force to stop the shear frames and gig mills to no purpose so they are trying this method now'.[96] In June 1812 a draft petition to Parliament presented to a Manchester meeting attacked the House of Commons' refusal to sanction wage regulation even though prices were rising, and pointed out that the Combination Act prevented workers from 'unitedly attempting to advance their wages' so that they might keep pace with prices.

---

92 Gravener Henson in evidence to the Select Committee on Artisans and Machinery, Fourth Report, *PP* (1824) V, p. 282. The previous March Henson, as leader of the framework knitters, had attempted to persuade magistrates to act against hosiers cutting prices paid for finished work. Their refusal was 'the immediate cause' of Nottingham Luddism (John Stevenson, *Popular Disturbances in England 1700-1832*, second edition (1992), p. 194). The attribution, widely repeated, that Henson himself was King Ludd was made by Francis Place (Gustave d'Eichthal, 'British society in 1828', (1828), reprinted in B. M. Ratcliffe and W. H. Chaloner (eds.), *A French Sociologist Looks at Britain* (1977), p. 55). This was fanciful, but Henson was sufficiently close to the movement for his relation to it to have remained a potent source of historical controversy, see R. A. Church and S. D. Chapman, 'Gravener Henson and the making of the English working class', in E. L. Jones and G. E. Mingay (eds.), *Land, Labour and Population in the Industrial Revolution* (1967), and E. P. Thompson, *The Making of the English Working Class*, pp. 924-34. Henson subsequently wrote a *Civil, Political and Mechanical History of the Framework-Knitters* (1831) which contains a sustained eulogy to the benefits of trade guilds: 'few systems conferred so much happiness and solid content' (p. 232).

93 E. P. Thompson, *The Making of the English Working Class*, p. 603.

94 *Records* 1952, pp. 141, 147, 151, 154.

95 HO 42/128, 7 October 1812.

96 Quoted in John R. Dinwiddy, *Radicalism and Reform in Britain*, p. 399.

In an interesting reiteration of the classic conception of property in skill it added: 'the object of all political institutions ought to be the general good, the equal protection and security of the person and property of each individual, and therefore labour (the poor man's only property) ought to be held as sacred as any other'.[97]

Luddism has sometimes suffered from an interpretive blinkering that, by simplistically interpreting it as about opposition to new technology, fails to locate it in the context of the broader concerns of the trades involved. Equally, a fixation with the drama of Luddism can deafen us to the steady background noise of workplace complaint and grievances. If less dramatic and leaving a lighter trace on the historical record, this was arguably more important for the evolution of trade unionist mentality. As one contemporary sympathizer recalled: 'ever since I can remember, feuds and quarrels have subsisted betwixt the Employers and the Employed respecting apprentices and *illegal men*; and also an *allowed* number of *Apprentices*: and the proper, or *lawful time* of servitude in Apprenticeships, &c. &c.'.[98] To apprenticeship we now turn.

THE REPEAL OF STATUTORY APPRENTICESHIP[99]

The repeal of the apprenticeship clauses of the Statute of Artificers provides a neat illustration of how radicalism and trade unionism did not necessarily intersect. The dogged adherence to apprenticeship on the part of engineering trade societies, especially the millwrights', at a time when its centrality in other trades was slipping was a source of considerable frustration to employers (it was an engineering masters' lobby of Parliament that had initiated the 1799 Combination Act). Because of new technologies — especially the power-driven lathe — it was possible to introduce less-highly trained workers to the shop floor. Early in the nineteenth century the trades' defence of apprenticeship included the successful prosecution of two engineering employers for infringing 5 Elizabeth. One of the two was Alexander Galloway who, not surprisingly, subsequently took a leading role in the campaign to secure the repeal of the statute's apprenticeship clauses. Galloway was one of five engineering employers who sent a 'memorial respecting combinations and benefit societies' to the government and press in May 1813. A campaign for repeal was thus initiated, managed by a committee of which Galloway was chairman.[100]

At the same time that he was leading the employers' campaign to reform apprenticeship, Galloway was one of a group of London radicals seeking contact with France and exiled United Irishmen there. Galloway was, in fact, one of the most politically radical Londoners of his age. He had been a leading member of the London Corresponding Society, a link man between it and the Nore naval mutineers and he was deeply involved in the revolutionary United Englishmen, for which he had been imprisoned in 1798-1801. Galloway was an early member of the society Thomas Spence

---

97 *Report of the Proceedings on the Trial of Thirty-Eight Men, on a Charge of Administering an Unlawful Oath ... at Lancaster, on Thursday, 27th August 1812, with an Introductory Narrative by John Knight* (Manchester, 1812) p. 98, cited in John R. Dinwiddy, *Radicalism and Reform in Britain*, p. 401.

98 [George Beaumont], *The Beggars Complaint, against Rack-Rent Landlords, Corn Factors, Great Farmers, Monopolizers, Paper money Makers, and War, and Many Other Oppressors and oppressions. Also, Some Observations on the Conduct of the Luddites in reference to the Destruction of Machinery* (1812), p. 102.

99 Iorwerth J. Prothero, *Artisans and Politics in Early Nineteenth-Century London: John Gast and His Times* (1979), and T. K. Derry, 'The repeal of the apprenticeship clauses of the Statute of Apprentices', give complementary accounts of the events leading up to the repeal of the apprenticeship legislation of 1563, the first strongest on the artisans', and the second on employers' involvement. The metropolitan bias of both is balanced to some extent by John Rule, *The Experience of Labour in Eighteenth Century Industry*, pp. 114-19.

100 T. K. Derry, 'The repeal of the apprenticeship clauses of the Statute of Apprentices', p. 77.

founded to promote his ideas and also the brother-in-law of Thomas Evans who led it after Spence's death in 1814. He largely co-ordinated the defence of those arrested after the great Spa Fields demonstration of 1816: as an old Jacobin later recalled, 'Mr Galloway showed his true patriotism in the case of young James Watson' (who, waving a tricolour, had led the Spa Fields rioters into the capital) whom he helped to hide and escape to America.[101]

As an employer Galloway did not permit collective wage bargaining in any form at his works but struck an individual contract with every worker. In this way he hoped to frustrate any combination, believing that 'in all those trades where the men have made their own individual engagements, we never see anything like combinations'.[102] The memorial of 1813 contained a strongly worded claim that friendly societies 'have created, cherished and given effect to the most dangerous Combinations among the several Journey men of our district'. The employers saw this as integrally linked to apprenticeship: 'Benefit Societies have made a successful weapon, and the Statute of the 5th of Elizabeth a constant and prosperous rallying point to further the measures of the Journeymen against their employers'.[103] When the authors wrote that 'a convention of delegates has been sitting in the Heart of the metropolis for some months composed of two persons from every Trade and Profession ... solely to Consider of the best means of applying to the legislator to enlarge the powers and to extend the operation of the Statute of the 5th of Elizabeth', they did so perhaps in light of knowledge Galloway acquired via his contacts in radical circles. For the trades' campaign to consolidate and extend the apprenticeship provisions of the 1563 Statute illustrates workers' organization at its most extensive yet most opaque.

Engineering employers were not alone in facing prosecution by trade unions for breaching 5 Elizabeth during the years the Combination Act was in force. In 1813, Allen Davenport, like Galloway a leading Spencean but also a shoemaker and a trade unionist, recalled:

> The women's men acquired great strength as to numbers, and a considerable increase in pecuniary means. We had at one time fourteen divisions in London; besides being in union, kept up by a well regulated correspondence, with the trade in every city and town, of any importance, throughout the kingdom. But about this time the trade commenced a law suit against a master, for employing an illegal man, and refusing to discharge him. The case was conducted by two intelligent shop-mates, Messrs. Oldfield and Bent, assisted by an attorney in the court of King's Bench, Westminster. We gained the day, but the prosecution cost the trade a hundred pounds.[104]

The women's men's action was no isolated episode. Apprenticeship control had been the subject of agitation in the English and Scottish textile industries since the beginning of the century. Furthermore the shoemakers' case was one of at least twenty brought to the London courts between 1809 and 1813, involving thirteen different trades and employing the same attorney in every case. Such court cases were expensive, indicating that even trades less organized than the women's shoemakers must have had fairly sophisticated means to collect sufficient funding as well as considerable collective commitment to the cause: even successful prosecutions (eight of the twenty) cost more than they

---

101 Quotation from a letter from Thomas Preston in *Northern Star* 18 December 1845. For Galloway and the revolutionary circle of which he was part see Malcolm Chase, *'The People's Farm'*.
102 Galloway, evidence to the Select Committee on Artisans and Machinery, First Report, *PP* (1824) V, p. 27.
103 HO 42/133, 27 May 1813.
104 Allen Davenport, *The Life and Literary Pursuits of Allen Davenport. With a further Selection of the Author's Work*, compiled and edited by Malcolm Chase (1994, originally published 1845), pp. 18-9.

recouped through the fine levied on the guilty master. Fines had to be shared with the Crown and courts consistently set them at nugatory levels, and legal costs were not recoverable. Systematic research outside London would undoubtedly yield many more examples: for example Carlisle weavers pressed magistrates on the apprenticeship issue in 1812, while the following year Bath shoemakers successfully struck on the issue.[105]

The London women's shoemakers' case of 1813 was the last of its kind. Cross-trade co-ordination is obvious in the chronological concentration and employment of the same lawyer in these court actions. Even before Davenport's union went to court an Artisans' General Committee had been set up by the London trades to prepare a campaign by which, it was hoped, Parliament could be persuaded to strengthen and extend the apprenticeship clauses of 'the law Queen Betty made':

> Her memory still is dear to journey men,
> For shelter'd by her laws, now they resist
> infringements, which would else persist:
> Tyrannic masters, innovating fools
> Are check'd, and bounded by her glorious rules.
> Of workmen's rights she's still the guarantee.[106]

The Artisans' General Committee met weekly, emboldened by legal opinion that their activities did not constitute an offence under either Common Law or the 1800 Combination Act. It maintained a considerable provincial correspondence and an adjunct committee possibly sat in Bristol. It was apparently responsible for the publication of a newspaper, the *Beacon*, and it saw itself as having a wider role as 'the means of keeping up the Spirit of Mechanics'.[107] Though petitioning Parliament to enforce statutory apprenticeship was a new tactic, the case made by the committee was rooted in traditional arguments in favour of a property in skill, upheld by communal values and state legislation alike:

> The apprenticed artisans have, collectively and individually, an unquestionable right to expect the most extended protection from the Legislature, in the quiet and exclusive use and enjoyment of their several respective arts and trades, which the law has already conferred upon them as a property, as much as it has secured the property of the stockholder in the public funds: and it is clearly unjust to take away the whole of the anciently established property and rights of any one class of the community, unless, at the same time, the rights and property of the whole commonwealth should be dissolved, and parcelled out anew for the public good.[108]

The Committee's deliberations were given added urgency by the repeal of the wage-fixing clauses in the Statute of Artificers in 1813 — a rebuttal to the Lancashire cotton spinners who had petitioned magistrates to enforce them. The Tory MP George Rose, whose paternalistic and protective economic ideas were very much in accord with the trade societies and who had sponsored the path-breaking

---

105 June Barnes, 'The trade union and radical activities of the Carlisle handloom weavers', *Transactions of the Cumberland and Westmorland Antiquarian and Archaeological Society*, 78, (1978), p. 154; R. S. Neale, *Bath: A Social History or; A Valley of Pleasure, yet a Sink of Iniquity* (1981), p. 327.

106 From a 1811 trial report of an apprenticeship case involving the London saddlers, quoted in E. P. Thompson, *Customs in Common: Studies in Traditional Popular Culture* (1991), p. 62.

107 Iorwerth J. Prothero, *Artisans and Politics*, pp. 54-5. See also Iorwerth Prothero's note, 'The Beacon: the first trade union newspaper?', *BSSLH* 24, Spring 1972, 33-4.

108 Quoted in T. K. Derry, 'The repeal of the apprenticeship clauses', p. 78.

1793 Friendly Societies Act, was secured as the Committee's parliamentary spokesman. Rose was not exactly adroit in his management of the issue in parliament, but the pressure to end statutory apprenticeship was in any case inexorable. This was partly because of the prevailing tide of *laissez faire* opinion in government circles but also because the apprenticeship campaign had unfolded against the background of unprecedented labour unrest in the capital[109] and in the country at large. The national context suggested that the existence of statutory apprenticeship was a significant factor in the power of organized trades which — in spite of the Combination Acts — were increasingly public and assertive.

A few examples must suffice of the growing momentum shown by trades organization at this time. 'The men are all associating together for an increase of wage ... they are writing upon the walls, "Cutlers stand true". Their plans are, I understand, very well organised', wrote a Sheffield magistrate, adding that the grinders maintained 'a regular Committee appointed to examine the work; and if it is sufficiently well done, as they suppose, they send a note to the masters signifying their approval of it'.[110] Blackburn employers pointed to a local committee of weavers circulating handbills similar to those in other Lancashire towns, proof of 'a Degree of System and Combination which in our opinion ought immediately to be checked'.[111] In 1811 Whitehaven miners met 'publickly now twice a week to collect subscribers and to swear them to be true to each other'.[112] The title alone of the 'General Association of Operative Weavers of Cumberland, Westmorland, Northumberland and Durham and the Southern Counties of Scotland' indicates a broad measure of supra-regional organization. However, communication between the Scottish and English textile trades extended well beyond it, 'the intercourse being carried on in an organised and expeditious manner' according to the Scottish Lord Advocate.[113] Details of the United Feltmakers of Manchester only reached the Home Office from Scotland, new regulations regarding tramping having been addressed to the 'journeymen hatters of Glasgow with speed' where they were intercepted by the Post Office.[114] Two months later woolcombers' societies 'in union' held a national delegate meeting in Coventry. The extensive articles agreed by it were then published by a further 'meeting of the Worsted Manufacturers' in Keighley, West Yorkshire, that November. These emphasized 'legal apprenticeship', closely regulated tramping, called for closed shops and provided for a central register of fair men and the dissemination of any job vacancies notified by employers.[115]

The woolcombers' initiative was a further indication of the interconnectedness of Luddism and trade unionist objectives, an issue that preoccupied authority in the regions most concerned. Early in 1813, acting in the light of 'combinations among the journeymen in almost every branch of trade', Lancashire magistrates framed a bill 'to prevent the Friendly Societies from being perverted to purposes of public mischief'.[116] This would have made any meeting of an unregistered society unlawful and tightened magistrates' powers to regulate registered bodies. It is hardly surprising, therefore, that engineering employers bracketed trade unions, friendly societies and Luddism together. It is also conceivable that some of the national trades' correspondence, which the Home

---

109 David R. Green, 'Lines of conflict: labour disputes in London, 1790-1870', *International Review of Social History*, 43/2, (1998), p. 213.
110 HO 42/106, paper titled 'Disposition to combination amongst the workmen at Sheffield' enclosed with Effingham to Beckett, 14 April 1810.
111 HO 42/108, 23 August 1810.
112 Michael W. Flinn, *The History of the British Coal Industry Volume 2: 1700-1830: The Industrial Revolution* (1984), p. 397.
113 Arthur Aspinall, *The Early English Trade Unions*, p. 123.
114 Ibid, p. 121.
115 Ibid, p. 127ff.
116 HO 42/132, 4 February 1813.

Office linked with the 'disturbances', related to statutory apprenticeship and was being conducted under the aegis of the Artisans' General Committee. Equally, of course, contact made about this issue would have facilitated the subsequent exchange of information on others.

Conventionally, narratives of the repeal of statutory apprenticeship have stressed parliamentary factors influencing its progress, the fact that opposition to it was swamped by interest in the Corn Bill at home and the fall of Napoleon abroad. Furthermore, opposition from the provincial trades, extensive while the bill lay before the House of Commons, melted away when it was sent to the Lords. Further research into apprenticeship as a political issue in the English regions is certainly needed if the episode is ever to be fully understood. By the end of April 1814 an estimated total of 300,000 had signed petitions to retain and enforce the Elizabethan legislation, and a further 27 petitions (Bristol journeymen alone sent 5,811 signatures) were received by the Commons shortly before the bill was sent to the Lords.[117] However, it is hard to believe that the Luddite disturbances of 1811-12 had been forgotten at Westminster as Parliament deliberated on statutory apprenticeship. Luddism and trade unionism were more closely associated than many historians have allowed, not least in the mind of contemporary authority.

Alexander Galloway believed that the repeal of the apprenticeship clauses of 5 Elizabeth, 'broke the neck of all combinations'. He was wrong. Yet this particular piece of legislation (54 George 3, c. 96) redefined the landscape for trade unionism as much, even more perhaps, than the repeal of the Combination Acts ten years later. As we saw in the previous chapter, apprenticeship had been subject to a process of erosion going back over at least a century. Yet while statutory apprenticeship remained a legal fact (if not always a social reality) it shaped artisans' self-awareness and sense of respectability and property in skill. It held out a prospect, receding but nonetheless tangible, of becoming one's own master. The repeal of the Statute of Artificers was one more brick in a wall being erected between employers and employed, as William Crawford, a bookbinder who had served an apprenticeship at the turn of the century, affirmed in 1843:

> The trade is carried on now in a different manner from what it was many years ago. Formerly, when a man was bound to the trade he was taught the whole of the business; but now the binding of a book is so subdivided into many branches, and each man does only one of them. For instance, one man puts on the boards, another man does the back, a third puts on the leather, another does the lettering, another the general finishing. Thus an apprentice now only learns exceedingly little and is unfit to get his living setting up for himself; or to work anywhere, except in large shops, where the work is done on a large scale, [and] can be so subdivided.[118]

---

117 T. K. Derry, 'The repeal of the apprenticeship clauses of the Statute of Apprentices', p. 80; Iorwerth J. Prothero, *Artisans and Politics*, p. 60.
118 Evidence of William Crawford, Royal Commission on Children's Employment, *PP* 1843, XIV, p. 806. Another consequence of the de-skilling he describes was the ease with which employers were able to introduce child and female workers into trades hitherto largely adult male preserves: see George Dodd, *Days at the Factories: or, the Manufacturing Industry of Great Britain Described ... Series I.—London*, (1843), pp. 362-84, for a detailed portrait of just a bindery as Crawford described.

4

'A Young and Rising Commonwealth'

WATERLOO TO PETERLOO

The situation of the trades after the repeal of 5 Elizabeth in 1814 varied enormously. Most obviously and crucially the end of the war against France brought a severe depression to the economy that lasted to the end of the decade. Around 350,000 troops and seamen were demobilized. The distress of the post-war years represented the sternest test yet for industrializing society. Protective tariffs for agriculture were introduced in 1815, in the form of corn laws prohibiting the import of foreign grain until the domestic price exceeded eighty shillings a quarter. They were met with massive petitions and by rioting in London on a scale not seen since the 1780s. Revolutionary currents accelerated in intensity and produced, in the Spa Fields meeting of December 1816 and the Cato Street conspiracy of 1820, two highly disturbing — if never very realistic — attempts at a *coup d'état*. Of greater long term significance was popular support for constitutional reform, 'the most impressive radical mobilization in pre-Chartist history'.[1] The tragic climax of this movement came at Peterloo, the name immediately and universally given to the forcible dispersion on 16 August 1819 of a meeting of some 60,000 reformers at St Peter's Fields, Manchester. Peterloo exposed weaknesses in popular constitutionalism: massive popular indignation did nothing to prevent the exoneration of those responsible for eleven deaths and hundreds of injuries. Furthermore the Whig opposition rather than popular radicalism benefited most from the anti-government propaganda victory, as the latter passed the repressive Six Acts and imprisoned Henry 'Orator' Hunt, whose personification of the mass platform agitation was at once one of its greatest strengths and weaknesses.

Trade unionism overlapped these agitations. It seems likely the mass petitioning against the Corn Laws owed something to the trades' apprenticeship campaign the previous year. On that occasion at least 300,000 had signed petitions to the House of Commons, a proportion of the total population (around 2.5 per cent) that compares well alongside the infinitely better resourced and experienced Chartist movement's first petition of 1839 (signed by just under 7 per cent of the total population). Many trade societies were sympathetic to the aims of the revolutionary underground. Some took sympathy a stage further: coachmakers, tailors, typefounders and shoemakers were among the London trades ready to act had the Cato Street conspiracy succeeded in assassinating the Cabinet.[2] In the less-opaque arena of popular constitutionalism, trade societies were enthusiastic participants in the political theatre of parades and demonstrations. For example, on Tyneside the Winlaton

---

1 John Belchem, *'Orator' Hunt: Henry Hunt and English Working-Class Radicalism* (2012), p. 69.
2 Malcolm Chase, *'The People's Farm': English Radical Agrarianism, 1775-1840* (2010), p. 103.

ironworkers led a 16,000 strong procession onto Newcastle's Town Moor to join a monster meeting condemning Peterloo in October 1819.[3] Artisans were well-disposed towards Hunt's insistence that 'all what the radicals required was a reformed parliament which would act for the benefit of the people ... It was said that property should be represented: so he said [as well], for labour was the property of the people'.[4]

Industrial disputes during the post-war years added to a sense of popular expectation of change. There was a renewed spate of machine-breaking in Lancashire during 1816-17, but far more significant was a series of mass strike actions by cotton textile workers in the region the following year. These turn-outs were on an unprecedented scale.[5] They were well organized (delegates from each mill elected a central committee which in turn drew down financial assistance from other trades both regionally and nationally) and they were disciplined. 'The peaceable demeanour of so many thousand unemployed men is not natural', commented the local military commander, 'their regular meeting and again dispersing shows a system and organisation of their actions which has some appearance of *previous tuition*'.[6] 'The funds of the Benefit Societies', complained one magistrate, were 'openly applied to the support of the obstinately idle'.[7] What began as a spinners' dispute spread to power- and hand-loom weavers, dyers, 'bricksetters and their labourers', carpenters and joiners, glassworkers and colliers.

In August some nineteen Manchester trades formed 'a Union of all Trades called the PHILANTHROPIC SOCIETY'. Its purpose was to assist any affiliated body of workmen in defensive or offensive strike action, or against 'being oppressed or illegally used'.[8] The Society's history is somewhat opaque, being bound up with the radical-political underground of the period. In the minds of both Whitehall and the Manchester magistracy it was closely associated with local members of the clandestine ultra-radical network. 'The system of support from one trade to another is carried on to an amazing extent, and they regularly send delegates out to the different towns who are in work to receive their subscriptions.'[9] In September 1818, at a meeting held at Todmorden in the West Riding of Yorkshire, delegates from Lancashire, Yorkshire, Nottingham, Birmingham and Somerset met to discuss extending the union. No organization emerged from this proposal (conceivably what delegates meant by 'general union' did not require one).

However, three months later in London there was formed the Philanthropic Hercules, 'a union of Journeymen (as suggested by the Manchester Men)'. Its president was the shipwrights' leader and Spencean sympathizer John Gast. The Philanthropic Hercules called 'upon all Trades, desirous of becoming free and respectable, to send their Deputy with proper instructions, to consolidate the GENERAL UNION'. Its title was resonant with more than just the Manchester body. Four years before, the ultra-radical Thomas Spence had published *The Giant Killer*, with references to 'the

---

3 John Belchem, *'Orator' Hunt*, p. 96.
4 Ibid. p. 151.
5 A modern study of the Lancashire strikes of 1818 is much needed. The best accounts remain the Hammonds, *The Skilled Labourer 1760-1832* (1919), pp. 47-119, and that compiled from Home Office papers by Arthur Aspinall, *The Early English Trade Unions: Documents from the Home Office Papers in the Public Record Office* (1949), pp. 246-312. For brief accounts see John Stevenson, *Popular Disturbances in England 1700-1832*, second edition (1992), pp. 255-7 and John Rule, *The Labouring Classes in Early Industrial England 1750-1850* (1986), pp. 270-4.
6 HO 42/178, 26 July 1818.
7 HO 42/180, 17 September 1818.
8 Handbill in HO 42/179 and 181, quoted in Arthur Aspinall, *The Early English Trade Unions*, p. 273.
9 James Norris, JP to Sidmouth (Home Secretary), HO 42/178, 29 July 1818.

philanthropic giant-killers, the deliverers of mankind'. (In popular literature of the time Hercules was often portrayed killing giants.) Spence's circle called themselves the Spencean Philanthropists and members of it were the fulcrum of covert and revolutionary politics in the capital.[10] Both these early attempts at general union, in Manchester and London, emerged out of the ultra-radical political culture of the Regency years.

The strike movement is of considerable historical interest though it was ultimately unsuccessful. Manchester's Philanthropic Society survived the strike but was broken by the prosecution of the strike leaders. The Philanthropic Hercules, comprising delegates from between thirty and forty trades, lasted slightly longer and, as we shall see, had a greater impact through the London campaign to support the Lancashire strikers. No other industrial disputes in the immediate post-war years matched the intensity of Lancashire in 1818. It was also unmatched in the vigorous extent to which employers responded to the strikers. The cotton spinners' strike ended after seven weeks with funds perilously low and the entire organizing committee arrested on charges of conspiracy. Officers of the weavers were prosecuted under the Combination Act, two of them receiving two years' imprisonment and a third one year. These sentences were handed down in February of 1819, by which time the small advances made in the previous autumn's strike had been lost. The experience of defeat lent fresh impetus to the reform agitation in Lancashire, especially on the part of the handloom weavers who thereafter retreated from the use of trade unionism to improve their situation. The Combination Act seems always to have been applied sparingly, but events in Lancashire in 1818-19 reveal how profound its effect could be.

THE LAST YEARS OF THE COMBINATION ACT

At the close of the previous chapter we heard bookbinder William Crawford lament in 1843 how the demise of regular apprenticeship three decades earlier had reinforced the de-skilling of labour. It was echoed in many trades. Coventry watchmakers complained to a Parliamentary Select Committee in 1817 that 'a movement or spring maker is not able to work at any other branch of the business' because the trade was being flooded with outdoor apprentices. They also contrasted the recruitment of these non-resident juniors, who had little prospect of learning all the branches of the trade, with the regular apprentices some masters still maintained: William Mayo treated his apprentice 'both for protection and teaching his art' just like his own son. When he himself had come out of his time in 1800, 'persons using the trade lived in respectability and were looked up to with regard; no person of this trade was known to take parish support; if any watchmaker was reduced by affliction or other casualty, if he wanted support, a weekly subscription was made by the trade, as it was thought discreditable to allow a watchmaker to be in distress'.[11] The same point on behalf of his 'Brother Artisans' was taken up by an anonymous pamphleteer: before repeal, when parents 'put their children to the Watch Trade, they considered that by so doing they had given them the pledge of future comfort and respectability'. Now, Parliament was told, a 'multitude of apprentices are brought into the trade, far beyond the probability of employment when they become journeymen, either in

---

10 Quotation from the addresses of the Philanthropic Hercules taken from Iorwerth J. Prothero, *Artisans and Politics in Early Nineteenth-Century London: John Gast and His Times* (1979), pp. 69 and 101. For the intermingling of trade unionist and radical politics in these years Prothero is the best guide. On the Spencean dimension see Malcolm Chase, *'The People's Farm'*.

11 Quoted in Paul Sutton, 'Soup and supervision: the metropolitan watch and clock trade, 1797-1817', *Journal of Historical Sociology*, vol. 9, no. 3 (September, 1996), p. 331.

Coventry or elsewhere in the country'.[12] The abolition of statutory apprenticeship three years before represented, thought the watchmakers, those same 'pretensions to the allowance of universal uncontrolled freedom of action to the individual' that had marked the French Revolution.[13]

> The apprenticed artisans have, collectively and individually, an unquestionable right to expect the most extended protection from the Legislature, in the quiet and exclusive enjoyment of their several and respective arts and trades, which the law has already confirmed on them as a property, as much as it has secured the property of the stockholder in the public funds.[14]

The desire to maintain respectability is the keynote of the watchmakers' ideology, as it was in other skilled trades. When Parliament, in a further move to liberalize labour laws, removed wage-fixing in the Spitalfields silk industry in 1824, some weavers starved to death rather than go on the parish.[15] Petitioning for the restoration of the Spitalfields Act, the journeymen broad silk weavers warmed to a familiar theme:

> All persons whose incomes are derived from landed property, the funds, tythes, law-fees, and from monopolies of every kind, are subject to, and protected by legislative or conventional regulations ... as the Artisan's power of labour is his only property, it is irreconcilable with every sense of justice, and of *common right*, that the incomes and property of all other classes should be protected, whilst the Artisans and Labourers alone are left a prey to be plundered by needy, rapacious, and unprincipled Employers.[16]

Artisans who joined the Philanthropic Hercules did so 'from a just sense of his or their respectability'. A 'Brother Mechanic' in 1818 complained of 'the progressive reductions of our means of supporting that decent and respectable appearance in society as becomes valuable members', and he called on his readers to 'unite in the mutual support of your reputation and respectability'.[17] The maintenance of reputation and respectability was closely allied to the ideal of the male breadwinner. The outlook of the brushmakers' society was vividly captured by its historian William Kiddier, himself a 'brother panhand' and saturated in the ethic of the trade:

> The root of the movement is in the home. The living wage concerns the whole family to the babe just born. What movement is so essential as this? — that men shall work and wives and children shall be fed! What could be more sacred!
>
> Enter not the philanthropist. Profane not the temple of homelife by your free gifts. Attempt not to destroy the ideal of the skilled workman by sundry offers for the care of his children. The man wants work. His ideal is a home with the man as wage-earner. The approach of the philanthropist is a mockery to this.
>
> Besides! The nation's strength lies not in free soup but in wages.
>
> What the nation loses by the continuous opposition to men's Trade Societies cannot be known.[18]

---

12 Quoted in Margaret Lane, *Apprenticeship in England 1600-1914* (1996), pp. 162-3.
13 Quoted in John Rule, 'Trade unions, the Government and the French Revolution, 1789-1802', in John Rule and Robert Malcolmson (eds.), *Protest and Survival: The Historical Experience — Essays for E. P. Thompson* (1993), p. 114.
14 Quoted in John Rule 'General introduction' to J. L. and Barbara Hammond, *The Skilled Labourer*; new edition (1979), p. xii.
15 Iorwerth J. Prothero, *Artisans and Politics*, p. 27.
16 *The Petition of the Journeymen Broad Silk Weavers of Spitalfields, and its vicinity, for a 'Wages Protection Bill'* [1828?], pp. 6-7.
17 BL Add. MSS 27799, fols. 143-4.
18 William Kiddier, *The Old Trade Unions, From Unprinted Records of the Brushmakers* (1930), p. 191.

This same sense of respectability, decidedly not to be confused with Victorian middle-class values but rather derived from the aspirations of the 'middling sort' of the previous century, of which skilled workers had always seen themselves as part, led many workers to prefer to pay for their children to attend private working-class venture day schools rather than charity schools.[19] To some extent almost all workers subscribed to this ethic, the crucial difference for artisans being that its realization lay within their grasp, or seemed to do so if only adverse legislation and the decline of custom could be overcome. Respectability's most pervasive expression is to be seen in working people's almost universal desire to avoid the indignity of a pauper's grave, provision against which was the commonest motive for joining a friendly society. Distaste for charity, though, came a close second. Skilled workers made little distinction between private philanthropy and parish relief. We saw in Chapter 2 that benefit functions lay at the heart of most early trade societies. A rigid distinction between friendly and trade societies is as impractical as it is unhelpful to our understanding of the early industrial worker's world.

The symbiosis of trade and friendly society function was intensified by the Combination Act. To speak, as historians often do, of trade unions masquerading or disguised as friendly societies to evade this legislation is misleading, since friendly society functions were in any case a central part of most of them. But the Acts undoubtedly restrained trades from making public the existence or development of other functions. For example, the Birmingham button burnishers' Loyal Albion Lodge had been founded in 1810: 'we had a sick and burial club, our only legal hold in those days, but our principal object was to keep up wages'.[20] Given that the responsibility to prosecute infringements of the Combination Act lay with employers, there was also widespread tacit acceptance of trade unions' existence. Societies formed before 1799 and whose existence had therefore already been officially approved, usually continued with impunity even if — as for example the Friendly Associated Cotton Spinners (whose rules were approved by Manchester's Quarter Sessions in 1795) — their regulations made it clear that they had an overt industrial function, in this case through the attempted enforcement of closed shops in the industry.[21] In Oxford the Acts of 1799 and 1800 were regarded as so ineffectual that master shoemakers, with the support of their guild, raised a subscription to secure a private act 'for abolishing and suppressing the societies of journeymen boot and shoe makers and for the more effective preventing of unlawful combination'.[22] In 1816 the Maidstone-based Original Society of Papermakers petitioned Parliament for legislation to control mechanization; this was in spite of both the general proscription on combination and legislation specific to papermaking of 1796.[23]

---

19 The literature on respectability is extensive and intersects with the contentious concept of 'labour aristocracy'. As such it features most centrally on the literature of the Victorian period, see for example Neville Kirk,*The Growth of Working-class Reformism in Mid-Victorian England* (1985), Patrick Joyce, V*isions of the People: Industrial England and the Question of Class, 1840-1914* (1991), Trygve Tholfsen, *Working-class Radicalism in Mid-Victorian England* (1976). On this earlier period see Iorwerth J. Prothero, *Artisans and Politics* and Paul Sutton, 'Soup and supervision'. On working-class venture day schools see Phil Gardner, *The Lost Elementary Schools of Victorian England* (1984).

20 Quoted in John Rule, *The Labouring Classes in Early Industrial England 1750-1850*, p. 286.

21 *Articles, Rules, Orders, and Regulations, Made, and to be Observed, by and between the Members of the Friendly Associated Cotton Spinners* (1795). The society was governed by 'arbitrators' each nominated by the members in their shop. Members undertook not to instruct anyone in cotton spinning who was not a member of the society.

22 M. J. Walker, 'The extent of guild control of trades in England, *circa* 1660-1820: a study based on a sample of provincial towns and London companies', unpublished Ph.D thesis (University of Cambridge, 1985), pp. 343-4.

23 Peter Clark and Lyn Murfin, *The History of Maidstone: the Making of a Modern County Town* (1995), p. 86.

The evasion of the Combination Act was most widespread in the capital. 'The Congress' (delegate committee) in hatmaking operated a structure of closed shops which obliged masters to obtain 'a certificate of his cleanliness' before employing any worker.[24] We saw in the previous chapter how the London women's shoemakers' trade society prosecuted infringements of the Statute of Artificers in 1812. Some London trades, notably tailors, cabinetmakers and compositors negotiated collectively with employers to agree elaborate price lists for wages in their trades. In the various processions honouring Queen Caroline (the wife whom George IV was seeking to put aside) in 1820, London tradesmen, grouped in specific societies and often led by elaborate banners, featured prominently. As in radical politics, the campaign in Caroline's support provided an unimpeachable opportunity for public organization and the assertion of collective identity.[25]

The social dynamic of London was not necessarily repeated elsewhere. In 1812 the Midlands framework knitters sent a deputation to the capital where they sought the advice of the London carpenters who had successfully prosecuted employers for infringing 5 Elizabeth.

> They thought we possessed a fund on the permanent principle to answer any demand, at any time, and if that had been the case, would have Lent us two or three thousand pounds, (for there is £20,000 in the fund belonging to that Trade) but when they understood that our Trade kept no regular fund to support itself, Instead of Lending us money, their noses underwent a Mechanical turn upwards, and each saluted the other with a significant stare, Ejaculating, Lord bless us!!! what fools!!! they Richly deserve all they put! and ten times more!!! We always thought stockeners a sett of poor creatures! Fellows as wanting of spirit, as their pockets are of money. What would our Trade be, if we did not combine together? perhaps as poor as you are, at this day, Look at other Trades! they all Combine (the Spitalfield Weavers excepted, and what a Miserable condition are they in) see the Tailers, shoemakers, Bookbinders, Gold beaters, printers, Bricklayers, Coatmakers, Hatters, Curriers, Masons, whitesmiths, none of these trades Receive Less than 30/- a week, and from that to five guineas this is all done by Combination, without it their Trades would be as bad as yours.[26]

Doubtless the carpenters' teasing gained in the telling. Yet the conclusion that the Combination Acts 'were something but not much'. Orth[27] is only tenable from a metropolitan perspective. Especially in industries, like framework knitting, that were dispersed rather than concentrated in urban communities, they retarded the evolution of a corporate ethic and may even have contributed to a continuing adherence to traditional forms of protest; and, as we have seen, their selective use broke the unionist spirits of the Lancashire handloom weavers in 1818.

On the other hand, such was the range of legal redress available to employers, the 1824 repeal made little difference to the practical situation of those trades too weak to withstand employer hostility. Since the early eighteenth century, prosecution of workers' combinations under the common law of conspiracy had been available to those who chose to employ it, Conspiracy was often preferred even while the Combination Acts had been in force, including not only the Lancashire spinners in 1818 but also the high-profile prosecution of *The Times* printers in 1810. Other prosecutions included London hatters and coachmakers, Coventry silk weavers and Manchester

---

24 David R. Green, *From Artisans to Paupers: Economic Change and Poverty in London, 1790-1870* (1995), p. 92.
25 Iorwerth J. Prothero, *Artisans and Politics*, p. 142.
26 Thomas Large to the Framework Knitters' Committee, 24 April 1812, quoted in *Records* 1952, p. 143.
27 J. V. Orth, 'The legal status of English trade unions, 1799-1871', in A. Harding (ed.), *Law-Making and Law-Makers in British History* (1980), p. 197.

engravers. Trial for conspiracy was generally the only recourse available in Scotland where the Combination Acts did not apply, until a crime of combination was recognised by the courts in the case of a Weavers' Association in 1813.[28]

It is a tribute to those who masterminded the 1824 repeal of the Combination Act that they succeeded in persuading Parliament to remove trade disputes from the law of conspiracy as well. The story has often been told of how Francis Place, in 'a masterpiece of adroit diplomacy, lobbying and skilled argument'[29] led the campaign for the repeal of the Combination Acts. One should not under-rate the tenacity and skill of the Charing Cross tailor in securing support inside the House of Commons, co-ordinating the evidence submitted to the Select Committee and winning the backing of trade societies who were — not unnaturally — highly suspicious both of parliamentary legislation in all its forms and of Place himself. Place had after all supported the repeal of statutory apprenticeship in 1814 and argued (probably disingenuously) that repeal of the combinations laws would actually lead to the diminution of trade union activity. Furthermore, Gravener Henson and Peter Moore, the radical MP for Coventry, had made substantial progress with an alternative repeal measure. This bill (admittedly not well-drafted) was defeated not by outright parliamentary opposition but by the finesse of Place and Joseph Hume, who managed support inside the Commons. With a trade-union sponsored measure removed and, as we shall see, the law of master and servant newly tightened, it is scarcely surprising that Parliament felt able to pass the Combination Laws Repeal Act in 1824.

Yet even this victory was short-lived, for the repeal measure was substantially amended the following year. Trade disputes were once again subject to the common law of conspiracy, an exception being made for peaceable moves to increase wages or reduce working hours. The 1824 Act's prohibition of violence, threats and intimidation was extended to embrace 'molesting' and 'obstructing'. In a move to restrain labour's capacity to control entry to a trade or enforce closed shops, the 1825 Act added a new prohibition against any 'endeavour to force' an employer 'to make any alteration in his mode of regulating, managing, conducting or carrying on such manufacture, trade or business, or to limit his number of apprentices, or the number or description of his journeymen, workmen or servants'. In the years to come it became abundantly clear that concepts like molesting, obstructing and endeavouring to force left wide latitude for judicial interpretation.

Nonetheless, trade unions, if not yet exactly legal, were no longer explicitly illegal: and the 1824-5 legislation has always therefore been viewed as a watershed in the evolution of British trade unionism. Rather less attention has been paid by historians to the application of the Master and Servant Act of 1823. The law of master and servant derived, like so much else in the sphere of industrial relations in early nineteenth century England, from the Statute of Artificers; but unlike wage fixing by magistrates and the regulation of apprenticeship it was not something authority was minded to abolish, nor disinclined to enforce when asked by employers to do so. Thus in November 1818 fifteen striking linen weavers from Barnsley were committed to the Wakefield House of Correction 'on a charge of leaving their work in an *unfinished state*'.[30] The Tudor law had conceptualized the wage contract as centred on the performance of a discrete object and made it an offence for a worker to leave off labour without an employer's permission until the object they were employed to make (or help to make) was complete. Be it a piece of cloth or a ship, the law was the same: unless wages were overdue, to stop work before the item was complete was to risk criminal

---

28   W. H. Fraser, *Conflict and Class: Scottish Workers, 1700-1838* (1988), p. 95.
29   John Rule, *The Labouring Classes in Early Industrial England*, p. 285.
30   *The Gorgon*, 14 November 1818

prosecution and up to a month in gaol and a fine of £5. Eighteenth-century statutes introduced piecemeal modifications to this aspect of 5 Elizabeth. In particular, an act of 1766 imposed up to three months' hard labour on 'any artificer, callicoe printer, handicraftsman, miner, collier, keelman, pitman, glassman, potter, labourer, or other person' who 'shall absent himself from his service before the term of his contract shall be compleated'.[31] By then the concept of 'service' no longer related to the fulfilment of an obligation to complete a particular task but had embraced the whole contractual relationship between employer and employee. 'The combination Act is nothing: it is the law which regards the finishing of work, which masters employ to harass and keep down the wages of work people', wrote one critic (possibly Gravener Henson) in 1823. 'Very few prosecutions have been made to effect under the combinations Acts, but hundreds have been made under this law, and the labourer or workman can never be free, unless this law is modified.' In a revealing comment he added that 'by repealing the combination Acts, you leave the workman, in 99 cases out of 100, in the same state you found him, — at the mercy of his master.[32]

The 1823 Master and Servant Act upheld the potential sentence of three months' hard labour but it also provided the alternative for workers to be fined part of their wages or sacked. It made explicit that a contract between employer and employee need only be oral and controversially placed alleged offences within summary justice. Procedures under the Act against workers were a matter of criminal law, whereas masters were only liable in a civil action. Once a complaint against an employee was made on oath, a magistrate was obliged to issue an arrest warrant, not a summons, in contrast to the law of combination, both before and after repeal. The prospect of prosecution and imprisonment until brought to trial was often sufficient to discourage workers from leaving off work. More generally the 1823 Act hobbled trade unionism by making strike action a daunting prospect indeed for every participating individual.

Let us set aside the unfathomable question of what merely threatening action under the Master and Servant Act might have achieved. With prosecutions in Staffordshire alone averaging around three a week in the late 1850s and early 1860s[33] it is hardly exaggerating to say that this was the single most serious legal issue that confronted labour in the nineteenth century. Yet few historians notice it and systematic study of the law's application is conspicuously lacking, especially in the first decades of its history.[34] Meanwhile, as we have seen, Parliament lost some of its *laissez-faire* nerve in 1825 and significantly amended the terms of the 1824 repeal measure. To understand why authority continued to find workers' organizations so unsettling we have to explore further the breadth and increasing sophistication of trade unionism at this time. For it was this, as much as any lurid accounts of violence linked to trade unions, that explains the decision by Parliament to tighten up the law. It had, after all, been assured by Francis Place that repeal would *diminish* the number of trade combinations. Yet not only was an increase in the number of organizations readily apparent, so too

---

31 J. V. Orth, *Combination and Conspiracy*, (1991), pp. 108-9.

32 [George White and Gravener Henson] (1823), *A Few Remarks on the State of the Laws, at Present in Existence, for Regulating Masters and Work-People*, p. 51.

33 Daphne Simon, 'Master and servant', in J. Saville (ed.), *Democracy and the Labour Movement: Essays in Honour of Dona Toor* (1954), p. 195.

34 John Saville, *The Consolidation of the Capitalist State, 1800-1850* (1994), pp. 20-3, provides a short summary and assessment of the law. See also John Saville, 'The "crisis" in labour history: a further comment', *LHR*, 61/3, (1996), p. 326, who points out that Daphne Simon, 'Master and servant' remains the standard account in spite of her concentration on the later Victorian period. See though John Orth, *Combination and Conspiracy*, ch. 7, for the legal history and dimensions of the legislation, Trygve Tholfsen, *Working-class Radicalism*, pp. 180-6, D. C. Woods, 'The operation of the Master and Servants Act in the Black Country, 1858-75', *Midland History*, 7, (1982), Raymond Challinor and Brian Ripley, *The Miners' Association: a Trade Union in the Age of the Chartists* (1968, new edition (1990), and also the Conclusion below.

was an emerging sense of shared purpose and ideology that went beyond long established notions of artisan respectability and property in skill. This was abundantly evident in the material collected by the 1825 parliamentary Select Committee when it reviewed the 1824 repeal.

'Like a young and rising commonwealth': Trade Unionism in 1825

This material affords a unique insight into the ideology and character of early trade unionism. The original repeal of the Combination Act had coincided with a period of economic prosperity which was in itself propitious for the formation of trade societies. A rash of offensive strikes and a disturbing level of violence, apparently arising from the activities of unions, led to the formation of the 1825 Select Committee on Combination Laws.

In its report the Committee reprinted the rules and regulations of thirteen unions, mostly of those whose activities it had particularly investigated.[35] These documents show considerable consistency, yet with little repetition of stock formulae, suggesting an underpinning common culture that pre-dated the repeal of the Combination Acts, and they are both sophisticated and substantial: the preamble and fifty-five regulations of the Shipwrights' Provident Union of the River Thames, for example, comprise nearly 7,000 words.

Hardly surprisingly, these documents picture 1824 as an epochal moment, in the words of the Ayrshire Colliers' Association: 'the remains of Gothic barbarism and feudal tyranny, known by the name of the Combination Laws, have been swept from the statute book'. 'The iron grasp of the Combination Laws paralyzed every effort', recalled the General Association of Weavers in Scotland: 'these laws are now removed … Let us then gather ourselves together like a young and rising commonwealth, and form a strong compact establishment against every encroachment'.[36] 'Now', declared the committee of the Rochdale Association of Journeymen Woollen Weavers, Man Spinners and Others, 'you may become men and consider your own importance in the trade'.[37]

The response of the trades in 1824 was not just to form unions, or make public organizations that had previously existed covertly before, but to proclaim their right to do so, stressing the philosophical, legal and social justification for their actions:

> We, the Shipwrights resident in or near the town of South Shields, in the county of Durham, who by ourselves or our respective agents shall sign and execute these presents, taking it into our serious consideration that man is formed a social being, and that the Sovereign Ruler of the World has been pleased to place us in life dependent upon each other, and in continual need of mutual assistance and support, Do severally agree to form ourselves into a Friendly and Benevolent Association.[38]

These documents were clearly designed to invest unionisation with an air of solemnity. The north-east unions adapted the format of statute law to add weight to the legal status they held to have been conferred on them, for example the Seamen's Loyal Standard Association of North Shields:

> ARTICLES of agreement made this 5th day of October, in the year of our lord 1824, and in the 5th year of the reign of our Sovereign Lord George the Fourth, by the Grace of God of the

---

35 *PP*, 1825 (437) IV, The effect of the Act of 5 Geo. IV c. 95, Select Committee Report, appendix.
36 Ibid, p. 52.
37 Ibid, p. 37.
38 South Shields Shipwrights Union Society, p. 24

United Kingdom of Great Britain and Ireland, King, Defender of the Faith, and so forth; by and between several creditable seamen, resident in or near North Shields, in the county of Northumberland.[39]

A strongly religious tone was evident in other statements, for example the South Shields shipwrights' and the Stockport Cotton Jenny Spinners' Union Society. The Rochdale Association quoted from the Book of Jeremiah, 'woe unto him ... that useth his neighbours labour at reduced wages, and giveth him not for his work'.[40] Many preambles contained highly politicized statements, for example that to the articles of the Scottish weavers:

> It is with certain orders of civilized society, having no common centre to act upon, as it is with nations, in a state of nature, without landmark, and without law. They are equally the prey of every ambitious and avaricious adventurer. In such a state did the Europeans find the original inhabitants of North America, and drove them, piece by piece, into the very bosom of the wilderness. The fate of the cotton weavers in this country has been somewhat analogous.[41]

'That we are a suffering body is beyond all doubt', claimed the Rochdale union, 'and that there are men that would sink us still lower, if by that means they could augment their store, is equally true'. The Ayrshire Colliers Association gave the most forcible indication of its proposed course of action:

> Is it not evident that there are masters in the coal trade who are constantly running a race in the reduction of wages, and are never satisfied unless they are paying below their neighbours; and by forcing the measure far above the common standard, to find a sale, and outsell their neighbour colliers? This is a case that requires immediate attention, and it becomes the duty of this association to point out such masters; and after being duly warned, if they still continue in such a career, so hurtful to the trade in general, then it will be our duty to try every way that prudence may dictate to put them out of the trade.[42]

Much in these rules and regulations is resonant with the trade societies of the previous century or more. There is much talk of 'the trade' and even 'the profession' (Thames shipwrights and Ayrshire miners). Rules are emblazoned with coats of arms, emblems and mottoes: 'Union of sentiment is the strength of society', 'Hand-in-Hand', 'United to support but not combined to injure', 'Love as brethren'. All nine unions specifying a place of meeting used public houses. 'The Friends of Humanity' (a society of London coopers) rewarded its officers with 'one shilling each to be spent at the house of meeting', while Rochdale committeemen were allowed a pint from union funds whenever they met; at all general meetings a junior steward was appointed to administer a 'liquor account'.

The majority of the unions were pledged to uphold regular apprenticeship, generally of seven years but of unspecified length or three years in the case of the Scottish unions, in line with the national custom. In England, of course, no basis in law had existed for apprenticeship since 1814, but the Journeymen Paper Makers particularly revealed an understanding of legality that was rooted in custom rather than statute:

---

39 Select Committee Report, p. 31.
40 Ibid, p. 36.
41 Ibid, p. 52.
42 Ibid, p. 55.

No one shall be entitled to the business unless he has served a legal apprenticeship of seven years and can produce his lawful indenture, (except the eldest son of a paper-maker, who is deemed to be a worthy member at the age of twenty-one, provided that he is brought up to the trade), also a card of freedom.[43]

The most extensive regulation of entry to the trade was attempted by the Thames shipwrights (who spoke of 'regular bred shipwrights') and the Rochdale weavers and spinners. The latter stipulated that members working in shops 'where there is a hireling employed' were to leave and be relieved from the union's funds until they had secured another position. The same procedure was to apply 'at any shop where there is any woman, or woman weavers that has come or had come into the trade since the 12th of March 1824'.[44] 'We consider that setting women to weave has been injurious to the men,' explained a weaver interviewed by the committee, 'it has deprived them of an opportunity to work when they want it'.[45]

All but the papermakers and the Coal Miners' Union of Sheffield had extensive friendly society functions, though the latter provided for tramping. Stockport's jenny spinners spoke of 'the frequent instances that we have seen of distress, and the removal of many industrious families from the town and neighbourhood of Stockport, to their respective parishes', a reference to the right of settlement in a parish necessary to claim poor relief.[46] Most rules specified appropriately elaborate procedures for the security of the society's box, of three or four locks and with the landlord of the pub where meetings took place usually holding one key. Benefits ranged from unemployment, sick, widows' and funeral payments to the replacement of clothes or tools lost at sea or by fire. South Shields shipwrights undertook to auction a deceased member's tools on club night for the benefit of his widow. The West Riding Fancy Union operated as a 'house of call' placing unemployed members with new masters.

Committee membership was by rota and often office-holding too. Rules were punctilious about the timing and conduct of meetings. West Riding fancy weavers could be fined a shilling for 'quarrelling, swearing, or using abusive language' and a penny for not being silent when asked by the chairmen to be so. South Shields Shipwrights were enjoined not to 'curse, blaspheme, [or] take the Almighty's name in vain', on pain of a sixpenny fine. Sunderland seamen and London coopers were not to 'stir up strife and confusion' nor Rochdale textile workers to lay wagers in the club room. 'Should any member or members speak contemptuously of the present King and Constitution, in the club-room, he or they shall be fined 5s' (Sunderland and North Shields seamen); similar clauses, also prohibiting discussion of religion, were included in the Rochdale union's and Thames shipwrights' regulations. A more general concern with propriety is also much in evidence. The seamen's unions withdrew the benefits of membership from anyone sentenced to a term in prison while the Sheffield colliers applied the same sanction to any member 'who shall lose his employment in consequence of not executing his work in a proper manner'. Sound workmanship clearly meant much in mines where lives were at risk if standards were lax, but a concern with behaviour and workmanship is everywhere evident. Stockport spinners withheld benefits from any member who became unemployed through drunkenness, idleness 'or wilful neglect of his business'. The aim of the Thames shipwrights union

---

43 Ibid, p. 57.
44 Ibid, p. 39.
45 Ibid, p. 153.
46 Ibid, p. 33.

was 'a moral system, to support their respectability in society, and keep up the rights of their trade'.[47]

Six of the unions had clear federal structures with shops, yards or districts sending delegates to a central executive, though only the papermakers aspired to national (English and Welsh) coverage. The Thames shipwrights had resolved that 'a correspondence be opened with the several maritime ports of England'.[48] Correspondence, however, was one of the issues about which the evidence given to the Select Committee was most opaque. The two seamen's unions, for example, were linked with cognate societies the length of England's east coast in the Seamen's Loyal Standard Association but this is nowhere apparent in their rules.[49] Only the papermakers were so frank about the past as to refer in their published rules to activities prior to the repeal of the combination laws (freely admitting that until 1812 it had been accepting fees in lieu of 'servitude' from those whose apprenticeships had been interrupted by military service).

Though the Select Committee was particularly concerned with actions of the shipwrights and seamen, and with allegations of violence and intimidation more generally, its minutes of evidence add a further dimension to what can be gleaned from the rules and regulations. Several witnesses, both trade unionists and employers, thought that the 1824 repeal, by eliminating a tendency to secrecy, had made workplace organization less opaque. Old structures and attitudes, however, endured as the coopers exemplified. The rules of their largest society, the Friends of Humanity, embracing around 700 of London's estimated 1500 coopers, did not even specify a connection with the trade. Asked if his workers had formed a society, a master cooper admitted, 'We have no doubt they have, although we cannot trace it home'.[50] Questioned if there were 'any men in your yard not belonging to the union', one of his workers, Robert Raven, replied, 'I do not think there are'. At the same time he was at pains to emphasize that the Friends was a benefit society: a strike fund was maintained by separate subscriptions of 10d monthly. Decisions on industrial issues were taken by 'the men in employ', including any case of a newcomer to a shop who had not previously joined the society: 'We meet together and advise him to do it, and I have never seen a case of resistance for my own part made to it; they do it, and willingly'.[51] In questioning him, Committee members freely spoke of 'the union' but Raven scrupulously distinguished between shop meetings and the benefit society. He did though state that 'His Majesty's coopers in Portsmouth and at Deptford are in union with us';[52] and also that he had been a member of an untitled body (to which he referred elsewhere just once as 'the union') since its establishment in 1821.[53] Members of the Committee clearly had problems grasping that the Friends of Humanity was not a union, not least perhaps because it had been instituted in September 1799, one month after the Combination Act became law.

Similarly overlapping, almost synonymous associational cultures were also evident in the Ayrshire coalfield, in the Colliers' Association and colliery Brotherhoods. 'Brothering' was an initiation ceremony for young colliers on attaining the status of 'a full man' and it seems clear that the concept of Brotherhood embraced traditions of workplace solidarity and control of entry as effective as any formally constituted trade society. Outsiders, including the Duke of Portland's collieries manager whom the Committee interviewed, confused the union and Brotherhood; but another

---

47 Ibid, p. 44.
48 Ibid, p. 45.
49 D. J. Rowe, 'A trade union of north-east coast seamen in 1825', *Economic History Review*, 25, (1972).
50 Select Committee Report, p. 33.
51 Ibid, p. 45.
52 Ibid, p. 46.
53 Ibid, p. 52.

interviewee, a Kilmarnock collier, made a clear distinction:

> Are you sure whether there are any secret oaths taken by any person on joining the association? — I am sure there never was one taken or required ...
>
> Any secret signs by which you know one another? — Yes, but that does not belong to the association.
>
> What does it belong to? — That is the Brotherhood of the Colliery, that has nothing to do with the association.
>
> What is the nature of the Brotherhood of the Colliery? — It is the same as Free Masonry.
>
> How far does it extend? — It extends just among colliers themselves.
>
> What is the intention of it? — Just to make them friendly and true to each other.
>
> Has it anything to do with striking? — Nothing in the world ...
>
> Do you conceive it the same as Free Masonry? — It is the same.
>
> Are you a Free Mason? — Yes.[54]

Alan Campbell[55] has shown how quasi-masonic traditions of solidarity infused early Scottish mining unions and notes an Ayrshire delegates' meeting in 1817 taking place in a masonic lodge. Details of secret initiation rites, first obtained by Scottish authorities in 1818, were claimed to be still current by Portland's agent, but the collier denied recognizing them and declined to divulge other details to the Committee.

The Committee had similar problems distinguishing between various elements in the associational culture of the north-east seamen. Like the Friends of Humanity, the articles of the Seamen's Loyal Standard Association made great play of its being a benevolent society plus, as we have already seen, an effusive declaration of patriotism; but its role in serious stoppages in the Tyne and Wear collier fleet was widely known: 'In consequence of the union of the seamen', complained one North Shields shipowner, 'we are not the directors or owners of our property in any respect'.[56] It was precisely because the Loyal Standard was a well-resourced friendly society that it was able to lay a firm claim on members' support when it sanctioned industrial action, as they would not wish to jeopardize their investment in its funds. Moreover the seamen's unions enjoyed extensive support in the wider community: in Berwick, for example, a strike-breaker was covered in paint, his face blackened and paraded round the town, while 'a mob of women hooting and threatening' gathered on the quay to express displeasure at a ship whose crew included non-unionists.[57] Directives concerning industrial action from the Loyal Standard were communicated to members in the form of printed broadside dialogues, a familiar form of popular radical and loyalist propaganda. *A DIALOGUE between Tom and Harry; on the Duties of Seamen, and the just and equitable Rewards for their services, addressed to the Seamen of the Tyne and Wear*, which the Select Committee reprinted, contained a detailed discussion about what the minimum rates of pay for voyages of particular lengths should be.[58] 'Tom and Jerry' broadsides, commented a South Shields shipowner, were 'the real rules guiding them as a combination'.[59]

A similar degree of communal solidarity is also apparent in evidence relating to the West Riding

---

54 Ibid, p. 76.
55 Alan Campbell, *The Lanarkshire Miners: a Social History of their Trade Unions, 1775-1874* (1979), p. 60.
56 Select Committee Report, p. 87.
57 Ibid, p. 164.
58 Ibid, pp. 108-9.
59 Quoted in D. J. Rowe, 'A trade union of north-east coast seamen', p. 87.

Fancy Union. This was, explained one of its vice-presidents, a federation of 'boxes' each of fifty to a hundred members, all of whom worked in their own homes. The difficulties of communicating with this highly dispersed membership were overcome by posting handbills 'on every church door round the neighbourhood'. The union claimed to be able, via the same means, to call on non-members, 'workmen who wish well to the trade', to black masters who put out work at rates below its demands. The trade had benefited from the economic upturn that had coincided with the 1824 repeal: 'Have not the union taken advantage of that to raise the wages? — Undoubtedly', replied the vice-president.

The Emerging Sense of a Trade Union Movement

The trade unionists who gave evidence to the 1824 and 1825 parliamentary select committees acquitted themselves impressively. Some, notably the shipwright John Gast, were questioned at considerable length. Select committees were not courts of law but the context was hardly conducive to the quietly confident manner in which they testified, which comes through in the written minutes of the committee. Although critics of workers' freedom to combine referred to the provisions of the 1824 repeal as ushering in a 'period of Saturnalian liberty', there was a general sense that the previous status quo should not and could not be restored: 'all counter-revolutions are injurious when they attempt to restore things exactly to their former state. Allowance must be made for the feelings which have been generated, and the ideas which have grown up in the minds of the workmen during this period.[60]

Trade unions were scarcely a recent evolution. However, only in the 1820s does it become possible to conceptualize trade unionism as a 'movement'. That this is so was very largely due to the accumulated experiences of the post-war period. Britain had avoided revolution while it had seen a hardening of political attitudes along increasingly socially differentiated lines. The interest in general unionism that emerged in these years reflected this mood. When workers initially spoke of general union they were struggling to refine a vocabulary of *class* as much as they were anticipating any imminent formal organization. Consider this letter written during the Lancashire strike wave of 1818, sent 'for the Staley Bridge Spinners and by their Order' to all colliers in the vicinity of the town:

> The spinners of Manchester have authorized me to solicit you to join in their union of trade, as all trades in England are uniting in one body for Trade and Reform, and you are desired to send a delegate to all Meetings to consult matters over and to inform you that you will be supported in your Trade in turn; A letter was received from London this day from the Silk Weavers wishing to join them and offer their support, they have taken all the big piecers in pay lest they should do mischief and their numbers is 800, they have no less now on pay than 3000 in the whole, we must try our Friends in every corner of the Land wherever they can be found and which every exertion is now making to accomplish and hope it will contribute to carry them into ultimate success they seem quite determined not to return to their Egyptian Slavery and haughty language and cruel usage for the same terms they quitted for, and indeed nothing less than a serious determination will ever bring their employers to any reason for if Manchester is obliged to give way at last the Work People in this and every other Town may bid an everlasting farewell to having any comfort or above one half of the Wages that will supply the common necessaries of Life.[61]

---

60 *Monthly Review*, 3rd series, no. 1 (1826), quoted in J. V. Orth, *Combination and Conspiracy*, p. 85.
61 HO 42/179, 7 August 1818.

Trade unionist activity intersected with radical politics and the communication lines of radicals and revolutionaries were very often those of the organized trades. Furthermore, the explosion of popular political publishing in these years heightened awareness of common interests across regions and occupational categories. *The Gorgon, A Weekly Political Publication*, which appeared from May 1818 to April 1819, is a good example of this process of widening awareness at work and of the cultural environment in which significant support was forthcoming for trade unions from outside the movement. The paper was edited by John Wade, a former journeyman woolsorter, and initially published by Richard Carlile, formerly a tinsmith. Carlile was already well known as a London radical journalist: he was soon to become a prolific publisher of Paine's works and the self-appointed guardian of his memory. Carlile was succeeded as publisher by John Fairburn, whose previous publications included a biography of the popular millenarian prophetess Joanna Southcott; but his most notable contributions to the London book trade were to be polemics in support of Queen Caroline and anti-clerical pornographic literature. Wade's career followed a less disreputable trajectory (in old age he was granted a Civil List pension). Much of his reputation rested on his compilation of *The Black Book; or Corruption Unmasked!* (dedicated to 'the Working, the Agricultural, the Commercial, and Manufacturing Classes of the Community'), the first of many editions of which appeared in 1820, published by Fairburn.[62]

Wade aimed *The Gorgon* at a popular readership, but unlike its more celebrated contemporaries *Black Dwarf*, *Cobbett's Political Register* and the *Republican*, members of trades organizations were a key target group. Factual content and editorial 'line' were tailored to this readership:

> Labour is the superabundant produce of this country; and is the chief commodity we export ... Of the four staple manufactures, namely, cotton, linen, cloth, and iron, perhaps on an average, the raw material does not constitute one-tenth of their value, the remaining nine-tenths being created by the labours of the weaver, spinner, dyer, smith, cutler, and fifty others, employed in different departments. The labours of these men form the chief article of traffic in this country. It is by trading in the blood and bones of the journeymen and labourers of England, that our merchants have derived their riches, and the country its glory and importance.[63]

This was the Ricardian labour theory of value, writ very large indeed for a journeymen readership, accustomed to thinking in terms of property in their skill and who doubtless warmed to the idea that capital was stored up labour. Ricardo's apparent influence upon plebeian economic thinking is an issue to which we shall return.

The Gorgon was the only periodical publication to offer effective support to the cotton textile workers in 1818. It enjoyed a substantial Lancashire readership as a result. Though its circulation beyond the North-west and London was in all likelihood slender, it attempted to offer a national coverage. Besides covering the situation in Lancashire, it carried a major series of articles on the state of various trades, plus items about wages in Coventry and the Black Country, the prosecution of Birmingham workers under the Combination Act and Barnsley weavers for leaving work unfinished contrary to 5 Elizabeth, and the condition of West Country agricultural workers. *The Gorgon*

---

62 There is an extensive literature on Carlile: the entry in the *DLB*, vol. 6, pp. 46-53 is a good starting point. Wade is less well covered, apart from a *Dictionary of National Biography* entry, but on the *Black Book* particularly see notes in *LHR* vol. 59 (1994), no. 2, pp. 55-7 and no. 3, p. 10. Fairburn is much neglected, though see Iain McCalman, *Radical Underworld: Prophets, Revolutionaries and Pornographers in London, 1795-1840* (1998), *passim*. For *The Gorgon* see E. P. Thompson, *The Making of the English Working Class* (1968), pp. 845-51, but there's no substitute for reading the paper itself; quite widely accessible thanks to a Greenwood Press reprint (1969).

63 *The Gorgon*, 12 September 1818.

publicized the London defence fund for the Manchester spinners and through provincial correspondence, initiated with King's Lynn, Norfolk, it facilitated provincial subscriptions as well. Such fund-raising would soon be a valuable but unremarkable function of the radical press but, as with the circulation of national labour news, Wade was a pioneer of the practice.

The political affiliations of *The Gorgon* are also interesting. According to Place the paper was supported financially by the most prominent of the utilitarians, Jeremy Bentham. There is little doubt that Wade's politics were Benthamite but he was unusual at this time in aiming for a readership of working men and focusing so clearly on trade issues. He thus became an important ally for Francis Place and should share with him some of the credit for the ultimate success of the anti-combinations law agitation. Place used the paper extensively as a medium for his own thinking on the subject and circulated it widely among MPs: 'This paper induced Mr. Hume to come into my project much more than he had hitherto done ... *The Gorgon* was not altogether such a publication as I should have preferred, but it was the only one which could be used with any considerable effect'.[64] Place's reservations presumably stemmed first from Carlile and Fairburn's wider publishing interests and second from Wade's talent for political invective. However, the one would never have troubled a popular readership at this time, whilst the other enhanced the appeal of the paper: for example Wade described 'that detestable paper', *The Times*, as 'howling like a starved and blood-thirsty wolf at the Manchester Spinners' (10 October 1818). Place was also ambiguous about trade unionism, an ambiguity that found its way into the pages of *The Gorgon*: 'Both masters and journeymen, ought in all cases to act *individually*, not *collectively*. When either party has recourse to *unnatural* or *artificial* expedients they produce unnatural effects' (12 September 1818). If Wade subscribed to these sentiments, however, he shortly afterwards changed his mind. It appears that the outcome of the 1818 Lancashire strikes was instrumental in this:

> Perhaps of all the manufactures that have been carried on in this country, the cotton manufacture has been the most profitable for those who have embarked their capital therein; yet have the masters in that business violated their *solemn engagements*, and kept their workmen at wages which would not purchase the necessaries of life ... Now it remains to account for this paradoxical fact; for it is certainly contrary to theory, and the opinions we *once* entertained; for we had always thought that the prosperity of masters and workmen were simultaneous and inseperable. But the fact is not so; and we have no hesitation in saying, that the cause of the *deterioration* in the circumstances of workmen generally, and the different degrees of deterioration among different classes of journeymen, depends entirely upon the degrees of perfection, that prevails among them, which the law has pronounced a crime — namely, COMBINATION. The circumstances of workmen do not in the least depend on the prosperity or profits of the masters, but on the power of the workmen to *command* — nay to *extort* a high price for their labour; and this again depends on the degree they are combined together, so as to act in concert. The masters are united to a man to keep down wages; it is their interest; and if workmen are not united likewise to oppose them, there is no limit to their degradation.

The article goes on to praise the tailors for their 'most masterly Combination, which does the highest honour to the intelligence and harmony which prevail among them, and which all journeymen ought to cultivate' (21 November 1818). As E. P. Thompson[65] observed, 'This can scarcely be Place', who would tell the 1824 Parliamentary Select Committee on Artizans and Machinery that 'no principle of

---

64 BL Add. MSS 27,798, fol. 14
65 E. P. Thompson, *The Making of the English Working Class*, p. 850.

political economy [is] better established than this of wages: increase of wages must come from profits'. *The Gorgon* reflected the range of positions on trade unionism among reformers, but more than this it also revealed the working-out of trade unionist theory and inter-trade awareness during the Lancashire strikes. When the spinners' leaders were arrested for illegal combination, *The Gorgon* told its readers the dispute was 'Their Cause!!! and your Cause!!! the Cause of every Friend of Impartial Justice, and every Mechanic in England: on its issue will probably depend the fate of every Benefit Society in England; and the Right of every industrious and labouring man' (9 January 1819).

In combining well-researched articles on labour issues with focused political campaigning, the whole wrapped up with journalistic flair, *The Gorgon* set a standard for subsequent periodicals in the field. The early 1820s saw a flurry of papers aimed at an artisan readership: the *Artisan, or Mechanics Register*; the *Journeyman and Artizan's London and Provincial Chronicle*, the *Labourer's Friend and Handicraft Chronicle*, the *Mechanics' Chronicle, Mechanics' Magazine* and *Mechanics' Weekly Journal*. However, the most influential of these papers was the *Trades' Newspaper and Mechanics Weekly Journal* (subsequently retitled *Trades' Free Press*) which appeared from 1825 to 1828. Unlike *The Gorgon*, the *Trades' Newspaper* was owned and funded by trade unionists, through a consortium of London societies. However, the paper enjoyed a significant provincial circulation. Shares were brought by shipwrights' societies in Bristol, Cork, Dublin, Dundee, Leith, Liverpool, South Shields, Southampton, Sunderland and Yarmouth, by sawyers' societies in Oldham and Liverpool, and by unspecified workers in Carlisle, Cambridge and Manchester. The prevalence of shipwrights points to the key role played in the management of the paper by their London leader John Gast. To him especially should be credited much of the interest among the trades in federation and general union, not only in London but also beyond it.

The *Trades' Newspaper* emerged from the London trades' committee on the combination laws and was seen by them as potentially laying the foundation of a general union through its educational and information exchange functions:

> We have begun to call up the power of our *minds* to assist in the improvement of our humble lot But it is not enough that Mechanics have begun to exercise, like other men, the right of thinking, and acting for themselves; it is necessary, in order to the achievement of any general good, that they should *think and act together*, not, however, by any secret or mysterious confederation; not by delegating to the few the privilege of thinking for the many (a concession excusable only when it cannot be helped); but simply by availing themselves of the same public medium to which other classes of men have recourse to make their sentiments known to, and respected by, the public. What the British Mechanics still want is a Press — a Newspaper of their own — a common organ which may give better effect to their common appeal to the hearts and understandings of men, and which may, under all changes of circumstances, through good and through evil report, advocate and uphold the interests of the working classes, as before all others entitled to consideration and protection.[66]

As the concentration of provincial shareholding among the shipwrights suggests, the *Trades' Newspaper* never achieved its objective of an extensive general national readership to underpin its aims. It was also dogged by circulation problems, some of them doubtless proceeding from the

---

[66] *Laws and Regulations of the Trades' Newspaper Association* [1825], p. 3, quoted in Iorwerth J. Prothero, *Artisans and Politics*, p. 186. Prothero provides a detailed account of the paper to which this section is much indebted. See also Patricia Hollis, *The Pauper Press: A Study in Working Class Radicalism of the 1830s* (1970), pp. 100-1, David Stack, *Nature and Artifices the Life and Thought of Thomas Hodgskin, 1787-1869* (1998), *passim*, and Dorothy Thompson, *The Chartists: Popular Politics in the Industrial Revolution* (1984), pp. 124, 129.

inexperience of its owners in the production of newspapers, a business that was becoming increasingly capitalized and competitive. It was also experimental (in March 1826 the Trades' Newspaper Association set up its own printing works to produce the paper) and launched in an economy that was still highly regionalised and in which a national railway network was still some way off — hence perhaps the relative ease with which it attracted coastal as opposed to inland readers. On the other hand it sold around a thousand weekly copies at its peak, even though it eschewed the sensationalism that other publishers, political radicals among them, were discovering helped sustain large circulations. Nor was it afraid of confronting either political or intellectual controversy. One of the fascinating features in the *Trades' Newspaper* is a recurring counterpoint of arguments by and against Francis Place. He was initially hostile to the paper on account of an antipathy to its first editor (with whom he had clashed over the management of the London Mechanics' Institute), but from November 1825 became a regular contributor.

The *Trades' Newspaper* also introduced to a wider readership the ideas of the economist Thomas Hodgskin, whose book *Labour Defended against the Claims of Capital* (subtitled *The Unproductiveness of Capital proved with Reference to the Present Combinations amongst Journeymen*) appeared in 1825.[67] This was a critical moment in the evolution of economic thought for, as his biographer points out, 'Labour Defended was the first radical text both to recognise the centrality of the critique of capital, and make the conflict between labourers and capitalists more important than that between labourers and landlords'.[68] Purporting to be written by 'a Labourer' to one of his own kind, *Labour Defended* was trenchant and topical. The acceleration of industrial unrest that followed the repeal of the Combination Acts had increased hostility to trade unions. Hodgskin attempted to legitimize them by developing the case for the right of workers to the products of their labour. Economic activity, he argued, is essentially 'co-existing', synchronized labour, using fixed capital that is itself purely the product of past synchronized labour. Capital *per se* plays no part in the process of production. The illusion that it does depends upon what Marx would later describe as the fetishization of capital. 'One is almost tempted to believe', Hodgskin wrote, 'that capital is a sort of cabalistic word, like Church or State, or any other of those general terms which are invented by those who fleece the rest of mankind to conceal the hand that shears them. It is a sort of idol before which men are called upon to prostrate themselves.' The capitalist, in Hodgskin's view, violates the natural laws of distribution and exchange by the imposition of profit. Not only are workers cheated at the point of reward for their endeavours (since they do not receive the full value of their labour), they are also cheated as consumers, having 'to give over and above the quantity of labour nature demands ... a still larger quantity to the capitalist'.

It follows from this part of Hodgskin's argument that the interests of workers are integrally joined and integrally opposed to those of capitalists. Furthermore, capitalists,

> have long since reduced the ancient tyrant of the soil to comparative insignificance, whilst they have inherited his power over all the labouring classes. It is, therefore, now time that the reproach so long cast on the feudal aristocracy should be heaped on capital, and capitalists; or on that still more oppresive aristocracy, which is founded on wealth, and which is nourished by

---

67 For Hodgskin see David Stack, *Nature and Artifices*, Dorothy Thompson, *The Chartists*, also the entry on him in *DLB*, vol. 9 (1992), pp. 130-8. Some of the following argument first appeared in my entry on Hodgskin in G. Kelly and E. Applegate (eds), *Dictionary of Literary Biography*, vol. 158. *British Reform Writers* (1996), pp. 141-7.

68 David Stack, *Nature and Artifices*, p. 132.

profit.[69]

This was an attack on Ricardo's theory of rent, which saw landlords' ability to profit from the finite nature of land as a threat to national prosperity. It was also, though the author (a retired naval officer) was possibly unaware of its significance, a powerful critique of the agrarianism that was a central element of radical politics. *Labour Defended* also made a significant advance in the conceptualization of social relations and did much to sweep away the notion of social orders. Hodgskin's taut prose was readily intelligible to a readership unversed in political economy. He was to prove highly influential in the popular radical movement as its focus widened beyond parliamentary reform and 'old corruption', especially among those who thought most deeply about trade union issues.

It is important, though, to establish the limits of Hodgskin's vision. First, the notion that labour was the source of all value was scarcely a novelty, least of all to the skilled craftsmen who made up the overwhelming majority of trade union members. Place's assessment, that Hodgskin 'induced thousands to believe that every thing produced belonged to the individual producers each in his own right',[70] was wide of the mark in the sense that it ascribed to Hodgskin's agency alone a train of thought that he had simply strengthened. It had recently also been expressed by Cobbett (in his 1816 *Address to the Journeymen and Labourers*) and, as we have seen, by *The Gorgon*. Edward Thompson[71] pointed out that John Thelwall put the same argument in his *Rights of Nature* as early as 1796, though we might be cautious about Thelwall's influence in this particular respect. Secondly, Hodgskin was careful in his use of terminology: *capitalists* were criticized rather than *employers*. He believed that the latters' managerial functions were properly accommodated within the realm of labour; it was the capitalist system that drove a wedge between masters and men, between whom 'the contest now appears to be … but it will soon be displayed in its proper characters; and will stand confessed a war of honest industry against idle profligacy'. These sentiments were well-suited, perhaps, to artisan readers that might still nurse ambitions of becoming their own masters. Such aspirations had become progressively more remote for industrial workers, but as an idealized notion they still played a part in the psychology of craft trade unionism. Hodgskin's influence here reinforced existing assumptions, helping to soften the perceived line between employers and employees at the very point when in practice it was hardening, and strengthening the tendency for radicals to locate the fundamental conflict within society not between workers and employers, but between the economically productive and the idle. A third limitation to Hodgskin's vision that should be noted is that it was the exchange process and not capitalist production itself that was perceived to lie at the root of economic injustice. Rather than arguing for workers to control the means of production, he argued for market forces to be liberated as a means to render exchange relations equitable. It is hard, therefore, to discern any real grounds for the Webbs' claim about 'Hodgskin's illustrious disciple Karl Marx'.[72]

Yet it is readily apparent that Hodgskin's defence of workers' interests meshed well with ideas that were to prevail in the labour movement for some time to come. David Stack,[73] following

---

69 Thomas Hodgskin, *Labour Defended against the Claims of Capital or the Unproductiveness of Capital proved with Reference to the Present Combinations of Journeymen* (1825), p. 19.
70 Quoted in David Stack, *Nature and Artifices*, p. 141.
71 E. P. Thompson, *The Making of the English Working Class*, p. 175.
72 Sidney and Beatrice Webb, *The History of Trade Unionism*, revised edition (1920), p. 162.
73 David Stack, *Nature and Artifices*.

Saville,[74] rather laments that the anti-capitalist force of Hodgskin's ideas lost momentum in their adoption by other writers. But this should not be allowed to obscure how influential he was, on, for example Bronterre O'Brien, the *Poor Man's Guardian* and the National Union of the Working Classes, concerning the contribution of unjust legislation to workers' miseries and, particularly, capital's command over labour as being rooted in legal force; or Hodgskin's influence on the 'natural' versus 'artificial' conceptual framework deployed within Chartism (notably by Feargus O'Connor). Above all, by centralizing capital within radical economic analysis, Hodgskin provided intellectual reinforcement to the social and political processes that had brought trade unions and radicalism close together during the first quarter of the century. In doing so he also claimed for trade unions a natural place in industrial society:

> The most successful and widest-spread possible combination to obtain an augmentation of wages would have no other injurious effect than to reduce the incomes of those who live on profit and interest, and who have no just claim but custom to any share of the national produce.[75]

INDUSTRIAL DISPUTES IN THE WAKE OF REPEAL

Labour Defended, like the *Trades' Newspaper*, appeared in July 1825, shortly after the amended Combination Laws Repeal Act. Together they constitute strong evidence of a growing sophistication in trade unionist circles. Hodgskin himself was a retired naval officer and professional journalist, but the paper's six front page articles extracting and commenting upon his work, in addition to the substantial letters he wrote to it, ensured that his ideas quickly achieved wide familiarity. By itself, however, this would have mattered little had industrial disputes not increased and intensified in the wake of the 1824 repeal (which received royal assent on 21 June). Some 130 petitions for repeal had been received by Parliament. Many had been facilitated by Place, but from beyond London petitions had been received from the weavers of Norwich and nearby Wymondham, mechanics in Barnsley, Sheffield and Tewkesbury, Lancashire cotton spinners and shoemakers at various centres. In addition trades delegates attended the parliamentary committee of enquiry from Lancashire, Yorkshire, Glasgow, Hawick, Macclesfield and Dublin.[76] All this was indicative of Place's organizing ability (though these trades were far from unanimous in their support for him) and, of course, of the depth of feeling the laws concerned evoked among workers; but the extent of organized lobbying also indicates the relative health of trade organization at this time.

This became more apparent in the months that followed, a period of high employment and rising food prices that led inevitably to demands for wage increases and, in turn, strike action. In particular, there was a wave of industrial unrest among the Lancashire cotton spinners; but also, for example, 'in Hyde alone in January … successful strikes by weavers, colliers, dyers, farriers and shoemakers'.[77] Something of a moral panic engulfed sections of the establishment. The Dublin Police Office reported that 'not less than 60 or 70 cases have occurred of violence committed in the streets, — that 30 or 40 persons have had their skulls fractured, a great number have had been assaulted and beaten, and two persons have died of the wounds inflicted upon them', the connection between all this and

---

74 John Saville, *1848: the British State and the Chartist Movement* (1987) p. 216.
75 Thomas Hodgskin, *Labour Defended*, p. 28.
76 Iorwerth J. Prothero, *Artisans and Politics*, p. 176.
77 Ibid. pp. 177-8.

combinations 'appears ... hardly to admit of question'. Similar evidence was produced for Scotland.[78] The consequence of all this was, as we have seen, the establishment in March of a Parliamentary Select Committee to review the repeal of the combination laws. Although predictably emphatic use was made of the evidence of trade society violence, it was a strike by the Thames shipwrights that weighed heaviest on Westminster. A Thames Shipwrights' Provident Union had been formed from the societies at various yards in August 1824, with John Gast as its secretary, and had spread rapidly to include not only virtually all mercantile yards but even some of the naval builders. Iorwerth Prothero has skilfully delineated the history of this union and the ways and means by which it managed its members' interests through support of discrete disputes at individual yards, backed where necessary by financial support for any shipwright sacked for industrial action. The culmination was a lock-out by employers designed to break the power of the union, timed — almost certainly deliberately — to coincide with the first sittings of the Select Committee. Though the union was singled out for censure by the committee, the amended Repeal Act, as we have seen, refined rather than reversed the legislation of 1824. The Commons did agree, though, to waive for two years the requirement that British-registered vessels had to be repaired only in British yards, a move designed to strengthen the employers' hand. Subsequently the largest naval yards, including Devonport and Portsmouth, were authorized to undertake merchant shipping repairs, at which point 'the strike was doomed to fail. ... So ended what was long remembered on the Thames as "the great strike", which "lasted so long, that the grass is said to have grown up in the building slips"'.[79]

The other major industrial dispute in the wake of 1824 occurred in Bradford among the combers and weavers of the woollen and worsted industry. We have seen, apropos of the combers particularly, that there was a long history of efficient organization in the woollen trade. Although the Brief Institution, the remarkable pan-regional union of combers' societies in Yorkshire and the West Country, had ceased to operate at the beginning of the century, the collapse of federalization did not take with it the constituent societies. A national congress of 'the United Societies of Woolcombers' was held in Coventry in 1812. It resolved to regulate tramping more closely, and to enforce apprenticeship even to the exclusion of second and subsequent sons of combers unless their father was himself a master owning his own stock of wool.[80] The constraints upon entry and the intricacy of its precautions against the abuse of tramping, coupled with a resolution to exclude Irish entrants under all circumstances, indicate that all was not well with the combers. The erosion of craft prerogative had been masked by relatively good remuneration due to an overall increase in activity in the trade.[81] This had seen a population explosion of some 150 per cent in Bradford between 1811 and 1831, accompanied by the tentative introduction of some machinery into the weaving and combing sectors during the early 1820s. The immediate consequence of the 1824 repeal was an amalgamation of weavers' and combers' societies into one union. It was this body that, at the peak of a cycle in the worsted trade, called for a stand out against three firms paying low wages in June 1825. By August the dispute had engulfed the region as manufacturers resolved 'to counteract a combination which, if not repressed, would strike at the root of the prosperity of the town and neighbourhood'.[82] Threats of mechanization and refusal to employ union members were used by the employers. The strikers

---

78 *PP*, 1825 (437) IV, The effect of the Act of 5 Geo. IV c. 95, Select Committee Report, minutes of evidence, p. 8.
79 Iorwerth J. Prothero, *Artisans and Politics*, pp. 170-1.
80 Arthur Aspinall, *The Early English Trade Unions*, pp. 127-37.
81 J. A. Jowitt, *Mechanization and Misery: the Bradford Woolcombers' Report of 1845* (1991), p. 9.
82 Quoted in Jonathan Smith, 'The strike of 1825', in D. G. Wright and J. A. Jowitt (eds.), *Victorian Bradford. Essays in Honour of Jack Reynolds* (1981), p. 70.

launched an abortive attempt to establish a combers' co-operative and 'developed an intellectual critique of the political economy of *laissez-faire*' in a series of addresses that received widespread attention both within and beyond the West Riding.[83] As the strike evolved into essentially a dispute about union recognition, it assumed a totemic status for other workers. Prothero has pointed out how even striking London shoemakers and the extremely depressed Spitalfields weavers and dyers managed to raise subscriptions when the *Trades' Newspaper* appealed: 'It is all the workers of England against a few masters at Bradford'.[84]

The dispute ended in November when, having failed to secure wage increases, the strikers settled for an offer by the Bradford manufacturers to recognize the union. This suggests that issues of entry to, and control of, the trade may have weighed more heavily than the maximization of income in the minds of workers, though the onset of winter was also doubtless a keen factor. It saw a further deterioration in the trade and widespread unemployment, though the union endured until 1827, when it was defeated in a further strike.[85] This marked the end of more than a century of trade organization among the combers. Thereafter they and the Bradford weavers devoted their energies in turn to general unionism, the anti-poor law agitation and Chartism. Strategies based on trade organization had ceased to be feasible for these occupations, for whom regulation of entry to their trade and control of production were an increasingly distant memory.

There were further industrial disputes during the economic downturn that coincided with the winter of 1825-6. Those in London tended to be 'largely defensive actions against wage cutting' rather than aggressive in character,[86] and doubtless this was true outside the capital also. Machine-breaking by Lancashire handloom weavers the following spring was sufficiently serious to have been termed a 'rising'.[87] Though these disturbances were impressive for their degree of organization, it seems fairly clear that they were rooted in community solidarity rather than in a union organization. The idea of a Lancashire textiles general union had apparently been discussed when the Combination Acts were repealed, but abandoned because, in the words of one Rochdale worker, 'they could not agree about the necessary arrangements'.[88] The relevance of the 'rising' to the history of trade unionism lies chiefly in its demonstrating how the desperate plight of the weavers was making trade organization increasingly irrelevant. This was demonstrated less dramatically, but no less remorselessly, to the Yorkshire weavers and combers in the wake of their strike in 1825. Nonetheless, as in Luddism (to which the events of 1826 bore more than a superficial resemblance) elements of the unionist mind-set can be discerned. For example, a committee of Bolton weavers agreed a price-list with local masters before going on to campaign for wage-fixing by a joint-committee of employers and employed, to be backed by statutory enforcement.

The most eloquent exponent of this potential solution to industrial unrest was William Longson, a Manchester weaver who earlier had co-ordinated support for Moore and Henson's alternative Combination Act repeal measure. Longson's campaign for legally binding arbitration and conciliation received the backing both of the *Trades' Newspaper* and of Francis Place. It narrowly missed

---

83 Ibid, pp. 74-6.
84 Iorwerth J. Prothero, *Artisans and Politics*, p. 160.
85 Jonathan Smith, 'The strike of 1825', p. 76.
86 David R. Green, 'Distance to work in Victorian London: a case study of Henry Poole, bespoke tailors', *Business History*, 30, (1988), p. 213.
87 Andrew Charlesworth *et al.*, *An Atlas of Industrial Protest in Britain, 1750-1990* (1996), p. 48.
88 R. G. Kirby and A. E. Musson, *The Voice of the People: John Doherty 1798-1854: Trade Unionist, Radical and Factory Reformer* (1975), p. 41.

becoming the subject of a parliamentary select committee in April 1827.[89] This interesting amalgam, of the once-prevalent philosophy of state regulation with a rapidly emerging culture of trade society federation and collective bargaining, was part of the much wider debate about wages and political economy at this time. Some, including the Spencean Shoemaker Allen Davenport, proposed that the price of the workers' dietary staple, bread, should be used to determine the level of wages. 'No Union, however organised,' believed Davenport, 'can prevent the poor half-starved man, with his children's cry for bread ringing in his ears, from working for whatever wages he can obtain, be they high or low'.[90] Others campaigned for the repeal of the Corn Laws, believing that any significant decrease in bread prices would augment real wages. Without some sort of minimum wage, however, it seemed apparent to many workers that a reduction of wages would follow. Higher wages, on the other hand, would increase demand for British products, thereby diminishing industry's dependency upon the export trade that benefited capitalists and not labour. By a similar argument, the introduction of machinery, in leading to unemployment, also led to a contraction in the market and a dependency on exports which was potentially ephemeral and the benefits of which would be unevenly distributed. Such issues were a central preoccupation for the *Trades' Newspaper* as they were for the 'General Association', a regular meeting of London trades delegates in 1827-8.[91]

The General Association is further evidence of how interest in effecting the 'widest spread possible combination' was growing in the late 1820s. John Gast was a pivotal figure in this development. He led the Association and was also supportive of a 'Union of Unions' proposed during a five-month strike in the Kidderminster carpet-weaving industry in 1828.[92] In addition, Gast was probably in touch with the 'Associated Trades' of Sunderland who in 1825, significantly took as their name 'The Philanthropic Hercules'.[93] Yet the Sunderland and Kidderminster projects were only two of several provincial general unions that emerged in the wake of the repeal of the combination laws. An Artisans' General Committee, described by the cotton spinners' leader John Doherty as an attempted general union, was established in Manchester. The Birmingham, Nottingham and Sheffield trades formed similar associations. A 'Grand Union of England', comprising these four provincial associations plus the Staffordshire potters was also mooted in 1825. This was not a formal federation: rather, they were 'in union' with one another in much the same way that many societies within a single trade were beginning to recognize each other. In 1827 woollen weavers in the Rochdale area, confronted by the threat of a lock-out, drew up plans for 'a general union of the whole trades'.[94] It is also worth noting that general committees of delegates were formed in industrial centres across England in 1828, in response to parliamentary proposals for the closer regulation of friendly societies.[95]

In the mid-1820s, as in 1818, the nervous anticipation of those who had most to lose from concerted industrial action outstripped the organizational reality that confronted them.

> The manufacturing interests of the country are in fact, at this moment, under the immediate

---

[89] For Longson see his book *An Appeal to Master, Workmen and the Public, shewing the Cause of the Distress of the Labouring Classes* (1827), also R. G. Kirby and A. E. Musson, *The Voice of the People*, and Iorwerth J. Prothero, *Artisans and Politics*.
[90] *Trades' Newspaper*; 12 March 1826.
[91] Iorwerth J. Prothero, *Artisans and Politics*, pp. 218-25.
[92] L. D. Smith, *Carpet Weavers and Carpet Masters: The Handloom Carpet Weavers of Kidderminster 1780-1850* (1986), p. 109.
[93] Iorwerth J. Prothero, *Artisans and Politics*, p. 182.
[94] R. G. Kirby and A. E. Musson, *The Voice of the People*, p. 154.
[95] Iorwerth J. Prothero, *Artisans and Politics*, pp. 232-8.

> control of the grand union of Trades, formed by a committee of delegates from each trade, and it is in their power to destroy, whenever they are pleased to do so, any branch of manufactures; and there is no power to restrain them.

Whilst this 1825 *Stockport Advertiser* editorial[96] gave exaggerated credence to the potency of general unionism, it does convey something of the alarm of many contemporary observers. In Lancashire this was strengthened by contemporaneous moves to establish a federal union of cotton spinners. As early as 1810, delegates from each Manchester spinning shop and districts beyond had attended 'a General Congress'. The latter co-ordinated the Lancashire spinners' strike and lock-out that same year. Defeat on this occasion presumably inclined cotton spinners to seek wider support as the industry approached its next crisis in 1818, hence the formation of the Philanthropic Society; but the spinners did not abandon their interest in federation: there were further moves in this direction in 1825-6, 1829-30 (the Grand General Union of Cotton Spinners), 1836 and more effectively in the 1840s. Partly because of their position at the 'leading edge' of industrialization, and partly because of their almost routine linkages to wider political developments, federal associations of the cotton spinners have attracted most attention on the part of historians. Along with London, the Lancashire region preoccupied those responsible for domestic security and is therefore the most extensively documented.[97]

National or regional affiliation of societies from within a single trade was one of the distinguishing features of these years and the phenomenal general unionist movement considered in the next chapter is only fully intelligible when viewed alongside this development. 'Trades-Unions advance a step further, and invite those in similar trades in all the great marts ... to join in a more extended union', wrote the Irish-born economist and socialist William Thompson in his influential book *Labor Rewarded*.[98] The journeymen papermakers' national structure was long-established by the time it was scrutinized by parliamentary select committee in 1825. The General Union of Carpenters and Joiners (which disappeared only through amalgamation in 1921) was formed in 1827.[99] The Steam Engine Makers' Society spread steadily from Liverpool, where it was founded in 1826, to embrace both London and the North-east by the early 1830s. By 1826, despite its name, the Newcastle and County Tanners, had branches the length of eastern Britain from Aberdeen to Sussex.[100] The Society of Journeymen Brushmakers, founded in London in 1806, had spread across England as far north as Lancashire and York by 1829 through the accretion of local societies on an established tramping route. The Friendly Society of Ironfounders provides another example. By 1824 it covered all England north of a line from the Severn to the Wash, and also had branches in London, Glasgow, Belfast and Dublin.[101] As a result of the process evident in each of these trade bodies, the term 'union' became an established part of the vocabulary of labour as, for example, in this

---

96 Quoted in R. G. Kirby and A. E. Musson, *The Voice of the People*.
97 R. G. Kirby and A. E. Musson, *The Voice of the People*, pp. 18-152; 'Mule spinner societies and the early federations', in Alan Fowler and Terry Wyke, *The Barefoot Aristocrats: a History of the Amalgamated Association of Operative Cotton Spinners* (1987); H. A. Turner, *Trade Union Growth, Structure and Policy: A Comparative Study of the Cotton Unions* (1962), pp. 44-107.
98 William Thompson, *Labor Rewarded*, p. 79.
99 Properly titled the Friendly Society of Operative House Carpenters and Joiners. See S. Higenbottam, *Our Society's History* (1939), pp. 25-44, and R. W. Postgate, *The Builders' History* (1923), pp. 53-4, 58 and 67.
100 There are no histories of either the Steam Engine Makers or the Tanners, but see Humphrey Southall,'Towards a geography of unionization: the spatial organization and distribution of early British trade unions', *Transactions of the Institute of British Geographers*, new series vol. 13, (1988), *passim*.
101 H. J. Fyrth and Henry Collins, *The Foundry Workers: a Trade Union History* (1959).

declaration by Bath ironfounders:

> This society is desirous of opening a correspondence with any Society who may feel disposed to form a Friendly Union with them on the following terms:
> That if any free member of a society in union with us should travel to Bath for work, he shall be entitled to supper, lodging and breakfast the next morning. The same rules to be observed towards members of our society, by societies in union with us.[102]

Federation of societies, both within an individual trade but more particularly between different trades, worried the authorities. It was hard to monitor, being largely effected through tramping with its natural emphases on secrecy and solidarity. It was also a highly political development. Loans between societies would in all likelihood be invisible to authority. However, the public declaration of affinity and shared purpose that general unionism entailed was in itself a profoundly political statement, emphasizing as it did the commonality of *labour* above the particularism of individual trades. In the words of William Thompson, a 'Central Union of All Trades' would 'extend its operations, and enlarge its sympathies' to 'comprehend All the Industrious, agricultural and day-laborers, in the sphere of its operations'.[103]

---

[102] Loyal Vulcan Society, *Rules* (1823), cited in Humphrey Southall, 'Towards a geography of unionization', p. 472.
[103] William Thompson, *Labor Rewarded: The Claims of Labor and Capital Conciliated or How to Secure to Labor the Whole Products of its Exertions* (1827), p. 82.

5

Across the Frontier of Skill: General Unionism

The Economic and Political Context, 1829-34

From the mid 1820s it is possible to be cautiously optimistic about the impact of industrialization on workers' standards of living, though there were considerable variations according to locality and trade (and for almost everyone a marked deterioration in old age). Economic historians' 'downsizing' of Britain's experience of industrialization in recent years looks rather contrived when read against the 1820s and 1830s. Urbanization, the feature of British society that had for some time distinguished it from its continental neighbours, seemed almost rampant. It has been estimated that, as a proportion of Britain's gross domestic product, expenditure on housing in the 1820s reached an all-time peak.[1] Rates of population growth in many industrial centres almost defy the modern imagination, touching as they did 25 per cent in Nottingham, 42 per cent in Birmingham, 45 per cent in Manchester and 63 per cent in Bradford in this decade. 'They make machines in this country as we plant cabbages in ours', wrote a French visitor, Gustave d'Eichthal, in a letter home in 1828. 'They are afraid of nothing, so plentiful are funds; they raze hills, fill in valleys, to open up communications they dig tunnels under towns and they don't consider such things worthy of mention.' He immediately added, however: 'The physical condition of the working class is very uneven'.[2]

Having spent time in Lancashire and Clydeside, d'Eichthal, a sociologist, concluded that the repeal of the Combination Act had enabled spinners to resist increases in the hours of their labour, and helped workers generally to resist the erosion of wages and leisure time. He did not, though, underestimate the extent to which even spinners remained poverty-stricken, despite earning more than double the ten shillings per week a female power-loom weaver might receive (handloom weavers of either sex rarely earned more than six to eight shillings). Moreover the working day was still long: Robert Owen's mills at New Lanark were accounted unusual in requiring only eleven hours' labour. In a situation such as this, though workers' association in the broadest sense might help secure their position, formal organization through trade unionism was still largely the preserve of those workers able to exploit a relative scarcity of their labour; and thus trade unionism tended to fluctuate with the trade cycle. An upturn in trade in 1833 was a significant factor behind the increased interest in trade unionism which is the focal point of the second part of this chapter.

In economic terms the years 1829-34 were relatively unremarkable compared with what had gone

---

1 Richard Rodger, *Housing in Urban Britain, 1780-1914* (1995), p. 19.
2 Gustave d'Eichthal, 'British society in 1828', reprinted in B. M. Ratcliffe and W. H. Chaloner (eds.), *A French Sociologist Looks at Britain* (1977), p. 7.

before or indeed would come after. Politically, however, the years 1829-34 constitute one of the most eventful episodes in modern British history, perhaps the only one about which it can legitimately be asked how close the country came to revolution. Certainly, the reform legislation of these years was nothing short of a constitutional revolution. The process began in 1828 with the comparatively uncontroversial (but hugely symbolic) restitution of full civil rights to those Protestants who were not members of the state Church of England and then proceeded — through somewhat choppier political waters — to a similar measure for Roman Catholics in 1829. The controversy surrounding Catholic emancipation, however, was but nothing compared to that engendered by the movement for parliamentary reform.

The pulse of British political radicalism was quickened by the French Revolution of 1830. Even more disturbing, however, were the riots, arson attacks and machine-breaking that spread through rural England during the same year. The Swing revolt (after 'Captain Swing', the pseudonymous author of many threatening letters connected to the outbreak) was concentrated upon the corn belt of southern and eastern England. Yet it is difficult to underestimate its importance for government policy as a whole in these years. Swing lent dramatic impetus to the contemporary debate over the Poor Laws, whilst it instilled in the recently formed Whig government a suspicion of popular agitation as deep-seated as that of its Tory predecessor. Swing was no random or unfocused outburst of violence but an organized movement for improved wages and conditions. Its suppression, spearheaded by military force, and the subsequent execution of nineteen rioters, transportation of nearly 500 others and gaoling of 640 more, had a deep psychological impact that extended far beyond rural southern England. 'Whig', hitherto a political term, became part of the popular vocabulary of abuse.[3]

In South Wales memories of the Merthyr Rising in June 1831 held a similar potency. The repression of a miners' and ironworkers' riot, in which upwards of twenty were killed and 70 wounded and which provoked a four-day rebellion, proved a seminal step in the emergence of Welsh trade unionism.[4] A similar chain of causation linked Swing and the agricultural trade unionists of Tolpuddle; but whereas Welsh trade unionism was only stilled by an employers' lock-out, in rural England it was to be all but extinguished for three decades.

Awareness of political division and social dislocation intensified as a result of the events of 1830-31. The Manchester free-trader Archibald Prentice wrote that 1829, having commenced 'disastrously for both masters and men, ended, without an interval of relaxation from distress, scarcely with an interval of hope, in a depression of trade almost unexampled ... the two classes were arrayed against each other in a hostility which daily became more bitter'.[5] In the minds of Prentice and other middle-class radicals, the two classes should have been united to oppose trade protection and high taxation. Indeed the appearance of Parliament as dominated by the landed interest and deaf to the interests of provincial manufacturing was a powerful constituent of the reform agitation of these years and it did much to secure middle-class opinion in favour of parliamentary reform. Against a background of economic dislocation and intensifying demand for parliamentary reform, the government introduced

---

3   Eric J. Hobsbawm and George Rudé, *Captain Swing* (paperback edition, 1973), remains the standard work on Captain Swing but it exaggerates the extent to which Swing riots were essentially local phenomena. Subsequent research has both located Swing in a broader chronological focus and revealed its wider contemporary context. See for example John E. Archer, *'By a Flash and a Scare', Arson, Animal Maiming and Poaching in East Anglia, 1815-70*, (2010); Andrew Charlesworth, *Social Protest in a Rural Society*, Historical Geography Research Series, 1 (October, 1979); and Mick Reed and Roger A. E. Wells (eds.), *Class, Conflict and Protest in the English Countryside, 1700-1880* (1990).

4   Gwyn A. Williams, 'Merthyr 1831: Lord Melbourne and the trade unions', *Llafur*, vol. 1, no. 1, (1972), and *The Merthyr Rising* (1978).

5   Archibald Prentice, *Historical Recollections and Personal Recollections of Manchester*, (1851), pp. 344-5.

a reform bill. It was defeated in the House of Lords in October 1831. Large-scale rioting followed in which parts of Derby and Nottingham were burnt down and control of Bristol lost by the authorities. A second bill was similarly defeated the following spring and, King William IV having declined to create sufficient peers to reverse the situation, the government resigned. By this time much of Britain was also afflicted by epidemic cholera.

The Reform Act was finally passed under a reinstated Whig government in June 1832. The extent to which its safe passage was secured by the apparent threat of revolution, and the likely consequences had it been defeated, have intrigued historians ever since. Limited though the Act might appear with hindsight, it seemed to signal a sudden and massive potential for further political change. Not all reformers, particularly working-class ones, believed with Prentice and those of similar outlook that the defeat of the landed interest in 1832 had essentially completed the process of reform. Even before the Act reached the statute book, an important minority of radicals rejected it as a cynical and highly partial palliative; they were also increasingly inclining towards a socio-political analysis that emphasized the iniquity of concentrations of property, not just in land, but in the means of industrial production too. Few politically aware workers heeded talk of the Act being a final settlement of the reform issue. Pressure from without Parliament had at last secured significant political change: the political landscape appeared to have shifted as a consequence. A dawning realization that finality was indeed what the government had intended was a powerful factor in shaping popular agitation over the next decade. Furthermore, by effectively detaching commercial and manufacturing interests from the popular reform movement in the *political* sphere, the Reform Act also sharpened the perception among workers that the *economic* interests of those who now enjoyed the vote were opposed to their own.

Attempts at general unionism in these years have to be read against this background, as does Chartism (a movement which must have included virtually all those who, a few years before, had lent their support to the idea of general trade unions). Moreover, much of the legislation enacted by the reformed Parliament reinforced working people's sense of a need to construct their own institutions, thus carving out a separate space within which to defend their independence. Parliament's patent antipathy to the interests of ordinary working people (evident in 1833 in the Irish Coercion Act, a massive curtailment of civil liberties, and the rejection of the Ten Hour Bill to limit the working day for children), culminated in the New Poor Law of 1834. This much-despised measure cut deeply into popular notions of the rights and status of working people. It replaced the haphazard but essentially undemeaning system of parish poor relief with the workhouse system. The agitation against the New Poor Law is conventionally cited as one of the constituents of Chartism. But the debate that preceded its introduction also shaped the outlook of those who, in 1834, supported the Grand National Consolidated Trades' Union (GNCTU), perhaps the best known of all early labour organizations.

The GNCTU, however, was very far from being an isolated phenomenon. This has long been recognized by specialist historians, but hardly at all in school textbooks and general literature on the nineteenth century. Furthermore, it owed a great deal less to Robert Owen and Owenism than is often supposed. Enduring interest in the 'Tolpuddle Martyrs', combined with long-debated questions about the influence of Robert Owen on this particular phase of trade union history, have arguably been allowed to obscure the fuller picture. John Harrison's verdict[6] still stands: 'The complex story of the development of British trade unionism in the years 1831-34 has never been satisfactorily unravelled.'[7]

---

6   J. F. C. Harrison, *Robert Owen and the Owenites in Britain and America* (1969), p. 208.
7   W. H. Oliver, 'The Consolidated Trades' Union of 1834', *Economic History Review*, 17, (1964), remains the standard study, but should be

Although Harrison also observes that in this brief period 'the British working-class movement was saturated with Owenism', the roots of what was happening in the early months of 1834 went much deeper than the response to Owen's involvement in it. Indeed, as we shall see, his interest was so short-lived as to be almost ephemeral. Whilst it is the case that workers' interest in Owenite thinking had been gathering pace since the end of the previous decade (London followers of Owen, most of them printers, established a community as early as 1821), the idea of general unionism itself had a different and longer pedigree. As we saw in the previous chapter, it emerged in the fevered but fertile post-Waterloo years.

Nor was general trades' unionism, as Musson claims, 'a mainly endogenous trade-union movement'.[8] It certainly drew on the same network through which the apprenticeship campaign of 1814 had been organized nationally; and it further consolidated the established practice whereby a financially secure society might make a loan to a society in another trade. However, it is difficult to draw sharp or meaningful distinction between general trades' unionism and the more ambitious political organizations of these years. All might deploy the term 'union' to summarize and convey the spirit of their activities. Thus the Metropolitan Trades' Union of 1831, formed initially as a general union of trades for collective assistance mutated into the National Union of the Working Classes, the foremost ultra-radical association of its day in the capital. The idea of general unionism was intensely political: John Gast admitted as much when, two decades later, he looked back to the general union movement of 1818:

> He wanted to see, not merely isolated unions in the several trades, but a general union made up out of the whole. In 1818, he proposed a society which he had called the Philanthropic Hercules; it being, in fact, a Parliament of working men. He proposed that each trade should elect delegates, in proportion to its extent; and that the delegates thus elected should constitute a working man's Parliament. He would never be satisfied until he had seen that project realized; for then, and then only, should he feel assured of the complete emancipation of the working classes.[9]

How the term 'union' was used in these years is itself highly informative. More than anything, its usage conjured a spirit of unanimity of purpose, as for example when William Benbow (influenced, like Gast, by revolutionary ideas associated with Thomas Spence) wrote, 'The spirit of union possessed our ancestors, they resolved to be free, and their liberties were confirmed'.[10] Besides the National Union of the Working Classes and the Grand Union of England, there was the Union Exchange Society (an early London co-operative store) and upwards of 130 Political Unions formed within the reform movement in the late 1820s and early 1830s.[11] The Glasgow Trades' Committee's *Herald to the Trades Advocate* (1830-1) suggested that independent newspapers were themselves a

---

supplemented by Iorwerth J. Prothero, *Artisans and Politics in Early Nineteenth-Century London: John Gast and His Times* (1979), pp. 300-9, John Rule, *The Labouring Classes in Early Industrial England 1750-1850* (1986), pp. 301-7, and Gregory Claeys, *Citizens and Saints: Politics and Anti-Politics in Early British Socialism* (1989), pp. 194-207. Though dated, G. D. H. Cole, *Attempts at General Union: A Study in British Trade Union History, 1818-1834* (1953), is still useful for its longitudinal study of the theme of general unionism and also contains helpful appendices.

8   A. E. Musson, *British Trade Unions, 1800-1875* (1972), p. 70.
9   *Constitutional*, 25 November 1836, cited in Iorwerth J. Prothero, *Artisans and Politics*, p. 102.
10 William Benbow, *Censorship Exposed* [1818], p. 5.
11 Nancy LoPatin, *Political Unions, Popular Politics and the Great Reform Act of 1832* (1999).

form of 'working-class union'.[12] The word retained a broad sense of moral and political momentum for many years. This can be seen in the titles of periodicals which were far from being specialist trades' papers: for example, *Union* (1831-2), advocating class co-operation and published by Carlile; or the *Political Unionist* founded (30 June 1832) 'to create a medium of communication between the various Unions of the kingdom'; and finally, a decade later, *The Union: A Monthly Record of Moral, Social and Educational Progress* (1842-3). That sense of crabbed particularism, associated with the term 'trade union' in the mid-Victorian period as organized workers strove to defend or extend their sectional interests, was unknown in the early 1830s. Instead 'union', like Chartism after it, came close to being the idea of its age. 'Going into union started off as being an ambitious, even a total enterprize'.[13] 'Senex' (the collaboration of J.E. Smith and James Morrison) told readers of the *Pioneer*,

> To us, brethren, it matters little who or what may be the men that direct the crazy machine called *the state*. We have little to do with them ... While we adhere to *our union*, we have nothing to apprehend either from them or their precious legislature ... You have worked in pain and want, for society; you have resolved to constitute the society for whom you work.[14]

In the Grand National Consolidated Trades' Union, the chosen terminology indicated that inter-trades activity was firmly located within this broader and highly politicized spectrum.

The notion of general union between different trades presaged a new kind of way of seeing work itself, the solidarities and commonality of a single craft being extended beyond the frontier of the skill concerned. For this reason, the general unionism of 1829-34 has always attracted the attention of historians. For the Webbs, the events of these years were the substantial initiation of 'the revolutionary period'. For E. P. Thompson the 'consciousness of the identity of interests between working men of the most diverse occupations and levels of attainment ... was expressed on an unprecedented scale in the general unionism of 1830-34'.[15] The Oldham general strike of 1834, in Foster's interpretation[16] a carefully premeditated consequence of general unionism, was a watershed in the history of the town. Enthusiasm for general unionism indicated a critical shift in perceptions of the way society was ordered. This is one reason why the government, more or less reconciled to the existence of trade unionism since the Combination Acts repeal in 1824, devoted considerable energy to monitoring the development of general unionism. Trade unionism suddenly became a subject of general political discourse:

> There is an important distinction now made by the Working classes themselves, between the classes that live by the wages of labour, and those who live by the return to capital ... The labouring, or Working Classes, believe that they have interests which are common to themselves as labourers, which interests are opposed to interests of the other classes of society.[17]

Such perceptions are integral to the notion of *class consciousness*, a term so far not used in this study. The concept of class has sometimes proved a blunt instrument for the analysis of nineteenth-century

---

12 Patricia Hollis, *The Pauper Press: A Study in Working Class Radicalism of the 1830s* (1970), p. 272.
13 Stephen Yeo, 'Organisation and creativity: mere administration and mere theology', *Journal of Historical Sociology*, 9/2 (June, 1996), p. 256.
14 *Pioneer*, 22 March 1834.
15 E. P. Thompson, *The Making of the English Working Class* (1968), pp. 887-8.
16 John Foster, *Class Struggle and the Industrial Revolution* (1974), pp. 107-14.
17 J. A. Roebuck, *Trades' Unions: Their Advantages to the Working Classes*, (1834), p. 2.

society, and in a few hands arguably obscures more than it illuminates; but a terminology to denote the growth of a shared awareness among working people of commonality — of both situation and political purpose — is necessary for an historical analysis of these years. This is not to surrender to a metaphysical concept of *class*, in which 'the middle' or 'the working' class become historical actors in their own right, capable — or so it almost seems — of thought and action born of an independent volition. Nor is it to suggest that the perception of commonality was uniformly shared across all occupations or localities. Even a superficial examination of the two greatest general unions, the National Association for the Protection of Labour (NAPL) and the GNCTU, explodes that notion. However, the history of social movements in the 1830s and 1840s is extraordinary compared to anything that had gone before (or arguably went after) for reasons of their national scope, political ambition and intellectual reach. Bound up within that history is a transition within the trades' awareness of themselves. Workers' associations, from being essentially reactive responses to economic circumstances, were becoming increasingly pro-active in pursuit of a creative role in the shaping of those circumstances.

To a great extent this transition derived from a growing realization that, while the process of economic change was not to be stemmed, there was scope for labour to adjust its pace and direction. It is posterity that invented the concept of the 'industrial revolution', the popular heroic view of which depends upon a foreshortened historical perspective: industrialization was not achieved precipitately, nor was it a process of undeviating linear progression. Thus the economy appeared more capable of accommodating the culture and values of labour than we, with the benefit of hindsight, are apt to assume. It was as natural for the trade unionist of 1834 to believe in a new moral world as it was the trade society member of the eighteenth century to believe in the preservation or restitution of an old one. The general unionism of 1829-34 was about more than just mutual support.

For many observers this perception was strengthened by contemporary socialist economic writing, especially Hodgskin and Thompson, and by popular radical journalists such as the tailor trade unionist George Petrie ('Agrarius' of the *Man*), James Morrison (editor of *Pioneer*) and J. E. Smith, a collaborator with Morrison and editor of the *Crisis*. The considerable emphasis once placed on Robert Owen's role in the labour movement of 1829-34 is now generally recognised as having been misplaced: but Owenism (within which there were a number of strains of thought, not all of them agreeable to Owen himself) permeated the thinking of many workers during these years. The economist Thomas Hodgskin, whose influence on popular political economy was examined in the previous chapter, was struck by general unionism's potential for redrawing the map of industry. So too was William Thompson, the Irish-born economist closely associated with the Owenite movement. Part of the appeal of both writers to a popular readership was that they wrote as if existing relations of economic production were not immutable. In contrast to Hodgskin, Thompson was primarily concerned to assimilate trades associations to co-operation and communitarianism, but in doing so he also advanced the view that trade unionism could only be effective if comprehensive and general. Such views powerfully reinforced the arguments of those within the radical movement like Bronterre O'Brien:

> These two classes never had, and never will have, any community of interest. It is the workman's interest to do as little work, and get as much possible for it. It is the middleman's interest to get as much work as he can out of the man, and to give as little for it. Here then are their two respective interests as directly opposed to each other as two fighting bulls.[18]

---

18 *Destructive*, 9 March 1833.

Hodgskin and O'Brien cannot in any meaningful sense be described as Owenites. Even Thompson, a close associate of Owen, was stringently critical of him on a number of occasions.[19] Hodgskin, Thompson and O'Brien's views both indicated and reinforced a growing climate of opinion within the radical and labour movements which meant that attempts at general union from 1829 were considerably more purposeful than those of 1818 and the early 1820s.

THE NATIONAL ASSOCIATION FOR THE PROTECTION OF LABOUR (NAPL)

We saw in Chapter 4 that the timing of attempts at general union was often influenced by a specific industrial dispute which required support. The two great movements of 1829-34 were no exception: the NAPL had roots in moves to formalize support for fine spinners in Manchester, while the GNCTU coalesced round the cause of the Derby spinners' turn-out.

On 30 September 1829 over 1,000 workers from twenty different trades gathered in Manchester to hear speeches by delegates from the dyers and cloth dressers, smallware weavers and cotton spinners in favour of 'a general co-operation and combination of all the working classes of the kingdom'. The 'Catholic Rent', instigated by the popular Irish leader Daniel O'Connell to finance the recently successful campaign for Roman Catholic Emancipation, was cited as a model for general unionism. A common concern was 'the document' — the customary term for a legally enforceable agreement to renounce trade unionism that employers could require workers to sign as a condition of employment. From this meeting the NAPL emerged. The underlying reasons for this were specific to the experience of the Manchester trades, especially textile manufactures, rather than to an intellectual commitment to Owenism. It had been the spinners' misfortune, despite their well-established tradition of collective action and a relatively sophisticated trade union, once again to have failed to counter a reduction in wages. By consolidating labour's capacity for resistance, the NAPL was intended to prevent the piecemeal introduction of reduced wages by making it impossible for employers to pick off individual towns or districts, factories or sectors of industry; it was also seen as the only effective answer to combinations of employers, and the only realistic form of unionisation in a period of depression.

Given this context, it is hardly surprisingly that the NAPL drew its greatest support from workers in the textile industry, not just the cotton spinners but also calico printers, power- and hand-loom weavers (particularly from the Rochdale flannel industry) and textile machine makers. The support the NAPL received outside of the Lancashire and Cheshire manufacturing district was limited. Contributions to the Association from the whole of Yorkshire barely reached £20, a sum comfortably exceeded by numerous small industrial townships west of the Pennines, though there is some evidence to suggest that Yorkshire played a larger role in the organization than its finances suggest. The NAPL did, however, draw significant support from the textile districts of Nottinghamshire, Derby and Leicestershire. Outside these counties financial support was forthcoming only from Carlisle, Bradford, Dewsbury and Knaresborough, until the Potteries became a focal point for activities in the final phase. However, financial contributions only tell part of the story. For example, though there are no recorded subscriptions, the NAPL enjoyed support in Belfast and *Rushlight*, an Irish radical paper, publicized the Association. Nor was its membership necessarily coterminous with its sphere of influence. Attempts to set up NAPL districts in the West Midlands were unsuccessful, though there was a co-ordinating committee in Birmingham and promotional work for the idea of

---

19   Richard Pankhurst, *William Thompson (1775-1833): Pioneer Socialist* (1991), pp. 120-6.

general unionism probably smoothed the path for the Operative Society of Builders later.

The NAPL's influence can also be traced across the northern coalfields and into Wales. Delegates to the Friendly Associated Coal Miners' Union Society attended a meeting of the 'Coal Miners' Union' in Bolton in April 1831, from Cheshire, Lancashire, Staffordshire, Yorkshire, Flintshire and Denbighshire. The meeting agreed they should 'immediately join the Trades' Union', that is the NAPL. The financial contributions on which Cole[20] relies show only two miners' bodies actually subscribing to the Association, both from Blackrod, north of Wigan.[21] However, as Sykes[22] points out, the miners' resources were needed to sustain strike actions and stave off the union's dissolution (in which, ultimately, it failed). From the north-east Welsh collieries a missionary, William Twiss, accompanied by Welsh interpreters, was sent to South Wales to capitalize upon the industrial unrest that existed there, particularly in Merthyr Tydfil. The party arrived shortly before the Merthyr Rising. It is a moot point whether the NAPL 'might even have served as a detonator' of the rising, as Gwyn Williams suggested.[23] He makes a more plausible case, though, for the government's handling of the episode — particularly the decision to hang a young miner, Richard Lewis (Dic Penderyn), as a supposed ringleader — having been influenced by the spectre of the NAPL elsewhere at this time. Oblivious to its existence while alive, Dic Penderyn probably died 'a martyr to the National Association for the Protection of Labour'.[24] There was a flurry of trade union activity in the wake of the rising, as lodges (sometimes described as a 'Friendly Society of Coal Mining') were formed across the region from Newport westwards to Swansea. Presumably this was a resumption of the work the emissaries from the north-east coalfield had intended before the rising engulfed the area, for Twiss was still there in November, preaching on a text from Isaiah: 'And it shall come to pass in that day that the Lord shall punish the host of the high ones that are on high and the kings of the earth upon the earth. And they shall be gathered together as prisoners are gathered in the pit and shall be shut up in the prison.'[25] It is doubtful how aware, if at all, these new-found collier trade unionists were of the existence of the NAPL: but the timing of this, the earliest trade union development in the South Wales coalfield, seems to have been influenced by the NAPL. The episode also illustrates the opaque quality of unionist activity at the time. It is only as a result of the close-grained and imaginative research of Gwyn Williams that the NAPL's links into South Wales are known at all, the standard history of the Association arguing 'there is no evidence' of them.[26]

The history of the NAPL is rather less dramatic than that of the GNCTU and this is possibly one reason why it has suffered relative neglect. Similarly, in its full-time secretary, John Doherty, it had a leader of manifest ability and commitment, but a somewhat paler figure than Robert Owen, putative leader of the later movement. As Sykes[27] points out, the NAPL 'lasted much longer than the GNCTU,

---

20 G. D. H. Cole, *Attempts at General Union*.

21 Gwyn A. Williams, *The Merthyr Rising*, is the main source for the Welsh dimension to the NAPL. See also his earlier article, 'Merthyr 1831: Lord Melbourne and the trade unions', R. G. Kirby and A. E. Musson, *The Voice of the People: John Doherty 1798-1854: Trade Unionist, Radical and Factory Reformer* (1975), pp. 231-2 and Emlyn Rogers, 'Labour struggles in Flintshire, 1830-50', *Flintshire Historical Society Publications*, (1953-5).

22 Robert Sykes, 'Trade unionism and class consciousness: the "revolutionary" period of general unionism, 1829-1834', in John Rule (ed.), *British Trade Unionism, 1750-1850: The Formative Years* (1988).

23 Gwyn A. Williams, *The Merthyr Rising*, p. 112.

24 Ibid, p. 201.

25 *Monmouthshire Merlin*, 12 November 1831, cited in Gwyn A. Williams, *The Merthyr Rising*, p. 219.

26 R. G. Kirby and A. E. Musson, *The Voice of the People*, p. 231.

27 Robert Sykes, 'Trade unionism and class consciousness', p. 180.

had a larger paying membership, developed a firmer organisational structure and in many respects achieved a broader coverage in terms of different trades and geographical extent'. What it lacked in Owenite thrust, (not necessarily an unmitigated blessing), it more than compensated for in an economic analysis that was already familiar to supporters in its Lancashire textile heartlands. Excessive competition between employers was driving down wages, and if competition was mitigated it was only because employers themselves combined to depress rewards to labour further. So strong was this belief that the inaugural resolutions of the Association, agreed by a delegate meeting in Manchester in June 1830, stipulated 'that the funds of this Society shall be applied only to prevent reductions of wages, but in no case to procure an advance. Any trade considering their wages too low may exert themselves to obtain such advance, as they may think necessary and can obtain by their own exertions.' Individual membership was precluded and 'no trade can be admitted members of this Association that is not regularly organised and united to itself'.[28]

However, two key problems dogged the NAPL almost from its inception. The first was financial: its first general secretary absconded with £160 from the funds, not in itself sufficient to sink the NAPL but enough to require revised (and unwieldy) financial procedures. Many affiliates seem to have ignored the requirement to subscribe altogether. Despite a membership that may have reached 80,000 at its peak, the Association never accumulated at any one time sufficient funds to sustain the systematic withdrawal of labour from employers reducing wages. Lock-outs and strikes had to be supported by *ad hoc* appeals which inevitably drained the commitment and confidence of subscribers, especially when — as was all too frequently the case — the outcome was a defeat for the workers involved.

The NAPL's second key problem centred on the influence of the cotton textiles trades in its direction. Without the cotton spinners' union there would have been no NAPL: but its 'general Committee, consisting of one delegate from every 1000 members' met only twice a year, executive power being vested in a Manchester-based Provisional Council the composition of which inevitably tended to favour the cotton textile and allied trades. This committee inclined to greater caution than did John Doherty, the energetic Irish-born spinner who, driven by a vision of a truly national organization, sought to extend its reach to the Midlands, Yorkshire and London. In the Midlands he was successful; in Yorkshire he was an effective proponent of general unionist ideals, but this yielded little in the way of formal affiliation or subscriptions. London would have to be the fulcrum if the NAPL was to become a national organization, Doherty believed; but his attempts to move the NAPL's paper *Voice of the People* to the capital foundered amidst difficulties in attracting advertisers, the hostility of the Manchester committee to the proposal, and the strains placed on Doherty's time which, the committee felt, was best concentrated in the north. The *Voice of the People* folded, Doherty resigned his post with the union and the provisional committee proved unable to replicate either his energy or vision. Doherty became increasingly absorbed in factory reform. Ailing from the autumn of 1831, in the spring of 1832 the NAPL 'disintegrated totally'.[29]

What were the underlying reasons for the Association's failure? The NAPL's leverage upon its non-Lancashire affiliates had always been slight. Artisan trades outside the textile industry, even in Lancashire, were lukewarm in their support. However, Kirby and Musson's account[30] of the NAPL places too great an emphasis on trade particularism and aloofness to explain the pattern of its support

---

28 *United Trades Co-operative Journal*, 10 July 1830.
29 Robert Sykes, 'Trade unionism and class consciousness', p. 180.
30 R. G. Kirby and A. E. Musson, *The Voice of the People*.

satisfactorily. In an important commentary on the pattern of support for the NAPL, Robert Sykes observes that, 'in many of the largest artisan trades, which remained overwhelmingly unmechanized and orientated to the domestic market, wage reductions were frequently not the critical issues'.[31] The defence of apprenticeship and control over the labour process were what most mattered here, and these trades limited industrial action in depression, preferring to exploit the advantages of labour in boom periods. Significantly, the one non-textile artisan trade to support the NAPL was the hatters, who were confronted by exactly that erosion of wage levels that the Association intended to counter. 'It was the relevance of the NAPL to the precise economic needs of individual trades', Sykes concludes, 'which most satisfactorily explains its patterns of membership'.

Beyond the NAPL

Where the Association was highly effective was in spreading the general principle that each trade should be 'regularly organised and united to itself', as its founding resolutions expressed it. This ideal, energetically promoted by Doherty in lecture tours, spread through Yorkshire. The NAPL also politicized trade affairs further. Nowhere is this clearer than in its influence upon London. William Carpenter, formerly editor of the *Trades' Free Press*, successor to the *Trades' Newspaper*, ascribed the origins of the National Union of the Working Classes (NUWC) to the attendance of delegates from the capital at a NAPL conference in Manchester in 1830. When the Metropolitan Trades' Union was set up through the collaboration of London co-operators and members of the General Union of Carpenters in March 1831, the NAPL was the model they took. Within a few weeks, and with the Reform Crisis breaking all around it, the organization changed its title to NUWC, swept up in the campaign for radical reform. The NUWC became the dominant ultra-radical organization in London between 1831 and 1833, with extensive (and under-researched) provincial branches. As the Webbs observed, 'it occupies, during the political turmoil of 1831-2, by far the largest place in the history of working-class organization, and was largely implicated in the agitation and disturbances connected with the Reform Bill'.[32] It quickly extended the basis of its membership to include individual enrolment as well as trade society subscription; but the NUWC's trade unionist origins and orientation remained clear:

> The Rights of Man in society, are liberty — equality before the laws — security of his person — and the full employment of the produce of his labour ... The objects of the NATIONAL UNION are ...
>
> To obtain for every working man, unrestricted by unjust and partial laws, the full value of his labour, and the free disposal of the produce of his labour.
>
> To support, as circumstances may determine, by all just means, every fair and rational opposition made by societies of working men (such societies being part of the Union), against the combination and tyranny of masters and manufacturers; whenever the latter shall seek, *unjustly*, to reduce the wages of our labour, or shall institute proceedings against the workmen.[33]

It is unrealistic to separate off the NUWC from trade unionism as 'exclusively political'.[34] As John

---

31 Robert Sykes, 'Trade unionism and class consciousness', p. 183.
32 Sidney and Beatrice Webb, *The History of Trade Unionism*, revised edition (1920), p. 156.
33 *Carpenter's Monthly Political Magazine*, January 1832, quotation from pp. 180-1. See also Patricia Hollis's introduction to the Merlin Press reprint of the *Poor Man's Guardian* (1969), p. xi, and Iorwerth J. Prothero, *Artisans and Politics*, pp. 270-5.
34 R. G. Kirby and A. E. Musson, *The Voice of the People*, p. 244.

Betts, secretary of the Ashton spinners and one of John Doherty's key lieutenants, saw it: 'Trades Unions and Political Ones were now so intimately blended that they must be looked upon as one'.[35] Though few seem to have followed Betts' lead in unfurling the tricolour at union meetings, his belief that workers' unionisation had reached a new threshold was widely shared. Given the sometimes chameleon-like complexities of popular radicalism, and the manner in which the idea of 'union' infused working men and women's thinking in these years, it is hardly surprising that clear demarcation between trades' unionism, co-operation and political unions is impossible.

Nowhere is the constitutional untidiness of general unionism more obvious than in Yorkshire. In December 1832 an inquest was conducted into the death of a Farsley woollen weaver, allegedly murdered by trade unionists because he was a blackleg. The coroner observed:

> So extensive and alarming is the Combination called the Trades Union. It extends through every manufacturing town and village in the West Riding ... this Union is composed of branches of the different trades. The Clothiers, Stone Masons, Potters etc., I have reason to believe have each their separate Societys and all centre in the Trade Unions.[36]

The coroner's remarks show an appreciation that pre-existing trade societies had a loosely connecting affiliation with each other. It was this affiliation which at various times was called 'the Yorkshire Trades' Union', 'the Trades Union', 'the Union' or 'the Leeds Union'. The driving force behind it was the largest trade society in the region, the Leeds Clothiers Union, also confusingly known as the Leeds Trades' Union but often called 'John Powlett' after a (probably fictitious) officer. Much that was popularly ascribed to the Yorkshire Union was actually due to the exertions of 'John Powlett'. It was the model for the Linen Trades' Union (covering Barnsley, Knaresborough, Leeds and York) and was itself a federal body. Most of the divisions of the trade were represented, not only in Leeds and its satellite communities, but also in Batley, Dewsbury, Halifax, Holmfirth, Morley and Slaithwaite.

The Leeds Union had parallels elsewhere. Sheffield's Trades' General Union, which was extant by March 1830,[37] was quite distinct from the Leeds body. However, the Bradford Trades' Union (also known as the Bradford Order) was closely associated with the Leeds body, so much so that Cole regarded it as the worsted section of the Yorkshire Trades' Union.[38] The Bradford Order spread its net widely. It is known to have formed lodges as far south as Banbury in Oxfordshire and it was deeply involved in prosecuting a strike over union recognition at Dolphinholme, near Lancaster. Both its officers and those of the Leeds' body may have consciously seen themselves as continuing the work of the NAPL, for Doherty had developed close links with west Yorkshire during the Association's final stages.[39]

Another, if less vigorous, parallel to the Yorkshire Trades' Union could be found in the Leicester Union. A 'Trades Union Secret Committee' existed here in September 1833 (and very possibly earlier). It appears to have been the linear successor to the NAPL District which had been established in the county in March 1831, and which seceded (if so formal a term is appropriate in the circumstances) from the NAPL when Doherty severed his connections with the Manchester organizing committee in January 1832. The Leicester Union aligned itself with the new mood that

---

35 HO 40/27, 8 November 1830.

36 HO 52/20, 24 December 1832, cited in John R. Sanders, 'Working-class movements in the West Riding textile district, 1829-39, with emphasis on local leadership and organisation', University of Manchester, D.Phil. Thesis, (1984).

37 NAPSS 1860, 536-8.

38 G. D. H. Cole, *Attempts at General Union*.

39 R. G. Kirby and A. E. Musson, *The Voice of the People*, p. 200.

culminated in the GNCTU, its component lodges becoming in their turn lodges of the latter in January 1834. Among other things it supported a co-operative of striking framework-knitters 'at the sign of the Trades Union' in Bond Street, Leicester, and organized extensively among female textiles workers. It is unclear what happened to the Leicester Union as the GNCTU folded, but the problems of nomenclature are vividly apparent in September 1834 when the Operative Cordwainers vigorously repudiated belonging to a trades union: their society, they said, had no connection with any other.[40]

Interest in general unionism was not confined to England and Wales, as the discussion so far might seem to imply. Whilst Irish trade unionism in these years lacked the drama of its British counterpart, its history exhibits a number of points of affinity. These were years of accelerating trades activity in Ireland, responding to the stimulus of the repeal of anti-combination legislation, and to similar movements of the economic cycle. There was decidedly less interest, however, in the idea of general unionism and federation with British associations was rare. We saw in Chapter 2 that printers' chapels were relieving Irish tramps as early as 1715, and that the tramping network formalized by the shoemakers in 1784 probably included Ireland for Thomas Preston regarded his tramp there in 1792 as completely unexceptional. In evidence before the 1824 Select Committee on Artizans and Machinery, the Chief Constable of Dublin spoke of trade societies' passes having a common currency on both sides of the Irish sea, and tramping was doubtless the medium through which the 'regular correspondence with London' of which another witness spoke, was maintained by Dublin. However, attempts at any affiliation more sophisticated than this were apt to founder, though a United Kingdom-wide correspondence was maintained by the hatters, via which price lists and strike relief were circulated.[41] Nine Irish 'Societies in the House Furnishing Department' affiliated with their English counterparts in 1833: the Dublin and Londonderry societies each sent a delegate to an annual meeting held that year in Manchester; but by 1837 the Cabinet Makers' Society (as it had become) resolved that 'we do withdraw from union with Ireland altogether, excepting the usual acknowledgement of their tramps, provided their societies act reciprocally with ours, as the expense of communication was so great and the connection found too unwieldly to conduct'.[42] British bricklayers' and carpenters' unions maintained Dublin branches in the early 1830s, but the one paled in comparison to the local Irish society, the Old Body of Bricklayers, whilst that of the General Union of Carpenters seems not to have endured beyond 1836.[43] The Belfast spinners' involvement in Doherty's Grand General Union, as we have seen, was cut short by the collapse of the organization as a whole, whilst their commitment to the NAPL was limited to involvement in a local committee formed to support the Ashton turn-outs. There were, however, links between the Leeds-based Linen Trades' Union and Ulster.[44]

A series of prosecutions of trade unionists, similar to those in England, took place in Ireland over the winter of 1833-4. In Cork and Belfast sentences of transportation were handed down for assaults arising from combination. Conspiracy charges were brought against members of combinations in Londonderry, Lisburn, County Antrim, Belfast and Dublin. Such was the climate of suspicion against trade unionism that in August 1834 police raided the meeting of a Cork burial society and secured the

---

40 A. Temple Patterson, *Radical Leicester: A History of Leicester; 1780-1850* (1975), p. 288.

41 *PP* 1824 (5 1)V — Select Committee on Artizans and Machinery, Second Report, 72, 295-6; John W. Boyle, *The Irish Labor Movement in the Nineteenth Century* (1988), p. 31.

42 Quoted in S. Higenbottam, *Our Society's History* (1939), p. 15.

43 John W. Boyle, *The Irish Labor Movement in the Nineteenth Century*, p. 101.

44 J. R. Sanders, 'Working-class movements in the West Riding textile district, 1829 to 1839, with emphasis on local leadership and organisation', (University of Manchester D.Phil. Thesis, 1984), p. 101.

prosecution of eight of its members under the same legislation. Hardly surprisingly, therefore, members of Irish trade societies perceived the Tolpuddle case as indicative of a wider hostility to trade unionism as well as a peculiar case of injustice. This was especially so in Belfast where George Kerr, a member of the city's cabinet makers' society, was arrested and tried the same year for the administration of illegal oaths, the alleged offence being committed when he was recruiting to a short-lived Londonderry Cabinet Makers' Society. The Belfast cabinetmakers were one of twelve trades that affiliated *en bloc* to 'the Belfast Branch of the General Trades' Union' (also known as the 'Northern Trade Union'). It was almost certainly connected to the GNCTU. Half its affiliates and two-thirds of its total membership were drawn from the building industry. The Union included neither coachmakers nor printers, both societies involved in prolonged strikes and bruising defeats in 1834. Nor were the textile industries represented, perhaps because Ulster linen workers' connections with England lay with the Leeds Linen Union and through it with the Yorkshire Trade Union, and before that possibly with the NAPL. In April 1834, the Northern Trade Union organized a rally of 1,500 trade unionists in St George's Market, Belfast, to protest at the treatment of the Tolpuddle martyrs. Though the Ulster dimension to support for the GNCTU has gone unremarked among British historians, as an indicator of the appeal of trades' unionism it is not without significance. Kerr's treatment whilst remanded in prison (his case, when finally heard, was thrown out) and the responses of Irish employers to the formation of trades societies in 1833-4 all indicate the extent of establishment unease at the growth of trade unionism, an unease equally in evidence in Britain. Like the GNCTU in England, the Belfast Union collapsed in the summer of 1834, its constituent trades embroiled in disputes about the right to union membership.[45]

The Scottish experience was rather different. Here the principal advocate of 'a union of all trades for the protection of labour' was Alexander Campbell, an Owenite joiner and journalist. The United Trades of Glasgow (of which Campbell was 'Interim Secretary') collected 30,000 signatures in support of the Dorchester labourers. However, in preference to union with the GNCTU (which sent delegates to Clydeside to raise support for the Derby turn-out) the Glasgow trades called for a Scottish Confederation of Trades, whose delegates would become a Scottish parliament of workmen.[46] Nothing came of the Glasgow proposal but their interest in general unionism was not isolated. Earlier, Campbell's response to the collapse of the NAPL had been to propose a Glasgow and West of Scotland Association for the Protection of Labour. Fraser points to the growth in mutual support among trades, particularly on Clydeside, in the early 1830s.[47] This included a Co-operative Union of women powerloom weavers and male dressers and tenters (mechanics). Meanwhile in Edinburgh a trades' committee published a monthly journal, cited by one of the city's newspapers as evidence of endeavours to form 'one general confederacy' which it compared to the 1831 revolt of the Lyon silk weavers. In Aberdeen the United Trades raised funds to support several strikes, including that of the Aberdeen Female Operatives' Union.

---

45 George Kerr, *Kerr's Exposition of Legislative Tyranny, and Defence of the Trades' Union*, Belfast, (1834), (reprinted in Andrew Boyd, *The Rise of the Irish Trade Unions*, second edition (1985), appendix 1); M. Doyle, 'Belfast and Tolpuddle: attempts at strengthening a trade union presence, 1833/4', *Saothar*, 2, (1976), p. 4. see also John W. Boyle, *The Irish Labor Movement in the Nineteenth Century*, pp. 40-1.

46 Gregory Claeys, 'Alexander Campbell and the GNCTU in Scotland: The Scottish Trades' Union Gazette', *BSSLH*, vol. 51, no. 3, (1986); W. H. Fraser, *Conflict and Class: Scottish Workers, 1700-1838* (1988), p. 148, and *Alexander Campbell and the Search for Socialism* (1996), p. 51.

47 W. H. Fraser, *Conflict and Class*, pp. 147-8.

The Grand National Consolidated Trades' Union (GNCTU)

Considering its short life, the GNCTU has enjoyed an extraordinary degree of interest from historians. In Robert Owen it provides one of the most widely recognized of labour leaders and in the Tolpuddle Martyrs one of the few episodes in British labour history to have truly gripped the popular imagination. (Neither Peterloo, Chartism nor the General Strike, after all, has been turned into a cinema box-office success, as were the Dorset farm labourers in *Comrades*, 1987.)

The history of the GNCTU cannot be treated like that of a conventional institution. It was scarcely an organization but rather a very loosely federal movement. Even the Webb's comparison of the GNCTU to the American Knights of Labour flatters it to some extent. Margaret Cole's comment that the GNCTU 'crashed almost before it was formed',[48] conveys something of the flavour of its chaotic history. During 1833 the idea embodied in the GNCTU was talked about extensively: groups formed with the intention of participating before even it existed. It was an emotional force even more than it was a physical reality. Yet at one point the GNCTU was reputed to have a million members. The Webbs put the total at half a million.[49] The basis of their calculation is as unclear as the figure is misleading. Yet more spurious is the drastically revisionist conclusion of Oliver, who calculated the 'total United Kingdom financial membership' to be 'a little over' 16,000.[50] This figure has tended to stick, even though it is based on a solitary surviving balance sheet. At best it is a snapshot of a particular category of constituents. No one would ever seriously suggest that support for Chartism was effectively limited to those who subscribed to the National Charter Association (some 50,000 in 1842). Formal membership is an injudicious means to assess support and even A. E. Musson, the fiercest historical critic of the enterprise, concedes that 'a larger penumbra may have been vaguely associated with it'.[51]

The key questions, then, are 'how large and how vague?' In what remains, frustratingly, the only local case study of the GNCTU, Haynes[52] has pointed out how the data from which Oliver computed his total membership for the GNCTU actually excludes Northampton. Yet using Oliver's own criteria for estimating membership, the total number of GNCTU affiliates in Northampton alone would number 1,300. On purely procedural grounds, then, the now commonly accepted membership figure is fatally flawed. Northampton also demonstrates the difficulties of delineating the national general union movement, and of what actually constituted membership in the popular view. The town was among those Midlands centres where a branch of the NUWC had been established. This may have encouraged local shoemakers in 'struggling along against a host of oppressors, by a sort of Local County Union', to quote one local activist. It was solely or principally made up of shoemakers. Early in 1834 the 'Co-operative Boot and Shoemakers' resolved to 'arrange themselves into Lodges, after the manner, and under the Rules and Regulations of the National Trades' Union'.[53] The GNCTU still did not formally exist at this stage and, according to another Northampton radical, 'the whole of the workmen in the shoe trade had joined the Manchester order in mistake'. The error was only acted

---

48 In Sidney Pollard and John Salt, *Robert Owen, Prophet of the Poor: Essays in Honour of the Two Hundredth Anniversary of his Birth* (1971), p. 211.
49 Sidney and Beatrice Webb, *The History of Trade Unionism*, p. 152.
50 W. H. Oliver, 'The Consolidated Trades' Union of 1834', *Economic History Review*, 17, (1964), p. 85.
51 A. E. Musson, *British Trade Unions, 1800-1875* (1972), p. 33.
52 M. J. Haynes, 'Class and class conflict in the early nineteenth century: Northampton shoemakers and the Grand National Consolidated Trades' Union', *Literature and History*, 5, (1977), p. 88-9.
53 John Harrison, *Pioneer*, 15 March 1834; Josh. Johnson 'Chairman', letter to the editor, *Pioneer*, 11 January 1834.

upon in the light of local arrests for swearing loyalty oaths: many northern trade unions were continuing to insist upon these while the GNCTU did not. Subsequently 'the whole body ceded by acclamation, and joined the London Consolidated Trades' Union'. It says a great deal about the enthusiasm for general union that a substantial and politically aware body of workers could enrol in one body by mistake for another; it is no less salutary to learn that the same body then joined the GNCTU apparently with no more formality than by acclamation. This does not make for the kind of neatness that the once dominant institutional approach to labour history sought. Reading Cole's *Attempts at General Union*, one can almost hear sighs of irritation as the author seeks in turn to fit the deluded Northampton shoemakers into 'some remnant of the N.A.P.L.', then 'merely the Manchester Order of Cordwainers' and finally 'some section of the Yorkshire movement'.[54]

When it emerged in the early weeks of 1834 the GNCTU was the product of two forces. The first was popular enthusiasm for general unionism which had not been stinted by the decline of the NAPL, though it would be fair to say that enthusiasm was greatest among those who had not been involved in the earlier movement. The second force was Robert Owen. He was a recent convert to trade unionism, and his conception of it would never match those of trade unionists themselves, but no other figure in radical politics commanded the attention Owen did at this time. Cobbett and Hunt were long past the peak of their powers, neither enjoying good health; Feargus O'Connor was as yet untried and largely unknown. But 'Robert Owen, wise and good, / Better known than understood', as a poem in the *Poor Man's Guardian* of 20 September 1834 aptly put it, presented a dynamic fusion of benevolent philanthropy, intellectual engagement and social vision. He was also a leader in search of a movement. Having returned to Britain in 1829 after five years in America including an unsuccessful communitarian experiment in Indiana, Owen discovered that in his absence his ideas had been taken up by small but enthusiastic groups of working-class intellectuals. Their involvement in radical and trade politics, education and, especially, retail co-operatives was a conduit through which Owen reached a wide popular audience. During 1833, with the idea of producer co-operation assuming growing prominence and attracting considerable trade union support, Owen effectively became head of a national movement of the trades.

The argument put by Harrison[55] in his seminal study of Owen and the Owenites bears repetition. Owenism could only 'capture' trade unionism because it seemed to offer a solution where the various movements for economic and political reform, self-help, the factory agitation and trade unionist endeavour had failed. After the almost apocalyptic expectations raised during the Reform Crisis, the Owenite vision 'of a complete transformation of the whole society ... found a receptive audience'. The idea of 'union' suggested a new route: loose federation along the lines of the NAPL and the GNCTU seemed capable of uniting under one political umbrella co-operative and benefit societies together with a diverse range of trades societies, many of which had proud traditions of protecting their sectional interests through job control and wage bargaining. A few societies, chiefly in printing and engineering, took no part in general unionism: 'no such connexion does exist, or ever can exist, until the principles of our Union are wholly changed' decreed the council of the London Society of Compositors.[56] On the other hand, under the Owenite impulse, the embrace of trade organization was extended further than ever before, and notably to women and farm workers. This fever of recruitment, Harrison suggests, 'should perhaps be related to the millenarian hopes' that were never

---

54 'Further persecution of the unions', *Poor Man's Guardian*, 17 May 1834; G. D. H. Cole, *Attempts at General Union*, pp. 68-9.
55 J. F. C. Harrison, *Robert Owen and the Owenites in Britain and America* (1969), pp. 212-14.
56 Ellic Howe (ed.), *The London Compositor: Documents relating to Wages, Working Conditions and Customs of the London Printing Trade, 1785-1900* (1947), p. 225.

far from the surface of popular culture at this time. Owen's millennial rhetoric has proved a fruitful subject for academic interpretation; but however metaphysical his notions of change and its agency may have been, it is hard to believe that in speeches like the following he did not have a form of general strike in mind.

> I now give you a short outline of the great changes which are in contemplation, and which shall come suddenly upon society, like a thief in the night, for not one in a hundred of our population has the least idea of what is approaching. This change is to be accomplished not by violence, bloodshed, or any species of injustice ... It is intended that national arrangements shall be formed to include all the working classes in the great organization, and that each department shall become acquainted with what is going on in other departments; that all individual competition is to cease; that all manufactures are to be carried out by national companies ... This national organization shall be accomplished by simplification and combination: we shall retain all the advantages of division of labour and union. All trades shall first form associations of lodges ...[57]

In this lecture Owen set the course that was to steer, erratically and ultimately disastrously, the GNCTU. Yet even from this point it is easier to trace the nature of the enterprise than it is to identify a precise organizational entity. As early as 20 April 1833, when the first plans for labour exchanges were drawn up, a National Association of the United Trades was also suggested, to be formed 'by a union of Trade, Benefit, and Co-operative Societies' (this was the embryonic National Equitable Labour Exchange). The following week the *Crisis* abandoned its masthead depicting a socialist community and adopted as a subtitle the *National Co-operative Trades' Union, and Equitable Labour Exchange Gazette*. Thereafter Owen's speeches are littered with phrases such as 'a national moral union of the productive classes'[58] and references to 'the Union' recur in the radical press. However, they did so in the loose way one might use 'movement' rather than as denoting a precise organization. Moral union implied a unity of purpose rather than constitutional form and it was not until January 1834 that a formal constitution and rules for the Grand National Consolidated Trades' Union were distributed. There is a sense in which the brevity of the GNCTU's history hardly matters: it is the general unionist *mood* that was most significant. It was this which continued to draw in both organized trades and the hitherto uninvolved, even after the NAPL and Yorkshire Union faded; but it was precisely because these earlier initiatives had dissolved leaving their constituents sceptical about the practicalities of general union that the GNCTU could never be the grand, national or consolidated body its promoters hoped.

Owen's interest in general unionism was in this sense belated. He was carried along by general unionism, never impelling it forward himself, until with support ebbing away in the autumn of 1834 he abandoned it for a new vehicle: the British and Foreign Consolidated Association of Industry, Humanity and Knowledge, reorganized in the spring of 1835 under the yet more immodest but less prolix title of the Association of All Classes of All Nations. This new banner also made explicit Owen's abhorrence of class antagonism, one of the reasons why he had severed his links with the GNCTU. Yet Owen's outlook was neither apolitical nor cast in the mould of establishment politics. There was much in his personal vision for the GNCTU that appealed to trade unionists: 'partnership manufactories' in which masters would be replaced by superintendents, 'elected for their skill and

---

57 *Crisis*, 12 October 1833.
58 *Crisis*, 15 June 1833.

integrity' by the workers; a national structure of parochial, county and provincial lodges, where the grouping of individual trades would be paralleled at each tier by united trades committees with delegates and officials selected by ballot.[59] In the trade union and Owenite press this vision was developed into the 'House of Trades', closely anticipating — as Claeys points out[60] — syndicalism, extra-parliamentary workers' control of the means of production.

The syndicalist dimension to Owenite thinking struck a chord with trade unionists who had always been concerned with upholding a culture in which skill received more than merely pecuniary recognition. What is also striking, however, is the manner in which trade organizations intermeshed not only with the politics of the communities of which they were part, but also subscribed to a broader vision of comprehensive social changes. Union became the watchword for a whole range of activities, some of them only indirectly linked to immediate workplace issues. Conventionally historians have ascribed this to Owenism. The working-class movement of 1829-34 appears, in John Harrison's words, 'saturated with Owenism'. However, much was the result of a drawing-out of strands from within workers' own experience, rather than of the direct influence of Owen or the wider movement that took his name (not all adherents of which were at ease with Owen's tutelage, nor he with them). Any understanding of trade unionism in these years requires an appreciation of its relationship to wider issues. Agrarianism, co-operative production and exchange and the concept of general strike relate primarily to the intellectual milieu of contemporary radicalism; but another cluster of issues, centring on women, the idea of skill and the ritual of trade societies, were closely linked to the 'inner life' of trade unionism. The remainder of this chapter is devoted to these two clusters of issues. It then concludes by examining in some depth the episode for which trade unionism in this period is most often remembered, the Tolpuddle Martyrs.

TRADE UNIONISM IN A BROADER CONTEXT

The agrarian tradition within English radicalism had a long pedigree. Since the 1770s, land reform and land resettlement had continuously been part of the popular political spectrum. The most prominent British agrarian theorist was Thomas Spence, Newcastle-born son of poor Scottish parents, who rose to a position of some prominence in the London Corresponding Society and of even greater influence in metropolitan revolutionary circles in the early years of the nineteenth century. The agrarian tradition, however, was wider than Spenceanism. It seemed to many that issues of contention at the work-place might be resolved, in part at least, through the land. Even in the eyes of urban workers, industrialization only slowly eroded the relevance of land reform and resettlement. Agrarian fundamentalism peaked in the 1830s and 1840s (the Chartist Land Plan could marshal 70,000 weekly subscribers at its peak, for example) and inevitably, in the radical intellectual maelstrom of these decades, trade unionism was affected by it.

Appropriately, therefore, one of the most widely read trade unionist journalists of the early 1830s, the tailor George Petrie, wrote under the pseudonym of 'Agrarius'. Petrie was a key figure both in his trade society and in the GNCTU, for whom he acted as a missionary to the Midlands and Lancashire. His introduction to radical politics had been through Spenceanism and from 1832 until his premature death in 1836 he lived in one of the many small agrarian communities contemporary to, but overshadowed by, the Owenite Harmony Hall and Chartist land colonies. However, for George Petrie the crucial context in which the agrarian vision might be fulfilled was trade unionism. He built a

---

59 *Man*, 13 October 1833.
60 Gregory Claeys, *Citizens and Saints*, p .198.

coherent case that the abolition of private property in land — long a Spencean objective — could and ought to be applied to other means of production, concluding that 'until machinery of every description is appropriated to the general welfare ... all the evils which we now complain of will progressively accumulate'. The objective of trade unions should be to 'STRANGLE COMPETITION' and general unionism should be 'the focus for the fulfilment of our designs'.[61]

Petrie was not alone among London trade unionists in his agrarian views. Similar ideas were advanced by Allen Davenport, another Spencean, formerly active in the London ladies' shoemakers' trade society. Both one of the London lodges of the Operative Builders' and the brassworkers' society accumulated funds with the intention of settling under- and unemployed members on the land. The practice was probably more widespread than surviving examples suggest, for in January 1835 a committee of the London trades drew up plans for a co-ordinated approach, 'viewing the absolute necessity OF THE CONNECTION of the various Trade Societies to employ their unemployed, to possess Land, as one of the the only fundamental elements which Man is heir to'.[62]

Most trade unions at this time, especially those within the orbit of the GNCTU, would have sympathized with the Grand Lodge of United Operative Tailors' view that 'Man must return to the breast of his mother earth for nurture'.[63] More widely dispersed than actual land schemes, however, were trade-society based initiatives in co-operative production, initiatives deserving more systematic investigation by historians than they have so far received. It might be supposed that this is clear evidence of Owenite influence but in many cases it seems to have been spontaneous. Skilled artisans had not entirely lost the traditional world-view in which the male life-cycle naturally progressed from apprentice to journeyman to small master. Furthermore many trades were accustomed to exercise considerable autonomy at the workplace. In any case, temporary ventures in manufacturing were a well-established strike tactic and in London had been established by breeches makers in 1793, bookbinders in 1794 and pipemakers in 1819. At various times Bristol, London, South Shields and Sunderland shipwrights' societies had all rented vacant yards to build vessels 'on spec' as an alternative to sending members on the tramp.[64] In 1831 London carpenters, through their houses of call, similarly commenced production of a complete house. The Kidderminster Weavers' Co-operative Association employed workers blacklisted after the 1828 strike to make carpets which were then sent to the London co-operative labour exchange. Striking Ashton spinners, Manchester sawyers, cloth dressers and dyers opened their own establishments in 1830.[65] Other associative producers included societies of Leicester hosiers and London coach and livery-lace weavers.

John Sanders[66] has pointed out how the Leeds shoemakers' society opened a 'large and commodious Work Shop for Our Men' in 1836, in the wake of the collapse of the national federation for their trade. In doing so, Sanders argues, they were following a strong but largely undocumented

---

61 Quotations from 'Agrarius', *Man*, 25 August, 10 November and 1 December 1833. For Petrie see particularly T. M. Parssinen and I. J. Prothero, 'The London tailors' strike of 1834 and the collapse of the Grand National Consolidated Trades' Union: a police spy's report', *International Review of Social History*, 22, 1, (1977), Malcolm Chase, *'The People's Farm': English Radical Agrarianism, 1775-1840* (2010) and *DLB*, vol. 10.

62 Malcolm Chase, *'The People's Farm'*, p. 143.

63 *Official Gazette of the Trades' Unions*, 14 June 1834.

64 Iorwerth J. Prothero, *Artisans and Politics*, p. 250; David Dougan, *The Shipwrights: The History of the Shipconstructors' and Shipwrights' Association, 1882-1963* (1975), p. 14.

65 Robert Sykes, 'Popular politics and trade unions in south-east Lancashire, 1829-42' (University of Manchester D.Phil. Thesis, 1982), pp. 193, 300-1, 332.

66 J. R. Sanders, 'Working-class movements in the West Riding textile district', p .95.

tradition in which trade unions established 'commercial orders', operations which drew on union finance to set up manufactories in which members could be employed. 'Every day adds to the numbers of these Commercial Orders', claimed the *Voice of the West Riding* (22 February 1834). There survives in the Home Office papers for these years a placard proposing that Staffordshire colliers should establish 'Political and Commercial Union ... for the purchasing, renting and working of pits of their own account'.[67] Such enterprises were especially strong in the West Riding of Yorkshire and Sanders suggests[68] that Owen's own vision of a 'Grand Moral Union', which preceded the GNCTU and in which he posited that partnership manufactories could take over the national manufacturing base 'by simplification and combination' was inspired by meetings with Huddersfield trade unionists in April 1833.

The logical concomitant of trade-union directed co-operative production was co-operative exchange. As well as direct trade union involvement, contemporary enthusiasm for co-operative exchange drew on that generalized vision of union we have already noted. Thus in 1827 a small London group set up the Union Exchange Society whose members exchanged goods via cash or barter, dividing the commission on transactions between them.[69] This was followed in 1829 by the Lambeth Co-operative Trading Union and in 1830-1 by at least four further exchanges in the capital, the best known being Owen's 'National Equitable Labour Exchange'. 'The public mind was completely electrified by this new and extraordinary movement', recalled Davenport,[70] who even moved house to be nearer the exchange. The extent to which these various establishments were kept supplied by trade societies rather than individual initiative is unclear. The British Association for Promoting Co-operative Knowledge, frequently referred to as the 'Trades' Co-operative Society', ran a bazaar that seems to have drawn almost totally on unionist products. Two tailors' societies supplied the Western Union Exchange, but the National Equitable had to make a specific effort to draw in the products of trade societies. Eventually, the societies involved formed the United Trades' Association to facilitate co-operative production. The Association was one of the bodies involved in re-launching the exchange bazaar in July 1833 after it had come close to closing due to poor management, but a combination of factors — not least an improvement in the economy which tempted producers (including trade societies) to sell on the open market and skewed the supply of goods available from the exchange — led to its closure in the early summer of 1834. Outside London, exchanges had only ever been established in Birmingham and Glasgow, neither of which survived the early 1830s.[71]

It is easy with the privilege of hindsight to ridicule the labour exchange movement and the economic naïvety upon which it was based. Had it been successful it could only ever have been of direct relevance to artisan-based commodity production. The lack of interest among northern industrial workers is therefore hardly surprising, but the labour exchange idea was important for what it symbolized, as much as for what it managed to achieve in practical terms. It held out the prospect that the labour movement might step outside of the capitalized industrial system and, as it were, un-

---

67 HO 40/31, f. 110.
68 J. R. Sanders, 'Working-class movements in the West Riding textile district', pp. 301-10.
69 Iorwerth J. Prothero, *Artisans and Politics*, p. 241.
70 Allen Davenport, *The Life and Literary Pursuits of Allen Davenport. With a further Selection of the Author's Work*, compiled and edited by Malcolm Chase (1994, originally published 1845).
71 For the National Equitable Labour Exchange see J. F. C. Harrison, *Robert Owen*; Iorwerth J. Prothero, *Artisans and Politics* is an essential supplement for the wider London exchange movement; there is limited material on the Birmingham and Glasgow initiatives in J. F. C. Harrison, *Robert Owen*, and W. H. Fraser, *Conflict and Class*, respectively. *Crisis* is the main contemporary source for the National Equitable Labour Exchange, of which Allen Davenport, *The Life and Literary Pursuits*, pp. 23-4, provides a most vivid description.

make it. A similar prospect was embodied in general unionism, especially the GNCTU which was the linear institutional successor to the National Equitable Labour Exchange.

Nowhere is belief in the transformative potential of trade unionism clearer than in contemporary usage of the word *jubilee*. In an unbroken tradition stretching back to John Milton, the word was heavy with a sense of epochal change. This was not the dominant modern usage which couples the word almost exclusively to monarchy and anniversary, but rather a radical reading of the highly politicized biblical original (at which the land was to be restored to its original occupiers, slaves released and debts annulled). The progressive accretion of meanings, by which jubilee came to be almost synonymous with the idea of general strike, however, was partly the result of specifically Spencean influences and partly of a general tendency to equate the idea with millenarian and revolutionary change. The seminal *Grand National Holiday and Congress of the Productive Classes*, issued in 1832 by William Benbow, a former Manchester shoemaker turned London radical publisher, was greatly indebted to this radical concept of jubilee. So too was another pamphlet issued in these troubled years, *Trades Triumphant or Unions' Jubilee!*[72] Benbow did not actually use the term 'general strike', though it is clear enough that this is exactly what his grand national holiday would have been:

> The grounds and necessity of our having a month's Holiday, arise from the circumstances in which we are placed. We are oppressed, in the fullest sense of the word: we have been deprived of everything; we have no property, no wealth, and our labour is of no use to us, since what it produces goes into the hands of others.

This 'Holiday' was to be the occasion 'for a CONGRESS of the working classes ... To reform society [and] to obtain for all at least expense to all, the largest sum of happiness for all'[73].

So, almost from its inception, the economic destabilization that was endemic to the idea of general strike was charged with the strongest possible emphasis on far-reaching, even revolutionary political and social reform. The notion of a national congress or convention was a long-established element in radical political thinking, rejecting the authority of an unrepresentative parliament for an alternative which the whole people would elect. It was a recurring theme during the Reform Crisis and a radical National Convention did meet in Manchester in December 1831, the month before Benbow issued his pamphlet. The Huddersfield Political Union called for 'great and simultaneous meetings' on the 26th of that month to make it 'a grand National Holiday'. 'Every wheel and every wheel's connection shall rest from their labour, and that the whole population shall shout with an irresistible voice, and that the country shall reverberate the glorious sound — Liberty! .'[74] John Doherty was a key participant in the events of December 1831 in Manchester. While (like Benbow) not actually using the term, he too called for a general strike:

> Let a day be fixed upon: let that day be well-known and fixed — say one month or six months

---

72 F____. K____. S____., *Trades Triumphant or Unions' Jubilee! A Plan for the Consolidation of Popular Power, and Restoring to the People their Long Lost Rights*, (1834). For Benbow and the idea of general strike see Iorwerth J. Prothero, 'William Benbow and the concept of the "general strike"', *Past and Present*, 63, (1974) and *DLB* vol. 6. For radical and labour usage of 'jubilee' see Malcolm Chase, 'From millennium to anniversary: the concept of jubilee in late eighteenth- and nineteenth-century England', *Past and Present*, 129 (November, 1990).

73 William Benbow, *Grand National Holiday and Congress of the Productive Classes* (1832).

74 *Poor Man's Guardian*, 10 December 1831. Information about the idea of national convention can be found throughout the extensive secondary literature on radicalism, but the best starting point remains T. M. Parssinen, 'Association, Convention and Anti-Parliament in British Radical Politics, 1771-1848', *English Historical Review*, 88, (1973), pp. 504-33.

hence; and when it arrives, *let every Workman in the United Kingdom* REFUSE TO WORK ANOTHER STROKE *until his class are permitted to exercise their due share of influence in the affairs of their country and the same justice is meeted out to them which has hitherto been dispensed to others.*[75]

Visiting London the following month Doherty urged the tactic of simultaneous meetings at gatherings of the NUWC. Place somewhat tartly observed that Doherty, 'one of the most malignant men I ever knew ... associated himself with a congenial spirit, William Benbow, and these two ran in couples'.[76] By April 1834, if not earlier, Doherty was explicitly using the term 'general strike'[77] and it soon entered into common parlance.

The spectre of general strike was all the more disturbing because of the scale of contemporary industrial unrest that outstripped all precedent. Among London labour disputes between 1790 and 1870, the year 1834 ranks third highest, with only the strike waves of 1853 and 1865 exceeding it.[78] Even the briefest analysis of the years 1833-4 has to take into account this unrest, the chronological context for which was a number of high profile disputes in the preceding four years. Taking just the major disputes in Lancashire, for example, these included in 1829 a six-month strike by 10,000 spinners and power-loom weavers in Stockport, a combined strike and lock-out of Manchester spinners and a particularly bitter dispute in Rochdale which began when the flannel weavers' union forcibly removed shuttles from mills paying below its list prices. Troops were brought in from Manchester, more than twenty arrests were made by police and there were at least six fatalities as troops fired on the crowd during an abortive attempt to rescue the prisoners. Thirteen men were eventually gaoled and one transported.[79] During 1830 there were further wide-scale strikes by a variety of trades in Ashton (spinners, hatters); Manchester and its environs (mechanics, spinners, fustian cutters, brickmakers), Oldham (sawyers, tailors) and a substantial and successful strike across the whole Lancashire coalfield, leading into the following year. Labour relations were further embittered by a benchmark legal judgement in a connecting case brought against a miners' activist (*R v Bykerdyke* 1832) in which the common law offence of conspiracy was applied to workers threatening to leave employment if other workers were not discharged.[80]

We have already considered the events at Merthyr in 1831, the same year in which there was high-profile turn-out by engineers at Bolton.[81] The greatest industrial dispute of 1831, however, was a nine-month strike by textile workers in Leeds, commencing at Gotts' mills. This secured wage rises, principally because strikers were supported by fellow members of the Leeds Clothiers' Union working at other premises. The Union then turned its attention to other mills. 'In the first eight months of 1832, each firm was picked out individually and none chose to fight a battle which Gott had lost'.[82] Huddersfield members of the same union were similarly successful.[83] The year closed

---

75 *Voice of the West Riding*, 17 September 1831.
76 Iorwerth J. Prothero, 'William Benbow', p. 152.
77 R. G. Kirby and A. E. Musson, *The Voice of the People*, p. 290.
78 David R. Green, 'Lines of conflict: labour disputes in London, 1790-1870', *International Review of Social History*, 43/2, (1998), pp. 213-14.
79 Robert Sykes, 'Popular politics', p. 254.
80 J. V. Orth, *Combination and Conspiracy: A Legal History of Trade Unionism, 1721-1906* (1991), pp. 92-5.
81 E. W. Daniels, 'A "turn-out" of Bolton machine-makers in 1831', *Economic History*, 1, (1926-9).
82 R. J. Morris, 'The rise of James Kitson: trades union and mechanics' institution, Leeds, 1826-51', *Thoresby Miscellany*, 15, (1973), p. 189.
83 Alan J. Brooke, 'Labour disputes and trade unions in the industrial revolution', in E. A. H. Haigh (ed.), *Huddersfield a Most Handsome Town: Aspects of the History and Culture of a West Yorkshire Town* (1992), p. 226.

with a massive strike across the north-east coalfield.[84]

Hamish Fraser comments that 1832-4 constituted 'two years of quite unprecedented industrial activity' in Scotland.[85] In London and the provinces disputes, involving workers in the building trades, were assuming increasing prominence from 1832.[86] By 1833 Lancashire employers were responding with 'the document' with the aim of suppressing the Operative Builders' Union. As many as a thousand Bolton weavers struck successfully to prevent wage reductions, but their union foundered when attempts were made to spread an agitation for Bolton prices throughout north Lancashire.[87] There were further disputes in the Leeds textile industry, including a lock-out of all trade unionists by master dyers who all entered into a bond for £500 to be forfeit by any one of them employing unionists in the future.[88] This tactic was successfully followed by mill owners the following year. In Leicester, a strike at a worsted-spinning factory against the dismissal of female workers became a test of the strength of the Leicestershire Union. Employers combined to enforce the document and lock-outs engulfed almost all sections of the local textiles workforce.[89] Leicestershire unionists complained that the Derby turn-out had diverted attention from their cause. Important though it was, not least in its contribution to the downfall of the GNCTU, the Derby spinners' strike should not be allowed to eclipse the general extent of industrial unrest in 1834. There were general turn-outs in Manchester by shoemakers and tailors; by tailors in Bolton (lasting twenty-three weeks and breaking the union);[90] by the joiners' society in Preston; and in Rochdale by ironmoulders. The hatters', coopers', tailors' and builders' strikes in London have been well documented.[91] There were extensive strikes in the Glasgow building and furniture trades; in both Todmorden and Salford successful strikes by mechanics to reduce hours and in Leamington the first documented industrial dispute in the town's history as the builders' union sought to enforce closed shops in local firms.[92] The Oldham 'general strike' of April 1834 is among the best-studied of industrial disputes,[93] but there were also unsuccessful actions by ironmoulders, hatters and sawyers. In Leeds the Clothiers' Union dissolved following further disputes and the application of the document by employers. The year ended with a successful general strike in the Potteries to enforce its list by the newly founded potters' union.[94]

Attitudes and Mentalities

The ideology of the early trade unions was emphatically gendered. A recurrent theme in earlier chapters has been union resistance to the dilution of skill, and the power it conferred, by regulating admission to their trade. The construction of notions of skill was intimately bound up with the definition of masculinity, honour and respectability; with the male breadwinner ideal; and the notion

---

84 Robert Colls, *The Pitmen of the Northern Coalfield: Work, Culture and Protest, 1790-1850* (1987), pp. 88-93, 248-56.
85 W. H. Fraser, *Conflict and Class*, p. 140.
86 J. R. Sanders, 'Working-class movements in the West Riding textile district', pp. 90-3; A. J. Peacock, *Bradford Chartism, 1838-1840* (1969), p. 8; R. W. Postgate, *The Builders' History* (1923); Iorwerth J. Prothero, *Artisans and Politics*, pp. 301-2.
87 Robert Sykes, 'Popular politics', p. 238.
88 R. J. Morris, 'The rise of James Kitson:', p. 190.
89 A. Temple Patterson, *Radical Leicester*, pp. 284-8.
90 Robert Sykes, 'Popular politics', p. 304.
91 Iorwerth J. Prothero, *Artisans and Politics*, pp. 302-6; T. M. Parssinen and I. J. Prothero, 'The London tailors' strike of 1834'.
92 T. H. Lloyd, 'Chartism in Warwick and Leamington', *Warwickshire History*, 4/1 (Summer, 1978), pp. 2-3.
93 John Foster, *Class Struggle*, pp. 110-14; R. G. Kirby and A. E. Musson, *The Voice of the People*, pp. 291-4; Robert Sykes, 'Popular politics'.
94 Harold Owen, The Staffordshire Potter; (1901), pp. 24-6.

of the workplace as masculine space. Though Doherty's spinners did concede that women might form a separate union of their own, they excluded women from membership as part of their strategy to control the labour supply.[95] Even where masculine control of a trade was no longer a norm, the ideals upon which it was based continued powerfully to inform male thinking. The introduction of power-spinning, for example, substantially reduced the skill level and strength required in the process. In theory this could have permitted wide-scale female participation in mule spinning. In practice the strength of trade union organization, and a claim that women were by temperament unable to discipline subordinate workers, allowed male spinners substantial control of the sector.[96]

The extent to which these attitudes remained ingrained even among Owenite working men is evident in the differential allowance made to male and female producers by the National Equitable Labour Exchange.[97] The distaste of skilled workmen for competition from female labour and the very real experience of declining wages in the face of the feminization of certain trades, made women's unionisation a delicate issue within the GNCTU. The comprehensive nature of the Union and a commitment, influenced by Owenism, to diminishing inequality between the sexes, opened it up to large-scale female membership. Female participation in co-operative production and exchange was already well established by the time Owenite socialism moved into its trade unionist phase. The GNCTU called for the formation of 'lodges of industrious females' wherever practicable. Those that were formed included female glovers, lacemakers, straw hatmakers, shoebinders, stockingers, glass-cutters, cotton spinners, laundresses, milliners and tailoresses. There was a lively women's page in the trade unionist *Pioneer* and a strong editorial line in favour of women's participation there and in the movement's other main paper, *Crisis*.

On the other hand, the majority of the GNCTU's affiliates remained not just male trade societies but organizations whose rationale hinged on their being masculine domains. With very few exceptions, women became involved in the GNCTU through female-only societies. Even where men and women worked alongside each other in the same occupation, the tendency was still to separate union lodges. Many female lodges may have been pre-existing women's friendly societies. This would explain the prodigious growth in female participation from what was otherwise a very low organizational baseline. This would logically parallel the development of men's trade unions which, as we have seen, was integrally linked to box clubs and benefit societies. The mobilization of female friendly societies would also have been consistent with the GNCTU's origins in calls for a single 'grand moral union' that would include all mutualist associations.

The gender division within the GNCTU might not in itself have been a problem had there not also been considerable hostility within the movement to the idea of women's unionism and to their participation in 'male' trades at all. 'There is a great number of men that cannot bear the idea of a women's union, and yet they are unionists themselves', wrote an 'initiated weaver's wife' to the *Pioneer*.[98] Some men resented an activity that took wives away from family responsibilities. 'Men's business, in a general way, is done away from home; but "wive's and matrons'" business is at home', wrote one tailor, 'and, in my opinion, none but lazy, gossiping, drunken wives will wish to go to meetings'.[99] But a perceived need to defend the frontier of skill against female intrusion was no less important. Barbara Taylor has skilfully explored this theme with particular reference to the tailors,

---

95 Anna Clark, *The Struggle for the Breeches: Gender and the Making of the British Working Class* (1995), p. 209.
96 William Lazonick, 'Industrial relations and technical change: the case of the self-acting mule', *Cambridge Journal of Economics*, 3, (1979).
97 Barbara Taylor, *Eve and the New Jerusalem: Socialism and Feminism in the Nineteenth Century* (1983), p. 97.
98 *Pioneer*, 15 March 1834.
99 *Pioneer*, 29 March 1834.

demonstrating that the 1834 London strike was substantially about the introduction of female labour. 'Have not women been unfairly driven from their proper sphere in the social scale, unfeelingly torn from the maternal duties of a parent, and unjustly encouraged to compete with men in ruining the money value of labour?' asked the Operative Tailors' secretary.[100] Attitudes soured further when the large merchant employers introduced female workers to break the strike. Even the *Crisis* felt ambiguous about this. 'The masters seem determined to feminize the whole trade, rather than yield' it commented, adding sarcastically 'we have no doubt that a female tailor would succeed gloriously, more especially if she did not entrust the measuring department to the masculine gender'.[101] On the streets masculine humour was heavier-handed: Anna Clark cites the testimony of an eighteen year-old Manchester tailoress at this time: the tailors, 'pointed out to her all the unfortunate girls on the street, and said that when they [the turn-outs] went to work she would have to go on the town for a living. They said if they ever caught her in the dark they would squeeze her.'[102]

Flawed though it was, the accord between skilled male trade unionists and female workers reached under the aegis of the GNCTU would not be equalled again in the nineteenth century. It fell away quickly, though it informed attitudes in early Chartism about the nature of female participation in political activity. Another aspect of the general unionist movement of these years, scarcely less notable (or ephemeral) than its partial feminization, was the culture of the trade unionist funeral: 'a proof of the growing intelligence and morality of the people, and an ominous warning to our relentless law-givers'.[103]

> The members of the different lodges, headed by their respective officers, walked in procession, the secretary first with the Bible open on black velvet cushion, supported by two other district officers with scarves and hatbands, and rosettes on their left breasts, followed by eighty-five presidents and vice-presidents, having on surplices as white as snow. Then upwards of one-hundred females dressed in white, with hoods, black scarfs, and bands; next came the members of the different lodges, both of town and country, headed by the wardens, having on black gowns, and the treasurers with their dispensations. The whole of the members had a rosette of black and white ribbon on their left breasts.[104]

The funeral of 'poor Daniel Law, a Unionist of Leicester' on 17 February 1834 was extraordinary by almost any standards except that of the trade union movement of which he had been a member. Lavish funerals, trades' union-directed and dominated, with mass attendances (Law's was estimated at 2,000) were almost commonplace in 1833-5.

Most trade societies made, and always had made, some form of provision for the death of a member even if it was simply a contribution towards the cost of burial. Burial societies were the most basic, and as far as can be judged ubiquitous, form of friendly societies. Guilds had always observed members' deaths, even perhaps with greater ostentation in the eighteenth century than at any time since the Reformation. Trade societies were highly conscious of this inheritance. When the Bolton ironmoulders formed a society in 1809, the precedent on which they drew was clear. It was

> an ancient and most laudable custom for divers Artists, within the United Kingdom, to meet and

---

100 Barbara Taylor, *Eve and the New Jerusalem*, p. 110.
101 *Crisis*, 17 May 1834.
102 Anna Clark, *The Struggle for the Breeches*, p. 201.
103 *Pioneer*, 5 April 1834.
104 *Pioneer*, 1 March 1834.

form themselves into Societies, for the sole purpose of assisting each other in case of Sickness, Old Age, and other infirmaties, and for the Burial of the Dead.[105]

Their purpose, of course, had more mundane and immediate relevance than simply the observation of tradition. Even before the hated Poor Law Amendment Act of 1834, a fear of going to a pauper's grave was endemic to plebeian culture. Even if attendance at organized acts of worship was declining, early nineteenth-century Britain remained a profoundly religious society and it was of course one in which death was all too familiar.

So the involvement of trade societies in the funeral arrangements of deceased members was natural and even necessary. It was one reason for joining such a society in the first place. Ruth Richardson has speculated that the nature of trade union funeral observance was influenced by the 1832 Anatomy Act[106] (a deeply unpopular measure which made available for medical dissection the corpses of those who died alone in the workhouse). The Act certainly focused more sharply the way in which working people regarded death. However, a more specific stimulus was Owenism's 'religion of brotherliness'.[107] Even here, Owenite influence took the form more of drawing out existing strands of workers' experience and practice, rather than proposing new forms. Funerals of members of the larger affiliated orders of friendly societies were already often lavish. Even more than these, however, the trade union funeral was a profoundly political statement. Like rituals of initiation it emphasized that death was the ultimate leveller whilst, at the same time, affording to the departed a degree of dignity and ceremony that would not have been out of keeping at a funeral of the highest social rank.

These funerals were also unimpeachable in their respectable appearance and good order, no mean consideration in what were uncertain times for trade unionism. Furthermore, they were also promoted as a forceful argument in favour of enrolment. 'If this be union I will be made a member next Saturday night', was allegedly the reaction of many who witnessed the Barnsley Linen Operatives' Union obsequies for a deceased brother, 'and some that had got the name of being black did promise to become white'.[108] 'Our correspondent from Tunbridge informs us', James Morrison wrote, following a Kent funeral, 'that before the procession they only initiated about four or five members a-week; but since the procession they have initiated in two nights twenty-two, and expect a dozen or fifteen more next week'. Men 'very naturally enquire', the Tunbridge trade unionist had added, 'what new system of union is this, in which so many different trades can unite in such love and friendship towards each other, not only through life, but even to the grave?'[109]

The practice of formal trade union attendance at members' funerals endured long into the twentieth century in some communities. However, the ceremonies described here were products of a very specific moment. General unionism was imbued with a breadth and ambition that surpassed any previous radical or labour movement. Amidst almost millenarian aspirations, it momentarily seemed poised on the brink of realizing its ambitions: these funerals can be seen as symbolizing these transformative aspirations. They routinely involved not only the trade society of the deceased but all those trades with which it was in union. The results were public celebrations of identity, 'theatrical

---

105 Quoted in H. J. Fyrth and Henry Collins, *The Foundry Workers: a Trade Union History* (1959), p. 16.
106 Ruth Richardson, *Death, Dissection and the Destitute* (1987), p. 275.
107 For which see E. J. Yeo, 'Robert Owen and radical culture' in Sidney Pollard and John Salt, *Robert Owen, Prophet of the Poor: Essays in Honour of the Two Hundredth Anniversary of his Birth* (1971).
108 *Pioneer*, 29 March 1834.
109 *Pioneer*, 1 March 1834

events which dramatized social bonds transcending place and craft'.[110]

TOLPUDDLE

Led by George Loveless, six farm workers from the Dorset village of Tolpuddle established a Friendly Society of Agricultural Labourers in October 1833. Even early histories, apt both to patronize the labourers by ascribing to them the very simplest of motives and to emphasize their isolation, could not ignore Loveless's own account that his body had been founded with the assistance of 'two delegates from a Trade Society'. Extensive Home Office enquiries failed to establish who they were. The Tolpuddle Society's role within the GNCTU was as the projected local hub ('grand lodge') for the unionisation of south Dorset farmworkers.[111] However, its formation pre-dated by some weeks that of the Consolidated Trades' Union, though it is commonly assumed that the two delegates were from the GNCTU.[112] Tolpuddle's place within a wider unionist network deserves teasing out.

Visits by tramping trade unionists in Tolpuddle were doubtless a useful stimulus to the formation of a trade society (Tolpuddle lies on the main highway into Dorchester from the east, and just off the Salisbury road to the north). As we saw in Chapter 3, trade unionist activity in agricultural districts had been an occasional feature of rural life since the 1790s (also the decade in which nuclei of political radicals began to appear in country towns in the rural South). By the early 1830s political life in many of the towns and larger villages of the rural South approached that of smaller manufacturing centres in the Midlands and North. The lord lieutenant of Sussex claimed the countryside 'swarms with tramps and travellers who converse with the Cottagers & their wives & always speaking of the Revolution'.[113] In north Hampshire in the autumn of 1832 several political clubs existed, their rules modelled on those of the NUWC which, as we have seen, combined trade unionist with overtly political objectives.[114] There had been disturbances in Dorset during the Reform Crisis and the area around Tolpuddle had figured in Captain Swing, with a member of the Loveless family among those arrested. The diffusion of Swing incidents was often linked to clusters of rural political radicals and, as Wells argues, 'Unionist mentalities were central to Swing'.[115] George Loveless traced his interest in trade union affairs to 'the years 1831-2, when there was a general movement of the working classes for an increase in wages' and he was appointed a labourers' delegate to local magistrates' arbitration of a long-running pay dispute in his parish, in which his brother James was also involved.[116] Another brother, John, was a member of a unionised trade, the flax dressers, in Bridport: when George Loveless was arrested in 1834 he was found to possess a printed address, 'To the Flax and Hemp Trade of Great Britain', dated Leeds, 30 November 1832, which among other things referred to the Leeds Clothiers' Union. This was one of several circulating in the West Country, for a further copy was sent to a village near Yeovil, Somerset, in July 1833,

---

110 Thomas Lacqueur, 'Bodies, death and pauper funerals', *Representations*, 1, (1983), p. 118.
111 See the 'General Laws of the Agricultural Union', *Pioneer*, 29 March 1834: 'the grand lodge shall be held at Toll-puddle'.
112 e.g. Sidney and Beatrice Webb, *The History of Trade Unionism*, p. 145.
113 Quoted in Roger A. E. Wells, 'The development of the English rural proletariat and social protest, 1700-1850', *Journal of Peasant Studies*, vol. 6, no. 2, (1979), p. 185.
114 Ian Dyck, *William Cobbett and Rural Popular Culture* (1992), pp. 192 and 268.
115 Roger A. E. Wells, 'Tolpuddle in the context of English agrarian labour history, 1780-1850', in John Rule (ed.), *British Trade Unionism, 1750-1850: The Formative Years* (1988). p. 118.
116 George Loveless, *The Victims of Whiggery; being a Statement of the Persecutions Experienced by the Dorchester Labourers...*, second edition, (1837), pp. 5-6.

bearing the endorsement of a trade unionist from the Yorkshire linen-weaving centre of Barnsley requesting the recipient to form a trade society and pass the notice on.[117] Little is known of a further brother, Robert, who lived in London, though George recollected receiving from him a letter in which he wrote that 'he thought the Society would be a good thing'.[118] George and James Loveless were not, therefore, political bumpkins.

Nor were they acting in isolation. In the general unionist movement of which the GNCTU was simply the final phase, the unionisation of agricultural labour was seen as a constituent part. For example, a fortnight or so before the Tolpuddle society was formed, a 'Friendly and Protective Agricultural Association' was established with its headquarters in Covent Garden, London. Its stated objects were 'to protect and support its members when sick, or out of employment, or under other contingencies of distress', principally by settling them and their families on the land. This in itself was not unusual: interest in land settlement schemes had paralleled the growth of trade organization. But this Association seems to have been established with a wider object in view. Its secretary, James Tucker, was a leading Owenite co-operator and later a Chartist.[119] In a letter enclosed with its rules to *Crisis*,[120] Tucker suggested that friendly societies withdraw their money from the funds and invest instead in land, thus denying revenue to the government. He then went on to call for a 'general union' of all such societies, electing delegates through a county structure to 'their own parliament... But, what would be an infinitely superior union than this ... is for each and all of those societies immediately to unite with the Trades' Unions'. Tucker saw Owen's proposal for grand moral union, put to the Co-operative Congress the previous week, as the ideal model for this purpose.

It is difficult to tell how far Tucker was articulating a wider vision of what rural trade unionism might be, but it is worth noting that when the Sussex 'United Brothers of Industry' was formed early in 1835 it had an alternative title. This 'Agricultural Labourers' Conjunction Union Friendly Society' was promoted in part as a replacement for paternalistic village friendly societies.[121] Nor was it the only 'Labourers' Conjunction Union'.[122] It seems probable, therefore, that the two delegates received by the Tolpuddle farm workers in October 1833 came either from the Friendly and Protective Agricultural Association or were promoting a movement close in spirit to that for which Tucker called. One thing is certain: they could not at that date have been acting as representatives of the GNCTU for this had yet to be formed. The week before Tucker's statement was published, *Pioneer* printed an open letter from 'Concord' to Lord Melbourne, the Home Secretary.[123] Its focus was the attempted suppression of the Leeds Clothiers' Union and the Operative Builders' Union through the masters' concerted use of 'the document'; but it predicted that farm workers might 'form a union', adding 'It is possible, my lord, in a very short time, by a combination among the agricultural labourers, to make the whole landed property of the country change hands'. This could be read as evidence of a covert and possibly highly politicized union movement in rural England: at the very least it confirms that the unionisation of farm workers was actively discussed in industrial trade unionist circles prior to the formation of the GNCTU.

Fleeting evidence of other farm workers' trade societies within the orbit of the general union

---

117 It is preserved in HO 40/31.
118 Joyce Marlow, *The Tolpuddle Martyrs* (1971), p. 42.
119 Malcolm Chase, *'The People's Farm'*, p. 173.
120 9 November 1833.
121 Andrew Charlesworth (ed.), *An Atlas of Rural Protest in Britain, 1549-1900* (1983).
122 e.g. *Pioneer*, 22 February 1834.
123 *Pioneer*, 2 November 1833.

movement strengthens this supposition: for example the United Brothers, already mentioned, or the 'First Lodge of Operative Agriculturalists' at Farnley Tyas, south of Huddersfield. The latter was likely to be the result of the Leeds Clothiers' Union rather than the GNCTU.[124] The *Poor Man's Guardian* drew attention to a 'ploughman's Union' in the Carse of Gowrie, between Perth and Dundee.[125] There had been farm servants' combinations here in the Regency years; in a coincidental parallel to Dorset, one of the Dundee trade unionists who helped the 1834 initiative was a flax dresser.[126] There is also patchy evidence for agricultural unionisation in the English Midlands. The April 1834 Quarter Sessions in Northampton was charged to be vigilant against rural unionism: 'there are persons going about the country under the name of Delegates from Trades' Unions, swearing in persons to join these unions. The evil has not found its way much into agricultural districts, but in some parts it has a little extended even among the agricultural labourers'.[127] However, Captain Swing's country was less diffident. There were reports of 'upwards of 150 agricultural labourers' collecting GNCTU rulebooks from Brighton in a single week in April 1834. Strikes by farm workers took place in Bedfordshire, Devon, Essex, Hertfordshire and Sussex. The formation of Dorset trades societies, in the plural, was noted by magistrates in January 1834. They swiftly became the subject of an extensive correspondence with the Home Office:

> Much encouragement has been given to these Societies by communications from Strangers who have passed thro' the Villages at different times, and who appear to have districts allotted to them, and one great object of these Strangers and of the leaders of the Society seems to be to instil into the minds of the Labourers that these meetings are not illegal and that the Justices have no authority to put a stop to them.[128]

Insofar as the law on combinations was concerned, this was a correct summary. Hence the selection of the Unlawful Oaths Act of 1797, passed in response to the Naval Mutinies earlier that year, as the means to suppress Dorsetshire trade unionism. The use of the Act for this purpose was by no means isolated: elsewhere in 1834 there were similar prosecutions in Belfast, Cambridge, Northampton, Oldham and Stafford. Prosecution of trade unionists under the Act had also been mooted in Leicester the previous October (it had been used in Glasgow as far back as 1818). The significance of the Tolpuddle prosecution, however, was that it was intended as a swift and effective strike against rural radicals apparently in correspondence with London, at a time when dissatisfaction with the government was mounting in both the capital's radical press and in rural centres. The government was fully aware from intelligence reports that the GNCTU was 'trying to get up a Union among the agricultural labourers' and that 'the subject of wages [is] only a subterfuge ... they have an ulterior object'. Home Secretary Melbourne therefore agreed to prosecution of the Tolpuddle farm workers 'for the sake of promptitude in bringing the offenders to justice, for the greater publicity of the proceedings, and for the most authoritative exposition of the law'.[129] Melbourne's handling of events in Merthyr three years before suggests he was particularly mindful of the potential threat of general trade unionism and of its overlap with radical and even revolutionary politics.

---

124 *Pioneer*, 29 March 1834.

125 *Poor Man's Guardian* 26 July 1834.

126 George Houston, 'Labour relations in Scottish agriculture before 1870', *Agricultural History Review*, 6, (1958).

127 R. W. Shorthouse, 'Justices of the Peace in Northamptonshire, 1830-45', *Northamptonshire Past and Present*, vol. 5, no. 3, (1975), p. 246.

128 Frampton to Melbourne, 5 March 1834, HO 52/24, reprinted in Arnold Walter Citrine et al., *The Book of the Martyrs of Tolpuddle, 1834-1934* (1934), p. 176.

129 Ball to Rowan, February 1834, HO 64/15; Phillips to Frampton, 6 March 1834, HO 52/24, reprinted in ibid, p. 177.

The successful prosecution of the Dorset labourers, and the draconian sentence of transportation for seven years that they received, had the desired effect in dampening the development of rural trade unionism. Agricultural trade unionism after Tolpuddle was inevitably far patchier, more clandestine and ephemeral than before, as the short histories of the United Brothers in Kent and Sussex in 1835[130] and Essex unions in 1836 demonstrate.[131] As the judge who sentenced the Tolpuddle labourers observed, 'the use of all punishment is not with a view to the particular offenders or for the sake of revenge — that is not the view of those who administer the law, nor the intention of the law itself; it is for the sake of example'.[132] That example was felt to be necessary because of the potent destabilizing nature of politically conscious farm worker trade unionism in the eyes of the rural establishment. The mood in the parlours of the home counties magistracy in the mid-1830s was similar to that which, during the previous period of incipient farm unionism of the late 1790s, had helped secure the general Combination Acts. The curate of the Essex parish of Wormingford, a centre of strikes and incendiarism before, during and after 1836, 'preached on "the evil tendency of Unions among the working class", arguing that rural unions must always be beaten because farmers would replace those joining them with Scots and Irishmen imported by steamer; the military would put down any serious unrest; and in any case the Bible taught submission'. Five Essex labourers, imprisoned for intimidating a blackleg, were reminded that 'the combination of labouring men who had no property to direct their masters in what way they are to employ their capital is a subversion of the principles of civilized society'.[133]

The impact of the Tolpuddle trial and verdicts was not restricted to rural labour alone. Urban workers saw it as blatant legal victimization, and assistance was forthcoming from all over the British Isles and from Ireland. The Tolpuddle case, however, was about more than solidarity. It posed two direct and immediate issues for trade unionists. The first was the continued viability of a culture of secrecy and oath-taking. The second concerned how the status of trade unionism itself was altered by the affair. This chapter concludes by looking at each of these in turn.

As we have seen in previous chapters, the roots of trade union ritualism lay deep: it was no superficial borrowing from masonic or friendly society sources, but rather a common legacy that continued to bind all three mutualist (and still sometimes overlapping) movements. Mutual-aid associations, even those within the remit of the Friendly Societies Act, were self-disciplining and self-auditing. The need to impress new members was practical as well as quasi-recreational: ritual was a form of cultural mortar that bound memberships together in shared sense of purpose, responsibility and obligation. For trade societies there were additional elements: work was important, skill defined status and rituals proclaimed it. There was also a need to re-enforce loyalty and solidarity that might be tested under the duress of strike action and employer hostility, as well as practical issues of financial security (necessary to an effective tramping system) and confidentiality.

Ritual was especially prominent in the GNCTU. The Union had a chaplain, the Revd Dr John Wade, vicar of Warwick, who attended major meetings 'dressed in full canonicals, and wore the red badge of a Doctor of Divinity, which corresponded with the Union ribbon'.[134] Supporters emphasized

---

130 Roger A. E. Wells, 'Tolpuddle in the context of English agrarian labour history, 1780-1850', pp. 124-5.
131 J. P. D. Dunbabin, *Rural Discontent in Nineteenth-Century Britain* (1974), pp. 70-1; Roger A. E. Wells, 'Rural rebels in southern England in the 1830s', in Clive Emsley and James Walvin, *Artisans, Peasants and Proletarians, 1760-1860* (1985), pp. 143-5; A. F. J. Brown, *Meagre Harvest: The Essex Farm Workers' Struggle Against Poverty 1750-1914* (1990), pp. 13-14.
132 *The Times*, 21 March 1834.
133 A. F. J. Brown, *Meagre Harvest*, p. 13.
134 *Pioneer*, 26 April 1834.

the 'moral dignity' his presence brought to Union proceedings. But business at 'grassroots' level also sought moral dignity and this was a potential hostage to fortune. Contemporary society regarded organized religion in its many forms with great seriousness; equally it looked on heterodoxy with much suspicion. As James Obelkevich, in a perceptive analysis of popular belief at this time, observes: 'the disjuncture between Christianity and popular religion was at the same time a social and cultural one between the elite and the poor. Christianity, a "higher" religion, was closely linked with the higher ranks in society, while its place in the life of the poor was tenuous and problematical.'[135] So when, from the widely reported trial proceedings, polite readers learnt of George Loveless having commissioned a life-sized painting of a skeleton and of its use in an admission ceremony along with blindfolds, Bible readings and the wearing of surplices by the lodge's officers, they doubtless experienced a certain frisson of dread. The ceremony cannot be explained away as the product of the overheated minds of rural methodists. Woolcombers' rites of initiation were long-established and very similar to the procedure adopted in Tolpuddle, suggesting that links with Yorkshire trades unionism, glimpsed in the papers found on Loveless at his arrest, were more than coincidental.[136] Lodges within the Operative Society of Builders spent heavily on regalia, gilded axes and the like, as Raymond Postgate long ago recognized:

> For the unionists of 1833 the oaths and ritual were not things to laugh at. The law offered them no protection against thieving officials. Spies might at any time bring disaster upon any and every member of the lodge. No other protection against internal treachery could be devised but an oath, made as terrible as form and ritual could make it.[137]

Such rituals, however, were not merely a response to the legal situation of trade organization. The image of the human skeleton was integral to union ritual as much as anything because it symbolized human equality beyond the grave. The admission ceremony of the Operative Stonemasons' Society, for example, climaxed when the initiate removed his blindfold to be addressed by the president:

> Stranger, mark well this shadow which now you see:
> 'Tis a faithful emblem of man's destiny.
> Behold this head once filled with pregnant wit;
> These hollow holes once sparkling eyes did fit.
> This empty mouth no tongue or lips contains,
> Of a once well-furnished head see all that now remains,
> Behold this breast where a generous heart once moved;
> Mark well these bones; the flesh hath left its place,
> These arms could once a tender wife embrace;
> These legs in gay activity could roam;
> Alas, the spirit fled, and all is gone.
> O Death, O Death, thy spirit strikes us with dismay;
> 'Tis only the just spirit that has left its earthly clay
> Can set there at defiance, and in triumph say:
> The sting of death is sin, and we are sinners all;
> The heavy stroke of death must one day on us fall;

---

135 James Obelkevich, *Religion and Rural Society: South Lindsey 1825-1875* (1976), p. 262.
136 W. H. Oliver, 'Tolpuddle Martyrs and trade union oaths', *Labour History*, 10 (May, 1966).
137 R. W. Postgate, *The Builders' History*.

O death, where is thy sting, O grave, where is thy victory?[138]

'Workmen have sometimes been unable to recover their proper senses, and usual composure of mind for some weeks after admission', claimed — somewhat implausibly — the Lancashire factory commissioner Edward Tufnell.[139] Tufnell did more than anyone to expose trade union ritualism. But it was the repercussions of the Dorchester trial itself that was mainly responsible for the rapid process of secularization within trade unionism. More exactly the process was de-sacramental, for scriptural references and the invocation of God were generally retained in trade unionist ritual (as was a culture of secrecy). However, the use of the Bible diminished sharply. Candidates for admission to the Boilermakers, for example, who had once made 'a vow unto the Lord' were simply required to 'accord, attest and promise, on the principle of a man, and in accordance with the laws of my country'.[140] Friendly societies similarly reformed their ritual in response to Tolpuddle, though lecture books retained skull and crossed-bones ornament.[141] The Roman Catholic Church's attitude to trade unionism was also significantly influenced by Tolpuddle. The Church was already hostile to Ribbonism, a secretive Irish protest movement, sustained by oath-taking, which offered migrant workers from Ireland tramp relief through its British cells. The effect of the Dorchester labourers' case was to associate Ribbonism and trade unionism yet more closely in the minds of the Church authorities, which 'inevitably led to an intensification of the Church's attack against combinations of workmen'.[142]

The de-sacramental process was rapid, though swearing oaths certainly endured in the Scottish collieries with their close association with freemasonry. The consequences were of considerable symbolic importance in a society where religious issues assumed great magnitude. Tolpuddle, however, had wider repercussions still. The mood of trade unionism and of working people themselves was altered by the affair. It was seen as compelling evidence that trade organization faced a renewed threat from central government. 'There is an open and declared hostility evinced, by all who have a little wealth, against "Union of the Working Classes"', claimed the *Pioneer*.[143] As a consequence Tolpuddle called forth displays of trade union solidarity on a huge scale. There was a mass-petitioning movement, at the organization of which the trades were by now rather adept. The usual focus at each provincial centre was a public meeting to memorialise Parliament. That in Coventry, 'very numerously attended by the Members and friends of the Trades' Union' was typical

---

138 Ibid, pp. 64-6, reprinted a substantial part of this ceremony, the complete document of which is now in the University of Warwick Modern Records Centre (MS78/05/BR/16/1/1). The ritual and iconography of early trade unionism deserves further research, though see the useful sketches by W. H. Oliver, 'Tolpuddle Martyrs and trade union oaths', and Andy Durr, 'Ritual of association and the organizations of the common people', *Ars Quatuor Coronatorum* (*Transactions of the Quatuor Coronati Lodge, No. 2076, London*, 1987). Unfortunately the most comprehensive available study of British trade union iconography has never appeared in English: Christian Muller, *James Sharples und das Zertyfkat der Amalgamated Society of Engineers. Studien zur Bildkultur Britischer Gerwerkschahen*, Hamburg, 1978.

139 [Edward Carleton Tufnell], *Character, Object, and Effects of Trades' Unions; With Some Remarks on the Law concerning them* (1834), p. 66.

140 Order of Friendly Boiler Makers, 'Branch Ceremony' (1834) quoted in J. E. Mortimer, *History of the Boilermakers' Society: Volume 1, 1834-1906* (1973), p. 19; United Society of Boilermakers and Iron and Ship Builders, 'Initiatory Ceremony' (1852), quoted in Andy Durr, 'Ritual of association and the organizations of the common people', p. 102. David Vincent, *The Culture of Secrecy: Britain, 1832-1998* (1998), p. 59, suggests that 'oath-taking persisted well beyond the period of outright repression'. How far is unclear, underlining the point just made about the need for further research.

141 Edwin Crew, *Loyal Order of Ancient Shepherds Friendly Society: Centenary Souvenir*, (1926), Heywood, p. 109. Oddfellowship, see James Spry, *The History of Oddfellowship* (1867), pp. 36, 39, and 50.

142 J. H. Treble, 'The attitude of the Roman Catholic Church towards trade unionism in the north of England, 1833-42', *Northern History*, 5, (1970), p. 99.

143 *Pioneer*, 26 April 1834.

in its agreement that there was a 'manifest disposition to suppress the endeavours of the Working Classes to promote their interests, by peaceable and moral means, exhibited in the opposition to and persecution of Trades' Unionists'. In Manchester, the issue stimulated the formation of an inter-trades committee.[144] Bradford demonstrators heard that the issue 'was to all intents and purposes a trial of the strength of the working-classes, as well as their spirit'.[145] John Doherty addressed a Manchester meeting: 'the condition of these unfortunate men might be that of any individual here present, for they were all members of Trades' Unions — he had been so himself, and was proud of it, and that man who would not support his union, under whatever circumstances, was a traitor to the common cause of industry'.[146]

At Copenhagen Fields, London, the GNCTU organized a public meeting on 21 April 1834 which, given all that was at stake, was a remarkably peaceful occasion. William Benbow, prominent in the Tolpuddle Martyrs agitation, had recently reissued his *Grand National Holiday*. Calls for a general strike had been prominent in the radical press during the weeks leading up to the demonstration and the organizing committee had seriously considered calling a 'general holiday' on the same day.[147] Though it is unlikely it gathered the 400,000 demonstrators claimed for it, it did set a new standard in peaceful public protest. In the Pennine textile region, however, the case of the Dorsetshire labourers became entwined in a volatile local political situation. Yorkshire people, according to the *Poor Man's Guardian*, 'treated the Dorchester case *as personal to themselves ... a blow at the entire body of the working classes*',[148] Sykes[149] has argued that the Oldham general strike of 1834, far from being the result of concerted local organization as Foster[150] contends, can only be understood in the context of national issues, principally Tolpuddle. It began as a spontaneous protest against the 'Dorchester-style arrest' of two officials of the spinners' union. Police also found documents linked to oath-making at the lodge room. Early the following day (15 April) a crowd, chanting 'no more Dorchester', rescued the arrested men. It was at this point that a movement formed which widened first to attack a local mill and then to a general strike. Clearly, the Oldham general strike was not just about Tolpuddle, but it is noticeable that when strikers from the town visited Huddersfield four days later to address a 5,000-strong supportive rally, their main theme was a call for a national stoppage until the Dorset labourers were brought home.[151]

Several prominent Chartists, among them the charismatic Peter Bussey, a clothiers' union leader in Bradford, cut their political teeth on the Dorchester campaign. Feargus O'Connor's links with Yorkshire began with his appearance on the platform of a Tolpuddle rally at Huddersfield in July 1835. He subsequently made the campaign to pardon the martyrs a central subject of his first northern tour later that year.[152]

The Tolpuddle affair was one of the hinges on which nineteenth-century labour history turned. The pardon granted to the Tolpuddle Martyrs in 1836 affirmed the potential effectiveness of extra-

---

144 Robert Sykes, 'Popular politics', p. 155.
145 *Leeds Times*, quoted in J. R. Sanders, 'Working-class movements in the West Riding textile district', p. 410.
146 R. G. Kirby and A. E. Musson, *The Voice of the People*, p 290.
147 Iorwerth J. Prothero, *Artisans and Politics*, p. 170.
148 *Poor Man's Guardian*, 11 July 1835.
149 Robert Sykes, 'Trade unionism and class consciousness', p. 190.
150 John Foster, *Class Struggle*.
151 Alan J. Brooke, 'Labour disputes and trade unions in the industrial revolution', p. 229.
152 J. R. Sanders, 'Working-class movements in the West Riding textile district', pp. 481-2; cf. James Epstein, *The Lion of Freedom: Feargus O'Connor and the Chartist Movement, 1832-42* (1982), p. 18.

parliamentary agitation. On the other hand it was only a pardon and not an overturning of the verdict against them. The essential problem of the legal vulnerability of trade organization remained.

6

Trade Unionism and the Early Chartist Movement

Introduction

Chartism is one of the most intensively researched episodes in modern English history.[1] It continues to capture the imagination of historians at the level of detailed monographs and general interpretative treatments alike. All agree that there was much more to this movement for parliamentary reform than the six points of the People's Charter, issued by the London Working Men's Association in May 1838. So great was its motivational force and so imaginative the popular response to it, that Chartism was the structure within which for a time the majority of industrial workers pursued their political and even cultural activities. This was particularly the case in the years 1839-42. The new-born child of Chartist parents might be received into the movement at a special ceremony presided over by one of its leaders, and possibly given his name. Subsequently they might attend a Chartist Sunday School or have a subscription to the Chartist Land Plan taken out on their behalf. Meanwhile the parents would be immersed in the political and social life of the local branch of the National Charter Association, maybe the father also in one of its trade localities and the mother in a Female Charter Association. They might shop at a Chartist joint stock provision (i.e. co-operative) store. If a ratepayer, the father might be able to support Chartist candidates in local elections; if teetotal, the family could enlist in a Chartist Temperance Association. Prints of Chartist leaders would adorn the home and spare pence subscribed to support Chartist prisoners and their families. The family's main source of national news would be a Chartist weekly paper, usually the *Northern Star*. Male Chartists might join a clandestine group for arms drill. And men and women would participate in the great nocturnal mass meetings, such as these in south Lancashire, described by the Chartist Robert Gammage:

> At the whole of them the working people met in their thousands and tens of thousands to swear devotion to the common cause. It is almost impossible to imagine the excitement caused by these manifestations. To form an adequate idea of the public feeling, it was necessary to be an eye witness of the proceedings. The people did not go singly to the place of meeting, but met in body at a starting point, from whence, at a given time, they issued in huge numbers, formed into procession, traversing the principal streets, making the heavens echo with the thunder of their

---

1 See the two complementary bibliographies of the movement: J. F. C. Harrison and Dorothy Thompson, *Bibliography of the Chartist Movement, 1837-76* (1978), and Owen Ashton, Robert Fyson and Stephen Roberts, *The Chartist Movement: A New Annotated Bibliography* (1995); also Miles Taylor, 'Rethinking the Chartists: searching for synthesis in the historiography of chartism', *Historical Journal* 39 (2), (1996), pp. 479-95. Edward Royle, *Chartism*, 3rd edition (1998), is an excellent short introduction.

> cheers on recognizing the idols of their worship in the men who were to address them, and sending forth vollies of the most hideous groans on passing the office of some hostile newspaper, or the house of some obnoxious magistrate or employer. The banners containing the more formidable devices, viewed by the red light of the glaring torches, presented a scene of awful grandeur. The death's heads represented on some of them grinned like ghostly spectres, and served to remind many a mammon worshipper of his expected doom. The uncouth appearance of thousands of artizans who had not time from leaving the factory to go home and attend to the ordinary duties of cleanliness, and whose faces were therefore begrimed with sweat and din, added to the strange aspect of the scene. The processions were frequently of immense length, sometimes containing as many as fifty thousand people; and along the whole line there blazed a stream of light, illuminating the lofty sky, like the reflection from a large city in a general conflagration.[2]

As the reference to 'the idols of their worship' suggests, not all Chartists were entirely comfortable with the platform oratory that was central to the movement. And of course there were many who were opposed to Chartism or (one suspects rather fewer) indifferent to it. Few Britons at this time, however, were not touched by Chartism and it is inconceivable that there were any who never had heard of it. The largest of the three Chartist petitions to Parliament, submitted in 1842, marshalled 3,317,712 signatures (by way of contrast the Reform Act of 1832 had created a combined British and Irish electorate of approximately 813,000). Of course not all those signatories were immersed as deeply in Chartism as the hypothetical case described above: but support for the Charter was close to the norm among working men. In the words of one London tin-plate worker, 'although I am not a Chartist by enrolment, I am one from conviction; and there are very few working men who are not Chartists in that sense of the word'. 'I had always been a Chartist' recollected a West Riding workman, 'since I knew what politics meant'.[3]

The relationship of trade unionism to this multi-faceted phenomenon has long been an issue of some controversy. It cannot be assumed that all trade unionists were Chartists and it is certainly not the case that all Chartists were union members. 'There is no reason to believe', claimed the Webbs, 'that the Trade Unions at any time became part and parcel of the Movement, as they had, during 1833-4, of the Owenite agitation',[4] a view largely supported by A. E. Musson.[5] E. P. Thompson[6] argued that working-class consciousness emerged by the early 1830s as a direct consequence of converging organization both within and outwith the workplace. Early critics of Thompson argued that there was little credible evidence for such a convergence, an approach dubbed 'compartmentalist' by Donnelly.[7] Thompson's path-breaking work stopped short of Chartism but others have defended the ground covered in *The Making of the English Working Class* and extended it, notably Behagg, Goodway, Prothero and Sykes.[8] All four have presented meticulously documented cases that

---

2   R. G. Gammage, *History of the Chartist Movement, 1837-54* (1969, first published 1854-5), pp. 94-5.

3   *Northern Star*, 22 April 1848; Joseph Lawson, *Letters to the Young on Progress in Pudsey during the Last Sixty Years* (1887), p. 132.

4   Sidney and Beatrice Webb, *The History of Trade Unionism*, revised edition (1920), p. 175.

5   A. E. Musson, *British Trade Unions, 1800-1875* (1972).

6   E. P. Thompson, *The Making of the English Working Class* (1968).

7   F. K. Donnelly, 'Ideology and early English working-class history: Edward Thompson and his critics', *Social History*, 2, (1976).

8   Clive Behagg, *Politics and Production in the Early Nineteenth Century* (1990); David Goodway, *London Chartism, 1838-48* (1982); Iorwerth J. Prothero, *Artisans and Politics in Early Nineteenth-Century London: John Gast and His Times* (1979); Robert Sykes, 'Early Chartism and trade unionism in south-east Lancashire', in James Epstein and Dorothy Thompson (eds.), *The Chartist Experience: Studies in Working-Class Radicalism and Culture, 1830-60* (1982).

Chartism and 'the trades' did substantially intersect at the levels both of key personnel and formal organization. Simultaneously, however, another argument has emerged[9] stressing the extent to which industrial workplaces were sites of important compromises between skilled workers and their employers, compromises which undermined labour's appetite for political militancy at the time, just as they are held to undermine the concept of class consciousness now. This interpretation can be viewed as interlacing the influential thesis advanced by Stedman Jones[10] that Chartism, as a political ideology, offered little that was new. Pointing to linguistic and conceptual continuities between Chartism and pre-Chartist radicalism, Stedman Jones argues that because they sustained the traditional attack on 'Old Corruption', the Chartists offered only a limited critique of the causes and consequences of industrial capitalism. Once social and economic reforms were passed by an unreformed Parliament, as they were during Peel's ministry in the mid-1840s, the interconnection crucially stressed by Chartism between economic distress and political power began to unravel. With it unravelled the Chartist movement itself.

Criticism of Stedman Jones has drawn attention to the selectiveness of his documentation, his implicit reluctance to recognise the importance of class in explaining Chartism, and the continuing repressive capacities of the British state, much in evidence in its handling of the Chartist revival of 1848.[11] No one pretends that Chartism did not unravel, but the process was lengthier and more uneven than Stedman Jones implies. As an explanation for the failure of Chartism the argument he advances is at best partial (as would be an explanation that rested upon the repressive apparatus of the state alone). In a thoughtful analysis of the decline of Chartism, Dorothy Thompson comments how unsatisfactory explanations for its failure have been.[12] The upturn in the economy after 1848 was neither so sudden nor so extensive that social unrest was eliminated. Furthermore, though some workers came to share in the cultural and political ethos of the middle classes, they did so only partially and via a diverse and uncontrolled process. The incorporation of workers into the electorate was similarly prolonged and piecemeal.

Chartism was too ambitious to succeed. Its appeal hinged on the capacity claimed for it to change everything. Its comprehensive vision rested upon an appealingly simple (and for adherents ostensibly 'common sense') programme of parliamentary reform. As the prospect of reform appeared to recede rather than draw closer, many chose to explore local solutions to particular aspects of the economic and social issues that Chartism had aimed to resolve. This might include involvement in local government; the further development of 'self-help' — retail co-operation, friendly, assurance, land and building societies; and the further protection and cultivation of workers' autonomy at the workplace. The Chartist experience informed and shaped all these activities.

INTO CHARTISM

It would make a neat narrative to proceed from the agitation to pardon the Dorchester labourers, involving as it did several who would become leading Chartists, directly to Chartism. Indeed many accounts of the labour movement have done this. However, history, especially labour history, is

---

9 e.g. B. Elbaum *et al.*, 'The labour process, market structure and marxist theory', *Cambridge Journal of Economics*, vol. 3, no. 3, (1979); Patrick Joyce, 'Work', *The Cambridge Social History of Britain, 1750-1950*, vol. 2 (1990).

10 Gareth Stedman Jones, 'The language of Chartism', in James Epstein and Dorothy Thompson, (eds.), *The Chartist Experience*, and *Languages of Class: Studies in English Working-class History 1832-1982* (1983).

11 On which see especially see John Saville, *1848: the British State and the Chartist Movement* (1987).

12 Dorothy Thompson, *The Chartists: Popular Politics in the Industrial Revolution* (1984), p. 330.

rarely so neatly packaged and the events of the mid-1830s need some explication of their own. Several historians have made the deceptively simple point that the Webbs' inflation of the numbers involved in the GNCTU led them to exaggerate the subsequent decline in trade union activity. An upturn in trade in 1835-6 also provided good ground for an expansion in trade unionist activity. Some historians, notably Musson,[13] have viewed the general unionist movement of the early 1830s as a distraction from the central business of trade unionism. The resulting emphasis on continuities of mood and form has a certain appeal, particularly in a movement so historically rooted as trade unionism. However, we have also seen that the principal momentum behind general unionism was the federalization of already existing associations. Though the collapse of general unionism saw a marked diminution in the unionisation of female and of unskilled male workers, in other sectors of the economy its consequences were limited. Union organization among tailors and shoemakers, both crushed by unsuccessful strike action in 1834, fell away for example, but among other occupations it did not.

The most striking example of this was the potters. The Staffordshire centre of the industry had affiliated to neither the NAPL nor GNCTU, though Doherty and Owen had made close contact with the trade's activists in 1830-1 and 1833 respectively. The experience of trade union organization in the potteries had not been a happy one. The first attempt, in 1824-5, had also initiated a union-run pottery to absorb unemployed members; but both union and co-operative collapsed after an unsuccessful strike in 1826.[14] A small China and Earthenware Turners' Society did affiliate to the NAPL, but the main focus of the latter's activities in the area was in organizing meetings and subscriptions in support of strikes by the Ashton spinners and the Staffordshire miners. (The fact that the committee organizing this described itself as 'a committee of the Potters' Union' shows just how fluid contemporary understanding of the notions of Union and membership thereof could be.) There was a further unsuccessful attempt at producer co-operation in 1834. By this time a National Union of Operative Potters had been established a year, claiming 6,000 members in Staffordshire and 2,000 more in 'out-potteries' elsewhere. In 1834-5, the Union conducted a highly successful strike in Staffordshire to enforce its price list.[15] It then turned its attention to the out-pottery that most flagrantly paid below list prices, at Thornaby on Teesside. Here too it was successful, partly because of the resources it was prepared to deploy, especially strike pay, newspaper advertising and the energies of a full-time official, the Union's 'Grand Master'.[16] However, the Union's ambitions did not stop there. It seriously attempted to win control of the Poor Law Guardians in the Staffordshire pottery towns, a move which, had it been successful, would have enabled striking members of the Union to receive poor relief they were otherwise denied. Its central committee also made a conscious decision, rather than to split the Union, not to affiliate to the GNCTU. As Fyson stresses,[17] this should not obscure enthusiasm for the latter in Staffordshire. Four thousand signed a Tolpuddle petition in 1834 and it would appear that the Union began to organize other trades in rural Staffordshire. It was unaffected by the demise of the GNCTU and enjoyed the support of a continuing national trade-union network when, in 1836-7, it fought a 21-week strike against aspects of the annual binding of

---

13 A. E. Musson, *British Trade Unions, 1800-1875*, p. 29-35.
14 Harold Owen, *The Staffordshire Potter*, (1901), pp. 16-19.
15 Ibid, pp. 20-6.
16 Malcolm Chase, '"The labour depreciating system": the 1836 Thornaby turnout and its background', *North East Labour History Society Bulletin*, 23, (1989).
17 Robert Fyson, 'Unionism, class and community in the 1830s: aspects of the National Union of Operative Potters', in John Rule (ed.), *British Trade Unionism, 1750-1850: The Formative Years* (1988), pp. 207-8.

Staffordshire pottery workers.

In this, though, it was unsuccessful and the Union collapsed. Though brief, the history of the National Union of Operative Potters illustrates a number of significant aspects of trade unionism in the mid-1830s. First, and most obvious, was the continuation of inter-trade and cross-regional co-operation upon which both the NAPL and GNCTU had been built and which survived their demise. Second, was a greater openness towards women. A significant proportion of the potteries' workforce were women and, from its inception, the Union appears to have treated them on an equal footing with male members. In the 1836 strike at Thornaby, working conditions for female transferrers and painters were among the grievances specifically raised by the Union, even though apprenticeship and entry to the trade lay at the heart of the dispute. The Union had also sent a female official from Staffordshire to work at the pottery, specifically to organize women workers.[18] Third, the Union demonstrates how the physical reach of trade unionism was expanding. Rule[19] makes a similar point in an account of how the Operative Society of Stone Masons opened branches in a number of small Cornish towns between 1834 and 1840. The mid-1830s also saw prominent growth of union organization in engineering, with the first real interest in forming (as Bolton engineers expressed it in 1839) 'one concentrated union' for a trade that was divided between four national bodies and innumerable local societies. In Lancashire a United Trades' Association, comprising the 'five trades of mechanism, viz. Mechanics, Smiths, moulders, Engineers, and millwrights', was formed in 1840. It published a paper, the *Trades Journal*, aiming to 'improve Trades Unions generally'.[20] The key figure in the Association and editor of its paper was a Manchester smith, Alexander Hutchinson. He was a sceptical participant in the GNCTU but unequivocally committed to Chartism (an aspect of his career that the Webbs, if they were aware of it, chose not to mention).[21] Also in Lancashire, the Friendly Union of Mechanics amalgamated with the Yorkshire-based Mechanics' Friendly Union Institution in 1837. The resulting Journeymen Steam Engine and Machine Makers' and Millwrights' Friendly Society was a key force in the subsequent history of engineering trade organization. In London a joint committee of several engineering trade societies, supported by other trades, successfully conducted an eight-month strike during 1836 to shorten the working week to 60 hours and secure payment for overtime.

The ideas behind general unionism were far from defunct, as John Gast explained from the chair of a London meeting in support of the potters: 'he wanted to see, not merely isolated unions in the several trades, but a general union made up out of the whole… He would never be satisfied until he had seen that project realized; for then, and then only, should he feel assured of the complete emancipation of the working classes'.[22] Gast was prominent among those London trade unionists who unequivocally supported the Chartist movement. Chartism absorbed energies which had earlier been channelled into general unionism and, indeed, can arguably be seen as a form of general union itself: it had, in theory if not always in practice, a structure within which trade societies could be accommodated; and it was distinguished by similar ambitions to inclusiveness.

Beyond the unions, the great issue confronting workers in these years was the implementation of

---

18 Malcolm Chase, '"The labour depreciating system"', pp. 26-7.
19 John Rule, *The Labouring Classes in Early Industrial England 1750-1850* (1986), p. 318.
20 Sidney and Beatrice Webb, *The History of Trade Unionism*, pp. 207-8.
21 Ibid, pp. 207-8. A full appreciation of Hutchinson's career is much needed. See, however, Mick Jenkins, *The General Strike of 1842* (1980), esp. pp. 128-41, Paul Pickering, *Chartism and the Chartists in Manchester and Salford* (1995), *passim*, and John Charlton, *The Chartists: the First National Workers' Movement* (1997), pp. 27-8.
22 Quoted in Iorwerth J. Prothero, *Artisans and Politics*, p. 316.

the Poor Law Amendment Act passed by Parliament in 1834. It provides a good example of the manner in which trade unions might become involved, at the level of formal commitment, to agitations in the wider political sphere. The Barnsley Linen Weavers' Union, for example, provided the organizational framework and most of the leadership of the local anti-Poor Law campaign. The West Riding campaign reached its climax with a Whit Tuesday demonstration in 1837, in which participants marched behind the banner of their respective radical association, friendly society or trade union. The following year, the trades of Leeds, Newcastle and Manchester organized boycotts of Queen Victoria's coronation festivities, staging their own alternative processions to draw attention to the iniquities of state legislation. A handbill issued by 'the Officers and Members of the Trades Unions in Manchester and Salford' attacked Parliament for withholding 'the political rights and liberties of freeborn British subjects'.

> At the same time they call upon us to testify our allegiance to that very system of government which offers us no protection — which manifests no sympathy for the destitute poor of our country, but upon all occasions takes advantage of the power they possess to treat us as slaves, stigmatize us as combinators, and pursue us as criminals.[23]

Such rhetoric was identical to that of Chartism. The anti-Poor Law campaign, together with factory reform (another issue close to the heart of many trade unions), were the key constituents that enabled the Chartist movement to be built so quickly. Sykes[24] has suggested that the significance of the anti-Poor Law agitation has been exaggerated by historians at the expense of a proper understanding of the role of trade unionism, especially the campaign in support of the Glasgow spinners. The latter should be seen in the context of continuing cross-trade awareness in the mid-1830s, manifest both in continuing interest in the welfare of the Dorchester labourers following their pardon and in support for new causes such as striking fustian cutters in Manchester (1836), London and Edinburgh typefounders in 1837 (which led to the formation of the Central Association of London Trades) and, in the same year, for Lancashire building workers facing conspiracy charges. Below the level of these 'headline' disputes were innumerable local episodes, generally invisible to historians, in which trades assisted each other. The 1836-7 accounts of the Glasgow spinners' themselves, presented at their trial in 1838, reveal that they had contributed sums of £180 and £340 to cabinet-makers' and block-printers' societies respectively.[25]

The Glasgow spinners' action was itself rooted in the expansion of trades' activism in the region. Weavers' 'General Protecting Unions' were active in Paisley and Glasgow during the mid-1830s, even publishing a newspaper, the *Weavers' Journal* (1835-7). Against a background of wage reductions and widespread defensive strike action during the particularly hard winter of 1836-7, a standing committee of Glasgow trades' delegates had been formed. Among other issues it protested at the installation of Sir Robert Peel as Rector of the University, which ceremony had been the occasion for a loyal address from 'conservative operatives'. The trades' riposte was initiated by the recently formed Scottish Radical Association which had just organized Feargus O'Connor's first visit to the country.[26] This illustrates the close relationship between political and trade agitations in Glasgow, typical of the larger British cities. Since 1832 a weekly paper, the *Liberator*, had served both

---

23 Handbill in HO 40/3 8, fol. 59, quoted in John Knott, *Popular Opposition to the 1834 New Poor Law*, (1986), p. 2.
24 Robert Sykes, 'Early Chartism and trade unionism in south-east Lancashire', p. 156.
25 Leslie C. Wright, *Scottish Chartism* (1953), p. 223.
26 Alexander Wilson, *The Chartist Movement in Scotland* (1970), p. 35.

movements. In 1836 it assumed the title *New Liberator* continuing as the self-styled 'organ of the working classes' and now edited by the future Chartist leader John Taylor. When the Glasgow spinners were tried it emerged that their union had contributed £978 to the paper.[27]

The Glasgow spinners' case has tended to be underestimated in historical accounts. It was quickly swept up into Chartism and it lacks the poignancy of the Tolpuddle martyrs' cause while, problematically for subsequent historians, it centred on the use of violence for unionist ends. At the time, however, it was widely perceived by workers as a particularly worrying development in hostility to trade unionism. The complicity of employers and a politically motivated local establishment was no less obvious than in Dorset. Unlike Tolpuddle, however, the target this time was not a weak and relatively marginal group of workers but a well-organized union in a major manufacturing city. This union not only controlled entry to the trade but had recently secured a wage increase of 16 per cent, the first since 1827. If such an increase was to be sustained, however, wages at mills beyond Glasgow had to be brought into line and in October 1836 the union became involved in a sixteen-week dispute at a mill in Duntocher, midway between Glasgow and Dumbarton. Ultimately defeated, and having spent over £3,000 to support the strikers and their families, the union was in no position to offer effective resistance to the events that followed.

Unemployment had soared in the winter of 1836-7. At the same time changes in technology to larger spinning machines requiring more piecers (youths employed to piece together broken threads beneath the machinery and from whom spinners were largely recruited) was weakening the skilled operatives' control of entry to the trade. There is little doubt that a cartel of the city's major manufacturers elected for a trial of strength with the union. First, the wage increase of the previous year was removed without notice; then further reductions of almost one-third on 1827 rates were announced, together with changes in working practices and wage calculation associated with the new technology. There was no alternative for the Glasgow Operative Spinners' Association but to order an all-out strike, to resist both the wage reductions and the implications of technological change (it had previously spent £4,375 on assisted emigration, mostly in the form of £10 grants to members). Clydeside's mills were silent from April; but in May, and with snow still on the ground, strike-breaking labour was introduced. Almost inevitably, clashes with mass pickets (sometimes a thousand-strong) ensued. Financial aid was received from subscriptions across Britain, but the strikers' situation grew increasingly desperate and with it incidents of assault, discharging firearms and arson. A typical anonymous letter denounced one manager as a 'low tool or cringing sycophant of a greedy Tyranical [sic] Capitalist' opposed to spinners only 'engaged in the Protection of their labour, their only capital'.[28]

Yet negotiations for a settlement were already well-advanced when, in late July, eighteen members of the union's 'Guard Committee' were arrested and charged with 'illegal conspiracy to keep up wages by sending threatening letters, setting fire to mills, invading dwelling houses and assaulting and murdering workmen — or with Murder'.[29] The arrests had been triggered by the fatal shooting of an Irish strike-breaker the previous day. However, it was unclear how far, if at all, those arrested were connected to the acts of violence specified in the charge; neither was it obvious that the deceased had been the target of specifically union-instigated violence. Almost immediately, those

---

27 Leslie C. Wright, *Scottish Chartism*, p. 223.
28 Quoted in W. H. Fraser, *Conflict and Class: Scottish Workers, 1700-1838* (1988), p. 154.
29 Swinton, *Justiciary Cases, 1835-7*, (1838-42), pp. 530 and 550, quoted in Leslie C. Wright, *Scottish Chartism*, p. 30. This account of the dispute is based on Leslie C. Wright, *Scottish Chartism*, Alexander Wilson, *The Chartist Movement in Scotland*, and W. H. Fraser, *Conflict and Class*. See also W. H. Fraser, 'The Glasgow Cotton Spinners, 1837' in J. Butt and J.T. Ward (eds), *Scottish Themes* (1976), pp. 80-97.

committed for trial were whittled down to five: the four chief officers of the Association plus the alleged killer. The trial was directed by the local sheriff, Archibald Alison, a frequent antagonist of trade unionism during the previous decade.

At the trial, held in early 1838, it emerged that payments had been made to strikers 'to try to take out the new hands who were working at reduced rates', although this may have simply been enhanced strike payments for active pickets. Much was also made of the Association's previous encouragement of 'unshopping' non-unionists: though occasionally violent, the methods used differed hardly at all from long-established practices in workshops all over Britain. As the evidence relating to the murder charges looked more and more spurious, it was increasingly trade unionism that appeared to be on trial. Verdicts of not-proven were returned for all serious charges but the defendants were found guilty of conspiracy 'to keep up wages' and of instigating 'intimidation, molestation and threats'. The five were sentenced to seven years' transportation, the same sentence handed down at Dorchester and likewise out of proportion to the charges on which guilty verdicts had been returned. On the other hand, their acquiescence in the use of violent tactics in pursuit of Association interests made the transported unionists somewhat ambiguous figures. Hamish Fraser[30] has speculated that this was one factor that led to the distinctive character of Scottish Chartism, which (in comparison with England) was notably moderate in tone and opposed to the use of violence. Scottish trade unionism was 'effectively branded as a violent conspiracy ... It was an image that was to prove extremely difficult to shake off. For decades after 1838, Scottish unions were weak and failed to attract more than a small minority of workmen.'

Support for the Glasgow spinners, however, was by no means half-hearted. Public meetings were held in major towns throughout Britain; the largest of several parliamentary petitions for clemency totalled some 20,000 signatures; and the agitation in the south Lancashire textile district eclipsed both the anti-Poor Law and factory reform campaigns. Both prosecution and sentence were widely perceived as evidence of class-based hostility against workers and their institutions: 'We are all *guilty*', declared the Manchester stonemasons, 'of the *great crime* of uniting to protect our labour from the same class of assailants as those who prosecuted the Cotton Spinners and Dorchester Labourers'.[31] However, contemporaries, no less than posterity, applied the terminology of martyrdom to the Dorchester labourers but not to the Glasgow spinners. Trade unionists were acutely aware that once again they were subject to the most critical of scrutiny. In such circumstances support for the spinners from public platforms tended to be muted, O'Connor and the north-east Chartist leader Augustus Beaumont being important exceptions. Industrial workers themselves were less equivocal, as in this popular ballad from Newcastle upon Tyne:

> Ye working men of Britain come listen awhile,
> Concerning the cotton spinners who lately stood their trial
> Transported for seven years far, far awa'
> Because they were united men in Caledonia.
>
> When first we were arrested, and lodged in Glasgow gaol,
> They stripped us of our clothes, left us naked in our cell;
> No sympathy they showed us, not the least ava'

---

30 W. H. Fraser, *Conflict and Class*, p. 162.
31 *Operative Stonemasons' Fortnightly Return* 15 August 1839, quoted in Robert Sykes, 'Early Chartism and trade unionism in south-east Lancashire', pp. 176-7.

> Because we were united men in Caledonia.
>
> Success to our friends in Ireland, who boldly stood our cause,
> In spite of O'Connell and his support for whiggish laws,
> Away with his politics, they are not worth a straw
> He's no friend to the poor of Ireland or Caledonia.
>
> Success to O'Connor who did nobly plead our cause,
> Likewise to Mr Beaumont, who abhors oppressive laws,
> But after all their efforts, justice and law,
> We are banished from our country, sweet Caledonia.
>
> Whigs and tories are United, we see it very plain,
> To crush the poor labourer, it is their daily aim,
> The proverb now is verified, and that you all can knaw,
> In the case of those poor spinners in Caledonia.[32]

Sufficient uncertainty surrounded the safety of the verdicts that the Glasgow spinners were never transported. After two and a half years aboard a prison hulk in the Thames they were pardoned.

O'CONNELL AND THE 1838 SELECT COMMITTEE ON COMBINATIONS

The figure demonized by the anonymous author of 'The Cotton Spinners' Farewell' was Daniel O'Connell, whose attitude to trade unionism helped shape its relationship with Chartism. Daniel O'Connell's charismatic espousal of Roman Catholic emancipation and Irish home rule made him one of the great figures, not only of Irish but of British politics in the second quarter of the nineteenth century. O'Connell's attitude to organized labour was, however, decidedly cool. In 1833 he had drawn the teeth of the Dublin Trades' Political Union by engineering the domination of his middle-class supporters.[33] The organization had been founded by Dublin trade societies to demand the repeal of the Act of Union and to promote the interests of the working classes, the prevalent view among organized labour being that the Act had reversed the country's economic fortunes. Their perception of how a campaign for home rule should be managed, however, was not O'Connell's.

Furthermore, trade union and labour violence were a particularly disturbing feature of Dublin life in the years 1836-7, standing out sharply against the general background of political calm that O'Connell wished to exploit. Single-minded in pursuit of his objective, in May 1837 O'Connell abruptly reversed his support for radical factory reform. Of this he had long been a popular advocate, but he was prepared to set this aside to prolong the life of a government which he thought likely to favour Irish issues. Around the same time he also attacked the Glasgow spinners' strike, widening the assault in November to denounce unions as secret societies and castigate them for seeking to control entry to their trades, impose closed shops and inflate wages.[34] O'Connell made these moves partly as a firm believer in a free market economy, but also because not to criticize trade unionism at a time of unprecedented labour unrest might have compromised his standing with middle-class opinion on both

---

32 'The Cotton Spinners' Farewell' (1838), verses 1, 2, 4, 5 and 7, quoted in Roy Palmer, *A Ballad History of England* (1979), p. 115. Palmer points out that this ballad would have been sung to the tune of 'Jamie Raeburn', about an allegedly innocent man transported for theft.

33 Fergus D'Arcy, 'The artisans of Dublin and Daniel O'Connell, 1830-47: an unquiet liaison', *Irish Historical Studies*, vol. 17, no. 66 (September, 1970).

34 Ibid.

sides of the Irish Sea. Sectarian considerations influenced his later relations with the Dublin trades,[35] but at this point it was primarily the issue of violence which coloured his thinking, though he was always exercised by the appearance of trade unions to be secret societies. In February 1838 he called for, and subsequently became a member of, a parliamentary Select Committee on Combinations of Workmen.

In the event nothing was to come of this enquiry but, lacking the cosy assurance of retrospect, it seemed to many workers at the time to be a further stage in the repression of trade unionism. William Lovett, secretary of the London Working Men's Association (LWMA) which would shortly publish the People's Charter, was one of them. When a London trades committee was established to monitor the parliamentary enquiry, Lovett acted as its secretary (just as he had of the Dorchester Committee four years before):

> We have through all past times, been a persecuted and calumniated class; our oppressors have bound us to the earth, and scorned us because we were down — they have kept knowledge from our reach, and taunted us with our ignorance — they have goaded *some* to violence by their injustice, and sweepingly condemned *all* as participants in the guilt.
>
> We greatly question whether the violent proceedings of unionists were the originating motives for this parliamentary investigation. We rather suspect them to be *the anxious desire for cheapened labour; and for disuniting the people*. Unions of the people are the weakness of their oppressors, and the cheap labour of the industrious is the gain of the privileged orders of society — do we want any other reason to account for the inquiry?[36]

Ostensibly the ground looked well-cultivated for the close co-operation of trade unionists with Chartism. Here after all, is a committee set up to defend unions against parliamentary interference, in which the key figure is a member of the London Society of Cabinetmakers, secretary of the LWMA and co-author of the Charter itself. The following January the *Charter*, a newspaper funded by the trades through Lovett's Combination Committee, commenced publication. But Chartism, like all mass movements with a vital inner life, has a way of confounding the predictions of the sympathetic historian. The most prominent of the parliamentary spokesmen for the LWMA, and one of its honorary members, was none other than Daniel O'Connell. The complex interpersonal politics of British and Irish radicalism now came into full play, with trade unionism entangled within them. Feargus O'Connor (who had broken with O'Connell over Irish issues in 1836) accused Lovett and the LWMA of complicity in the establishment of the Select Committee. Lovett replied with a scorching condemnation: 'You carry your fame about with you on all occasions to sink all other topics in the shade — you are the great 'I AM' of politics, the great personification of Radicalism'.[37] As Lovett later conceded in his *Life and Struggles*, the origins of the parliamentary enquiry had partly lain in the trades' call for an official investigation into the treatment of the Glasgow spinners. O'Connor's motives, however, were opportunistic. In O'Connor's defence, though, the wire-pulling micro-politics favoured by Lovett (and his mentor Francis Place, also involved in the London Trades Committee) was completely at odds with the politics of the mass platform that O'Connor espoused and epitomized. Conflict between the two wings of the Chartist movement thus broke out even before the Charter had been published.

---

35 Jacqueline R. Hill, 'Artisans, sectarianism and politics in Dublin, 1829-48', *Saothar: the Journal of the Irish Labour History Society*, 7, (1982).

36 [William Lovett], *An Address from the London Trades' Committee, appointed to watch the Parliamentary Inquiry into Combinations, to the Working Classes* (1838), pp. 2-3.

37 [William Lovett], *An Address from the London Trades' Committee*, p. 166.

'Labour is the Source of All Wealth'

The relationship between trade unionism and Chartism was inevitably affected by the polarization of leadership and opinion from this early stage. How far the trades beyond London took any notice of the affair is debatable, for whatever the rights and wrongs of the LWMA's handling of O'Connell and O'Connor, the inescapable fact is that it was O'Connor, not Lovett, who quickly assumed the position of the movement's national figurehead. Lovett's influence was slender, in spite of all that was once written by more-traditional historians of Chartism. To consider trade unions' relationship to Chartism is in effect to speak of their relationship to O'Connorite radicalism. What was it? What within it might trade societies identify as kindred to their own aims and objectives?

In the midst of his dispute with Lovett, O'Connor spoke at a public meeting convened by the LWMA on behalf of the Glasgow spinners. 'The RUBICON of profit', he declared, divided the middle classes from 'the people' and he strenuously advised trade unionists 'not to court their own destruction; not to invite a Parliamentary inquiry into the construction, rules, objects and results of Trade Associations'. Any such committee would merely be 'a tribunal of capitalists'.[38] O'Connor had a sure sense of working people's opinions, prodigious energy and a commanding presence on the platform. All this, plus his willingness to place space in his newspaper the *Northern Star* at the disposal of the trades, made him a natural focus for the respect and allegiance of industrial workers. Several national industrial unions used the paper as their main medium of communication: even the highly organized stonemasons occasionally preferred it to their own *Fortnightly Circular* to draw attention, for example, to blacked construction sites. When O'Connor moved his paper from Leeds to London in November 1844 he added as its subtitle 'National Trades' Journal'. O'Connor's support for the Dorchester labourers had been an important factor in establishing his credentials with English radicals.[39] He also recognized that trade unions, as the country's largest secular workers' movement, should play a crucial role in Chartism. O'Connor saw the situation of trade unions in 1838 as a key factor behind the take-off of Chartism:

> Our meetings of late ... have been more numerous and more numerously attended, and more strongly characterized by determination of expression than public meetings are wont to be. You will naturally seek a reason. It is not, then, that a new spirit has arisen, but that an union of different spirits has taken place. Antecedently to the attack upon, and the threatened destruction of Trades Unions by the Government, the different bodies of trades considered their orders sufficiently protected by the rules of their respective associations, and they rested satisfied with the protection which those rules yielded to their society, and therefore became negligent of their political duties. ... The system of our government, however, cannot afford the surrender of any portion of industry, that can be ceded to the money-mongers as the price for their political support, and consequently at the instance of that party ... war was made against all labour-protecting schemes, the effect of which has been to throw the whole body of the hitherto disunited and different plan-trying community into one general force, for the assertion of their political rights by which alone their social and class regulations can be protected.[40]

The language might be prolix but the meaning is clear. The legal security of trade unionism was

---

38   *Northern Star*, 10 February 1838.
39   James Epstein, *The Lion of Freedom: Feargus O'Connor and the Chartist Movement, 1832-42* (1982), p. 18.
40   *Northern Star*, 7 July 1838.

illusory: Parliament acted in the economic interests of those who elected it and would not tolerate a strong labour movement for long. Trade unions therefore needed to become part of a broad alliance to protect working people's organizations and interests. And that alliance was Chartism. A parallel argument was made by Joshua Hobson, editor of the *Northern Star*, when he claimed that the government had 'transported the Dorchester Labourers ... for the purpose of breaking up Trades' Unions. That transportation had answered its purpose. They all knew that Trades' Unions had crumbled to nothing before it; and whilst working men were thus paralysed, the Poor Law Amendment Act was passed by the Whigs'.[41]

Obtaining the Charter was universally seen as the prelude to a comprehensive programme of further reforms. Chartism was saturated with that same ideology upon which trade societies had been based since their inception: an ideology centred upon property in skill. This property, in the words of John Campbell, secretary of the executive committee of the National Charter Association (NCA),

> must always be deteriorated, until the labourer shall have a voice in the institutions he is called upon to submit to; institutions that not only affect his labour, which is his only property, but also his liberty and life. Railway companies, shipping interests, bank companies, cotton mills, and every other species of property is protected by law, whilst labour is unprotected; and what is the reason? simply this: because all these interests are represented, whilst you, the industrious artisans, are deprived of any share in the making of the laws at all.[42]

Chartist thinking, then, was very much of a piece with the trade unionist outlook. 'In Great Britain', stated the paper of the Manchester smiths, who affiliated *en bloc* to Chartism, 'the only object of the law is, to protect the privileges, the person and the property of the capitalist and the aristocrat; hence the poor, the honest man, hath no protection for his labour'.[43] 'The miscalled Reform Bill', stated the Barnsley Chartists in 1838, 'will never mend the condition of the working people.' The solution was 'most assuredly [to] obtain a great Charter, namely the right to vote for Members of Parliament; then will the working man enjoy the fruits of his own industry and become a respectable member of society, and never till then'.[44] All these quotations, of course, come from considered and articulate public pronouncements. A Stockport spinner, imprisoned for Chartist activities in 1839, put it more simply: 'if the wages were what they ought to be, we should not hear a word about the suffrage'.[45]

The prolonged slump in the trade cycle between 1836 and 1842 accentuated the relevance of Chartism to trade unionists: along with the potency of political hostility, the Glasgow spinners powerfully demonstrated how strike tactics failed to protect organized labour during a period of high unemployment — though few workers would have needed reminding of this, 'Their trades, after maturely examining the subject', declared Manchester's hammermen, smiths and mechanics, 'had found that the trades unions had not accomplished that for which they had been formed, namely the protection of the labour of the working man'. Nor did unions 'possess sufficient strength to secure to the labourer a just and reasonable remuneration for his labour, and protect his rights', according to the

---

41 *Northern Star*, 3 February 1838.
42 John Campbell, *An Examination of the Corn and Provision Laws* (1841), cited in John Belchem, 'Beyond Chartist Studies: class, community and party in early-Victorian populist politics', in Derek Fraser (ed.), *Cities, Class and Communication: Essays in Honour of Asa Briggs* (1990), p. 114.
43 Quoted in Robert Sykes, 'Early Chartism and trade unionism in south-east Lancashire', p. 171.
44 F. J. Kaijage, 'The manifesto of the Barnsley Chartists', *BSSLH*, 33, (1976), p. 23.
45 Inspector of Prisons interview with Charles Davies, HO 20/10, quoted by Edward Royle, *Chartism* (1996), p. 106.

city's carpenters.[46]

At the grassroots level there was considerable synergy between Chartism and trade unionism, and often it becomes difficult if not pointless to distinguish between adherents of the two. The Manchester engineer Alexander Hutchinson has already been mentioned. John Gast, leader of the Thames shipwrights was another. In the West Riding the Dewsbury United Trades' Society was central to the establishment of Chartism locally.[47] The inaugural Chartist meeting in Nottingham (November 1838) was chaired by a framework knitters' union activist.[48] In his autobiography, Cheshire Shoemaker Thomas Dunning described a natural transition from his support for the GNCTU into Chartism, selling *Northern Star* from his master's workshop, which also became a Chartist meeting place.[49] In south Lancashire, 'the father of the movement' (to use O'Connor's description) was a textile unionist, Richard Pilling.[50] Oldham Chartists met in a pub run by trade unionist and NCA delegate James Mills. He had probably taken the pub when blacklisted by local employers.[51] Another Chartist publican, Peter Bussey, leader of the movement in Bradford, 1838-9, had joined the town's woolcombers' and stuff weavers' union in 1824-5 when he was a comber. He had been secretary of the Bradford Trades' Union in 1834 and a leader of the protest against the Tolpuddle sentences.[52] The management board of the now-defunct National Union of Operative Potters supplied one of the most effective of Staffordshire Chartist leaders, William Ellis.[53] Perhaps the most eloquent trade unionist support of all for Chartism came in the form of a letter read to a mass West Riding demonstration on Hartshead Moor in October 1838, which simply bore the popular name of the great Leeds Clothiers' Union of the early 1830s: 'John Powlett'.[54]

Trade union members, though, did not just join Chartism as individuals. 'Joining' Chartism, particularly before the formation of the NCA in 1840, was a matter of general commitment rather than taking out a formal subscription. Many trade societies supported the movement *en bloc*. This was especially so in 1838-9 when a 'declaration of adhesion in bodies' was made among others by the trades of Birmingham, Bury, Manchester, Newcastle and Oldham.[55] The trades of Birmingham, Glasgow, Newcastle, Norwich, Nottingham and Sheffield collected for the fund-raising 'National Rent',[56] as did individual societies such as the fancy trades' union at Kirkheaton, West Yorkshire. Huddersfield shoemakers joined the movement as a body[57] as they did at Stockport, Manchester and Bolton.[58] The great demonstrations of 1838 which did so much to mobilize support for the Charter depended to a significant extent on formal trade participation. Seventy trade unions marched in a

---

46 *Northern Star*, 16 July and 2 April 1842.

47 *Northern Star*, 17-24 March 1838.

48 J. V. Beckett, *A Centenary History of Nottingham* (1997), p. 312.

49 David Vincent, *Testaments of Radicalism: Memoirs of Six Working-class Politicians, 1790-1885* (1977), p. 134f.

50 *DLB* vol. 6, 221.

51 David Gadian, 'Class formation and class action in north-west industrial towns, 1830-50', in R. J. Morris (ed.), *Class, Power and Social Structure in British Nineteenth-Century Towns* (1986), p. 30.

52 A. J. Peacock, *Bradford Chartism, 1838-1840* (1969), pp. 8-9.

53 Robert Fyson, 'The crisis of 1842: Chartism, the colliers' strike and the outbreak in the Potteries', in James Epstein and Dorothy Thompson, (eds.), *The Chartist Experience*, p. 202.

54 Alan J. Brooke, 'Labour disputes and trade unions in the industrial revolution', in E. A. H. Haigh (ed.), *Huddersfield a Most Handsome Town: Aspects of the History and Culture of a West Yorkshire Town* (1992), p. 230.

55 Peter Taylor, *Popular Politics in Early Industrial Britain, Bolton, 1835-50* (1995), p. 147.

56 David J. V. Jones, *Chartism and the Chartists* (1975), p. 139.

57 Alan J. Brooke, 'Labour disputes and trade unions in the industrial revolution', p. 230.

58 Robert Sykes, 'Early Chartism and trade unionism in south-east Lancashire', p. 163.

procession that stretched almost two miles to Glasgow Green in May that year.[59] In June 'processions of the trades marched from the various quarters of the town', to Newcastle Town Moor, 'every trade contributing its separate staff, even the most aristocratic of those bodies did not hold aloof', added the author, noting that the exclusive local coachmakers participated.[60] On Manchester's Kersal Moor in September, participating trade unions included the Friendly Society of Operative Spinners, the Steam Engine and Machine Makers' Friendly Society, the Wheelwrights' and Blacksmiths' Society, the Friendly Society of Fustian-shearers, the Friendly Institution of Boot and Shoemakers, plus unnamed societies of ladies' shoemakers, carpenters and joiners, smiths, farriers and tailors, each behind their banner.[61] Another banner, of the United Suffrage Association, was inscribed 'Labour the source of all wealth', a popular Chartist slogan which, a decade later, would be painted on the platform at the London rally which accompanied the presentation of the final Chartist petition to parliament.

'THE SACRED MONTH': 1839

The first test of Chartism's effectiveness as a political movement came in 1839 and the experience was not a happy one. In May the movement's first petition, of more than 1.25 million signatures, was presented to Parliament but a proposal in July that the House of Commons consider it fell by 235 to 46 votes. Numerous local altercations, serious riots in Llanidloes and Birmingham, and attempts at large-scale risings in Bradford and South Wales exposed Chartism to extensive criticism and the logic of its strategy to searching internal scrutiny. Above all, the movement committed itself to the tactic of a general strike, in the form of 'the sacred month' and then had to pull back at the last moment, proroguing as it did so the National Convention which had been widely seen by Chartists as an alternative government.

There was always an unresolved tension at the heart of Chartism, namely what should its next actions be if Parliament rejected its peaceable calls for reform. The National Convention, which assembled in London in February 1839, was charged with little more than the responsibility of managing the petition's collection and presentation, but almost from its inception an influential caucus within it was prepared to think the unthinkable, and to do so aloud. The result was rancour even before the Convention moved to Birmingham in May and began to formulate the 'ulterior measures' to be implemented if the petition was rejected: exclusive dealing in order to bankrupt shopkeepers unsympathetic to Chartism, mass withdrawal of bank deposits to destabilize the currency and, most potent of all, a general strike. The refusal by the Commons to debate the Chartists' petition was bad enough, but the movement was already suffering under the impact of official containment: troops were on alert throughout the North and arrests of Chartist speakers were commonplace. Furthermore Lovett and another leading Chartist had been arrested after criticizing the authorities' handling of the Birmingham riots a few days before.

Five days after the parliamentary vote, the Convention called for the sacred month to commence on 12 August. The tactic had been widely canvassed over the preceding months. William Benbow himself had been on the stomp in Lancashire and copies of his *Grand National Holiday* were once more in circulation. Military preparations had been in hand in certain Chartist localities for some time. For example, at Crowley's massive ironworks at Winlaton on Tyneside, 'fowling-pieces, small cannon, stoneware hand-grenades, pikes and "craa's feet" or caltrops — four-spiked irons which

---

59 Alexander Wilson, *The Chartist Movement in Scotland*, p. 50.
60 R. G. Gammage, *History of the Chartist Movement, 1837-54*, p. 28.
61 *Northern Star*, 29 September 1838.

could been strewn in a road to disable cavalry horses' had been in clandestine production since the end of the previous year.[62] However, the consequences of calling a general strike and the logistics of sustaining it had never been considered in detail. There was no formal mechanism by which Chartism might officially discuss such issues with the trades and the authority of the now depleted Convention was much eroded. Its majority in favour was small. However intemperate their previous language, the most influential national Chartist leaders were now opposed to the strategy, O'Connor included: 'The evidence from nine-tenths of the Kingdom went to show that the people could not, without organisation, enter upon the proposed holiday'.[63] From the Chartist districts came reports of unpreparedness and of escalating official hostility. On 6 August Convention announced the cancellation of the sacred month and the substitution of a three-day national holiday of peaceable demonstration. It then suspended its sittings.

So it was that, for a few days in mid-August an attenuated form of general strike did take place in some centres of Chartist strength: in the North-east, Manchester, Bolton, the Bury area, Carlisle and its industrial hinterland, Macclesfield, Mansfield and Nottingham. In the north-east, the interpretation of the miners' strike of 1839 as purely a 'Chartist' one has been shown to be an exaggeration;[64] yet the Charter found its way into the objectives of the strike at many collieries, especially in south Durham. What one Chartist miner described as a 'Colliery war of extermination' followed,[65] with extensive dismissals of politically active miners extending, or so it was claimed, even to those merely found carrying Chartist circulars.[66] In Manchester on 12 August several large factories were turned out by crowds who were in turn driven off by police; two mills stayed out on 13 August but the next day normal working resumed. The most serious unrest occurred at Bolton where most mills were stopped and special constables forced to retreat to the supposed safety of Little Bolton Town Hall. The lower floor had been wrecked by Chartist sympathizers by the time troops arrived and, firing into the crowd, dispersed the riot, wounding one man.

The lesson supporters of the Charter drew from August 1839 was salutary. 'The National Holiday had destroyed so many of the myths which had sustained physical-force Chartism. It was seen that the troops would act against the Chartists, and fire on them, and that disciplined troops and often even police were more than a match for unorganized crowds'.[67] Moreover, outside the major manufacturing centres, the threat Chartism presented was as much in the eyes of nervous officialdom as anywhere[68] and, fatally, in terms of the movement's capacity forcibly to exert political change, in London it was weak and divided. The Newport Rising of November 1839 formed a tragic coda to the year. Isolated insurrectionary flickers in Newcastle and West Yorkshire in January 1840 only served to underline the difficulty of formulating an effective strategy for the movement.

---

62 A. R. Schoyen, *The Chartist Challenge: A Portrait of George Julian Harney* (1958), p. 42. Accounts of Chartist preparations for an armed rising in 1839 can be found in all general texts on the movement. See also A. J. Peacock, *Bradford Chartism, 1838-1840*, Robert Sykes, 'Early Chartism and trade unionism in south-east Lancashire', and W. H. Maehl, 'Chartist disturbances in northeastern England, 1839', *International Review of Social History* 8, (1963).

63 *Northern Star* 17 August 1839.

64 D. J. Rowe, 'Some aspects of Tyneside Chartism', *International Review of Social History*, 16, (1971), pp. 30-1.

65 *Northern Star*, 3 April 1841.

66 Keith Wilson, 'Chartism and the north-east miners: a reappraisal', in R. W. Sturgess (ed.), *Pitmen, Viewers and Coalmasters: Essays on North-East Coalmining in the Nineteenth Century* (1986), p. 96.

67 Robert Sykes, 'Physical-force Chartism: the cotton district and the Chartist crisis of 1839', *International Review of Social History*, vol. 30, part 2, (1985), pp. 232-3.

68 Malcolm Chase, 'Chartism, 1838-1858: responses in two Teesside towns', *Northern History*, 24, (1988), pp. 152-3.

In the heady days of 1838 trade unions had aligned themselves with a political movement that seemed capable of exerting massive moral force on the establishment of the country. Twelve months later the strategy espoused by that same movement was in disarray. The root cause of the failure of the far more serious mass strike of 1842 lay here, in 1839, when the Chartists failed to solve the problems that were contingent on rejection by Parliament of their peaceable demand for political reform.

THE MASS STRIKES OF 1842

Not the least of these problems was organizational. Up until the autumn of 1839 Chartism had been sustained by a widespread but often unstructured emotional attachment to the Charter. Righteous indignation and raw energy had to be harnessed to a legally constituted organization capable of administering Chartism whilst retaining the commitment — and as far as possible the pecuniary subscriptions — of those who called themselves Chartists. In July 1840 the answer that emerged was the NCA.

At the same time the movement was labouring under the considerable burden of the imprisonment of upwards of 550 Chartists on charges resulting from the events of 1839 and early 1840. Although sustaining the prisoners and their families was a useful focal point for continuing activity it could not take the movement forward. The intention behind the NCA was that it would co-ordinate the movement at a national level whilst permitting the affiliation of local Chartist and Working Men's Associations and other local radical groups. It was also possible for trade societies to become 'localities' of the organization in the same way as geographically specific branches. The idea was that of Peter McDouall, a Scottish surgeon practising in Lancashire whose vision of the marriage of trade unions and Chartism was perhaps the most complete of any Chartist leader. McDouall based the details on the structure adopted by the Dundee trades who had formed a federal Trades Democratic Universal Suffrage Association.[69] Theoretically, a trade's locality was distinct from the corresponding trade society, but usually comprised the same membership and officers and met at the same location.[70]

The procedure was widely adapted in Manchester where societies affiliating included boilermakers, bricklayers, carpenters, fustian-cutters, painters and hammermen. The latter were informed by delegates from the mechanics and smiths,

> that their trades after maturely examining the subject, had found that the trades' unions had not accomplished that for which they had been formed, namely the protection of the labour of the working man; and, therefore, they had come to the conclusion that nothing short of a participation in the making of the laws by which they were governed, would effectually protect their labour. Having come to this conclusion, they had joined the National Charter Association.[71]

In the years 1841-3, a third of all the NCA localities in London were in fact trade ones.[72] Yet it was only in the capital, Manchester and Dundee that affiliation appears to have taken place on a large

---

69 Keith Wilson, 'Chartism and the north-east miners: a reappraisal', p. 273.
70 F. C. Mather, *Chartism and Society: An Anthology of Documents* (1980), p. 247.
71 *Northern Star* 16 July 1842.
72 Iorwerth J. Prothero, 'London Chartism and the trades', *Economic History Review*, 24, (1971), p. 202.

scale, though there were instances of affiliation elsewhere: for example, tailors in Birmingham,[73] shoemakers in Stafford, Northampton and Nottingham[74] plus a separate Bristol Trades NCA.[75] This is not in itself an indication of any breach between Chartism and trade unionism, for the NCA's membership in April 1842 had only reached 50,000: Chartists by conviction rather than enrolment were far greater in number and this would have been true of the trades too. We also have to be mindful that Chartism had been widely presented by a hostile press and establishment as an insurrectionary movement. 'Their Trades Union was illegal enough at present', commented one London shoemaker in 1842, 'and they were unpopular enough with the masters, without making them more so'.[76]

The relative paucity of evidence for the formal affiliation of trade unions to Chartism has permitted a wide latitude of interpretation. At one extreme, trade unions have been presented as aloof from politics, the discussion of which they expressly discouraged. However, it was usually prudent for a trade society to put at least an appearance of distance between it and Chartism: but this does not mean that either the society or its members were politically disengaged. Mather[77] makes much of 'an unsuccessful bid to remove the ban' on political discussion at the Manchester Trades' Congress of August 1842: yet this same body voted for a general strike until the Charter was won. Furthermore David Morrison, the principal speaker *against* its removal, represented the mechanics, the second largest occupational group among known Manchester Chartists.[78] He was a delegate to the ensuing Chartist conference and was one of those subsequently tried with O'Connor for his role in the 1842 strikes. When Morrison picketed the Bridgewater Foundry, where he worked, he told his workmates 'that though we might think we were well off, yet ultimately the distress would reach us also; that it was our duty to sympathize' with striking mill hands.[79] The very format of union meetings seems sometimes calculated to encourage, not stifle, political discussion. 'When met the first hour is devoted to promiscuous conversation. At eight the newspapers of the day are produced. They are read aloud by one of the company. This occupies near an hour'. Only at nine o'clock, according to this description of a Paisley trade society, would the chairman call for silence for 'the report of trade' to be heard.[80]

Against this background significant politicization in all but a handful of societies seems assured, especially at times of peak unrest. Of course support for Chartism was not necessarily unanimous. Members of the Operative Stonemasons, for example, criticized the Birmingham Chartist who acted as their national secretary for introducing political comment in union literature: 'I have, however, yet to learn', he replied, 'what difference it makes to the working-man whether his employer reduces his wages 6d. per day or the self constituted "authorities of the land" impose a political tax on his food … or that there is more virtue in resisting the one than in resisting the other'.[81] The handful of

---

73 E. P. Thompson, *Writing by Candlelight* (1980), p. 193.
74 Ibid, p. 186.
75 David McNulty, 'Bristol trade unions in the Chartist years', in John Rule (ed.), *British Trade Unionism, 1750-1850*, p. 227.
76 Quoted in David J. V. Jones, *Chartism and the Chartists*, p. 138.
77 F. C. Mather, *Chartism and Society*, p. 244.
78 Paul Pickering, *Chartism and the Chartists in Manchester and Salford*, p. 212.
79 *Trial* 1843, 98.
80 W. Taylor (1809), *An Answer to Mr Carlile's Sketches of Paisley*, quoted in J. T. Ward and W. H. Fraser, (eds.), *Workers and Employers: Documents on Trade Unions and Industrial Relations in Britain since the Eighteenth Century* (1980), p. 13.
81 Quoted in Clive Behagg, *Politics and Production in the Early Nineteenth Century*, p. 109.

societies that explicitly rejected association with Chartism, all of them drawn from what Prothero[82] has termed the 'upper trades' distinguished by strong, successful unions, were principally the shipwrights, coopers, bookbinders and typographers. We have already seen that the participation of the coachbuilders in a Newcastle Chartist demonstration was sufficiently unusual to occasion comment. Trades with less secure but nonetheless active unions were usually much more active in both inter-trade activity and Chartism. These included all the building trades, the textiles industries (where, as in the case of the Glasgow spinners, even an apparently strong union was insecure in the face of new technology), shoemakers, tailors and also those trades where unionisation was relatively recent. The engineering trades fell into this category, whilst Clive Behagg[83] has shown that it also included a wide range of Birmingham's workshop-based industries. From the 1820s traditional workplace solidarity in the city was increasingly formalized to resist the erosion of incomes and of control over entry and of the work-process.

There were also important spatial variations in trade union responses to Chartism in the 1840s, the reasons for which have yet to be fully investigated. For example: do the debilitating consequences of the Glasgow spinners' case alone explain why the trades of Glasgow, so prominent in 1838, seem subsequently to have fallen away from Chartism? And why should those of Dundee have mobilized with such effect? The evidence suggests that where trade societies were a major force in local society Chartism worked with and often through them. In smaller towns, however, trade societies were often bypassed. Committed trade unionists might form the backbone of the movement locally, but unions were not the logical medium through which to reach a mass audience. Much more could be achieved simply by sending a bellman to tour the streets and announce a public meeting.

Recent experience of a collapse in effective unionism was also a factor that swelled the Chartist ranks. This effect was most noticeable in north Staffordshire, one of the areas where disturbances were particularly serious in 1842. 'In the summer of 1842 the Potteries were in the trough of the worst depression of the century: trade was at a low ebb, the workhouses were overcrowded, wages were low and prices high'.[84] At the beginning of June colliers from a local pit turned out in protest against a wage reduction and protested in the time-honoured fashion by parading the Potteries with loaves of bread on poles. They met with some local support and when, the following month, there was a similar turn-out at another pit a Committee of Operative Colliers was formed, and a process of systematic stoppages commenced across the north Staffordshire coalfield. Pickets stopped work at each pit, raking out the fires of colliery engines and pulling out the plugs from the steam chambers. As the water cascaded out on to engine-room floors steam engines were rendered instantly inoperable. The dispute widened to embrace not just the restoration of earlier wage rates but pay rises, an end to truck and a shorter working week. The potteries closed for want of fuel. Robert Fyson[85] has demonstrated how the dispute assumed a wider importance, as the strikers sent representatives to the coalfields (also strike-hit) of Cheshire, Lancashire, Shropshire and the Black Country. Plans for a national delegate meeting of Welsh and English miners were formulated. All of this took place against a background of increasing Chartist activity in the Potteries. At least five miners were Chartist committeemen, including the two most prominent leaders of the Hanley colliers, and leading Chartists spoke in support of the strikers at public meetings. The Committee of

---

82 Iorwerth J. Prothero, 'London Chartism and the trades', p. 209.
83 Clive Behagg, *Politics and Production in the Early Nineteenth Century*.
84 Robert Fyson, 'The crisis of 1842: Chartism, the colliers' strike and the outbreak in the Potteries', p. 197.
85 Ibid.

Operative Colliers had its headquarters at the Hanley pub which was also a Chartist meeting place. A Shoemaker called John Richards, the local NCA corresponding secretary, acted in the same capacity for the strike committee (he had also been a negotiator for the potters' union in its 1836-7 strike). Not all local Chartists were comfortable with the identification of the movement with the strike, however, and the colliers insisted 'we have nothing to do with any Political question; our dispute is simply upon the Price of Labour'. Clearly, the strike was not Chartist-inspired nor led: yet equally clearly, its resolve and effectiveness were stiffened by Chartists.

Though the miners drifted back to work, the strike contributed to the atmosphere of crisis that pervaded north Staffordshire during the following month. On 15 August John Richards and one of the miners' leaders proposed at a public meeting attended by 7,000 to 8,000 on Crown Bank, Hanley, 'that all labour cease until the People's Charter becomes the law of the land'.[86] Attempts to enforce a general strike followed, which escalated into widespread rioting, looting and attacks on Stoke workhouse, police stations and the homes of magistrates and Poor Law officials. In crowd actions that were charged with symbolism, pawnbrokers were broken into and pledges redeemed without payment and, on another occasion, a fire made of property deeds. After twenty-four hours in which authority had lost all control, special constables and dragoons finally restored order just as a large body of turn-outs from Cheshire entered the area. The 276 tried at the subsequent Special Commission (three courts sitting simultaneously for two weeks under the direction of the Lord Chief Justice) included large numbers of potters and colliers and nearly all the local Chartist leadership.

The 1842 disturbances in north Staffordshire demonstrate a great deal about the nature of strikes and social protest in the Chartist period. Chartism was both a symptom and a cause of social unrest in 1842. Chartist arguments and perceptions of labour's situation informed the actions of trade unionists, strikers and rioters alike. The majority of those arrested in 1842, in Staffordshire as elsewhere, were not known Chartists (though they included two key local supporters of trade unionism, John Richards and William Ellis). Colliers, whose disciplined strike action two months before had been achieved within a well-organized delegate structure, were particularly prominent among the leading rioters.[87] However, as two Chartist activists observed of their fellow prisoners following the Lancashire strikes of 1842, 'not withstanding there are so few who can be said to have belonged *directly* to the Chartist body, we can state, that the *whole* of them are Chartists in *principle* and at heart'.[88] Given the economic conditions of the time, and the nature of popular protest, it is hardly surprising that control of events on 15 August was slipping from the local Chartist leadership even as they made the call for a strike until the Charter was gained. Both the colliers' strike and the August disturbances were thick with the symbolism of traditional protest: title deeds had been burnt by rebels at least as far back as the Peasants' Revolt of 1381. On the other hand the retention of a local political and trade-union activist as secretary and spokesman for an as yet non-unionised group indicates a completely different organizational form. As in Chartism as a whole, a wide repertoire of activities is evident, ranging from highly traditional modes of protest, through the still relatively novel general strike, to trade unionist forms of organization. The form chosen varied according to circumstances and the resulting pattern was far more subtle than a simple division between peaceable, 'modern' sustained organization and 'traditional' (and often violent) protest.

North Staffordshire, however, was but one of thirty-two counties in Britain affected by strikes and

---

86 Thomas Cooper, *The Life of Thomas Cooper Written by Himself* (1872), p. 192.
87 Robert Fyson, 'The crisis of 1842: Chartism, the colliers' strike and the outbreak in the Potteries', p. 211.
88 Isaac Hoyle and James Williams, letter in *English Chartist Circular* 132 [August 1843], 317.

disturbances in August 1842. These events are among the most controversial in the interpretation of Chartism. What the *Leeds Mercury* greeted with foreboding as 'The Chartist insurrection' was subsequently seen by several influential interpreters as nothing of the kind. The Webbs' view[89] that the strikes were 'captured' by the Chartists was repeated in the seminal volume *Chartist Studies*.[90] However, Mather[91] pointed out that the local leadership of the strikes was often provided by active Chartists and that their involvement in trade disputes pre-dated the August strike wave. Subsequent research has consolidated this interpretation with reference not only to Lancashire[92] but also the Lanarkshire coalfield,[93] north Staffordshire[94] and Huddersfield.[95]

The result is a subtle and discriminating view of the role of Chartism, rather than the conspiracy theory apparently believed at the time by the Home Secretary. This had the advantage from the Government's point of view of implicating the Chartist leadership at the highest level, but it also reflected a very real perception on the ground. 'It is difficult for anyone not in the manufacturing districts to have any idea of the slender hold on the people of anything like allegiance to a faith in any way or shape of the existing Government and political institutions', wrote the Leeds manufacturer James Marshall. 'They look upon it as an Incubus to be removed, if possible without injury to Person or Property; but the belief is growing that it MUST fall to pieces.' On 16 August Marshall had witnessed a 'mob', he thought from outside the city, 'closing round Leeds'. However, he then discovered to his surprise that most of the prisoners taken in the ensuing disturbances 'belonged to this neighbourhood and were not strangers' and that 'work-people here, though well disposed to protect person and property, sympathize strongly with their fellows, whom they think their own'.[96]

The geographical extent of the 1842 strike wave was unusual. Since the main medium of information exchange among workers at this time was the *Northern Star*, it is perhaps inevitable that these events are sometimes seen as Chartist-inspired and even, as in Jenkins' spirited account,[97] as a national general strike. However, the extent of disturbance was modest in most counties, with the crucially important exceptions of Cheshire, Lancashire, Staffordshire, Yorkshire's West Riding and Lanarkshire. Isolated strikes such as that of the Norwich jacquard loom weavers were probably coincidental to events in the industrial districts. As in 1839, London was out of step with the mood of the industrial North: 1842 is one of only ten years in the period 1790-1840 in which a systematic sampling of newspaper reports has failed to reveal any metropolitan labour disputes.[98] Where the strike wave was concerted a close affinity between Chartism and the trades concerned was always

---

89 Sidney and Beatrice Webb, *The History of Trade Unionism*, p. 175.
90 Asa Briggs, (ed.), *Chartist Studies* (1959), p. 54.
91 F. C. Mather, 'The General Strike of 1842: a study in leadership, organisation and the threat of revolution during the Plug Plot disturbances', in R. Quinault and J. Stevenson, (eds.), *Popular Protest and Public Order: Six Studies in British History 1790-1920* (1974).
92 Mick Jenkins, *The General Strike of 1842*; Paul Pickering, *Chartism and the Chartists in Manchester and Salford*, pp. 68-72.
93 Alan Campbell, *The Lanarkshire Miners: a Social History of their Trade Unions, 1775-1874* (1979), p. 252.
94 Robert Fyson, 'The crisis of 1842: Chartism, the colliers' strike and the outbreak in the Potteries'.
95 Alan J. Brooke, 'Labour disputes and trade unions in the industrial revolution'.
96 University of Leeds, Brotherton Library Special Collections: MS 739/6, 3 September 1842; MS 739/1, 16 August 1842; MS 739/5, Thursday [18 August 1842].
97 Mick Jenkins, *The General Strike of 1842*.
98 See David R. Green, *From Artisans to Paupers: Economic Change and Poverty in London, 1790-1870* (1995), p. 118. There were in fact at least three strikes, in the spring by stonemasons employed by the contractor building the Houses of Parliament, Nelson's Column and Woolwich Dockyard, and later by employees of the building contractor Cubitt and by the Thameside coal-whippers (David Goodway, *London Chartism*, pp. 53 and 180). Serious disorder was limited to demonstrations around the mainline railway stations against the dispatch of troops from the capital to the Midlands and North.

manifest. This was inevitable: 'in the manufacturing districts there are, at least, four out of every five of the working classes, that either are actually Chartists, or hold Chartist principles', Richard Otley of Sheffield stated at his subsequent trial. 'This being the case, it is quite impossible that there should be a turn-out for wages, without having a great number of Chartists among the turn-outs'.[99]

However, the Chartists had once again run up against the refusal of the political establishment to vote for its own extinction: in May a petition for the Charter of more than 3.25 million signatures had been rejected by Parliament. Unlike 1839, though, Chartism was better able to weather the implications. Chartists at Luddenden, near Halifax, declared themselves 'not at all disappointed being persuaded that those interested in the present monopolizing system will never render to labour its just reward, namely equality before the law'.[100] Moreover, the trades in the North of England, with the 1839 national holiday fiasco doubtless in their minds, were no longer waiting on the Chartist national leadership. When the first mass meeting to approve the much-vaunted motion 'that all labour should cease until the People's Charter became the law of the land' (on Mottram Moor, south of Stalybridge, on 7 August), it was not the first stage of a co-ordinated Chartist programme but a spontaneous gesture reflecting the particular mood of industrial workers in Lancashire and Cheshire, triggered by the decision of local cotton employers to reduce wages. Over the ensuing week the motion was carried at meetings across the Pennine textile districts; and we have already seen it taken up in the Potteries on 15 August, the day on which a conference of trades' delegates assembled in the Manchester Carpenters' Hall and approved the following address 'to the trades of Manchester and the surrounding districts':

> No sufficient guarantee is afforded to the producers of wealth, but from adoption and establishment of the people's political rights, as a safeguard for their lives, liberties and interests of the nation generally. ... The meeting proposes appointing delegates to wait upon and confer with shopkeepers, dissenting clergymen and the middle classes generally, for the purpose of ascertaining how far they are prepared to assist and support the people in the struggle for the attainment of their political rights. ... We, your representatives, call most emphatically upon the people to discontinue the production of creation of wealth, until the result of our deliberations is made known to the people whom we represent. ... For ourselves, we have no other property than our labour.[101]

The following day, now meeting in the Owenites' Hall of Science, a majority of over 120 of the 134 delegates (only seven had spoken for restricting strikes to wages only) approved a 'resolution of ceasing labour until the Charter becomes the law of the land'.[102] It happened to be the anniversary of Peterloo and the executive of the NCA had arrived in Manchester for the unveiling of a statue of Henry Hunt. Thomas Cooper, chairman of the Potteries meeting on 15 August described earlier in this chapter, had made a judicious exit that evening and arrived in Manchester the following morning. On the train he met several Chartist delegates, among them John Campbell, secretary of the NCA

---

99 *Trial* 1843, 246.
100 *Northern Star*, 21 May 1842.
101 *Bolton Free Press*, 20 August 1842, quoted in Mick Jenkins, *The General Strike of 1842*, p. 152. The latter is the most extensive study of industrial unrest in 1842. F. C. Mather, 'The General Strike of 1842', reaches similar conclusions about the nature of the strike in a considerably less ideologically engaged fashion. For important regional case studies see Robert Fyson, 'The crisis of 1842', and Robert Sykes, 'Early Chartism and trade unionism in south-east Lancashire', Andrew Charlesworth *et al.*, *An Atlas of Industrial Protest in Britain, 1750-1990* (1996) and John Charlton, *The Chartists: the First National Workers' Movement*, provide useful short summaries and analysis.
102 Mick Jenkins, *The General Strike of 1842*, p. 154-6.

executive: 'so soon as the City of Long Chimneys came in sight, and every chimney was beheld smokeless, Campbell's face changed, and with an oath he said, "Not a single mill at work! something must come out of this, and something serious too!"'.[103] It's an illuminating anecdote: that there were strikes was of course known, but their extent and politicization had caught the NCA executive by surprise. Meeting later that day, several members actually voted against giving official NCA support to the strike. However, the majority, led by O'Connor and McDouall, prevailed, as the latter subsequently recalled:

> The question of having or not having a strike was already decided, because the strike had taken place: the question of making that strike political was also decided, because the trades had resolved, almost unanimously, to cease labour for the charter alone ... [the question was] whether chartism should or should not retain its ascendancy in its natural territory.[104]

There was then a fundamental gap between the perceptions of the movement's national leadership and activists in Lancashire. The same situation was simultaneously noted by a Scottish Chartist paper: 'there was no authorised or known source through which the opinions of the various localities could be gathered'.[105] Trade unionists such as the smiths' leader Alexander Hutchinson (who chaired the Manchester trades conference) and the spinner Richard Pilling had been involved in Chartism since its inception and they firmly established a link between the two. The link was less one of organization than of thought and outlook. For the trade unionist seeking to make sense of workshop issues in a wider political context, Chartism provided a tool 'to think with'.

This also applied to a significant extent to labour leadership in the as yet largely non-unionised mining industry. The concept of a 'Chartist enlightenment' in the North-east coalfield[106] has proved too rhetorical for some tastes.[107] However, Keith Wilson provides a more refined summary: 'for the miners Chartism provided an articulation of their problems, a potential avenue for their resolution, and a vision of how things might otherwise be ordered'.[108] The 1842 strike wave provides abundant evidence of this. Only the Shropshire coalfield appears to be an exception, 'though the Chartists were satisfied to accept the credit for the strike lavished upon them'.[109] To suggest that these were 'Chartist strikes' was a useful stratagem for coal-owners unwilling, or unable, to comprehend the extent of their own responsibility for the breakdown in industrial relations. Yet even in the Black Country coalfield, for which the strongest case has been made for discounting the influence of Chartism, it has been readily conceded that 'the Chartists played a significant part in the organization of the miners from the start, that Chartist speakers were prominent at mass meetings, and were successful in stirring up the miners against injustice and oppression, and were sufficiently influential to prolong the strike'.[110] In Scotland, 10,000 Lanarkshire colliers struck work in July and August 1842: the picture

---

103 Thomas Cooper, *The Life of Thomas Cooper*, p. 206.

104 P. M. McDouall, *Letters to the Manchester Chartists*, (1842), p. 9, quoted in Paul Pickering, *Chartism and the Chartists in Manchester and Salford*, p. 70.

105 Quoted in Alexander Wilson, *The Chartist Movement in Scotland*, p. 195.

106 Robert Colls, *The Pitmen of the Northern Coalfield: Work, Culture and Protest, 1790-1850* (1987), p. 302.

107 R. A. Church, 'Chartism and the miners: a reinterpretation', *LHR*, vol. 56, part 3, (1991), pp. 26-7.

108 Keith Wilson, 'Chartism and the north-east miners: a reappraisal', p. 92.

109 Barrie Trinder, *The Industrial Revolution in Shropshire* (1973), p. 390.

110 C. P. Griffin (1972), 'Chartism and the miners' strike of 1842 in the Black Country: a reply', *BSSLH* 25, 67. See also the preceding discussion in issues 22-4 of the same journal. The republication of Challinor and Ripley's study in 1990 revived the debate in the successor to *BSSLH*: see *LHR*, vol. 56, no. 2; vol. 57, no, 2 and vol. 58, no. 1.

that emerges again is of the key role of a local leadership politicized through Chartism.[111] The secretary to the Airdrie and Coatbridge miners, for example, was a delegate to the Scottish Chartist convention in January 1842, and Chartist speakers addressed colliers' meetings during the summer. On 13 August, striking Clackmannanshire colliers 'determined to strike for nothing less than the People's Charter'; but this pledge was significantly qualified. The miners would 'never again produce a pennyworth of wealth till the People's Charter be law', provided that the rest of the country fell in with the same plan by 23 August.[112] Airdrie and some Fife colliers adopted the same objective and Dunfermline Chartists immediately formed a 'Cessation-from-Labour Committee' to promote the plan on both sides of the border. But, of course, the strike wave in England was almost spent by the target date. The episode epitomizes how labour's capacity to effect political change in the August crisis was held in check not just by the actions of authority but by inadequate co-ordination and wide regional variation in the timing and intensity of militancy.

Inevitably, opposition to the strikes was often met with violence. Local circumstances sometimes tilted protest in a particularly ferocious direction. The Potteries were the worst afflicted but were by no means unique. Halifax was another centre of particularly violent confrontation between troops and demonstrators, with three deaths (one a soldier), eight wounded and thirty-six subsequently sent for trial.[113] Yet, given the economic circumstances and mood of the demonstrators, the 1842 strike wave was surprisingly peaceable. Plugging a boiler itself was a highly theatrical way to bring a mill to a standstill, but not an act of permanent destruction. Mill-owners who offered little resistance generally had the rest of their property left intact (their non-resistance formed part of the basis for the persistent rumour that the Anti-Corn Law League was behind the strike). Strikers then joined the march to the next mill along the way. Even in riot-torn Halifax, turning out the mills was generally well disciplined. 'Keep the peace and do violence to no man', the local Chartist leadership instructed.[114] In a few localities events confounded observers, no more so than in Oldham where the Chartists voted against striking for the Charter and some even enrolled as special constables to assist in policing public gatherings.[115] One might suppose that the Rochdale mill-owner John Bright, a leading member of the Anti-Corn Law League and thus firmly in the Chartist demonography, would have been singled out for particular hostility. His workers duly turned out when pickets arrived and the water was released from his mill's boilers. Then on the common opposite his home a crowd, estimated by Bright at 6,000 to 8,000, gathered and 'sang psalms or Chartist hymns' before dispersing peaceably.[116] One is reminded of the French composer Berlioz's comment, that the English knew no more of how to have a revolution than Italians did of writing opera.

In the words of one Halifax Chartist, 'the struggle was short but fierce'.[117] In Yorkshire, mills began to re-open from the end of the week and most were fully operational by the following Monday, when the drift back to work also became apparent in Manchester. Some Lancashire strikes were more

---

111 Alan Campbell, *The Lanarkshire Miners*, pp. 250-2.
112 Quoted in Leslie C. Wright, *Scottish Chartism*, p. 146.
113 For events in Halifax see Noel Thompson, *The People's Science: the Popular Political Economy of Exploitation and Crisis, 1816-34* (1984), pp. 292-5, and the eye-witness account published by Benjamin Wilson, *The Struggles of an Old Chartist* (1887), reprinted in David Vincent, *Testaments of Radicalism*, pp. 193-292.
114 Ben Rushton, quoted at a Chartist meeting by the *Halifax Guardian*, 20 August 1842. 'Rushton epitomised the type of the W. Riding local leader' according to Dorothy Thompson, *The Chartists*, pp. 225-6.
115 Michael Winstanley, 'Oldham radicalism and the origins of popular liberalism', *Historical Journal*, vol. 36, no, 3, (1993), p. 636.
116 Keith Robbins, *John Bright* (1979), p. 37.
117 David Vincent, *Testaments of Radicalism*, p. 201.

protracted and the powerloom weavers held out until 26 September. As they continued, however, strikes were no longer attended by demonstrations as they had been in mid-August. At the local level, strikes were defeated by effective, usually military, containment or by temporarily licensing unrest. Joseph Lawson of Pudsey observed this at close quarters:

> When the magistrates appeared at Bankhouse accompanied by the military — the mounted Lancers — and read the 'Riot Act', this man North stood up and addressed them, telling them that all his men had resolved to shed no blood in self defence, but had determined that no more work should be done till the 'People's Charter' was the law of the land. He bared his breast as he spoke, and told both the magistrates and soldiers, they might pierce his heart with bullets or lances, but the people were moved to no longer starve when there was an abundance in the land, kept from the producers of all wealth by bad and unjust laws. The magistrates then left, guarded by the military, whilst scores of stones and broken bricks were thrown at them over some cottage houses in Bankhouse Lane, where the road was much lower than the houses. The Bankhouse Mill boiler was plugged, and the Fulneck Bread Bakery emptied, as well as many other houses, to supply the hungry invaders. Much valuable property was destroyed, and scores of mill boilers in various places were plugged, and many mill dams let off.
>
> Being but a young man (though married at the time) and not having much experience of riots, from all I could hear and see it seemed to me that order and quiet would never be restored till the government was changed to pure Democracy. In this I was mistaken.[118]

Without extended credit from shopkeepers or donations from wealthy supporters, however, it was almost impossible to sustain strike action when otherwise supportive fellow trades were themselves in dispute. At the macro-level, the trades were in a comparable position to the Chartist Convention three years before. Once it became clear how little the middle classes 'were prepared to assist and support the people in the struggle for the attainment of their political rights' (to quote once again the manifesto of the Manchester Trades' Congress), the only plausible strategy was a systematic escalation of strikes elsewhere in the country. To wait on the spread of spontaneous strike action (which as we have seen was patchy) was hopeless. Moreover, trades in other regions were waiting on news from Manchester and the news, when it arrived, was not encouraging. At Merthyr Tydfil, with the miners seemingly on the brink of striking, the authorities posted news of the drift back to work in Manchester. 'Unless the news from the North be bad I do not apprehend an outbreak', commented Glamorgan's Chief Constable. 'I believe this to be a shadow of the Manchester affair and their object the Charter, and their cry is now or never.'[119]

Robert Fyson has aptly encapsulated 1842 as 'the point at which history failed to turn',[120] a supreme moment of crisis as the State faced down unprecedented popular resistance. The once prevalent interpretation of Chartism in 1848 as being little more than farce has, quite properly, been exposed as utterly fallacious.[121] However, in terms of trade unionism and Chartism converging in one potentially transformative force, 1842 was the point of no return. The two were not, however, thereafter completely divergent and the history of their subsequent relationship provides further evidence of Chartism's capacity to shape and inform the way in which workers thought about society.

---

118 Joseph Lawson, *Letters to the Young*, p. 132.
119 HO 42/265, 21 August 1842, quoted in F. C. Mather, *Public Order in the Age of the Chartists* (1984), p. 131.
120 Robert Fyson, 'The crisis of 1842', p. 216.
121 David Goodway, *London Chartism, 1838-48*; John Saville, *1848*.

7

Out of Chartism

The Mid-1840s

The strike wave of 1842 was a unique phenomenon. There was no further occasion in nineteenth-century Britain when strikes were either so extensive or so closely identified with political objectives. The result was a change in the outlook of trade unions, though this is chiefly apparent only with the benefit of hindsight for, as we shall shortly see, trade unionist activities continued to be marked by continuity well into the third quarter of the century. The Chartist and strike movements of 1842 constituted the last point in British history when a revolution in the nature of government, economy and society seemed not only imperative but actually achievable to many of the population. The subsequent history of Chartism bears this out. A substantial harvest assisted the recovery of the economy and some of the wage reductions which had occasioned the strikes were reversed. Nationally, the Chartist leadership was scattered. Some were in prison, notably Thomas Cooper. Some went to America, notably McDouall, the most powerful advocate of Chartism as a trades movement. Some intensified their involvement in related (or, depending on one's point of view, tangential and even distracting) initiatives: education, temperance, religion or the land question. 'Local Chartists were left high and dry, a dedicated rump without a mass following, who were to be most successful when they busied themselves with other things'.[1]

The land question, with the indefatigable O'Connor very much to the fore, came closest to infusing Chartism as a whole with a new spirit and purpose. The successful mobilization of Chartism in 1848 owed much to an infrastructure derived largely from the Land Plan, which had more than 270 branches and 70,000 members at its peak, and which facilitated the continuation of Chartism as a national movement with its own press, full-time executive and professional lecturers. The Plan was, however, an activity to which trade societies less readily related. With its aim of promoting the relative scarcity of labour by removing it altogether from the manufacturing sector, the Plan was consistent with trade unionism; but the latter, with its inevitable privileging of industrial work, sat uncomfortably alongside the agrarian fundamentalism of the Land Plan: 'we know of nothing but … that is capable of preserving the country from inevitable destruction'.[2] Whereas proponents of the Charter in 1839-42 had posited an essentially equal partnership between Chartism and the trades, the balance now was shifting. Sometimes trade unionism was even projected in a distinctly subordinate role, as for example in this *Northern Star* editorial:

> The pompous trades and proud mechanics, who are now willing forgers of their own fetters … we will embrace them in our national regeneration corps, and admit them to participation in the

---

1   Edward Royle, *Chartism* (1996), p. 32.
2   Quote in Malcolm Chase, '"We wish only to work for ourselves": the Chartist Land Plan', in Malcolm Chase and Ian Dyck (eds.), *Living and Learning: Essays in Honour of J. F. C. Harrison* (1996), p. 139.

> battle and its fruits, which must be the triumph of justice over injustice, of knowledge over bigotry and intolerance, and of liberty over tyranny, THE PEOPLE'S CHARTER AND THE LAND!³

It is noticeable that support for the Plan came principally from labourers (almost entirely unorganized) and occupational groups where union organization had largely collapsed (woolcombers, stockingers, handloom weavers) or which had recently reorganized with a strong Chartist orientation (shoemakers and tailors).⁴ Furthermore, there was no facility for corporate membership. Only one trade society, of East London shoemakers, seems actually to have invested its capital in Land Plan shares.⁵ A few placed funds in the National Land and Labour Bank, established to facilitate the purchase of estates for Chartist colonies, but equally there were some well-publicized withdrawals and prohibitions on investment, notably by the Journeymen Steam Engine, Machine Makers' and Millwrights' Society which ordered all branches to withdraw their funds from the Land Bank or else be expelled.⁶ The Operative Stonemasons' Society told the Bank's manager bluntly that 'they had not personal confidence in Mr O'Connor'.⁷ This was prescient: O'Connor's probity was manifest and the Plan was in many ways a remarkable initiative; but it was distinguished by neither sound financial nor actuarial management.

It would be wrong, however, to suppose that trade unionists could no longer relate to Chartism. Its fundamental premise remained unaltered: the protection of working people's interests could only be ensured through the creation of a participative democracy. Chartism continued to generate a climate which nurtured the further development of working-class culture and associational forms. Benefit, friendly and mutual instruction societies all prospered in the 1840s. This was the period in which life assurance and building societies took off as a truly popular form of mutual help. Trade unionism similarly benefited from this collectivist impulse. Bleak though it turned out to be, 1842 did not represent a point from which trade unionism declined and the years to 1847 saw an escalation of trade society activity. In London, registration of friendly societies — many of them actually trade societies — reached a peak in 1842-4.⁸ In Leicestershire a trade union presence was re-asserted in the hosiery industry, notably in the fine glove trade where, under the leadership of the Chartist Thomas Winters, a society was formed that embraced more than 1,200 of the 1,400 workforce.⁹ A number of major urban centres saw the formation of new bodies for inter-trade co-operation, a situation Koditschek describes in Bradford where political radicalism 'heightened militancy and mobilization' and 'breathed new life into trade unionism'.¹⁰ This became clear in 1843-5 when an umbrella organization was formed under Chartist auspices, called the United Trades: 'structured more loosely

---

3   *Northern Star*, 1 November 1845.
4   David J. V. Jones, *Chartism and the Chartists* (1975), pp. 128-37, provides the most detailed discussion of membership, See also Malcolm Chase, 'The Chartist Land Plan and the local historian', *The Local Historian*, 18 (2), May, (1988), pp. 76-9.
5   Malcolm Chase, *'The People's Farm': English Radical Agrarianism, 1775-1840* (2010), p. 149.
6   *Northern Star*,1 January 1848.
7   *PP* 1847-8, XIX. Select Committee on the National Land Company, Third Report and Minutes of Evidence, q. 2189.
8   David R. Green, *From Artisans to Paupers: Economic Change and Poverty in London, 1790-1870* (1995), pp. 99-100.
9   See Richard Gurnham, *200 Years: The Hosiery Unions, 1776-1976* (1976), pp. 15 and 19 and Alan Little,'Thomas Winters: Chartist and trade unionist', *BSSLH*, 49, 1984). Winters was a former member of the Leicester Shakespearian Chartists and played a leading role in the development of trade unionism in the region's hosiery industry after 1842. He gave evidence to the 1844-5 Royal Commission on the industry and became a key figure in the NAUT, giving evidence on its behalf to the 1854 Select Committee on Stoppages of Wages in the Hosiery Industry, and the 1856 and 1860 Parliamentary Select Committees on Masters and Operatives.
10 Theodore Koditschek, *Class Formation and Urban Industrial Society: Bradford 1750-1850* (1990), p. 481.

than the general unions of the thirties, this body proved more effective in maintaining some links between the skilled and the proletarianized, serving as a more militant and activist precursor to the trades councils of the mid-Victorian age'. Largely due to the energy of the local Chartist leader George White, a Woolcombers' Protective Society was formed along with a union of female powerloom weavers. Similar bodies were established elsewhere: for example, in Bristol the United Trades' Association in 1844[11] and in Birmingham a Central Committee of Trades, in 1845. The latter was chaired by John Mason, who had been a full-time Chartist lecturer in 1840. 'New societies appeared in trades that previously had been relatively unorganized', for example the fire-iron and edge-tool makers.[12] In 1846, Aberdeen trades formed a 'Delegated Committee of Sympathy' to 'support each other in the event of a strike of any of them, or when any general movement was required in support of trade unions'.[13] This may well have owed something to the extraordinary trades' demonstration that greeted O'Connor and Duncombe when they visited the city in the autumn of 1843.[14] In Sheffield that year a committee of trade societies proposed 'the formation of a union to embrace all the trades of Sheffield'.[15]

National networks were also revived. In Lancashire the engineers' United Trades' Association was resuscitated and extended in 1844 as the Mechanics' Protective Society of Great Britain, specifically to resist the use of the document by northern engineering employers.[16] The president of the Cordwainers' General Mutual Assistance Association was a London Chartist. By the end of October 1844 it embraced 120 societies nationwide and it is a reasonable supposition that most of them involved local Chartists in leadership roles: this was definitely so at Colchester, for example, where closed shops were enforced across the city.[17] The rival Philanthropic Society of Boot and Shoemakers also sought to create a national general union. The following spring the two bodies amalgamated.[18] Prominent among those calling for the move were Chartists who argued that old-style trade societies should give way to mutualism under a central executive.[19] Though the initiative foundered later in the decade, the principal shoemakers' organizations all affiliated to the National Association of United Trades (NAUT), which was closely associated with Chartism. This seems to have been a common means by which local societies co-operated while guarding their autonomy, being adopted for example by rival Wolverhampton tin-plate workers' unions.[20]

When the General United Tailors' Trade Protection Society was formed in 1844 it too exhibited a distinct Chartist hue and nominated the *Northern Star* as its official organ. The *soirée* that concluded its foundation conference was presided over by O'Connor's close associate William Prowting Roberts (solicitor to the Chartist Land Plan) and Thomas Slingsby Duncombe, the radical MP whom Robert Peel described as 'the organ of the Chartist party'.[21] 'Unless the trade generally adopt the principles of

---

11 David McNulty, 'Bristol trade unions in the Chartist years', in John Rule, (ed.), *British Trade Unionism, 1750-1850: The Formative Years* (1988), p. 229.

12 Clive Behagg, *Politics and Production in the Early Nineteenth Century* (1990), p. 115.

13 W. H. Fraser, *Trade Unions and Society: the Struggle for Acceptance* (1974), p. 43.

14 R. G. Gammage, *History of the Chartist Movement, 1837-54* (1969, first published 1854-5), pp. 251-2.

15 NAPSS 1860, p. 542.

16 James B. Jefferys, *The Story of the Engineers* (1945), p. 25.

17 A. F. J. Brown, *Chartism in Essex and Suffolk* (1982), p. 74.

18 David Goodway, *London Chartism, 1838-48* (1982), p. 165.

19 Iorwerth J. Prothero, 'London Chartism and the trades', *Economic History Review*, 24, (1971), p. 213.

20 Archibald T. Kidd, *History of the Tin-Plate Workers and Sheet Metal Workers and Braziers Societies* (1949), pp. 81, 84.

21 David Goodway, *London Chartism, 1838-48*, p. 56.

a General Union, there is no hope of making a successful stand against the encroachments of the principal capitalists', observed London tailors whose 'house of call' (see Chapter 2) was at the Three Crowns in Soho.[22] Large meetings were addressed by the Society's Chartist secretary when he toured the country in 1845, including three gatherings, the largest a thousand strong, in Birmingham.

The largest new union, however, to have been shaped by Chartism in these years was that of the miners. We saw in the previous chapter how the coalfield strikes of 1842, though the product of conditions in the pits themselves, were interleaved with Chartism, not least in the personalities of many of their leaders. The miners represent an interesting and especially controversial case study in the interrelationship between trade unionist activity and Chartism.[23] The close solidarity of the mine did not necessarily translate into trade union organization: sometimes, as in the Free Colliers of Lanarkshire, it hardly needed to, since other associational forms generated similarly close and mutually supportive organization with less risk than formal unionism brought. For partly the same reason, formal Chartist organization made only limited headway on the coalfields, though the extent to which it did does seem to have varied between regions. 'Miners in general provided more mass than leadership to Chartism' comments Rule,[24] but the relative absence of Chartist branch-life or large-scale NCA membership does not mean that the appeal of the Charter went unheeded. Mine-owners exercised significant control, directly or through their managers or sub-contractors, of many aspects of miners' lives besides work: the provision of housing, the administration of local government and justice, the availability of employment opportunities outside the mine. This may have made miners wary of overt political activity: it certainly encouraged judicious occasional displays of deference and it influenced the continued prevalence of violent and/or theatrical protest.

However, none of these factors fenced off mining communities from the influence of Chartism, which was manifest in the formation of the Miners' Association of Great Britain and Ireland (MAGBI) in 1842-3. The previous chapter noted how Staffordshire miners sought to build connections with other coalfields during their strike in the summer of 1842: this culminated on 31 July in a call by Hanley miners for a Staffordshire, Shropshire and Cheshire delegate conference to prepare for a national congress of English and Welsh miners.[25] Even at this early stage a national miners' network may have been more than just conjectural: at almost the same time colliers in Halifax held 'a preparatory meeting in order to secure a general organisation, previous to a universal strike'. They also voted, one is tempted to say inevitably, 'in favour of the People's Charter'. At a subsequent meeting in the Halifax Oddfellows' Hall, delegates from several other towns were present and all supervisory workers were excluded. 'The formation of a general union' was discussed along

---

22   Ibid, p. 173.
23   The fullest study, Raymond Challinor and Brian Ripley, *The Miners' Association: a Trade Union in the Age of the Chartists* (1968), has generated considerable debate. See reviews and letters in *BSSLH* 20 (1970), 23 (1971) and 24 (1972), and John Rule, *The Labouring Classes in Early Industrial England 1750-1850* (1986). Its republication in 1990 revived the debate in *LHR* (successor of the *BSSLH*), see vol. 56, no. 2(1991), vol. 57, no. 2 (1993) and vol. 58, no. 1 (1994). For a detailed survey of the literature on the relationship between coalminers and Chartism see R. A. Church, 'Chartism and the miners: a reinterpretation', *LHR*, vol. 56, part 3, (1991). A full-scale study of the miners' strikes of 1842 is still lacking, but see Alan Campbell, *The Lanarkshire Miners: a Social History of their Trade Unions, 1775-1874* (1979), pp. 250-2, Robert Fyson, 'The crisis of 1842: Chartism, the colliers' strike and the outbreak in the Potteries', in James Epstein and Dorothy Thompson, (eds.), *The Chartist Experience: Studies in Working-Class Radicalism and Culture, 1830-60* (1982), pp. 198-201, and R. Quinault, 'The Warwickshire county magistracy and public order, c.1830-1870', in R. Quinault and J. Stevenson (1974) (eds.), *Popular Protest and Public Order: Six Studies in British History 1790-1920* (1974). See also the biography of Roberts, Raymond Challinor, *A Radical Lawyer in Victorian England: WP Roberts and the Struggle for Workers' Rights* (1990).
24   John Rule, *The Labouring Classes in Early Industrial England 1750-1850*, p. 337.
25   Robert Fyson, 'The crisis of 1842', p. 200.

with 'a general strike so as to bring all machinery and all power requiring coals to a stand'.[26]

The first national miners' union emerged from consultations during and after the 1842 strikes. The lead was apparently taken by a local Miners' Philanthropic Society meeting at the Griffin Inn, Wakefield, in November 1842.[27] A correspondence with North-east pitmen was established the following February. What was initially referred to by the *Northern Star* (an important medium of communication between the coalfields) as 'the Pitmen's General Union' quickly evolved into the MAGBI with a membership which the most plausible estimates place at between 30,000 and 40,000. This figure comfortably made it the largest trade union of its day. It was comparatively weak in Scotland and made no progress in Wales, so these membership figures would suggest at least a third of the English mines workforce joined.[28] The proportion of face workers was probably even greater, especially among the most highly skilled for whom the trade unionist ethos would have had a particular appeal. For example, hewers (around 40 and 50 per cent of all colliery workers) exercised a significant degree of discretion and control over the work process in the North-east, 'buttressed by a well established, though not a formal, apprenticeship system, [and] a strictly demarcated division of labour':[29] but, as Colls[30] has shown, the independence of the 'true-bred pitman' was fast being eroded.

During its relatively brief yet impressive life, the leadership of the MAGBI was closely associated with Chartism. W. P. Roberts was its national legal officer. Its treasurer Martin Jude, at least two of its general secretaries and the editor of its journal the *Miners' Advocate* had all been active Chartists prior to the formation of the union. Among the rank and file of the MAGBI, however, attitudes were more ambivalent. In part this may simply have been one of the consequences of 1842. O'Connor was not permitted to address its 1844 conference; there was hostility to the circulation of Chartist handbills at the Glasgow conference the same year and serious criticism of Roberts' influence. Roberts could have made a comfortable living as a solicitor in his native Bath. Instead, driven by a deep contempt for employers and landowners of every persuasion, he devoted himself to a career largely spent fighting industrial cases, mainly in magistrates' courts, all over England. He was indispensable to both Chartism and the MAGBI, but this does not mean he was easy to get on with nor, even, politically adroit. Much of the responsibility for initiating the protracted and bruising 1844 strike in the Durham and Northumberland coalfields lay with him, a move in which he was opposed by the other leading Chartist connected with the Association, Martin Jude. The great strike of 1844 was heroic, desperate, tragic. Although the MAGBI lingered on it was broken by the strike. It had sustained the action but inadequately, and had done so in the face of competing claims it could not meet from countless other disputes in the British coalfields. These included a three-month strike in Lanarkshire and turn outs, some of similar duration, in Yorkshire. Here large numbers of blacklegs

---

26 *Leeds Times*, 6 August 1842; *Halifax Guardian* 6 August 1842. For a slightly different reading of events in Halifax, see Raymond Challinor and Brian Ripley, *The Miners' Association*, p. 62.

27 Raymond Challinor and Brian Ripley, *The Miners' Association*, p. 63.

28 The English collieries' workforce was approximately 103,000 in 1840 (John Benson, *British Coalminers in the Nineteenth Century: A Social History* (1989), p. 217). Scottish membership of the MAGBI was just over 6,000 in 1844 and probably declined thereafter (Alan Campbell, *The Lanarkshire Miners*, p. 252). For the problems the MAGBI encountered in Wales see Raymond Challinor and Brian Ripley, *The Miners' Association*, pp. 166-7. The latters' calculation of MAGBI membership as 50,000 in November 1843 and up to 10,000 more thereafter is far from implausible — unlike the Webbs' (Sidney and Beatrice Webb, *The History of Trade Unionism*, revised edition (1920), p. 130) figure of 100,000. The inclusion of Ireland in the union's title was a nice touch of grandiloquence: at no time in the nineteenth century is the northern Irish coalfield likely to have employed more than 1,100. The Irish Suffrage Union, however, did support the MAGBI in its efforts to prevent Cumberland mine-owners recruiting strike breakers from Ireland in 1844.

29 R. A. Church, 'Chartism and the miners', p. 30.

30 Robert Colls, *The Pitmen of the Northern Coalfield: Work, Culture and Protest, 1790-1850* (1987), pp. 11-74.

were employed, there were mass evictions of miners from their homes and a flat rejection by employers of any notion of negotiating with the MAGBI which they described as 'an unjust and uncalled for interference with the rights of masters and men'.[31] In County Durham the attitude of the mine-owner Lord Londonderry was even more vituperative. In the words of one eye-witness, strikers, 'pregnant women, bedridden men, and even children in their cradles, were ruthlessly turned out'. 'Multitudes of them resort to the sea shore, living & sleeping amongst the rocks, where they exist on refuse, fish, and any other eatable matter they can collect'.[32]

The MAGBI survived the 1844 strike but increasingly in only a vestigial form. 'Almost imperceptibly, centralized control withered away' its historians commented.[33] Independent county or coalfield unions survived or were revived and as late as 1863, when a national miners' conference was held at Leeds, the MAGBI remained a key point of reference. What might have helped hold the Association together would have been effective national inter-trades organization but this was only partly forthcoming. The miners had to endure lengthy prolonged strike action and the victimization that followed at that point when the Chartist movement was least able to help. For example on Teesside, a rapidly expanding conurbation just ten miles away at its nearest point from the Durham coalfield, there were no reports in either the local or Chartist press of activity in the years 1844-5.[34] The formation of the NAUT constituted a significant revival in inter-trades co-operation, but as we shall see its relationship with the miners was a troubled one.

The National Association of United Trades (NAUT)

> The trades have long tried local societies and found them powerless for good. They next tried general unions of particular trades and found that these could not successfully resist the encroachments of the task masters. They then attempted to form a National Trades Union; but it was broken to pieces through mismanagement before it had grown into a 'monster combination'.[35]

Sam Jacobs, secretary of the Bristol Chartists and of the city's cabinetmakers' society, was impelled by the belief that an inter-trades national organization was necessary if the original aims of local trade societies were to be fulfilled. Towards the end of 1842 he floated a proposal for a National Trade Benefit Society. This idea was probably rooted in disillusion with political action as a remedy for social and economic change that had begun after the August strikes had petered out. It subsequently became the motif of his uneven relationship with Chartism. In 1843 he took his own society into a Manchester-based federation in search of the 'one great society' that would 'maintain our wonted respectability and save our trade from that wretched fate that hath befallen too many of the hitherto flourishing and respectable occupations'. He was the driving force behind the United Trades' Association of Bristol and also instrumental in the formation of the NAUT in 1845. During 1846-7 he was a NAUT missionary in Scotland. Looking back at the GNCTU's failure to grow into a

---

31 Raymond Challinor and Brian Ripley, *The Miners' Association*, p. 163.

32 Quotations from Raymond Challinor and Brian Ripley, *The Miners' Association*, p. 163, and Robert Colls, *The Pitmen of the Northern Coalfield*, p. 300.

33 Raymond Challinor and Brian Ripley, *The Miners' Association*, p. 241.

34 Malcolm Chase, 'Chartism, 1838-1858: responses in two Teesside towns', *Northern History*, 24, (1988), p. 162. David Goodway, *London Chartism, 1838-48*, p. 54, speaks of 'massive solidarity' for the 1844 strike. There is indeed extensive coverage and subscription lists in the *Northern Star*, June-September 1844, but they are slender compared to the Glasgow spinners' campaign six years earlier.

35 *Northern Star*, 17 October 1846.

'monster combination', in the letter quoted above, Jacobs added: 'I thank God that the NAUT has arrived at that state'.[36]

The National Association of United Trades for the Protection of Labour, to give it its full title, was not exactly a monster combination but the title chosen for it, a conscious echo of the NAPL of 1829-31, indicated its aspirations to be so. Like the earlier body its policy was to support societies in strikes to resist wage reductions but not for advances. It was the largest umbrella organization of the trades in Britain since the NAPL and GNCTU, and it can be argued it was more successful than either. Yet it has tended to be obscured by other aspects of the history of Chartism in the later 1840s and by subsequent developments in trade union history. Musson's influential sketch[37] effectively dismisses it for failing to attract the larger industrial unions, adding it was 'much less class-consciously aggressive' than the GNCTU 'but it too proved a failure'. It has been said that it 'began a long decline into obscurity' from 1848,[38] was of little importance after 1851'[39] and that it 'received very little support and soon became transformed into a modest pressure group'.[40] There is some truth in all these comments yet they are unnecessarily disparaging. Members totalled more than 50,000 as early as October 1846[41] and probably continued to grow during the following year. Initially it attracted a wide spectrum of support from across the trades but its support base fell away from 1847 as 'higher trades', such as compositors and bookbinders who had initially taken an interest, declined to affiliate, likewise major industrial unions such as the power spinners. Their motives for doing so seem to have been prompted by the perception that the legislative threat to organized labour was receding. Weaker and/or localized unions remained loyal. For example the origins of support for the Association in Huddersfield lay with the iron moulders and engineers, but the only two local unions directly to affiliate to the Association in 1847 were the tailors and fancy weavers.[42]

In 1848 the Chartists organized a third monster petition. Its rejection, and perhaps even more decisively the Government's handling of the London demonstration intended to accompany its presentation to Parliament, once again cast Chartism adrift from the hope of an imminent realization of its immediate objectives. It was once almost commonplace to dismiss the Chartist movement of 1848 as an ephemeral revival, constituting little threat to the establishment. This is now recognized as very far from the truth, especially when the Irish dimension to political unrest in Europe's year of revolutions is also taken into account. In Britain there were serious disturbances in Ashton-under-Lyne, Bradford (and nearby Bingley), Halifax, London's East End and Manchester. There was nothing, however, to match the scale of the 1842 strike wave; nor was organized trade involvement in unrest anything but minimal. Chartism's real successes in 1848 lay in the field of local government. Here patient organization often yielded favourable results. Patchy and piecemeal though these appeared at a national level, they nevertheless represented real progress. However, local government

---

36 See David McNulty, 'Bristol trade unions in the Chartist years', pp. 229-32. Because he was among the very first to use the term 'aristocracy of labour', Jacobs attracted some attention in the late 1970s when its validity as an analytical concept in social history was widely debated. See Michael Shepherd, 'The origins and incidence of the term "labour aristocracy"', *BSSLH*, 37, (1978), and comments by other historians in subsequent issues of *BSSLH*, especially David McNulty in no. 38 (1979), 19.

37 A. E. Musson, *British Trade Unions, 1800-1875* (1972).

38 Michael Shepherd, 'The origins and incidence of the term "labour aristocracy"', p. 53.

39 W. H. Fraser, *Trade Unions and Society*, p. 43.

40 E. H. Hunt, *British Labour History 1815-1914* (1981), p. 204.

41 Michael Shepherd, 'The origins and incidence of the term "labour aristocracy"', p. 54.

42 Alan J. Brooke, 'Labour disputes and trade unions in the industrial revolution', in E. A. H. Haigh (ed.), *Huddersfield a Most Handsome Town: Aspects of the History and Culture of a West Yorkshire Town* (1992), p. 232.

reform in the 1830s had still left a complex array of boroughs, improvement commissions, Poor Law Unions, and parish authorities. Furthermore, the nature of local government franchises (which excluded not only women but also recipients of poor relief, those who were in arrears of rates, lived with their parents, were lodgers or who had recently moved house) was intrinsically divisive. Eligibility for inclusion on electoral rolls was subject to widely varying local interpretation. Most decisively, though, the political issues confronting labour did not fall within the remit of local government: formal trade unionist interest was therefore inevitably slender.

The fortunes of the NAUT from 1848 reflected the fortunes of Chartism as a whole. It relied heavily on the *Northern Star* to communicate with its affiliates, having initially acquired a controlling interest in the *Apprentice and Trades' Weekly Register* which promptly failed. O'Connor's 'monthly magazine of politics, literature, poetry etc', *Labourer* was also a significant source of support. The quickening political pulse in 1847-8 prompted the NAUT to issue its own *Monthly Report*, followed in August 1848 by a lively weekly, *Labour League*. This, too, failed in May 1849 and the Association then reverted to using the *Northern Star* whose editor, George Fleming, succeeded T. S. Duncombe as the NAUT's president in 1852. Fleming was a co-operator and Owenite of some distinction but he lacked the commanding presence in the labour movement that Duncombe enjoyed. His accession contributed to the erosion of the Association's breadth of appeal. For all his aristocratic lineage and reputation as the best-dressed man in the House of Commons, Duncombe had been no mere figurehead. He involved himself in the routine work of the NAUT's executive and was a skilled parliamentarian who, as we shall shortly see, continued to represent labour interests in Westminster to the end of the decade.[43]

In the 1850s it becomes difficult to discern a pattern in the Association's membership. In 1856 Thomas Winters, NAUT's corresponding secretary, said it consisted of between 5,000 and 6,000 individuals drawn from 'the wood trade, the iron trade, the salt trade, and the leather trade, and various other trades; I cannot call them all to mind ... dispersed over different parts of the country'.[44] Yet the NAUT was more than a token presence in the labour politics of the 1850s, though this has gone largely unnoticed, and it survived into the 1860s. It therefore has some claim to be considered the last institutional survival of the Chartist movement.

Like the GNCTU, the NAUT was not, properly speaking, a general union but a federation of trade societies (its official publications usually speak in term of 'adhesions'). The GNCTU was a frequent point of reference for those who supported the new body: 'ever since [the] Builders' and Consolidated Union were broken up,' declared a London silk weaver, 'the working classes had been going downwards, for the want of an institution of the same magnitude, that these bodies were'.[45] The NAUT was very much a Chartist body in origin and execution. Editorials in the movement's paper had been calling for a 'Trades Parliament' or 'General Confederation of Trades' Delegates' and successful opposition to a tightening of the already widely resented Master and Servant laws in 1844 formed the basis for its formation. The Master and Servant campaign had included a national petition reputedly marshalling two million signatures which owed much to Chartist organization. Thomas

---

43 A full appraisal of Duncombe is long overdue. His *Life and Correspondence*, edited by his son and published in two volumes in 1868, being noticeably deficient on his radical and labour sympathies. The contention that he 'picked up causes as rapidly as the weather changed' (Michael Shepherd, 'The origins and incidence of the term "labour aristocracy"', p. 55) is unfair. Information can be found in all the major accounts of Chartism but, brief as it is, the most rounded appraisal remains that of the Webbs (Sidney and Beatrice Webb, *The History of Trade Unionism*, p. 187).

44 *PP* 1856 (343) XIII: Select Committee on Masters and Operatives (Equitable Councils of Conciliation), qq. 2-4.

45 *Northern Star*, 23 October 1847.

Slingsby Duncombe had engineered the defeat of the parliamentary bill. A testimonial committee in his honour, formed by London artisans and Chartists, formed one of the elements from which the preliminary delegate meeting was established which set up the NAUT in March 1845. This was, though, far from exclusively a metropolitan initiative: men like Sam Jacobs, and especially the united Sheffield trades which corresponded with Duncombe about the proposal, made it a national organization from its inception, though its executive was a London body with Duncombe as its president.[46]

The NAUT had four main objectives: mutual assistance, protection and solidarity for the trades; monitoring labour issues in Parliament; provision of arbitration and conciliation in industrial disputes; and producer co-operation and land settlement. Promotion of the latter was the responsibility of a separate arm of NAUT until the depression of 1848 forced it to consolidate around the first three objectives. In spite of this the NAUT remained very much attuned to the agrarian emphasis of Chartism in the late 1840s, in seeking 'the employment of surplus labour, which constitutes the reserve in the competitive market, by means of which wages are always kept down to the lowest subsistence level'.[47] This alternative political economy, Prothero observes 'in intention and potential at least, posed the greatest challenge to capitalist economic organisation, a challenge not repeated after mid-century'.[48] It was resonant, of course, with the interest in producer co-operation so much in evidence in the early 1830s, but Prothero also draws attention to interest in the same ideas in France in 1848.

Ostensibly, the NAUT's greatest successes came in its earliest years when it capitalized on the frustrated aspirations of those who had supported the convergence of Chartism and trade unionism in 1838-42, and dispatched lecturers to address large audiences across Britain. They included Sam Jacobs, the Lancashire miners' leader William Dixon;[49] David Ross, a temperance Chartist and Leeds schoolmaster who had been arrested in 1842 for involvement in the strikes in Manchester where he formerly lived;[50] and two leading London Chartists, John Skelton of the shoemakers' union,[51] and John Parker,[52] general secretary of the London tailors and one of the driving forces behind the formation of a national union for the trade.[53] Its founding conference profoundly influenced the establishment of the Cordwainers' Mutual Assistance Association and in 1846 it supported the Association in establishing an 'associative workshop', run as a co-operative by London shoemakers who had been presented with the document forbidding union membership. As David Goodway[54] points out this was the precursor of a wide variety of associative projects, mainly assisted by the Christian Socialists, in trades as diverse as the bakers and the engineers across London in the early

---

46 A full study of the NAUT is sadly lacking. This account draws on officers' evidence to the 1856 and 1860 Parliamentary Select Committees on Masters and Operatives and on David Goodway, *London Chartism, 1838-48*, esp. pp. 54-6. See also G. D. H. Cole and A. W. Filson, *British Working-Class Movements: Select Documents, 1789-1875* (1951), pp. 469-74, George Howell, *Conflicts of Capital and Labour, Historically and Economically considered. Being a History and Review of the Trade Unions of Great Britain* (1878), pp. 139-41, Iorwerth J. Prothero, 'London Chartism and the trades', *Economic History Review*, 24, (1971), Sidney and Beatrice Webb, *The History of Trade Unionism*, pp. 186-96.

47 *Labour League*, 1 August 1848.

48 Iorwerth J. Prothero, *Radical Artisans in England and France, 1830-1870* (1997), p. 166.

49 Peter Taylor, *Popular Politics in Early Industrial Britain, Bolton, 1835-50* (1995), p. 179.

50 Paul Pickering, *Chartism and the Chartists in Manchester and Salford* (1995), p. 204.

51 Iorwerth J. Prothero, *Radical Artisans in England and France, 1830-1870*, p. 246.

52 Michael Shepherd, 'The origins and incidence of the term "labour aristocracy"', p. 53.

53 David Goodway, *London Chartism, 1838-48, passim.*

54 Ibid, p. 156.

1850s. When the Central Association of London Trades ceased in 1846, the NAUT also took over much of its function. It was the means by which London societies within the fragile shoemakers' and tailors' federations remained formally part of a wider trade union network and it attracted a wide range of trades in its early stages. These included the Boilermakers' Society, the Operative Typefounders' Association, the London bookbinders, the General Goldbeaters' Protection Society and the sawyers (reputedly a trade scarcely interested in politics). The National Typographical Association also sent delegates to the inaugural conference, a rare indication of interest in inter-trades organization by a union that has come to epitomize sectionalism.[55] A more serious weakness, already noted, was the failure of the Lancashire spinners to show an interest beyond sending a delegation to the first conference. Despite this the Association was vocally represented in the Lancashire towns, enjoyed some support among the powerloom weavers and keenly supported the Preston spinners' strike of 1853-4.

The strike in which the NAUT was most closely involved, however, was that of the Wolverhampton Society of Tin-plate Workers in 1851-2. Like Tolpuddle and the Glasgow spinners before it, this was one of the critical trade disputes of the nineteenth century. It reveals much about both the NAUT and the position of trade unionism at the time. The Society was endeavouring to enforce a standard list of prices, even though it was still in debt to the London Operative Tin-Plate Workers' Society for loans received during a protracted dispute in 1842.[56] The real cause of the dispute was more deeply rooted than the price-list, however, and hinged on the introduction of machinery into two local works as well as price cuts by the employers concerned. The dispute provides a rare documented example of an occasion when NAUT officers became involved in arbitration. When their efforts failed they gave approval on the Association's behalf for a strike. The arrest of the local leadership was accompanied by that of William Peel, Thomas Winters and Frederic Green, the NAUT officers handling the case. Peel was probably a member of the London Operative Tin-Plate Workers' Society, but Winters as we have seen was a framework glove knitter and Green a morocco-leather finisher.[57] The case against Winters was eventually dropped, but charges of conspiracy were brought against the others under the 1825 Combination Laws Repeal Act, which had firmly placed trade disputes within the reach of the common law of conspiracy.

This was an issue which was of particular concern to the NAUT, quite apart from the arrest of its officers, and a London Central Defence Committee was formed under its aegis to manage an appeal for funds to mount a defence. W. P. Roberts was engaged to defend the accused. The Association had been involved in an earlier conspiracy case, against twenty-six members of the Newton-le-Willows (Lancashire) branch of the Journeymen Steam Engine and Machine Makers' Society, plus the Society's secretary Henry Selsby, in 1847. The prosecution was brought to break a peaceable strike against 'illegal' men and apprentices. An indictment (57 yards long, it was said), was presented. Central to it was that simply calling strike breakers 'knobsticks' was actually a conspiracy to commit bodily harm. On appeal the case was dismissed without judgement, leaving the state of the law open to widely varying interpretation.[58]

---

55 A. E. Musson, *The Typographical Association: Origins and History up to 1949* (1954), p. 71.
56 Archibald T. Kidd, *History of the Tin-Plate Workers*, pp. 37, 41, 77-81.
57 David Goodway, *London Chartism, 1838-48*, p. 203.
58 Selsby's case was widely reported in the popular press as a case of particular concern to working people. For example, *Reynolds's Miscellany*, 26 June 1847, deployed the venerably ancient radical rhetoric of the Norman Yoke, arguing the case exemplified employers entering 'the lists under the Norman banner, [and] every true Saxon will grieve'. The trial proceedings were edited by W. P. Roberts and published by the veteran radical and Chartist publisher John Cleave. For a modern account see J. V. Orth, *Combination and Conspiracy: A Legal History of Trade*

The Wolverhampton case constituted a disturbing shift in legal interpretation. Whereas the Lancashire mechanics had been deemed to have made threats of bodily harm towards non-strikers, the Wolverhampton prosecution relied on a legally untested notion of a conspiracy to molest and obstruct an *employer*. Its use seems to have stemmed from the fact that the conduct of the dispute was exemplary. There was no picketing, even when strike-breaking labour was introduced from France. Instead, attempts were made to dissuade strike-breakers in subsequent discussions at public houses — heated and voluble perhaps but none of them apparently intimidating. In summing up, the judge conceded that 'there might be no threats or intimidation used by the defendants'. However:

> If a manufacturer has got a manufactory, and his capital embarked in it for the purpose of producing articles in that manufactory, if persons conspire to take away all his workmen, that would necessarily be an obstruction to him, that would necessarily be a molesting of him in his manufactory.

When sentences of three months imprisonment were handed down, the NAUT was described as 'of a very dangerous character ... there is nothing to be said for persons who belong to an association of that kind, and who, of their own accord, no doubt, go down to different parts of the country, to assist workmen who have, or think they have, any grievance'.[59]

'If this conspiracy against labour should be successful, farewell to trade combinations, in any form', predicted the central committee of the Operative Stonemasons.[60] The verdict and its implications have to be borne in mind in judging the NAUT. If it subsequently failed to match its early promise, as is generally asserted by historians, this was partly because its rationale was compromised by the Wolverhampton judgement. As the law stood after 1851, simply to offer advice or participate as a third party in attempted conciliation ran the risk of an indictment for conspiracy. Even more seriously, participation in any strike might be construed as conspiracy. An even stronger assertion has been made about the NAUT, namely that its policy became one of 'unilateral industrial disarmament ... By complete compliance with the law, the National Association became no threat to employers or government — and no use to workers either'.[61] In fact, NAUT reacted as vigorously as the prevailing mood of the labour movement and the law of the land permitted. A petition of nearly 80,000 signatures was presented to Parliament asking for the law to be changed. The NAUT drew up a bill early in 1852 and set about carefully cultivating public opinion. In this it was conspicuously successful and the Conservative government undertook not to oppose the measure. However, this short-lived, lacklustre administration, chiefly remembered as the 'Who? Who?' ministry (from the comment of the hard-of-hearing Duke of Wellington on failing to recognize names of its members), fell before the bill's first reading. Its passage through the new parliament was protracted and stormy, not least because it was seized upon by Conservatives as a populist cause with which to embarrass the new government. Lord Palmerston, the Home Secretary, was particularly opposed and the bill fell in the House of Lords in June 1853. It was unrealistic to expect a change of heart during the government's lifetime (and Palmerston himself became Prime Minister in 1855).

The return of a Conservative government to Westminster in 1858 altered the political landscape for the NAUT. A bill 'to amend and explain' the 1825 Combination Laws Repeal Act, presented by

---

Unionism, 1721-1906 (1991), *passim*, esp. pp. 95-7.

59 Quoted in J. V. Orth, *Combination and Conspiracy*, p. 98.
60 Quoted in Iorwerth J. Prothero, *Radical Artisans*, p. 96.
61 Raymond Challinor, *A Radical Lawyer*, pp. 182-3.

Duncombe, passed through the Commons without debate and the Lords with only a minor amendment.[62] More commonly known as the 'Molestation of Workmen Act', this measure is of some significance in the evolution of trade unionism and its sponsors deserve greater recognition than they have received. Judicial interpretation lessened much of its force but until 1871 it nonetheless constituted the legal basis for picketing and as a precursor to the more important and enduring reforms of the 1870s it remains something of a benchmark. The distinguished jurist A. V. Dicey saw it as the point where individualism began to give way to collectivism. It has also been seen as encapsulating what long remained trade unionism's overriding legal objective: the right of labour to be left alone in the exercise of its economic power.[63] The passage of the bill also illustrates important changes in the character of trade unionist strategies. The nature of the House of Commons was evolving and demarcation between the various political interests within it was considerably less fluid than it once had been. At the same time the free-market views of the 'Manchester School' largely prevailed among radical MPs and, as far as the trades were concerned, 'wire-pulling' had therefore to give way to lobbying. If the limit of the NAUT's ambition was 'to whittle away at the statutory crimes created in 1825', as John Orth has concluded, this reflected a calculated assessment of what was politically feasible. It was also a strategy that was central to trade unionist thinking thereafter. The dependence of the NAUT upon the sympathies of Conservatives in Parliament is also significant. It was the basis of a working relationship between Tories and trade unions that continued to the mid-1870s. It permitted the Conservatives to claim, as an influential Tory lawyer put it in 1868, that they had fought 'hard against the great Liberal party ... to the great joy of the Working classes and the chagrin of the Manchester Radicals'. The Act remained a Tory reference point in this respect as late even as 1906.[64]

The NAUT's other main sphere of activity in the 1850s was in continuing to promote arbitration and conciliation, which had been a central part of the NAUT's philosophy at its inception. Here, too, it can be seen as laying a basis for significant subsequent development. NAUT publicized and encouraged the establishment of arbitration boards in the Potteries, printing, shipbuilding and the silk industry[65] and unsuccessfully in the Kidderminster carpet trade.[66] When Winters gave evidence before the 1856 Select Committee on Masters and Operatives (Equitable Councils of Conciliation), NAUT membership had dropped to around 6,000. However, this obscures the extent of the Association's network of contacts in the labour movement and, through this Committee, it influenced an abortive bill to establish local councils of conciliation and arbitration in 1858. In evidence to an 1860 Select Committee on the same subject, Winters was able to give details of more than a hundred trade societies, plus six trades councils or delegate meetings (among them Glasgow and Manchester), who wanted to see 'equitable courts of conciliation' established. Symbolically, Winters lived to advise on the successful bill with this objective which was passed in 1867.[67]

---

62 See the account and analysis of the 1859 Act's legal significance in J. V. Orth, *Combination and Conspiracy*, pp. 97-8, 1 19-20, 125-8, and the sources cited there. Also the *Report of the Central Committee of United Trades on the Proceedings Connected with the Combination of Workmen Bill* (1853) and *Report of the Executive Committee of the National Association of United Trades on the Proceedings Connected with the Combination of Workmen Bill, 1859* (1859).

63 J. V. Orth, *Combination and Conspiracy*, p. 152.

64 Charles Sturgeon (1868), *Letters to the Trade Unionists and Working Classes...*, p. 2; cf Conservative Party, Scotland, Campaign Guide (1906), p. 255: both cited in J. V. Orth, *Combination and Conspiracy*, p. 127.

65 E. H. Hunt, *British Labour History 1815-1914* (1981), p. 282.

66 L. D. Smith, *Carpet Weavers and Carpet Masters: The Handloom Carpet Weavers of Kidderminster 1780-1850* (1986), p. 253.

67 W. H. Fraser, *Trade Unions and Society*, p. 109.

The NAUT of the late 1850s was a far cry from the organization of 50,000 or more that had briefly flourished in the late 1840s. Even as Chartism revived during the depression of 1847-8, the Association had not found it easy to create a united front among the trades and on its own admission encountered difficulties in 'inducing such a combination of trades, each having different pursuits, different rates of wages, and, at first sight, different interests, to unite in sufficiently large numbers to give these principles a fair trial'.[68] On the whole, enthusiasm for the NAUT was greatest among those trades which were prepared to align closely to Chartism itself, notably the tailors and shoemakers. There was also a tension between those who thought in terms of 'the trades' and those whose preferred means of organization was 'trade unions'. Supporters of the NAUT saw it firmly in the latter camp, as an exclusively trade union body. So assiduously was this policy pursued that Sam Jacobs' employment as a NAUT missionary was actually terminated because his own trade society had failed to affiliate to the Association. But such a policy rang hollow when significant trade unions failed to support the Association. 'Past experience has taught us that we have had general union enough, commented the Manchester lodge of the Operative Stonemasons' Society. 'It may be well for trades who are divided into sections and have no national organisation amongst themselves to join such an association — they have nothing to lose', added the Society's Central Committee, 'but it is a question for serious reflection whether a general union of each trade separately would not be far more effective than the heterogeneous association in question'.[69] Consequently the NAUT was, as the Webbs[70] pointed out, 'more a Parliamentary Committee for the whole movement than a federation of Trade Unions'. Assessed on these terms, it deserves something more than the condescension of posterity.

THE DEMISE OF CHARTISM

Although the position of the NAUT as the principal trades' representative body was unassailed, it was not what leading Chartists had hoped it would be in the early months of its existence. The relationship between later Chartism and trade unionism therefore took another institutional turn in the autumn of 1848 with the formation of the National Association of Organized Trades for the Industrial, Social and Political Emancipation of Labour (NAOT). This was essentially a metropolitan body, set up following the revival of delegate meetings of the London trades in 1848. Much of its history was encapsulated in a dispute with the NAUT about trade unionist strategy. This dispute was shaped by the internal politics of the London trades and need not concern us here.[71] NAOT policy was one of agitating for a range of legislative measures and its aim was to represent all workers, not just unionised ones. Even more than the NAUT in its early stage, land reform was central to the new organization's outlook and it received a predictably warm welcome from Feargus O'Connor who feared, though, 'that the full programme of the N.A.O.T. would probably prove "too vast, and too

---

68 *Monthly Report of the National Association of United Trades for the Protection of Industry*, 1 December 1847. The trades to which it specifically referred were shoemakers, whitesmiths, tinsmiths, basket makers, card-room operatives, iron-tinned spoonmakers, handloom weavers, framework knitters, painters, shipwrights, bleachers, chairmakers, bricklayers, type founders, bobbin turners, sickle and reap-hook forgers, pearl scale cutters and grinders.
69 *Stonemasons' Fortnightly Circular*, 14 May 1846, quoted in Sidney and Beatrice Webb, *The History of Trade Unionism*, p. 191.
70 Ibid, p. 194.
71 The only sources on the NAOT are Frances Elma Gillespie, *Labor and Politics in England 1850-67* (1927), pp. 38-41, and John Belchem, 'Chartism and the trades, 1848-50', *English Historical Review*, vol. 98, no. 388, (July, 1983). See also David Goodway, *London Chartism, 1838-48*, p. 70, who, however, believes the NAOT was projected but never realized.

radical, to enlist the hearty support of the Trades'".[72] The enthusiasm of the London trades for the NAOT early the following year persuaded him he was wrong: the trades had ceased to be 'the great stumbling block in the way of national improvement' and were instead hailed as 'pioneers in the march of progress'.[73]

This optimism was, however, shortly to be replaced by hubris. The two National Associations became involved in a slanging match in the pages of the radical press. The NAOT appeared to be aligning itself with protectionists, and this occasioned the final and, in retrospect, fatal rupture of Chartism. On the one hand were those who favoured 'the Charter and something more', with G. J. Harney and a recent arrival to the Chartist leadership, Ernest Jones, increasingly prominent among them. Albeit not without rancour, they retained control of the NCA, looking to extend it towards socialism. Alliance with middle-class opinion was anathema to these 'Charter-Socialists' though they did respect conservatives like the factory reformer Oastler. On the other hand were those who did look to some form of alliance with progressive middle-class opinion, and who were soon to form the National Charter League. This left O'Connor, who had tried to steer a middle course, stranded;[74] but by now his failing mental health and the humiliating collapse of the Chartist Land Plan was eroding his standing in the country. To this rich mixture were added the National Reform League (followers of Bronterre O'Brien, emphasizing land nationalization and currency reform) and the People's Charter Union (a moderate London-based group with strong inter- nationalist leanings). It is impossible to see where trade unions, even had they felt so inclined, might have lent their support. The one possibility, an attempt by Harney to create a 'fraternal union' of all these groups (except the League) failed almost before it began.

With Chartism divided and increasingly marginal, unions preferred a path of relative isolation from political agitation. Increasingly, trade unionists joined the 'drift to liberalism', whose version of popular constitutional reform was sufficiently close to that of Chartism, in language and content, for it to seem a natural progression.[75] 'Himself always the same, Times have changed' reads the gravestone (erected 1904) of one Kidderminster carpet-weaver, Chartist and Liberal activist.[76] However, there was never a total rupture between Chartism and individual trade unionists: cross-fertilization continued during the 1850s. Of those mentioned so far who bridged the two, Thomas Winters was perhaps the most important but there were many others. Arthur Brown[77] has identified a number of Chartist activists who assumed leadership or advisory roles in a wide range of East Anglian trade unions, including the engineers, the Amalgamated Society of Carpenters and Joiners, the Yarmouth seamen's movement and Joseph Arch's National Agricultural Labourers' Union. In Scotland the participation of well-known Chartists in trade unionism continued for a generation. It included Allan McFadyen in the Glasgow textile trades, Duncan Robertson among the coal and ironstone miners and W. C. Pattison, secretary of the Scottish Steam Engine Makers, which he led into the Amalgamated Society of Engineers in 1851.[78] Martin Jude continued to act as 'secretary to the miners' even when the unionisation of the North-east coalfield had crumbled. He was

---

72 John Belchem, 'Chartism and the trades, 1848-50', p. 572.
73 *Northern Star*, 10 March 1849.
74 John Belchem, 'Chartism and the trades, 1848-50', pp. 583-5.
75 John Belchem, *Industrialization and the Working Class: The English Experience, 1750-1900* (1990), p. 144.
76 L. D. Smith, *Carpet Weavers and Carpet Masters*, p. 251.
77 A. F. J. Brown, *Chartism in Essex and Suffolk* (1982), pp. 83-4, 119-21.
78 Alexander Wilson, *The Chartist Movement in Scotland* (1970), pp. 256-7.

instrumental in the revival of a regional pitmen's union from 1858.[79] Joseph Linney, one of the Chartists who took a leading role in the Staffordshire strikes of 1842, continued to contribute to the Black Country trades agitations.[80] Many Teesside Chartists made 'a strategic switch' into trade union activity in the early 1850s.[81] Halifax weaver and leading local Chartist Alexander Straddling was recruited by Rochdale carpet weavers to assist a strike at Brights in 1860, from which evolved a national union for the trade.[82] The architects of the Amalgamated Society of Engineers, William Newton and William Allan, both attended the last Chartist conference of 1858[83] and Newton contested the 1852 general election as a 'Chartist' candidate. Over-arching the activities of them all was W. P. Roberts (retained by almost every group of workers, unionised or not, needing to pursue a case or defend themselves in the courts) and, more sedately, Duncombe who maintained an interest in trade union affairs until his parliamentary career ended with his death in 1861. Adherence to the NCA, however, seems never to have been contemplated even by those unions who continued to support the NAUT. Chartist ideas remained, to repeat an analogy from the previous chapter, tools used by trade unionists to think with, but an institutional relationship was no longer seen as either feasible or desirable.

This was not necessarily, of course, how Chartist leaders saw the situation. Harney's watch-cry was *'the Charter and something more* — THE CHARTER, THE LAND, AND THE ORGANISATION OF LABOUR!'[84] Both he and, particularly, Jones allocated space to the trades in the papers which they edited (though by the spring of 1852 they too had quarrelled). The increasing extent to which trade unions held back from the NCA and the NAOT was a considerable frustration:

> Do we fight against class-government? Well, then? there is class-government in our own ranks, and we ought to fight against it, too. Do we fight against aristocratic privilege? Well, then — there is aristocratic privilege of the vilest die among the high-paid trades, and we ought to fight against it too. Truth is the best policy. THE ARISTOCRACY OF LABOUR MUST BE BROKEN DOWN, the same as an[y] other aristocracies.[85]

A month later, just as the NAUT was struggling to survive the Wolverhampton prosecutions, Ernest Jones wrote it off as 'a failing cause' before restating his general view even more crisply: *'All trades'-unions are lamentable fallacies'*.[86] His comments severed all that was left of the connections between the NAUT and the rump of the Chartist movement. Jones's biographer has suggested that his 'dogmatic sectarianism' impacted even 'upon the labour movement of the twentieth century'.[87] Jones's central target was a newcomer among British trade unions, the Amalgamated Society of Engineers (ASE), to the significance of which we now turn.

---

79 Bryan Rees, 'The lost years: Northumberland miners, 1844-62', *North East Labour History*, 19, (1985).

80 Paul Pickering, *Chartism and the Chartists in Manchester and Salford*, p. 200.

81 Malcolm Chase, 'Chartism, 1838-1858', pp. 166-7.

82 Gillian Oakley (1995), 'Post-Chartism: Halifax, 1860-1 ', unpublished BA dissertation, University of Leeds, pp. 19-20. Ex-Chartist weavers in the town also organized prosecutions under the Truck Acts (engaging, inevitably, Robens).

83 John Saville, *Ernest Jones: Chartist* (1952), p. 68.

84 *Democratic Review*, February 1850.

85 *Notes to the People*, February 1852.

86 Ernest Jones, 'The policy of truth' and 'To the iron trades', *Notes to the People*, vol. 2, February and March 1852, 862 and 976; substantial extracts from these articles can be found in John Saville, *Ernest Jones: Chartist*, F. C. Mather, *Chartism and Society: An Anthology of Documents* (1980) and J. T. Ward and W. H. Fraser, (eds.), *Workers and Employers: Documents on Trade Unions and Industrial Relations in Britain since the Eighteenth Century* (1980), but see also 'The Amalgamated Iron Trades', *Notes to the People*, vol. 2, January 1852, 829.

87 John Saville, *Ernest Jones: Chartist*, p. 47.

The Engineers

The ASE was the product of recent amalgamation in the engineering trades. We saw in the previous chapter how the 'five trades of mechanism' — millwrights, engineers, iron-moulders, smiths and mechanics — combined in Manchester to form a United Trades' Association, an action that was closely related to the synergy between Chartist and trade politics at the time. Its revival as the Mechanics' Protective Society of Great Britain and Ireland in 1844 was a more pragmatic response to the use of quittance papers by employers in the north. In spite of its title this was essentially a northern, in fact mainly Lancashire, federation. A similar, unconnected committee existed for London, established to campaign for shorter hours. Both federations dwindled away when their specific objectives were, at least in part, won.[88] However, the Newton-le-Willows prosecutions in 1847 reinforced a sense among engineers that even a comparatively large national union (such as the Journeymen Steam Engine and Machine Makers' Society with 7,000 members) might be unequal to the consequences of future prosecutions. To protect itself, the 1848 delegate conference of the 'Old Mechanics', as it was usually known, formally disassociated the Society from strike action, agreeing that conduct of any future dispute should be placed in the hands of a committee on which the officers and executive would play no part.

Some of the momentum behind the amalgamation of the engineers' societies in 1851, therefore, derived from reactions to the Newton-le-Willows case. Amalgamation was far from universally popular among unionised engineers, though, and the initial amalgamation included only a part of the Old Mechanics along with the General Smiths' Society. The Steam Engine Makers' Society, involved in the preliminary discussions, drew back completely and the United Friendly Boilermakers' Society rejected all advances. Other bodies subsequently merged into the ASE, however, including by the end of 1851 the Society of Millwrights and the London Engineers and Machinists, along with the rump of the Old Mechanics. The ASE, having commenced 1851 looking scarcely more secure than previous federations, therefore ended the year on a much sounder footing, having more than doubled its membership.

The writing of history favours survivors and winners, and early historians of trade unionism tended to exaggerate the importance and distinctiveness of the ASE. Amalgamation within craft unionism was noted in Chapter 4 as part of the context for the general unionist movement of the 1830s. The ASE's inaugural rulebook was clear: 'There is nothing novel in its constitution... By it we hope to protect our interests more effectively ... than is possible by any partial union'.[89] It was neither the first union to employ a full-time officer (a distinction probably due to Gravener Henson of the framework-knitters at the beginning of the century); nor was it the first whose branch structure achieved a genuine national reach. Its system of sick, unemployment and funeral benefits was no innovation at all. The boilermakers had met all the criteria commonly held to distinguish the 'new model' by 1845, except that of a London headquarters — having restricted branch financial autonomy as early as 1842.[90] In a series of reforms between 1832 and 1846, the Friendly Society of Operative Iron Moulders similarly reshaped itself in all respects except that of full-time leadership which was not established until 1853.[91] Like these earlier unions, the ASE was a genuine

---

88   James B. Jefferys, *The Story of the Engineers*, pp. 26-7.
89   Quoted in H. A. Clegg et al., *A History of British Trade Unions since 1889. Volume 1: 1889-1910* (1964), p. 7.
90   J. E. Mortimer, *History of the Boilermakers' Society: Volume 1, 1834-1906* (1973), pp. 41-2.
91   H. J. Fyrth and Henry Collins, *The Foundry Workers: a Trade Union History* (1959), pp. 36-9, 45.

amalgamation rather than a federal body. It was also the first successfully to sustain the incorporation of branches in Ireland.[92] Most obvious of all, however, it was far larger than any other trade union, embracing a membership of nearly 11,000 as early as May 1851. This marked out the ASE within months of its formation, but so too did the degree of centralization. Through regular and meticulous communications from its London headquarters, it succeeded in sustaining a lively branch culture whilst vesting key decision-making and financial control in a central executive. The benefits issue loomed large in the reckoning of both supporters and opponents because ASE subscriptions were higher than the norm, even for the most skilled trades, and its provision of benefits to members correspondingly greater too.

The Webbs coined the term 'new model unionism' to describe the ASE and to underline its importance in their longer-term schema of trade union history.[93] Ernest Jones unequivocally labelled it an 'aristocracy' whose antipathy to the interests of labour, he believed, was as fundamental a threat as any facing workers from beyond their own ranks. Yet if aloofness from broader labour and radical politics is the criterion of 'new model' unionism, the ASE measures up poorly compared, say, to some longer-established unions like the printers or the bookbinders. William Newton's declaration to the 1856 Select Committee on Masters and Operatives that 'we do not allow any political matter to be discussed at all or entertained among us' no more accurately reflected the engineers than the 'no politics' policies of earlier unions. Newton himself exemplified this: the *Operative*, which he edited and used skilfully to promote the ASE within the industry, showed a strong general unionist tendency in its aspiration to become the organ of a 'central committee' of all labour in Britain and the Empire. The *Operative* also published Newton's manifesto when he stood for Tower Hamlets in the general election of 1852, a manifesto so radical that records of the contest simply designated him 'Chartist'. In its early phase the ASE also very much shared in the NAUT's enthusiasm for co-operative production in associative workshops. 'The workers', declared the *Operative*, 'can never thoroughly emancipate their order until they gather capital and employ machinery for themselves'.[94] William Allan, the general secretary of the 'Old Mechanics' and then of the ASE from its inception until his death in 1874, was more cautious. Yet, with Newton, he attended the final Chartist conference in 1858, and was a prominent member of the Reform League, which revived the agitation among working people for parliamentary reform in the 1860s.[95]

If a reluctance to deploy the strike weapon is seen as the distinguishing qualification of new model unionism, then the ASE fails utterly. There were a few unions, notably the stonemasons and flint glass makers, which distanced themselves from strikes for reasons of principle as well as

---

92 Maura Cronin, *Country, Class or Craft? The Politicisation of the Skilled Artisan in Nineteenth-Century Cork* (1994), pp. 72-3.

93 Sidney and Beatrice Webb, *The History of Trade Unionism*, p. 202f., remains an indispensable starting point for the study of trade unionism in these years. Of subsequent historians the most supportive of the notion of 'new model' unionism have been R. W. Postgate, *The Builders' History* (1923), who dubbed the new model unionists 'the servile generation', and J. F. C. Harrison, *Robert Owen and the Owenites in Britain and America* (1969), esp. pp. 9-19. G. D. H. Cole, 'British trade unions in the third quarter of the nineteenth century', in E. M. Carus-Wilson, *Essays in Economic History: Volume 3* (1962), and A. E. Musson, *British Trade Unions, 1800-1875*, esp. pp; 50-6, are the most critical. See also 'The Webbs as historians of trade unionism', *BSSLH* 4 (1962). Most recent summaries see the notion as limited or misleading: e.g. Harry Browne, *The Rise of British Trade Unions, 1825-1914* (1979), pp. 23-8, Alan Fox, *History and Heritage: The Social Origins of the British Industrial Relations System* (1985), p. 124f., E. H. Hunt, *British Labour History 1815-1914*, pp. 259-64, Keith Laybourn, *British Trade Unionism, c.1770-1990: A Reader in History* (1991), pp. 80-103.

94 *Operative*, 4 January 1851.

95 The best source of information on Newton is his entry in the *DLB*, vol. 2. An account of his 1852 election campaign can be found in Frances Elma Gillespie, *Labor and Politics in England 1850-67*, pp. 100-3, but for his designation as a Chartist in the 1852 election see *McCalmont's Parliamentary Pollbook* (1879). For Allan see *DLB* vol. 1.

pragmatism. However, it was the ASE's frank admission that strikes were sometimes unavoidable and should therefore be financed on a regular basis that jeopardized its chances of success early in 1851. In many respects the central preoccupations of the ASE look very traditional: the control of entry to the trade to defend skill. The timing of the ASE's formation was integrally related to the arrival of new technology, in this case machine tools, large-scale investment in which was a recent innovation in the industry.[96] Employers sought to recoup the cost of this investment through higher production (which increased the prevalence of piece-work and overtime) and where possible cutting basic wage rates. This in the absence of effective opposition from workers they could do, since machine tools facilitated the division of labour in an industry that had once depended on the all-round skill of its workforce. Hence regulating apprenticeship and refusing to work with 'illegal' men were central objectives for engineering trade unionism. So too was resisting piece-work and overtime. It was the abuse of apprenticeship and employment of illegal men that had led the 'Old Mechanics' into the Newton-le-Willows dispute, and it was piece-work and overtime that led the ASE into a massive dispute in 1852.

So soon after its formation, the consequences of defeat could have been, and nearly were, enormous. A few days after its first anniversary, nearly 11,000 engineers were locked out in London and Lancashire after the rejection by employers of demands for an end to overtime and piece-work. With the exception of railway maintenance depots (where terms and conditions of employment precluded union membership) the dispute involved all the largest engineering employers. The affected shops had an average workforce of around 300. By contrast small shops, where investment in machine tools was slight, were not involved.[97] If the strike was to remain firm it was crucial that the ASE make payments to members and non-members alike, but its funds were unequal to the task. An additional levy was paid by many working members and nearly £9,000 subscribed by other trade societies and sympathetic individuals. It was not enough, not least because the employers' agenda was as much about breaking the ASE as it was resisting changes in working practices. Negotiation was therefore refused. The lock-out continued into May with strike payments halved and limited to members only. Funds, finally, were exhausted in June. The document was systematically presented to all those seeking to return to work:

> I, A_____ B_____ do hereby honestly and in its simplest sense and plainest meaning declare that I am neither now nor will, while in your employment, become a member or contributor to, or otherwise belong to or support, any Trade Union or society which directly or indirectly by its rules or any of its meetings or transactions of its business, or by means of its officers or funds, takes cognisance of, professes to control or interfere with the arrangements or regulations of this or any other manufacturing or trade establishment, the hours or terms of labour, the contracts or agreements of employer or employed, or the qualifications or period of service. I do also declare that I have no purpose or intention to call in question the right of any man to follow any honest calling in which he may desire to engage, or to make what arrangement and engagement of the workmen he pleases upon whatever terms they choose mutually to agree.[98]

'The working monopoly of the "society" is at an end', stated Ernest Jones with no pretence at disappointment. 'The monopolies of these "societies" and "unions" with their dictatorial trade-

---

96 Keith Burgess, 'Technological change and the 1852 lockout in the British engineering industry', *International Review of Social History*, 14, (1969).

97 Ibid, pp. 233-4.

98 Quoted in James B. Jefferys, *The Story of the Engineers*, p. 40.

regulations towards their poorer fellow-workmen, have been some of the most oppressive, unjust and tyrannical on record. They have estranged the feelings of the many, who were unable, or not permitted, to enter their privileged and aristocratic circle'.[99] However Jones — a barrister turned novelist, poet and journalist — underestimated the continuing emotional power of the concept of property in skill. He underestimated, too, the extent to which workers preferred to prioritize the protection of their property over the less-immediately pressing issue of political reform. Not only was it the means by which subsistence was secured, work occupied (as it tends not to now) the majority of one's waking hours. This study has already remarked at several points how crucial work was in defining the masculine sense of self. Even in trades which did not work piece rate there was a stigma against slacking and the sense of possessing skill extended deep even into those occupations that ranked low in the hierarchy of labour (see also Chapter 4 above). Workers of many kinds therefore empathized with the ASE's situation and, with a declining Chartist movement perhaps at the back of their mind, actively or tacitly endorsed the Society's handling of the situation.

The ASE rebuilt itself. There was one immediate advantage: however precarious its finances, it was not facing prosecution, unlike the Wolverhampton tin-plate workers and NAUT officials. This suggested that size mattered in facing down employer and establishment hostility. There had been no shortage of the latter. Sidney Smith, the lawyer who acted for the London engineering employers throughout the dispute, thought the support of *The Times* had been critical in defeating the union. Comparisons were also made between the actions of the engineers and the French revolutionaries of 1848. Perhaps part of the reason for Jones's hostility lay in his exclusion from an ASE rally in December 1851 for fear that 'the enemies of the Society might make a handle out of his presence'.[100] In rebuilding its finances and its reputation, it is hardly inexplicable that the ASE should have erred on the side of political caution. It sanitized its rules and with the support of the Christian Socialists devoted much energy to two associative projects in London — neither, as it happened, successful. It facilitated the emigration of members as a way of decreasing the labour pool. Finally, in a process that deserves further investigation for the light it might throw on mid-Victorian political and social 'equipoise', the ASE quickly rebuilt its membership base. This it could do because a majority of engineering firms chose not to enforce the agreements their workers had signed as a condition of re-employment.

James Jefferys the historian of the ASE, ascribed its survival to an amalgam of Allan's and Newton's genius with an almost inevitable lacing of destiny. This is typical of the explanatory method of early histories of trade unionism as, indeed, of other voluntary agencies. To suggest that it is an exaggeration need not exclude the importance of human agency from historical explanation. Allan was remarkable both for his tenacity and appetite for organizational detail. A lesser man might well have given up, as Henry Selsby, the 'Old Mechanics' secretary indicted in the Newton-le-Willows dispute, had done. However, Jefferys also commented in passing that the frailty of engineering employers' organizations also contributed to the revival of the ASE. Remarkably, it is more than half a century since a history of the ASE was published: in explaining its development Jefferys' aside is a line of enquiry that would still repay investigation. By 1856 the employers' organization was described as 'still, nominally, in existence; but its functions have nearly ceased'. Even during the lock-out itself, its solicitor observed, 'there was found the greatest difficulty possible

---

99 *Notes to the People*, March 1852, p. 976.
100 Quoted in James B. Jefferys, *The Story of the Engineers*, p. 38.

in keeping the masters in a state of union'.[101] Ironically, the success of the engineering employers' federation in 1852 is commonly held up as the inspiration for the robust concerted action of textile manufacturers later in the decade.[102] Yet even here, as the historians of the key Preston strike of 1853-4 concede, 'the cotton manufacturers did not maintain a continuous formal association after the successful conclusion of their struggle'.[103] Subsequent research has qualified this impression, but has also demonstrated how mutual organization among cotton employers was fractured by geographical and product specialization, and also by their jostling for competitive advantage. Furthermore, many cotton employers' associations 'disappeared or became moribund' during the American Civil War and Cotton Famine.[104] Elsewhere, manufacturers' associations in Sheffield were also usually short-lived.[105] By comparison to other aspects of the nineteenth-century economy (trade unionism included), the history of employers' organizations is neglected: but before the late 1860s such associations tended to be ephemeral. This clearly worked to the advantage of labour organizations. However, the absence of an effective employers' body was no guarantee of trade union development, as the Yorkshire woollen and worsted industry clearly demonstrates. The extent of trade union development in the various sectors of the economy is an issue the Conclusion will consider.

---

101 *PP* 1856 (343) XIII: Select Committee on Masters and Operatives (Equitable Councils of Conciliation), qq. 1353, 1369.

102 H. I. Dutton and J. E. King, *Ten per Cent and No Surrender: the Preston Strike, 1853-4* (1981), pp. 34 and 88; Arthur McIvor, 'Cotton employers' organisations and labour relations, 1890-1939', in J. A. Jowitt and A. McIvor, *Employers and Labour in the English Textile Industries, 1850-1939* (1988).

103 H. I. Dutton and J. E. King, *Ten per Cent and No Surrender*, p. 89.

104 Andre Bullen, 'Pragmatism versus principle: cotton employers and the origins of the industrial relations system', in in J. A. Jowitt and A. McIvor, *Employers and Labour in the English Textile Industries, 1850-1939*, p. 39.

105 Sidney Pollard, *A History of Labour in Sheffield* (1959), p. 134.

8

Conclusion: Trade Unions in the Early 1860s

'He knew there was an aristocracy among working men, and he deeply deplored it', Charles Murray, a bootcloser, veteran Chartist and socialist told a meeting of London co-operators in 1861.[1] We saw in the previous chapter how Ernest Jones used the idea of the labour aristocracy in the early 1850s in a series of attacks on trade unionism and the ASE in particular, for what he perceived to be diminishing political commitment. There is an extensive literature on social and political stability in the mid-Victorian period. Much of it has centred on arguments about how a 'labour aristocracy' — in seeking wider affirmation of status derived from the workplace — sought or had imposed on it some form of accommodation with the middle classes. The 1970s[2] represented the high-point in this literature, of which Gray, *The Aristocracy of Labour in Nineteenth-Century Britain, c.1850-1914*,[3] is a useful summary. Such explanations have the merit of conceptual neatness but rely upon an over-systematized view of processes and agencies that were blurred and fluid. One alternative interpretation of the history of skilled labour has suggested that de-skilling was so extensive that control of production was effectively a dead issue and replaced by wage conflict.[4] Another view[5] is that the extent of de-skilling has been exaggerated. Therefore wider political or cultural changes must have underlaid the quietening of working-class politics.

A partial explanation is that quiescence was always relative. The political calm of the third quarter of the nineteenth century has been almost habitually exaggerated, just as the extent to which Chartism constituted a plausible threat to the political establishment after 1842 is exaggerated. At the same time increased stability was achieved through the convergence of a number of trends. These included improvements in real wages and the standard of living from the late 1840s;[6] ameliorative reforms along the lines emphasized by Stedman Jones;[7] the containment of Chartism and thus dampened hopes that extensive reform was readily achievable; and the further development of the deep-rooted popular ethic of mutualism. The latter was particularly evident from the 1850s in the growth of retail

---

1   *Working Man*, 21 September 1861, quoted in Stan Shipley, *Club Life and Socialism in Mid-Victorian London*, (1983), p. 74.
2   Notably John Foster, *Class Struggle and the Industrial Revolution* (1974).
3   R. Q. Gray, *The Aristocracy of Labour in Nineteenth-Century Britain, c.1850-1914* (1981).
4   Gareth Stedman Jones, 'Class struggle and the industrial revolution', *New Left Review*, no, 90 (1975); Patrick Joyce, *Work, Society and Politics: the Culture of the Factory in Later Victorian England* (1980).
5   e.g. Royden Harrison and J. Zeitlin, (eds.), *Divisions of Labour: Skilled Workers and Technological Change in Nineteenth-Century Britain* (1985).
6   Charles Feinstein, 'Pessimism perpetuated: real wages and the standard of living in Britain during and after the industrial revolution', *Journal of Economic History*, 58/3, (1998).
7   Gareth Stedman Jones, *Languages of Class: Studies in English Working-class History 1832-1982* (1983).

co-operation, land and building societies, savings banks, friendly societies and, of course, trade unionism. E. P. Thompson's description of this cluster of activities was that it constituted 'the warrening' of industrial capitalism from end to end.[8] The metaphor seems increasingly appropriate, not least as the extent of friendly societies in Victorian Britain becomes more apparent.[9] The role of these societies also continued to be bound up with trade unionism.

This was especially the case with the many one-trade local societies who ran boxes in public houses across the country. Houses of call, as described in Chapter 2, had hardly changed a century later when Henry Mayhew interviewed London's 'honourable' tailors. Six distinct societies 'in Union' each met at a pub in the West End. Mayhew also encountered further societies not in union but likewise pub-based, governed by similar rules and functioning as houses of call. The skilled coopers operated a similar structure of pub-based societies as did carpenters, joiners and men's shoemakers. Less comprehensive societies existed for the various branches of the leather trades. Mayhew also identified a range of other one-trade societies, not 'in union' and without an explicit trade protection function, including Smithfield drovers, St Katharine's dock-coopers, Thames boatbuilders and chairmakers.[10]

By their very nature, local single-branch friendly societies left little bureaucratic trace. Many declined to register under the Friendly Societies Act. Friendly societies were also the common resort of occupational groups that desired to organize for mutual assistance but were unable or unwilling to establish explicit trade unions. Occasional glimpses suggest that this practice extended into almost every sector of the labour force. For example, at Stockton-on-Tees in south Durham, members of a 'Labourers' Burial Friendly Society' were locked out in 1866 by local builders. Charged with intimidating a blackleg, they promptly retained W. P. Roberts to conduct their defence.[11] Such societies were widely formed by railway workers. Employment on the railways routinely precluded trade unionism, through heavy penalties for misconduct, forms of remuneration that were contingent on good behaviour (such as loyalty bonuses and tied cottages) and company-sponsored friendly societies where eligibility to benefits was contingent on continued employment.[12] Militancy on the early railways, however, was sometimes linked to autonomous workmen's friendly societies. The Camden Town branch of a Steam Enginemen and Firemen's Friendly Society (meeting at the Railway Tavern, Hampstead Road) organized a footplate strike on the London and North Western

---

8 E. P.Thompson, *The Poverty of Theory and other Essays* (1978), p. 71; cf. John Saville, *1848: the British State and the Chartist Movement* (1987), p. 208.

9 For the continued ubiquity of small, unregistered friendly societies later in the nineteenth century see Paul Johnson, *Saving and Spending: the Working-Class Economy in Britain, 1870-1939* (1985), p. 14, and John Benson, *British Coalminers in the Nineteenth Century: A Social History* (1989), p. 185. For the large affiliated orders see P. H. J. H. Gosden, *Friendly Societies in England 1815-75* (1961), Simon Cordery, 'Friendly societies and the discourse of respectability in Britain, 1825-75', *Journal of British Studies*, 34 (1995), Shani D'Cruze and Jean Turnbull, 'Fellowship and family: oddfellows' lodges in Preston and Lancaster, c.1830-c.1890', *Urban History*, 22/1, (1995), also James C. Riley, *Sick not Dead: the Health of British Working-men during the Mortality Decline* (1987), pp. 27-123 and Martin Gorsky, 'Mutual aid and civil society: friendly societies in nineteenth-century Bristol', *Urban History*, 25 (3), December, 1998. The situation was different in Ireland, though Dublin, Belfast and the major coastal towns sometimes approached British levels of friendly society membership (Anthony D. Buckley, '"On the club": friendly societies in Ireland', *Irish Economic and Social History* 14, pp. 39-58, (1987)).

10 Tailors quoted in Henry Mayhew, *The Morning Chronicle Survey of Labour and the Poor: the Metropolitan Districts* (1981-1982), II, pp. 74-5; coopers, VI, p. 13; carpenters and joiners, II, p. 122; men's shoemakers, III, p. 122f.; leather trades, VI, p. 174f.; drovers, VI, p. 202; dock-coopers (excluded from skilled coopers' societies because they only repaired casks), VI, p. 7; boatbuilders, V, p. 234; chairmakers, V, p. 171.

11 Malcolm Chase, '"This tremendous conflict now raging between capital and labour": workers' organisations on Teeside in the mid-Victorian period', *Bulletin of the Cleveland and Teesside Local History Society*, 60 (Spring, 1991), p. 24.

12 Philip S. Bagwell, *The Railwaymen: the History of the National Union of Railwaymen* (1963), pp. 19-45.

Railway in 1848; and the call for a ten-hour day in 1860 was led by an enginemen's and firemen's benefit society.[13] Overt trade organizations only emerged in the industry in the late 1860s. Even then their development was slow. At the end of the century the social investigator Seebohm Rowntree found that trade union membership in the railway-dominated city of York was 25 per cent below the national average and that male friendly society members outnumbered trade unionists by a ratio of more than two to one. Unregistered groups accounted for more than a fifth of local male friendly society membership, a clear majority of which was to be found in 'societies connected with the railway workshops'.[14]

Single-trade benefit societies were common where trade union organization was non-existent or had failed. In 1828 the Kidderminster Friendly Society of Operative Carpet Weavers collapsed after a prolonged strike. The same day that the dispute was called off, a 'United Trades Burial Society' was formed, known informally as the 'Old Union'.[15] The first friendly society in the new town of Middlesbrough was established in the late 1830s by migrant Staffordshire pottery workers.[16] Oddfellowship was introduced to Scotland by woolcombers recently arrived from Yorkshire, who formed an exclusive lodge in Aberdeen in 1837. The 'failure of the Trades' Union Clubs' was held to be the reason for heavy recruitment by the Manchester Unity of Oddfellows in the South Wales coalfield.[17] The Leeds-based Grand United Order of Oddfellows had a number of effectively single-trade lodges in the 1840s. These included two near Bury, one for a printing works and the other for a cotton factory, 90 per cent of whose memberships were drawn from the two establishments concerned.[18] The Preston Weavers' Union started life in 1861 as an Operatives' Burial Society.[19] Clearly, the contribution of friendly societies to workplace solidarity in the later nineteenth century deserves further research.

Meanwhile trade unions continued to emphasize the benefit payments to which their members were eligible. By the early 1850s, trade unionists were seriously arguing that their benefit systems helped keep poor rates down.[20] A turning-point in relations between trade unions and the State came in 1855 when Parliament offered legal registration under a new Friendly Societies Act to trade unions operating benefit systems. An 1860 survey of the rulebooks of 58 trade unions revealed that 22 gave funeral allowances, 12 unemployment benefits and 10 accident payments. These figures almost certainly under-estimated the proportion who made benefit payments since some of those making a nil return were simply federations of autonomous local societies. Six unions paid pensions to retired members. The notably 'aristocratic' coach-makers were atypical in paying twelve shillings weekly. ASE superannuation payments were seven shillings weekly and the lowest rate, of two to three shillings was paid by the smiths.[21] Some larger unions like the ASE managed their benefit funds with

---

13 Ibid, pp. 31, 37; Arthur Marsh and Victoria Ryan, *Historical Directory of Trade Unions. Volume 3: Building and Allied Trades, Transport, Woodworkers and Allied trades, Leather Workers, Enginemen and Tobacco Workers* (1987), p. 165.

14 B. S. Rowntree, *Poverty: A Study in Town Life*, 4th edition, (1902), pp. 348-50, 356-62. 'Male friendly society members' excludes members of trade unions.

15 L. D. Smith, *Carpet Weavers and Carpet Masters: The Handloom Carpet Weavers of Kidderminster 1780-1850* (1986), p. 214.

16 Malcolm Chase, 'Chartism, 1838-1858: responses in two Teesside towns', *Northern History*, 24, (1988), p. 160.

17 James Spry, *The History of Oddfellowship* (1867), pp. 29, 164-5.

18 James Staton, 'An essay on oddfellowship, V: the travelling system', *Magazine* [of the Grand United Order of Oddfellows], 7, September 1844, p. 7.

19 Patrick Joyce, *Work, Society and Politics*, p. 292.

20 Henry Mayhew, *The Morning Chronicle Survey of Labour and the Poor*, V, p. 91; J. Ginswick (ed.), *Labour and the Poor in England and Wales, 1849-51*, (1983), p. 215.

21 NAPSS 1860, pp. 141-5.

considerable actuarial skill. On the other hand, smaller trade societies often had developed little beyond the box-club stage, for example the Operative Tin-Plate Workers' Society which in 1853 discussed distributing its surplus funds to members on a regular basis,[22] or the Birmingham Operative Brass Cock Finishers' Trade, Sick and Dividend Society.[23] Meanwhile, meetings in public houses continued to be the norm for almost all workers' organizations. For example, in 1861, 85 per cent of all trade societies in Preston and Birmingham met in pubs, while in Newcastle and Nottingham no union at all met off licensed premises. But here Scotland contrasted sharply. One consequence of the Glasgow spinners' trial had been a distancing between trade unionism and licensed premises. Of the city's fifty known trade societies in 1861, only two appear to have met in pubs.[24]

The extent of trade union benefit systems was sufficiently large for them to be a matter of political concern. Critics claimed that benefit funds leaked away to support strikes. Workers in other trades should be using 'whatever influence they possess for withholding the men of their own order from fruitless struggles against the fixed laws which regulate human society', declared a critic of the 1858 anti-machinery dispute in Northamptonshire's shoe industry.[25] In practice, however, the support of the wider labour movement continued to be vital in sustaining major industrial disputes. It was especially prevalent in the 1859-60 lock-out in the London building trade. In July 1859, 24,000 building workers across the capital were locked out by employers responding to an agitation for a shorter working week. The Flint Glass Makers' Friendly Society sent a delegate to address a meeting of the amalgamated building trades:

> He had come from the battle-field where the glass-blowers had battled for thirteen weeks, and had received the sympathy and assistance of other trades in the country. The result had been that they had gained a complete victory over their masters; other trades came forward to assist them in the struggle, and now they had their trade society to assist those that wanted assistance and to lift the arm of the weak against their oppressors. (Cheers)[26]

The builders' lock-out lasted seven months and, although demands for a shorter working week were not met, the right to union membership upon which the dispute had turned was successfully defended. Among donors to the builders' cause was the newly formed Yorkshire Miners' Association, whose members had themselves weathered a dispute in the West Yorkshire coalfield in 1858, and the ASE, whose £3,000 was the largest element in a total subscription from trade societies of £23,000. Parliament responded by tightening the 1855 Friendly Societies Act to prevent loans or donations being made to bodies involved in trade disputes.

The successful resolution of the builders' lock-out became something of a watershed for trade unionism generally, not least because it flew in the face of those 'fixed laws' so dear to large sections of contemporary middle-class opinion. Many, like the writer of this *Leeds Mercury* editorial in 1864, regarded trade unions as a regrettable and unnecessary intrusion into the territory of industrial management and the logic of political economy:

---

22 Archibald T. Kidd, *History of the Tin-Plate Workers and Sheet Metal Workers and Braziers Societies* (1949), p. 41.
23 Arthur Marsh and Victoria Ryan, *Historical Directory of Trade Unions*, p. 27.
24 [London Trades Council], *United Kingdom First Annual Trades' Union Directory*, London: Thomas Jones, (1861), pp. 72-4, 80. For the circumstances surrounding this publication see Sidney and Beatrice Webb, *The History of Trade Unionism*, revised edition (1920), pp. 244-5.
25 NAPSS 1860, p. 9.
26 *Reynolds's Newspaper*, 18 September 1859, quoted in Takao Matsumura, *The Labour Aristocracy Revisited: The Victorian Flint Glass Makers* (1983), p. 143. For a detailed assessment of the 1859 builders' strike and its long-term significance for the industry, see Richard Price, *Masters, Unions and Men: Work Control in Building and the Rise of Labour 1830-1914* (1980), pp. 45-50.

> Without unions on either side the wages of the workmen ebb and flow with the prosperity of the master just as inevitably as the tides of the moon. The harmony is perfect, and strikes, lock-outs, discords, and the whole train of evils they bring after them are unknown. How different where the union enters. Both sides may be perfectly honest and just, but a false principle of regulation is brought in, a mode of calculation no more comparable in simplicity or exactness with what we have indicated, than the wild guesses and artificial systems of astrology are comparable with the beautiful accuracy and truthfulness of astronomy.[27]

The 1860 NAPSS survey, *Trades' Societies*, concluded that most masters 'agreed that Trade Unions have destroyed the proper relation — one of affectionate dependence — of the operative towards his master'.[28] This was as rosy and nostalgic a depiction of past experience as that of any other 'golden age', a concoction of half-truths intended as a criticism of the present. If employers believed that industrial relations were inevitably confrontational this was generally something kept to themselves. William Hopkins, a Teesside ironmaster, caused a local sensation in 1865 with the comment that 'the only mode, he thought, of dealing in these cases was brute force — active combination of employers and employed in opposition to each other'.[29] Hopkins's views were closer to those of trade unionists. 'Is not the interest of the employer and the employed to work together?', a member of the 1867 Royal Commission on Trade Unions asked William Allan. 'There I differ', the ASE secretary replied:

> Every day of the week I hear that the interests are identical. I scarcely see how they can be while we are in a state of society which recognizes the principle of buying in the cheapest and selling in the dearest market. It is in their interest to get the labour done at as low a rate as possible, and it is ours to get as high a rate of wages as possible, and you can never reconcile these two things.[30]

Allan's frankness rather grates against the reputation of the ASE and other amalgamated unions for 'an apparent addiction to arbitration'.[31] Few unions, however, were yet strong enough by 1860 to have secured institutionalized wage bargaining procedures. E. H. Hunt[32] suggests that enthusiasm for formal procedures after the mid-century was a sign of improved class relations. A note of caution, however, is necessary. First, formal conciliation procedures were often born of embittered dispute, for example in Lancashire cotton spinning following the 1853-4 strikes,[33] in Midlands hosiery during a period of trade union ascendancy[34] and in the North-east iron trade after the strike-ridden mid-1860s.[35] Second, trade unionists, especially officers of the larger national amalgamations, were apt to try and enhance their profile in society by stressing a commitment to arbitration. However, in the

---

27 Quoted in Trygve Tholfsen, *Working-class Radicalism in Mid-Victorian England* (1976), p. 271.
28 Ibid.
29 William Hopkins, *Middlesbrough Weekly News*, 3 March 1865, quoted in Malcolm Chase, '"This tremendous conflict now raging between capital and labour", p. 25. Hopkins's remarks caused much discomfort to the region's ironmasters and they prevailed upon him to deny having made them.
30 Quoted in *DLB* 1, pp. 15-16.
31 H. A. Clegg *et al.*, *A History of British Trade Unions since 1889. Volume 1: 1889-1910* (1964), p. 9.
32 E. H. Hunt, *British Labour History 1815-1914* (1981), p. 281.
33 Arthur McIvor, 'Cotton employers' organisations and labour relations, 1890-1939', in J. A. Jowitt and A. McIvor, *Employers and Labour in the English Textile Industries, 1850-1939* (1988), pp. 9-10.
34 Richard Gurnham, *200 Years: The Hosiery Unions, 1776-1976* (1976), pp. 26-30.
35 N. P. Howard, 'The strikes and lockouts in the iron industry and the formation of the ironworkers' unions, 1862-69', *International Review of Social History*, 18, (1973); Malcolm Chase, '"This tremendous conflict now raging between capital and labour".

early phases of these unions' development there was frequently tension between branches and central executives, not least over how far external intervention should supersede local practice in the settling of disputes. Most wage bargaining took place at the level of the individual workshop or, notably in engineering, the local district.

A further cautionary point is that contemporaries frequently used the terms arbitration, bargaining and conciliation imprecisely.[36] This was especially true of trade unionists, for whom formal procedures offered the prospect of official recognition of a right to collective bargaining and therefore of trade unionism itself. Institutionalized collective bargaining was usually achieved in situations of trade union strength, for example among London compositors where, as we saw in Chapter 3, the scale of prices agreed in 1805 remained the basis of piece-work rates for the rest of the century. This was only possible, however, because of enduring trade union strength. 'Believe me', wrote a print union activist in 1850,

> the preservation of the Scale rests more with ourselves than with our employers. Whilst we are united together its conditions will continue to be respected. ... But if the journeymen were to cease in their demands for an inviolable scale, and permit it to be broken with impunity ... reduction of wages would be forced upon them as a matter of necessity — and general depreciation would immediately set in.[37]

Institutionalized collective bargaining was sometimes established in situations where trade unions, if not strong, were dogged and persistent enough even in defeat not to be ignored. This was the case in the North-east iron trade: one of the most successful Boards of Arbitration and Conciliation was established here in 1869, in the wake of the bruising defeat of the National Association of Ironworkers in the 'Great Strike' of 1866. Where trade unionism was completely broken, as happened in the Scottish cotton industry after the Glasgow spinners' defeat in 1837, employers strenuously sought to exert direct managerial control over both work process and wage bargaining. The contrasting history of the Lancashire cotton spinning industry bears this out. 'The gradual acceptance of trade unions and the establishment of regional price lists and a formalized bargaining structure, which were distinct features of industrial relations in Lancashire, did not emerge in the Glasgow district'.[38]

We shall see in a moment that the strength of British trade unionism varied widely in the 1860s. This was the underlying reason for the patchiness of formalized bargaining and arbitration. Even at the end of the nineteenth century, more than three-quarters of all workers remained outside formal collective bargaining procedures.[39] However, we saw in the previous chapter the extent of the NAUT's commitment to arbitration and conciliation. During the 1850s boards of arbitration were established in sections of the printing, shipbuilding, silk and pottery trades. In December 1860 the establishment of the Nottingham Hosiery Board presaged further development in this direction, subsequently followed by similar arrangements in other branches of the Midlands clothing industry, some west midlands building trades, several coalfields and, as we have just seen, the North-east iron trade. Collective bargaining spread more rapidly, especially from the 1870s, with further growth in

---

36 H. A. Clegg *et al.*, *A History of British Trade Unions since 1889*, p. 10.

37 Quoted in John Child, *Industrial Relations in the British Printing Industry: The Quest for Security* (1967), pp. 137-8.

38 Per Bolin-Hort, *Work, Family and the State: Child Labour and the Organization of Production in the British Cotton Industry 1780-1920* (1989), p. 256.

39 E. H. Hunt, *British Labour History 1815-1914*, p. 388.

both trade union membership and size. This was the decade, especially with the downturn in the economy at its close, that saw a finally decisive swing away from smaller societies in the trade union movement. By 1900, the economist and historian William Ashley could note with astonishment that older craftsmen still remembered trade society regimes which closely resembled those of the eighteenth-century and earlier, but which 'have already passed away, and will soon be forgotten'.[40]

The vanished culture described by Ashley included workshop 'courts', houses of call, trade societies with publican treasurers, the payment of 'maiden garnish' and other drinking rituals. One central facet of this culture which had decidedly not vanished, however, was that associated with apprenticeship. The belief that a completed apprenticeship embodied a right to work was far from merely nostalgic. This was inevitable, not least because of the paucity of any alternative provision for technical education. As Charles More has demonstrated for early *twentieth*-century England, 'there were, at a very rough estimate, over 340,000 apprentices in any one year'.[41] The process of de-skilling conventionally associated with industrial capitalism was profoundly protracted in Britain. Although the bias of recent historical work on the centrality of skill in British industry has been towards the late nineteenth and early twentieth century, high levels of skill and workplace autonomy distinguished the mid-Victorian period also.[42] In certain industries, trade unions were largely responsible for ensuring this was so, the most obvious examples being the Lancashire cotton spinners[43] and the flint glass makers.[44] Even here, however, trade unions owed their success to a complex of factors. The achievements of Victorian industry are part of the mental furniture of anyone with even the most cursory interest in the past and it is therefore important to remind ourselves of the limitations of mid-Victorian technology. The pace and impact of de-skilling is easily exaggerated and, even where it occurred, new techniques and responsibilities were often created. Furthermore, the diminution of physical effort that accompanied mechanization was seldom paralleled by a significant reduction in the need for mental agility and knowledge of the capacities and characteristics of tools and raw materials.

The consequence was a fertile ground for the traditional ethos of skill. The ASE declared itself 'constrained to make restrictions against the admission into our trade of those who have not earned a right by probationary servitude'. The reasons it gave were that 'such encroachments are productive of evil, and when persevered in unchecked result in reducing the condition of the artisan to that of the unskilled labourer, and confer no permanent advantage on those admitted'.[45] The Railway Spring Makers' Society, representing an entirely new occupational group, adhered to the same outlook, essentially unchanged across the centuries covered in this study:

---

40 W. J. Ashley, 'Medieval urban journeymen's clubs', in his *Surveys, Historic and Economic* (1900), p. 259; originally published as 'Journeymen's Clubs' in the *Political Science Quarterly*, March 1897. Ashley's remarks were prompted by an account (appended to the 1900 edition) he had received from a hatter who had been secretary of the 'Blue Society', at the Anchor and Eight Bells in Bermondsey, south London, in 1858.

41 Charles More, *Skill and the English Working Class, 1870-1914* (1980), p. 64.

42 The literature on skill and British industrial workers is extensive, but see especially the essays in Royden Harrison and J. Zeitlin, (eds.), *Divisions of Labour: Skilled Workers and Technological Change in Nineteenth-Century Britain* (1985), William Lazonick, 'Industrial relations and technical change: the case of the self-acting mule', *Cambridge Journal of Economics*, 3, (1979) and Charles More, *Skill and the English Working Class, 1870-1914*. Alastair J. Reid, *Social Classes and Social Relations in Britain, 1850-1914* (1992), provides a useful critical overview.

43 William Lazonick, 'Industrial relations and technical change: the case of the self-acting mule'.

44 Takao Matsumura, *The Labour Aristocracy Revisited*.

45 H. A. Clegg *et al.*, *A History of British Trade Unions since 1889*, p. 4.

> Considering that the trade whereby we live is our property, bought by certain years of servitude, which give us a vested right, and that we have a sole and exclusive claim upon it, as all will have hereafter who purchase it by the same means, such being the case, it is evident that it is every man's duty to protect by all fair and legal means the property whereby he lives, being always equally careful not to trespass on the rights of others.[46]

It remains difficult to measure the practical impact of such attitudes because apprenticeship disputes seldom registered outside the immediate confines of the workplace concerned. They were certainly the subject of anti-trade union literature, aimed at working-class readers, into the late 1880s.[47] 'The story of apprenticeship control', John Rule points out, 'is not one of grand confrontation as much as running skirmish'.[48] The 'skirmish' lasted at least to the end of the nineteenth century, notably so in the engineering, shipbuilding, wood-working, printing and glass-making industries.

Of course unions in these sectors of the economy were not necessarily typical of trade unionism as a whole. The extent of trade union implantation in British industry at the end of the 1850s remained heavily biased towards the skilled trades. Even here unionisation was uneven. 'As a general rule', Mayhew remarked in 1850 of the non-metal working metropolitan crafts, 'I find the "society men" of every trade comprise about one-tenth of the whole'.[49] In the building, engineering and other metals-based trades the proportion of 'society men' would have been greater. A ratio of one-seventh for building workers suggested by the secretary of the General Builders' [Employers'] Association in 1867 seems plausible. In 1867, two well-informed observers put the total number of trade unionists in the United Kingdom at around 600,000, observing that while 'the trade-society men themselves estimate their number at 700,000; we shall certainly be under the mark if we reckon them at 500,000'. A total of 600,000 was likewise suggested by Harriet Martineau in 1859, suggesting that the trade-unionists' own calculation of 1867 may not have been far wide of the mark, since the intervening years had witnessed some growth in membership. As a proportion of the total population this represents 2.3 per cent. Given the nature of trade unionism at this time, however, it is more helpful to think in terms of the proportion of the total working male population, adjusted to exclude agricultural workers and the armed services. A membership total of 600,000 represents 11 per cent in 1861 and 9.3 per cent in 1871.[50] No less significant, it should be noted that trade union membership was concentrated in northern England, especially Lancashire, and to a lesser extent the industrial Midlands; that the vast majority of Scottish trade unionists were to be found on Clydeside, and that there were few trade societies in Ireland outside Belfast, Cork and Dublin. The slender nature of Welsh trade unionism is vividly apparent in the fact that there seems to have been more trade societies in Dublin alone in 1861 than in the whole of Wales.

Among female workers trade unionism could hardly be termed even slender. It was suggested in Chapter 5 that female friendly societies formed a basis for the momentary mobilization of women in the GNCTU; their possible subsequent contribution to female workers' solidarities merits

---

46 NAPSS 1860, pp. 131-2.

47 For example George Etell Sargent's heavily didactic novel *Our Ten Weeks' Strike*, first published by the Religious Tract Society in 1878 and republished in the late 1880s (London: Partridge, [1887]). See especially pp. 93-4 of the latter edition.

48 John Rule, *The Labouring Classes in Early Industrial England 1750-1850* (1986), p. 324.

49 Henry Mayhew, *The Morning Chronicle Survey of Labour and the Poor*, V, p. 168.

50 J. M. Ludlow and Lloyd Jones, *Progress of the Working Class, 1832-1867* (1867), p. 205; John Plummer, 'The economical results of trades unions', *Companion to the Almanac: or, Year-Book of General Information for 1868* (1867), p. 31; 'Secret organisation of trades', *Edinburgh Review*, 110, October 1859, p. 529. Percentages using recalculated figures based on the 1861 and 1871 population censuses in B. R. Mitchell and Phyllis Deane, *Abstract of British Historical Statistics* (1962), p. 60.

investigation. However, actions by women to defend or advance their position as wage earners tended to be 'informal and sometimes spontaneous. Drawing on existing social networks, their protest was independent of the trade union organization, and the meetings and structures which that implies'.[51] Existing trade unions were hardly an appealing model upon which women might base organizations of their own, bound up as they were with the masculine solidarities of workplace and public house and with upholding an exclusionary definition of skill. The period to mid-century had seen a rapid decline in married women's participation in the labour force.[52] The relative youth of the female industrial workforce made it even easier for male trade unionists to appeal to 'common sense' concerning the appropriate roles and capacities of women.

However, female incursion into trades that men had been accustomed to regard as their own did not recede, especially in lighter industries. Very few unions admitted women, even if they were clearly established in the trade concerned. During the 1860s, the all-male stockingers' unions were 'preoccupied with the actual or potential substitution of women for men'. Prompted by disturbances at a Nottingham factory where men had been discharged to be replaced by women, a local journalist commented that the latter could 'perform the duties connected with the rotary frame as efficiently as men. The pay of the females is, of course, very much less than that given to male operatives'.[53] In one industrial sector not segregated by sex, Lancashire cotton weaving, trade unions did exist which freely admitted both men and women. Yet even here trade union activists were, until the end of the century, invariably male and the weaknesses of integrated unions was frequently ascribed to their having female members. Outside Lancashire, there was no significant female involvement in trade unionism until the 1870s.

Reliable statistics for trade union membership in Britain would not become available until 1892: a careful estimate for 1888[54] puts the total at 750,000, or approximately 10 per cent of adult male workers. Statistically, figures for the memberships of the larger trade unions offer surer ground. In 1894 the Webbs compiled a series of this data which included the following membership totals for 1860 (all figures in thousands):[55]

ASE	20.9
Operative Stonemasons' Society	9.1
Friendly Society of Ironfounders	8.0
Society of Coachmakers	4.1
United Society of Boilermakers	4.1
London Society of Compositors	2.6
General Union of Operative Carpenters and Joiners	2.2
Steam Engine Makers' Society	2.1
Associated Ironmoulders of Scotland	2.1
Operative Brickmakers' Society	1.6
Typographical Association	1.5
Flint Glass Makers' Friendly Society	1.4

---

51 Charles More, *Skill and the English Working Class, 1870-1914*, p. 175.
52 Sara Horrell and Jane Humphries, 'Women's labour force participation and the transition to the male breadwinner family, 1790-1865', *Economic History Review*, 48/1, (1995), p. 112.
53 Sonya Rose, *Limited Livelihoods: Gender and Class in Nineteenth-Century England* (1992), p. 6.
54 H. A. Clegg *et al.*, *A History of British Trade Unions since 1889*, p. 1.
55 Sidney and Beatrice Webb, *The History of Trade Unionism*, p. 744-9.

Five other national societies (bookbinders, machine printers, machine grinders, blacksmiths and the newly formed Amalgamated Society of Carpenters and Joiners) had total memberships in the mid-hundreds. Returning to our best-guess total figure for this time of around 600,000 trade unionists, this suggests that more than half a million remained members of small local or regional societies. In 1859 Martineau estimated the likely number of these to be 2,000, but this would suggest an average membership per society of 250 which is almost certainly too high. The number of local trade bodies is therefore likely to have been appreciably higher.

With the special exception of the flint glassmakers,[56] entry to all the trades detailed above was by apprenticeship. In trades where entry was more open and progression via seniority, trade unionism tended to be less firmly implanted. In those areas where a single industry dominated the local economy, specialist trade societies could be found in various branches of the Midlands hosiery industry and, most extensively, in the spinning centres of Lancashire. Weaving towns were weaker but none the less ahead of the West Riding worsted and woollen districts where 'up to the 1870s, trade unionism, if indeed it can be referred to as such, was confined to the skilled and supervisory workers'.[57] Faintly paralleling this development were the handful of 'departmental combinations' in the late 1850s among what would now be called 'white-collar' workers in the Post Office and Civil Service.[58] In general, though, 'white-collar' unionism was a product of the last third of the nineteenth century. So too was the unionisation of the railways, though a Steam Enginemen and Firemen's Friendly Society, originating on the southern section of the London and North Western Railway, claimed 2,000 members by 1862 and had branches as far north as Leeds.[59] In the coal industry there were successive attempts during the 1850s to form Scottish miners' associations along with English miners' conferences in 1858-9. However, the disposition to union organization in Collieries themselves went largely unrealized at national and even district level until the mid-1860s.[60]

Among agricultural workers trade unionism was non-existent. Sick and funeral clubs offered an element of organization for unskilled workers and would be the major element from which Joseph Arch's National Agricultural Labourers' Union was created in the 1870s. However, it is unclear whether the Stockton Labourers' Burial Friendly Society, mentioned earlier, was in any way typical in operating as a *de facto* trade union for urban unskilled workers. Stedman Jones notes that early Thameside unions of the unskilled, such as coal and corn porters and stevedores, concentrated upon excluding interlopers from their members' traditional preserves.[61] In this they had more in common with the medieval and early-modern fellowships of labourers and porters, noted in Chapter 1, than with the general trade unions of the later nineteenth and twentieth centuries. Migrants from Ireland to Britain may have been better catered for as the Roman Catholic Church strove to establish a parish-based system of mutualist societies in place of Ribbonism, the secretive political movement that also functioned as a form of 'primitive trade unionism' among the Irish in Britain.[62]

---

56 See Takao Matsumura, *The Labour Aristocracy Revisited*.

57 J. A. Jowitt, 'The retardation of trade unionism in the Yorkshire worsted textile industry', in in J. A. Jowitt and A. McIvor, *Employers and Labour in the English Textile Industries, 1850-1939*, p. 88.

58 Arthur Marsh and Victoria Ryan, *Historical Directory of Trade Unions*, p. xii.

59 Arthur Marsh and Victoria Ryan, *Historical Directory of Trade Unions. Volume 3: Building and Allied Trades, Transport, Woodworkers and Allied trades, Leather Workers, Enginemen and Tobacco Workers* (1987), p. 165.

60 Alan Campbell, *The Lanarkshire Miners: a Social History of their Trade Unions, 1775-1874* (1979), pp. 254-7; Frank Machin, *The Yorkshire Miners: A History* (1958), p. 320.

61 Gareth Stedman Jones, *Outcast London : A Study in the Relationship between Classes in Victorian Society* (1984), p. 341.

62 John Belchem, *'Orator' Hunt: Henry Hunt and English Working-Class Radicalism* (2012).

We have seen that the process of mechanization left space for skilled labour to shape and defend a degree of autonomy at the workplace. So too did the nature of entrepreneurship. The partial and sporadic effectiveness of employers' associations worked to trade unions' advantage. Arguably this rescued the ASE in the wake of the great 1852 lock-out. Employers preferred, in modern parlance, 'quick and dirty' routes to profitability. Mid-nineteenth-century British industry was still operating with immense advantages over that of competitor nations. To take just one example which is particularly germane to trade unionism, capital-overheads remained relatively low. Limited investment in mechanization made economic sense as long as generally satisfactory profits were sustained. Moreover, product specialization, a dominant feature of the textile industry, was most-readily and cheaply maintained by deploying a skilled workforce rather than by improving plant and machinery. Workers had the additional advantage of being expendable in recession or even, as in the shipyards, during the interval between the completion of one job and the commencement of the next. The abundance of labour in all categories of skill in the mid-Victorian economy meant that minimal risks were involved for employers who adopted this strategy.

Having become detached from political radicalism, trade unionism also became less unacceptable to employers. Recognition was mostly grudging and seldom enthusiastic, but it was part of the cost of the entrepreneurial strategies just outlined. Offset against this cost were several factors working to the employers' advantage. Many trade unions continued to administer tramping systems which helped even out inequalities in labour supply while their payments to sick and unemployed members maintained the labour force without direct charge to employers. In so doing unions in the skilled trades shouldered a considerable burden. Between 1855 and 1884, for example, the percentage of members out of work in the Friendly Society of Ironfounders never fell below 6 per cent. In 1858 benefits were costing the Society 1s 10½d per member per week, almost double the weekly subscription.[63] Specialized unions lacking a national membership base (which spread financial risk in recession) might have to carry an even greater burden. The proportion of society members 'on the box' in the Sheffield trades during the 1860s was around a fifth, while for the Glassbottle Makers of Yorkshire in the years 1867-97 it was around a third.[64]

Less tangible, but none the less real, benefits accrued to employers from the work ethic trade unions promoted. 'As a matter of course', Thomas Winters told a parliamentary committee, 'skilled workmen who are in a society' taught everything they could to every youth 'who comes within their rules'. Society men would also be ashamed, he added, of 'executing unworkmanlike work'.[65] The stigma against slacking and shoddy workmanship has been noted several times in this study. Disciplinary measures against members who absconded from employment, or were dishonest in dealing with masters, are a little-appreciated aspect of British trade unionism. 'Employers as a class look with very little favour upon organizations like ours', observed the Typographical Association in 1877:

> One of the reasons why we are not subjected to greater antagonism on their part is the fact our Association offers great facility for obtaining men, either for regular or casual employment, and gives a kind of guarantee that such men have been taught the trade, and that they will attend to

---

63 H. J. Fyrth and Henry Collins, *The Foundry Workers: a Trade Union History* (1959), pp. 44, 56-7.

64 Raphael Samuel, 'The workshop of the world: steam power and hand technology in mid-Victorian Britain', *History Workshop Journal*, 3 (Spring, 1977), pp. 47-8.

65 *PP* 1860 (307) XXII: Select Committee on the Best Means of Settling Disputes between Masters and Operatives, 312-13. For trade union strictures against dishonest and absconding workers see para 321, and also Winters' evidence (minute 625) to the 1856 Select Committee.

the work they undertake, or be punished for their neglect.[66]

In the less fevered political atmosphere after mid-century, trade unionism's claim to employers' tolerance, if not whole-hearted approval, could be extended.

As far as the attitudes of the State are concerned, it is clear that trade unionism benefited from the demise of Chartism, or more accurately, the absorption of the broadest currents within Chartism into liberal versions of reform. We saw in Chapters 6 and 7 that relations between trade unions and Chartism had been close in the years up to 1842 but thereafter became distant. Popular radicalism of the 1850s was far from as quiescent as is sometimes supposed, but nothing approaching the spirit or scope of the Chartist movement of 1838-42 was seen after 1848. Fears that 'the scorned producers will take the law into their own hands'[67] diminished rapidly in the 1850s. The expansion of Friendly Society legislation in 1855, permitting trade unions operating benefit schemes to register, was one indication of a sea-change in parliamentary attitudes. Parliament's approval in 1859 of the 'molestation of workmen' bill, rejected in 1853 when legislators' memories of Chartism were still green, was another.

This measure has already been considered in the previous chapter, but it is worthwhile teasing out its significance further. The correct title is significant, 'an Act to amend and explain an Act of the Sixth Year of the Reign of King George the Fourth' (i.e., the 1825 Combination Laws repeal legislation). We noted in Chapter 4 that the 1824-5 repeal measures rendered trade unions not exactly legal but no longer explicitly unlawful. The legal status of trade union activity was so intimately bound up with the law of conspiracy that any more explicit recognition would have required extensive revision of an important area of criminal law. This is clear in the trade union reforms of 1871 which comprised both a Trade Union Act and a Criminal Law Amendment Act. In the interim, however, Parliament was content with a situation which allowed latitude for judicial interpretation. Like the 1824-5 repeal measures before it, the 1859 Act did not legalize trade unionism as such but instead set out to immunize it from prosecution for criminal conspiracy.[68]

In essence the intention of the 1859 Act was to reiterate the law of 1825 and unpick certain judicial interpretations of it. This it did by making explicit that neither combination nor peaceable persuasion could be deemed molestation or obstruction within the meaning of the 1825 Act 'and shall not therefore be subject or liable to any indictment or prosecution for conspiracy'. That Parliament could be persuaded that judicial construction was contrary to the intention of statute law was itself highly significant, an admission that the law of trade combination was neither settled nor immutable. However, it is also necessary to stress the restrictive amendments to the 1855 Friendly Societies Act, passed by Parliament in 1860 in response to the London builders' lock-out. Parliament's development of a less prescriptive policy towards trade unionism was cautious.

Furthermore, we are referring here to *parliamentary* attitudes. It is a moot point how far the attitude of the *State*, broadly defined, to trade unions had really changed since the mid-1820s. Care is necessary when speaking of 'the state' in Victorian Britain. It was not monolithic. This indeed was one of its greatest strengths. Significant disparities could and did exist between Parliament (the composition of which itself of course changed), the judiciary and those responsible for the application and interpretation of legislation locally. Such disparities disguised the pace of change and gave scope to those in authority to slow it altogether when circumstances appeared to them to require

---

66 Quote in John Child, *Industrial Relations in the British Printing Industry*, p. 152.
67 Slogan on a Chartist banner noted by Flora Tristan, *London Journal*, 1840 (1980).
68 J. V. Orth, *Combination and Conspiracy: A Legal History of Trade Unionism, 1721-1906* (1991), p. 121.

it. This was the case in the 1860s, a period of accelerating trade union activity which can be compared with that which followed the 1824 Combination Laws Repeal Act. This time, however, there was no new statute to still the movement but instead reinterpretation by judges of existing law. The case in 1866 of *Hornby* v. *Close* (when Bradford boilermakers were prevented from recovering embezzled funds on the grounds that their union, though registered under the 1855 Friendly Societies Act, was an illegal conspiracy) is the most-widely cited example of this. Judicial decisions amending the spirit of the 1859 Molestation of Workmen Act, however, were hardly less significant. By 1868 both silent picketing and the use of advertisements to give notice of disputes had been deemed conspiracies to restrain freedom of trade.[69]

Before the judicial reconstruction of the 1859 Act, employers who found it too bitter a pill to swallow could still resort to the 1823 Master and Servant Act which permitted considerable local autonomy in the treatment of strike action. During the 1860s its use increased as part of an attempt to curtail trade unionism.[70] As we noted in Chapter 4, this Act provided for the arrest of any employee that ceased work without their master's permission. After 1848 arrest was no longer mandatory and magistrates could instead issue a summons, but the extent to which this option was adopted was limited, especially when magistrates were themselves involved in the same industry as the employer concerned. 'In small strikes it was a common practice to have all the strikers arrested and then to confront them with the stark choice: either return to work at once on the employer's terms or go to prison'.[71] In larger strikes exemplary prosecutions were preferred. When strike action stopped one Northumberland pit in 1859 eight men — all teetotallers and six of them leading local Methodists — were gaoled for two months. 'I know they are respectable men', the colliery manager was said to have commented, 'and that is why I put them in prison. It is no use sending those to gaol who cannot feel.'[72]

Between 1858 and 1875 prosecutions in England and Wales averaged 10,000 a year. The general assumption has been that the Act's application was largely confined to 'the small-master sectors of the economy'.[73] More accurately, though, it was most commonly applied in two situations. The first was where trade union organization was non-existent, principally domestic service and agriculture. The second was where trade union organization did exist, but in circumstances where employers remained hopeful of extinguishing it. Thus, in the relatively settled spheres of printing and Lancashire cotton spinning, Master and Servant prosecutions were negligible; but for coalminers they were a near-constant affliction. This was also the case in building where employers took up the Act extensively following their failure to break trade unionism in 1859-60.

By itself the scale of firms in a sector is not a reliable indicator of whether the Act was used. It was deployed extensively, for example, in the Potteries, the iron trade and, as Woods shows,[74] by the largest Black Country employers. However, prosecutions declined rapidly on Teesside in the 1860s where the newly formed National Association of Ironworkers appears to have targeted its operation by local ironmasters. In 1864 the Act was used in an attempt to break a strike by nearly 2,000

---

69 Decisions in the cases of *R* v. *Druitt* 1867 (tailoring) and *Springhead Spinning Company* v. *Riley* (1868). See J. V. Orth, *Combination and Conspiracy*, pp. 132-3.

70 Philip S. Bagwell, *Government and Society in Nineteenth-Century Britain: Industrial Relations* (1974), p. 37.

71 Daphne Simon, 'Master and servant', in J. Saville (ed.), *Democracy and the Labour Movement: Essays in Honour of Dona Toor* (1954), pp. 171-2.

72 Quoted in William M. Patterson, *Northern Primitive Methodism*, p. 346.

73 John Saville, *The Consolidation of the Capitalist State, 1800-1850* (1994), p. 21.

74 D. C. Woods, 'The operation of the Master and Servants Act in the Black Country, 1858-75', *Midland History*, 7, (1982).

ironworkers employed by one Middlesbrough company. Their intransigence led to the withdrawal of all complaints made under the Act and the release of arrested leaders.[75] After this Master and Servant was little used in the region's iron trade, even in extensive disputes during the following two years which preceded the modification of the law in 1867. The 1867 Master and Servant Act, however, was indicative of the still tentative nature of State attitudes to trade unionism in that it was an annual act, extended from year to year. The final repeal of a measure which had done so much to constrain trade unionism came only in 1875.

Ambiguous though it remained, the legal situation of British and Irish trade unions after 1859 contrasted sharply with Germany and France where laws explicitly against trade combination were only relaxed from the 1860s. How far the legal context was primarily responsible for retarding the formation of trade unions and how far other factors were responsible is widely debated. As the British experience reveals, legal repression was not necessarily a sufficient condition for trade unionism to flounder. Christine Eisenberg suggests that the nature of workshop social organization was the key variable explaining the different trajectories of British and German labour.[76] In Germany the inhibiting legacy of continuing guild control of trade and the more-rapid character of economic change undermined craft workers' workplace-based solidarity. Evidence of continued guild control of trade in Britain, examined above in Chapters 1 and 2, suggests that this comparison may be overdrawn. There are also uncertainties about the veracity of the approach Eisenberg adopts, in extrapolating conclusions about the third quarter of the century from much earlier material.[77]

The situation is complicated further by revised assessments of the pace and nature of German economic change. Until recently it was generally assumed that the decline of *Handwerk* in Germany was a rapid process. The consequence was that a small residuum of largely self-employed artisans survived, but only outside the industrializing sector.[78] This clearly contrasted to Britain where industrialization left so much scope for the continuation of artisan traditions. However, as Breuilly points out,[79] small workshop-based production endured in the German economy longer than has often been supposed and workers from this sector were an important source of skilled factory labour. Wage and status differentials were widely maintained in German factories, notably so in engineering but also in iron and steel, mining and building. 'Workers who managed to form unions in the period 1850-80 in Germany were usually drawn from skilled occupations earning above average wages and with fairly narrowly defined concerns'.[80] The British experience would seem, then, to be not so very different; but the key phrase here is 'workers who managed to form trade unions'. Whilst there was some variation between the various German states, in the economic powerhouse of Prussia prohibition of combination and discussion or engagement in strike action was only relaxed in 1869. Furthermore, the freedom of assembly and expression of any organization engaged in public affairs was subjected to restriction, both before and after the 1869 reforms. John Breuilly suggests the use of these restrictions fulfilled a similar function to that of conspiracy and Master and Servant laws in Britain, to limit the effectiveness of trade unions.

A similar situation in which the nature of trade union membership mirrored Britain, but its extent

---

75 Malcolm Chase, , '"This tremendous conflict now raging between capital and labour", p. 25.
76 Christiane Eisenberg, *Deutsche und englische Gewerkschaften: Entstehung und Entwicklung bis 1878 im Vergleich* (1986).
77 John Breuilly, *Labour and Liberalism in Nineteenth-Century Europe: Essays in Comparative History* (1992), p. 18.
78 J. Kocka, 'Problems of working-class formation in Germany: the early years, 1800-75', in I. Katznelson and A. R. Zolberg (eds.), *Working-Class Formation: Nineteenth-Century Patterns in Western Europe and the United States* (1986).
79 John Breuilly, *Labour and Liberalism in Nineteenth-Century Europe*.
80 Ibid, p. 46.

was more tightly constrained by the State, is evident in France. Iorwerth Prothero has meticulously explored the many similarities between British and French artisans and their trade societies. Although controls were temporarily loosened at the Revolutions of 1830 and 1848, it was only in 1864 that legislation was passed permitting associations of workers explicitly to discuss and organize for improvements in wages and hours of work. Government policy during the 1850s was particularly repressive: but the trade unions that surfaced in the 1860s were the same occupations as those which were best organized in 1830-48 — masons, carpenters, tailors, hatters, shoemakers, printers and engineers.[81] As the Paris Typographical Society told its London counterpart in 1862, 'they had previously been obliged to have their Society enrolled as a Benevolent Institution only, as any Society for the maintenance of wages is not tolerated by the laws of France'.[82] Benefit societies were not only made legal but officially encouraged in the 1840s, but the phenomenon of their being used to front trade unionist operations long pre-dated this. Marseille's dockworkers, for example, formed a 'Society of St Peter and St Paul and of Our Lady of Mercy' in 1817, with the approval of local officials. 'Officially a mutual benefit society, it was actually a reconstitution of the dockworkers' corporation, or guild, from the old Regime'. It controlled entry to the trade with notable efficiency.[83]

Around the same time as the Marseille dockworkers formed their mimic guild, certain Baltimore and New York artisans secured state recognition of their incorporations.[84] They were not necessarily typical in so doing, but their actions do underline the artisan-based roots of trade unionism in America and the extent to which early unionism operated there, as in Britain and Ireland, with an idealized if 'shadowy image of a benevolent corporate state'.[85] In the America of the 1850s trade unions remained, even more so than in Britain, 'exclusive craft unions of skilled mechanics'.[86] The vast majority of unions were local in character and, although 'some eight or ten national unions were formed' between 1852 and the onset of the Civil War in 1861, only three survived.[87] Numerous local societies also fell away in the depressions of 1854 and 1857 while the Civil War itself impeded any revival. Although national unions in a dozen or more trades were formed between 1863 and 1865, it remained the case in America that the labour movement 'operated at the local rather than the regional or national level'. There were also fewer unionised workers — 300,000 or so in the early 1870s (a density of about 0.75 per cent of the population) — compared to Britain.

Whilst exhibiting some obvious parallels with their continental European and American counterparts, by 1860 British trade unions had clearly covered much further ground. They were generally larger. A significant number had achieved national coverage. Density of membership, as well as the gross number of trade unionists, was greater. Relationships with the State were still equivocal but the stance of the latter had for some time been regulatory rather than directly repressive. Of course, the attitudes of employers seldom signalled whole-hearted acceptance and outright hostility was not at all unusual. As we have seen, in its 1860 report, *Trades' Societies and Strikes*, the NAPSS observed that most employers 'agreed that Trade Unions have destroyed the

---

81 Dick Geary, *European Labour Protest, 1848-1939* (1981), p. 46.

82 Quoted in Iorwerth J. Prothero, *Radical Artisans in England and France, 1830-1870* (1997), p. 82.

83 William H. Sewell, 'Uneven development, the autonomy of politics and the radicalization of workers', in L. R. Berlanstein (ed.), *The Industrial Revolution and Work in Nineteenth-Century Europe* (1992), p. 152.

84 Mary Roys Baker, 'Anglo-Massachusetts trade union roots, 1130-1790', *Labor History*, vol. 14, part 3, (1973), p. 392.

85 Sean Wilentz, *Chants Democratic: New York City and the Rise of the American Working Class, 1788-1850* (1984), p. 89.

86 Pjilip S. Foner, *History of the Labor Movement in the United States, Vol. 1: From Colonial times to the Founding of the American Federation of Labor* (1972), p. 222.

87 Neville Kirk, *Labour and Society in Britain and the United States, Vol. 2: Challenge and Accommodation, 1850-1939* (1994), p. 81.

proper relation' between workers and their masters. The committee that prepared this report dissented but there is no reason to suppose that the statement misrepresented the situation. Clearly, trade unions continued to operate in a climate of hostility. Yet *Trades' Societies and Strikes* was itself a moderating influence on attitudes to trade unionism.[88] It also made at least one unusual convert. When it was received at the NAPSS conference, none other than Sir Archibald Alison, scourge of Lanarkshire trade unionism for almost four decades, opened the debate. Heckled by the veteran Scottish Owenite and labour leader Alexander Campbell, Allison observed that employers 'are of the opinion that trades' unions are the greatest social evils that now exist in society'. But he went on, 'trades' unions in themselves are not only proper, but are a necessary balance in the fabric of society. I think without them capital would become far too powerful, and workmen would be much beaten down'.[89] Coming as they did from the man who had prosecuted the Glasgow spinners in 1837, these comments suggest that the climate of hostility in which trade unions operated was becoming more civilized.

---

88 *Trades' Societies and Strikes* was intended to redress a situation whereby employers had 'better command of the avenues by which public opinion is influenced', quoted in E. J. Yeo, *The Contest for Social Science: Relations and Representations of Gender and Class* (1996, p. 345). The 700 page report has been praised as a source of historical information: Sidney and Beatrice Webb, *The History of Trade Unionism*, p. 227, described it as 'the best collection of Trade Union material and the most impartial account of Trade Union action that has ever been issued'. In the light of recent work demonstrating the significance of the NAPSS in British current affairs at this time (Lawrence Goldman, 'The Social Science Association, 1857-86: a context for mid-Victorian liberalism', *English Historical Review*, 100/1, (1986); E. J. Yeo, *The Contest for Social Science*, the contemporary impact of the publication merits further investigation.

89 NAPSS 1860, pp. 600-2.

Bibliography

Bibliographical note to the 2012 edition
A number of important studies have appeared since this book was written. Katrina Honeyman's, *Women, Gender and Industrialisation in England, 1700-1870* (2000) and Alastair J. Reid, *United We Stand: A History of Britain's Trade Unions* (2004) are indispensable overviews of their fields. Ian Gadd and Patrick Wallis have edited two useful collections of essays relating to guilds: *Guilds, Society and Economy in London, 1450-1800* (2002) and *Guilds and Association in Europe, 1200-1900* (2006). Another useful collection is Marie Cross (ed.), *Gender and Fraternal Orders in Europe, 1300-2000* (2010). However, the key work on British fraternal orders is now Simon Cordery's book *British Friendly Societies, 1750-1914* (2003). Three richly researched contributions to the history of employment law and industrial relations stand out: James Jaffe, *Striking a Bargain: Work and Industrial Relations in England, 1815-65* (2000), Mark Curthoys, *Governments, Labour, and the Law in Mid-Victorian Britain: the Trade Union Legislation of the 1870s* (2004), and Christopher Frank, *Master and Servant Law: Chartists, Trade Unions, Radical Lawyers and the Magistracy in England, 1840-1865* (2010). A broader treatment of the trade unionist dimension to Chartism can be found in Malcolm Chase, *Chartism: A New History* (2007). The journal *Labour History Review* provides an annual listing of additions to the periodical literature.

ARCHER, IAN W., *The Pursuit of Stability: Social Relations in Elizabethan London*, (Cambridge University Press, 1991)

ASPINALL, ARTHUR, *The Early English Trade Unions: Documents from the Home Office Papers in the Public Record Office* (London: Batchworth, 1949)

BAGWELL, PHILIP S., *The Railwaymen: the History of the National Union of Railwaymen*, (London: Allen & Unwin, 1963)

_____, *Government and Society in Nineteenth-Century Britain: Industrial Relations*, (Shannon: Irish University Press, 1974)

BAIN, EBENEZER, *Merchant and Craft Guilds: A History of the Aberdeen Incorporated Trades*, (Aberdeen: Edmond & Spark, 1887)

BAKER, MARY ROYS, 'Anglo-Massachusetts trade union roots, 1130-1790', *Labor History*, 14/3, (1973)

BARNES, JUNE, 'The trade union and radical activities of the Carlisle handloom weavers', *Transactions of the Cumberland and Westmorland Antiquarian and Archaeological Society*, 78, (1978)

BARRY, JONATHAN, 'Bourgeois collectivism? Urban Association and the Middling Sort', in Barry and Brooks, *The Middling Sort of People: Culture, Society and Politics in England 1550-1800*, (London: Macmillan, 1994)

BARRY, JONATHAN AND BROOKS, CHRISTOPHER (eds.), *The Middling Sort of People: Culture, Society and Politics in England 1550-1800*, (London: Macmillan, 1994)

BECKETT, J. V., *A Centenary History of Nottingham*, (Manchester University Press, 1997)

BEHAGG, CLIVE, 'Secrecy, ritual and folk violence: the opacity of the workplace in the first half of the nineteenth century', in Storch, *Popular Culture and Custom in Nineteenth Century England.*

_____, 'Masters and manufacturers: social values and the smaller unit of production in Birmingham, 1800-50', in Crossick and Haupt, *Shopkeepers and Master Artisans in Nineteenth-Century Europe.*

_____, *Politics and Production in the Early Nineteenth Century*, (London: Routledge, 1990)

BELCHEM, JOHN, 'Chartism and the trades, 1848-50', *English Historical Review*, 98/388, (July,

1983)

———, *'Orator' Hunt: Henry Hunt and English Working-Class Radicalism*, (Oxford: Clarendon Press, 1985; new edition: London: Breviary Stuff Publications, 2012)

———, *Industrialization and the Working Class: The English Experience, 1750-1900*, (Aldershot: Scolar Press, 1990)

———, 'Beyond Chartist Studies: class, community and party in early-Victorian populist politics', in Derek Fraser (ed.), *Cities, Class and Communication: Essays in Honour of Asa Briggs*, (London: Harvester, 1990)

———, 'The immigrant alternative: ethnic and sectarian mutuality among the Liverpool Irish during the nineteenth century', in Owen Ashton, Robert Fyson and Stephen Roberts (eds.), *The Duty of Discontent: Essays for Dorothy Thompson*, (London: Mansell, 1995)

BELLAMY, JOYCE AND SAVILLE, JOHN (eds.), *Dictionary of Labour Biography*, 10 volumes, (London: Macmillan, 1972-99)

BENBOW, WILLIAM, *Grand National Holiday and Congress of the Productive Classes*, (London: Benbow, 1832)

BENSON, JOHN, *British Coalminers in the Nineteenth Century: A Social History*, (London: Longman, 1989)

BERG, MAXINE, 'Political economy and the principles of manufacture', in Berg, Hudson, and Sonenscher, *Manufacture in Town and Country before the Factory*, (Cambridge University Press,1983)

———, *The Age of Manufactures, 1700-1820*, (Oxford University Press, 1985)

———, 'Women's work, mechanisation and the early phases of industrialisation in England', in Joyce, *The Historical Meanings of Work*.

———, 'Factories, workshops and industrial organisation', in Floud and McCloskey, *The Economic History of Britain Since 1700: Volume I — 1700-1860*.

BERG, MAXINE, HUDSON, PATRICIA AND SONENSCHER, MICHAEL (eds.), *Manufacture in Town and Country before the Factory*, (Cambridge University Press, 1983)

BERGER, RONALD M., *The Most Necessary Luxuries: the Mercers' Company of Coventry 1550-1680*, (Philadelphia State University Press, 1993)

BIERNACKI, RICHARD, *The Fabrication of Labour: Germany and Britain, 1640-1914*, (Berkeley: University of California Press, 1995)

BLACK, ANTONY, *Guilds and Civil Society in European Political Thought from the Twelfth Century to the Present*, (London: Methuen, 1984)

BLANKENHORN, DAVID, '"Our class of workmen": the cabinet-makers revisited', in Harrison and Zeitlin, *Divisions of Labour: Skilled Workers and Technological Change in Nineteenth-Century Britain*.

BOHSTEDT, J., *Riots and Community Politics in England and Wales, 1790-1810*, (Cambridge MS: Harvard University Press, 1983)

BOLIN-HORT, PER, *Work, Family and the State: Child Labour and the Organization of Production in the British Cotton Industry 1780-1920*, (Lund University Press, 1989)

BOYD, ANDREW, *The Rise of the Irish Trade Unions*, second edition, (Dublin: Anvil Books, 1985)

BOYLE, JOHN W., *The Irish Labor Movement in the Nineteenth Century*, (Washington DC: Catholic University of America Press, 1988)

BRENTANO, LUIGI, *On the History and Development of Gilds, and the Origin of Trade-Unions*,

(London: Trubner, 1870)

BREUILLY, JOHN, *Labour and Liberalism in Nineteenth-Century Europe: Essays in Comparative History*, (Manchester University Press, 1992)

BRIGGS, ASA (ed.), *Chartist Studies*, (London: Macmillan, 1959)

BROOKE, ALAN J., 'Labour disputes and trade unions in the industrial revolution', in E. A. H. Haigh (ed.), *Huddersfield a Most Handsome Town: Aspects of the History and Culture of a West Yorkshire Town*, (Huddersfield: Kirklees Cultural Services, 1992)

BROOKS, CHRISTOPHER, 'Apprenticeship, social mobility and the middling sort, 1550-1800', in Barry and Brooks, *The Middling Sort of People: Culture, Society and Politics in England 1550-1800*.

BROWN, A. F. J., *Essex at Work, 1700-1815*, (Chelmsford: Essex County Record Office, 1969)

_____, *Essex People, 1750-1900, from their Diaries, Memoirs and Letters*, (Chelmsford: Essex Record Office, 1972)

_____, *Chartism in Essex and Suffolk*, (Chelmsford: Essex Record Office, 1982)

_____, *Meagre Harvest: The Essex Farm Workers' Struggle Against Poverty 1750-1914*, (Chelmsford: Essex Record Office, 1990)

BROWN, HENRY PHELPS, *The Origins of Trade Union Power*, (Oxford University Press, 1986)

BROWNE, H. PHELPS AND HOPKINS, S. V., 'Seven centuries of the price of consumables, compared with building wages', *Economica*, vol. 23, (1956); reprinted in E. M. Carus-Wilson (ed.), *Essays in Economic History: Volume 2*, (London: Arnold, 1962)

BROWN, K. D., *The English Labour Movement, 1700-1951*, (Dublin: Gill and Macmillan, 1982)

BROWNE, HARRY, *The Rise of British Trade Unions, 1825-1914*, (London: Longman, 1979)

BUCKLEY, ANTHONY D., '"On the club": friendly societies in Ireland', *Irish Economic and Social History*, 14, (1987)

BULLEN, ANDREW, 'Pragmatism versus principle: cotton employers and the origins of the industrial relations system', in Jowitt and McIvor, *Employers and Labour in the English Textile Industries, 1850-1939*.

BURGESS, KEITH, 'Technological change and the 1852 lockout in the British engineering industry', *International Review of Social History*, 14, (1969)

BURKE, PETER, *History and Social Theory*, (Cambridge: Polity, 1992)

BURN, JAMES DAWSON, *The Autobiography of a Beggar Boy*, (1855); new edition with introduction by David Vincent, (London: Europa, 1978)

BYNG, JOHN, *The Torrington Diaries: Containing the Tours through England and Wales of the Hon. John Byng (later fifth Viscount Torrington)*, edited by C. B. Andrews, vol. 3, (London: Eyre & Spottiswode, 1935)

BYTHELL, D., *The Handloom Weavers: a Study in the English Cotton Industry during the Industrial Revolution*, (Cambridge University Press, 1969)

CALHOUN, CRAIG, *The Question of Class Struggle: Social Foundations of Popular Radicalism during the Industrial Revolution*, (Oxford: Blackwell, 1982)

CAMPBELL, ALAN, *The Lanarkshire Miners: a Social History of their Trade Unions, 1775-1874*, (Edinburgh: John Donald, 1979)

CARPENTER, KENNETH E., *Labour Problems before the Industrial Revolution: Four Pamphlets, 1727-1745*, (New York: Arno, 1972)

[CARTER, JOHN], *Memoirs of a Working Man*, (London, Charles Knight, 1845)

CHALLINOR, RAYMOND, *A Radical Lawyer in Victorian England: WP Roberts and the Struggle for*

Workers' Rights, (London: I. B. Tauris, 1990)

CHALLINOR, RAYMOND AND RIPLEY, BRIAN, *The Miners' Association: a Trade Union in the Age of the Chartists*, (London: Lawrence & Wishart, 1968; new edition: Whitley Bay: Bewick Press, 1990)

CHARLES, LINDSAY AND DUFFIN, LORNA, *Women and Work in Pre-Industrial England*, (London: Croom Helm, 1985)

CHARLESWORTH, ANDREW (ed.), *An Atlas of Rural Protest in Britain, 1549-1900*, (London: Croom Helm, 1983)

CHARLESWORTH, ANDREW, GILBERT, DAVID, RANDALL, ADRIAN, SOUTHALL, HUMPHREY AND WRIGLEY, CHRIS, *An Atlas of Industrial Protest in Britain, 1750-1990*, (London: Macmillan, 1996)

CHARLTON, JOHN, *The Chartists: the First National Workers' Movement*, (London: Pluto, 1997)

CHASE, MALCOLM, *'The People's Farm': English Radical Agrarianism, 1775-1840*, (Oxford: Clarendon Press, 1988; new edition: London: Breviary Stuff Publications, 2010)

_____, 'Chartism, 1838-1858: responses in two Teesside towns', *Northern History*, 24, (1988)

_____, '"The labour depreciating system": the 1836 Thornaby turnout and its background', *North East Labour History Society Bulletin*, 23, (1989)

_____, 'From millennium to anniversary: the concept of jubilee in late eighteenth- and nineteenth-century England', *Past and Present*, 129 (November, 1990)

_____, '"This tremendous conflict now raging between capital and labour": workers' organisations on Teeside in the mid-Victorian period', *Bulletin of the Cleveland and Teesside Local History Society*, 60 (Spring, 1991)

_____, '"We wish only to work for ourselves": the Chartist Land Plan', in Malcolm Chase and Ian Dyck (eds.), *Living and Learning: Essays in Honour of J. F. C. Harrison*, (Aldershot: Scolar Press, 1996)

CHILD, JOHN, *Industrial Relations in the British Printing Industry: The Quest for Security*, (London: Allen & Unwin, 1967)

CHRISTIE, IAN, *Stress and Stability in Late Eighteenth-Century Britain: Reflections on the British Avoidance of Revolution*, (Oxford: Clarendon Press, 1984)

CHURCH, R. A., 'Chartism and the miners: a reinterpretation', *LHR*, 56/3, (1991)

CHURCH, R. A. AND CHAPMAN, S. D., 'Gravener Henson and the making of the English working class', in E. L. Jones and G. E. Mingay (eds.), *Land, Labour and Population in the Industrial Revolution*, (London: Arnold, 1967)

CITRINE, ARNOLD WALTER, ET AL., *The Book of the Martyrs of Tolpuddle, 1834-1934*, (London: Trades Union Congress General Council, 1934)

CLAEYS, GREGORY, 'Alexander Campbell and the GNCTU in Scotland: The Scottish Trades' Union Gazette', *BSSLH*, 51/3, (1986)

_____, *Machinery, Money and the Millennium: From Moral Economy to Socialism, 1815-1860*, (Princeton NJ: Princeton University Press, 1987)

_____, *Citizens and Saints: Politics and Anti-Politics in Early British Socialism*, (Cambridge University Press, 1989)

CLARK, ANNA, *The Struggle for the Breeches: Gender and the Making of the British Working Class*, (London: Rivers Oram, 1995)

CLARK, PETER, *The English Alehouse: A Social History 1200-1830*, (London: Longman, 1983)

_____, 'Migration in England during the late seventeenth and early eighteenth centuries', in

Clark and Souden, *Migration and Society in Early Modern England*.

———, 'Migrants in the city: the process of social adaptation in English towns, 1500-1800', in Clark and Souden, *Migration and Society in Early Modern England*.

CLARK, PETER AND MURFIN, LYN, *The History of Maidstone: the Making of a Modern County Town*, (Gloucester: Alan Sutton, 1995)

CLARK, PETER AND SOUDEN, DAVID, *Migration and Society in Early Modern England*, (London: Hutchinson, 1987)

CLARKE, TONY AND DICKSON, TONY, 'Class and class consciousness in early industrial capitalism: Paisley, 1770-1850', in Tony Dickson (ed.), *Capital and Class in Scotland*, (Edinburgh: John Donald, 1982)

CLARKSON, L. T., 'Introduction: wage-labour, 1500-1800', in Brown, K. D., *The English Labour Movement, 1700-1951*.

CLAWSON, MARY ANN, 'Early modern fraternalism and the patriarchal family', *Feminist Studies*, 6/2, (1980)

CLEGG, H. A., FOX, ALAN AND THOMPSON, A. F., *A History of British Trade Unions since 1889. Volume 1: 1889-1910*, (Oxford University Press, 1964)

COLE, G. D. H., *Attempts at General Union: A Study in British Trade Union History, 1818-1834*, (London: Macmillan, 1953)

———, 'British trade unions in the third quarter of the nineteenth century', in E. M. Carus-Wilson, *Essays in Economic History: Volume 3*, (London: Arnold, 1962)

COLE, G. D. H. AND FILSON, A. W., *British Working-Class Movements: Select Documents, 1789-1875*, (London: Macmillan, 1951)

COLEMAN, D. C., *Myth, History and the Industrial Revolution*, (London: Hambledon Press, 1992)

COLLS, ROBERT, *The Pitmen of the Northern Coalfield: Work, Culture and Protest, 1790-1850*, (Manchester University Press, 1987)

COOPER, THOMAS, *The Life of Thomas Cooper Written by Himself*, (London: Hodder & Stoughton, 1872)

CORDERY, SIMON, 'Friendly societies and the discourse of respectability in Britain, 1825-75', *Journal of British Studies*, 34 (1995)

COULTON, G. C., *Social Life in Britain from the Conquest to the Reformation*, (Cambridge University Press, 1919)

CRAFTS, N. F. R., 'The industrial revolution: economic growth in Britain, 1700-1860', in Digby and Feinstein, *New Directions in Economic and Social History*.

———, 'The industrial revolution', in Floud and McCloskey, *The Economic History of Britain Since 1700: Volume I — 1700-1860*.

CRONIN, MAURA, *Country, Class or Craft? The Politicisation of the Skilled Artisan in Nineteenth-Century Cork*, (Cork University Press, 1994)

CROSSICK, GEOFFREY AND HAUPT, HEINZ-GERHARD (eds.), *Shopkeepers and Master Artisans in Nineteenth-Century Europe*, (London: Methuen, 1984)

DALY, SEAN, *Cork: A City in Crisis — A History of Labour Conflict and Social Misery 1870-72*, (Cork: Tower Books, 1978)

DANIELS, E. W., 'A "turn-out" of Bolton machine-makers in 1831', *Economic History*, 1, (1926-9)

D'ARCY, FEARGUS, 'The artisans of Dublin and Daniel O'Connell, 1830-47: an unquiet liaison', *Irish Historical Studies*, vol. 17, no. 66 (September, 1970)

_____, 'The National Trades' Political Union and Daniel O'Connell, 1830-48', *Eire-Ireland*, 17/3 (1982)

DAUNTON, M. J., *Progress and Poverty: An Economic and Social History of Britain, 1700-1850*, (Oxford University Press, 1995)

DAVENPORT, ALLEN, *The Life and Literary Pursuits of Allen Davenport. With a further Selection of the Author's Work*, compiled and edited by Malcolm Chase, (Aldershot: Ashgate, 1994; originally published 1845)

DAVIDS, KAREL, 'Seamen's organisations and popular protest in Europe, c.1300-1825', in Lis, Lucassen and Solly, 'Before the Unions: Wage Earners and Collective Action in Europe, 1300-1850', (1994)

D'CRUZE, SHANI AND TURNBULL, JEAN, 'Fellowship and family: oddfellows' lodges in Preston and Lancaster, c.1830-c.1890', *Urban History*, 22/1, (1995)

D'EICHTHAL, GUSTAVE, 'British society in 1828', reprinted in B. M. Ratcliffe and W. H. Chaloner (eds.), *A French Sociologist Looks at Britain*, (Manchester University Press, 1977)

DERRY, T. K., 'The repeal of the apprenticeship clauses of the Statute of Apprentices', *Economic History Review*, 3, (1931-2)

DICKINSON, H. T., *Liberty and Property: Political Ideology in Eighteenth-Century Britain*, (London: Weidenfeld & Nicolson, 1977)

_____, *The Politics of the People in Eighteenth-Century Britain*, (London: Macmillan, 1995)

DIGBY, ANNE AND FEINSTEIN, CHARLES, H., *New Directions in Economic and Social History*, (London: Macmillan, 1989)

DINWIDDY, JOHN R., *Radicalism and Reform in Britain, 1780-1850*, (London: Hambledon Press, 1992)

DOBSON, C. R., *Masters and Journeymen: A Pre-history of Industrial Relations*, (London: Croom Helm, 1980)

DONNELLY, F. K., 'Ideology and early English working-class history: Edward Thompson and his critics', *Social History*, 2, (1976)

DOUGAN, DAVID, *The Shipwrights: The History of the Shipconstructors' and Shipwrights' Association, 1882-1963*, (Newcastle upon Tyne: Frank Graham, 1975)

DOYLE, M., 'Belfast and Tolpuddle: attempts at strengthening a trade union presence, 1833/4', *Saothar*, 2, (1976)

DUNBABIN, J. P. D., *Rural Discontent in Nineteenth-Century Britain*, (New York: Holmes & Meier, 1974)

DURR, ANDY, 'Ritual of association and the organizations of the common people', *Ars Quatuor Coronatorum (Transactions of the Quatuor Coronati Lodge, No. 2076, London*, 1987), vol. 100 (publ. 1988)

DUTTON, H. I. AND KING, J. E., *Ten per Cent and No Surrender: the Preston Strike, 1853-4*, (Cambridge University Press, 1981)

DYCK, IAN, *William Cobbett and Rural Popular Culture*, (Cambridge University Press, 1992)

EISENBERG, CHRISTIANE, *Deutsche und englische Gewerkschaften: Entstehung und Entwicklung bis 1878 im Vergleich*, (Göttingen: Vandenhoeck & Ruptecht, 1986)

ELBAUM, B., LAZONICK, W., WILKINSON, F., AND ZEITLIN, J., 'The labour process, market structure and marxist theory', *Cambridge Journal of Economics*, 3/3, (1979)

EMSLEY, CLIVE, 'Repression, "terror" and the rule of law in England during the decade of the

French Revolution', *English Historical Review*, 100/397 (October, 1985)
_____, *Crime and Society in England. 1750-1900*, (London: Longman, 1987)
EPSTEIN, JAMES, *The Lion of Freedom: Feargus O'Connor and the Chartist Movement, 1832-42*, (London: Croom Helm, 1982)
EPSTEIN, JAMES AND THOMPSON, DOROTHY (eds.), *The Chartist Experience: Studies in Working-Class Radicalism and Culture, 1830-60*, (London: Macmillan, 1982)
EPSTEIN, STEVEN A., *Wage Labor and Guilds in Medieval Europe*, (Chapel Hill: University of Carolina Press, 1991)
_____, 'Craft guilds, apprenticeship, and technological change in preindustrial Europe', *Journal of Economic History*, 58/3, (1998)
EVANS, CHRIS, *'The Labyrinth of Flames': Work and Social Conflict in Early Industrial Merthyr Tydfil*, (Cardiff: University of Wales Press, 1993)
FARR, JAMES R., 'Cultural analysis and early modern artisans', in Geoffrey Crossick (ed.), *The Artisan and the European Town, 1500-1900*, (Aldershot: Ashgate, 1997)
FEINSTEIN, CHARLES, 'Pessimism perpetuated: real wages and the standard of living in Britain during and after the industrial revolution', *Journal of Economic History*, 58/3, (1998)
FELKIN, WILLIAM, *A History of the Machine-Wrought Hosiery and Lace Manufacturers*, (Newton Abbot: David & Charles, 1967; first published 1867)
FLINN, MICHAEL W., *The History of the British Coal Industry Volume 2: 1700-1830: The Industrial Revolution*, (Oxford: Clarendon Press, 1984)
FLOUD, RODERICK AND MCCLOSKEY, DONALD (eds.), *The Economic History of Britain Since 1700: Volume I — 1700-1860*, (Cambridge University Press, 1994)
FONER, PHILIP S., *History of the Labor Movement in the United States, Vol. 1: From Colonial times to the Founding of the American Federation of Labor*, (New York: International, 1972)
FOSTER, JOHN, *Class Struggle and the Industrial Revolution*, (London: Methuen, 1974)
FOWLER, ALAN AND WYKE, TERRY, *The Barefoot Aristocrats: a History of the Amalgamated Association of Operative Cotton Spinners*, (Littleborough: George Kelsall, 1987)
FOX, ALAN, *History and Heritage: The Social Origins of the British Industrial Relations System*, (London: Allen & Unwin, 1985)
FOX-GENOVESE, ELIZABETH, 'The many faces of moral economy: a contribution to a debate', *Past and Present*, 58, (1973)
FRASER, W. H., 'Trade unionism', in J. T. Ward (ed.), *Popular Movements, c. 1830-1850*, (London: Macmillan, 1970)
_____, 'Robert Owen and the workers', in John Butt (ed.), *Robert Owen, Prince of Cotton Spinners*, (Newton Abbot: David & Charles, 1971)
_____, *Trade Unions and Society: the Struggle for Acceptance*, (London: Macmillan, 1974)
_____, *Conflict and Class: Scottish Workers, 1700-1838*, (Edinburgh: John Donald, 1988)
_____, *Alexander Campbell and the Search for Socialism*, (Manchester: Holyoake Books, 1996)
FYRTH, H. J. AND COLLINS, HENRY, *The Foundry Workers: a Trade Union History*, (Manchester: Amalgamated Union of Foundry Workers, 1959)
FYSON, ROBERT, 'The crisis of 1842: Chartism, the colliers' strike and the outbreak in the Potteries', in Epstein and Thompson, *The Chartist Experience*.
_____, 'Unionism, class and community in the 1830s: aspects of the National Union of Operative Potters', in Rule, *British Trade Unionism, 1750-1850*.

GADIAN, DAVID, 'Class formation and class action in north-west industrial towns, 1830-50', in R. J. Morris (ed.), *Class, Power and Social Structure in British Nineteenth-Century Towns*, (Leicester University Press, 1986)

GALTON, F. W., *Select documents illustrating the History of Trade Unionism I: The Tailoring Trade*, (London: Longmans, 1896)

GAMMAGE, R. G., *History of the Chartist Movement, 1837-54*, (London: Merlin, 1969; first published 1854-5)

GEARY, DICK, *European Labour Protest, 1848-1939*, (London: Croom Helm, 1981)

GENT, THOMAS, *The Life of Mr Thomas Gent, Printer; of York; Written by Himself*, (London: Thomas Thorpe, 1832)

GEORGE, M. D., 'The Combination Laws reconsidered', *Economic History*, vol. 1, supplement, (1927)

_____, *London Life in the Eighteenth Century*, (Harmondsworth: Penguin, 1966)

GILLESPIE, FRANCES ELMA, *Labor and Politics in England 1850-67*, (Durham NC: Duke University Press, 1927)

GLEN, ROBERT, *Urban Workers and the Industrial Revolution*, (London: Croom Helm, 1984)

GOLDMAN, LAWRENCE, 'The Social Science Association, 1857-86: a context for mid-Victorian liberalism', *English Historical Review*, 100/1, (1986)

GOODMAN, JOCELYNE B., *Victorian Cabinet Maker: The Memoirs of James Hopkinson, 1819-1894*, (London: RKP, 1968)

GOODWAY, DAVID, *London Chartism, 1838-48*, (Cambridge University Press, 1982)

GORDON, GEORGE, *The Shore Porters' Society of Aberdeen, 1498-1969*, (Aberdeen: Reid & Son, 1969)

GOSDEN, P. H. J. H., *Friendly Societies in England 1815-75*, (Manchester University Press, 1961)

GRAY, R. Q., *The Aristocracy of Labour in Nineteenth-Century Britain, c.1850-1914*, (London: Macmillan, 1981)

GREEN, DAVID R., 'Distance to work in Victorian London: a case study of Henry Poole, bespoke tailors', *Business History*, 30, (1988)

_____, *From Artisans to Paupers: Economic Change and Poverty in London, 1790-1870*, (Aldershot: Scolar Press, 1995)

_____, 'Lines of conflict: labour disputes in London, 1790-1870', *International Review of Social History*, 43/2, (1998)

GURNHAM, RICHARD, *200 Years: The Hosiery Unions, 1776-1976*, (Leicester: National Union of Hosiery and Knitwear Workers, 1976)

HALL, ROBERT G., 'Tyranny, Work and Politics: the 1818 Strike Wave in the English Cotton District', *International Review of Social History*, 34, (1989)

HAMMOND, J. L. AND HAMMOND, BARBARA, *The Town Labourer 1760-1832: The New Civilization*, (London: Longman, 1917)

_____, *The Skilled Labourer 1760-1832*, (London: Longman, 1919)

HARRIS, TIM (ed.), *Popular Culture in England c. 1500-1850*, (London: Macmillan, 1993)

HARRISON, J. F. C., *Robert Owen and the Owenites in Britain and America*, (London: RKP, 1969)

HARRISON, MARK, 'The ordering of the urban environment: time, work and the occurrence of crowds, 1790-1835', *Past and Present*, 110, (1986)

HARRISON, ROYDEN, *Before the Socialists: Studies in Labour and Politics, 1861-81*, (London: RKP,

1965)

HARRISON, ROYDEN AND ZEITLIN, J. (eds.), *Divisions of Labour: Skilled Workers and Technological Change in Nineteenth-Century Britain*, (Brighton: Harvester, 1985)

HASKINS, CHARLES, *The Ancient Trade Guilds and Companies of Salisbury*, (Salisbury: Bennett, 1912)

HATCHER, JOHN, 'Labour, leisure and economic thought before the nineteenth century', *Past and Present*, 160 (August, 1998)

HAY, DOUGLAS AND ROGERS, NICHOLAS, *Eighteenth-Century English Society: Shuttles and Swords*, (Oxford University Press, 1997)

HAYNES, M. J., 'Class and class conflict in the early nineteenth century: Northampton shoemakers and the Grand National Consolidated Trades' Union', *Literature and History*, 5, (1977)

HEATON, HERBERT, *The Yorkshire Woollen and Worsted Industries, From the Earliest Times up to the Industrial Revolution*, (Oxford University Press, 1965)

HECHT, J. JEAN, *The Domestic Servant in Eighteenth-Century England*, (London: RKP, 1980; first published 1956)

HENSON, GRAVENER, *The Civil, Political, and Mechanical History of the Framework-Knitters, in Europe and America*, (Nottingham: Sutton, 1831)

HIGENBOTTAM, S., *Our Society's History*, (Manchester: Amalgamated Society of Woodworkers, 1939)

HILL, CHRISTOPHER, *Reformation to Industrial Revolution*, (Harmondsworth: Penguin, 1969)

_____, 'Pottage for freeborn Englishmen: attitudes to wage-labour', *Change and Continuity in Seventeenth-Century England,* (London: Weidenfeld, 1974)

HILL, J. W. F., *Georgian Lincoln*, (Cambridge University Press, 1966)

HILL, JACQUELINE R., 'Artisans, sectarianism and politics in Dublin, 1829-48', *Saothar: the Journal of the Irish Labour History Society*, 7, (1982)

HILTON, R. H., *English and French Towns in Feudal Society: a Comparative Study*, (Cambridge University Press, 1992)

HOBSBAWM, ERIC J., *Labouring Men: Studies in the History of Labour*, (London: Weidenfeld & Nicolson, 1964)

_____, *Primitive Rebels: Studies in Archaic Forms of Social Movement in the 19th and 20th Centuries*, (Manchester University Press, 1971)

_____, *Worlds of Labour: Further Studies in the History of Labour*, (London: Weidenfeld & Nicolson, 1984)

HOBSBAWM, ERIC J. AND RUDÉ, GEORGE, *Captain Swing*, (paperback edition, Harmondsworth: Penguin, 1973; first published 1969)

HODGKINS, J. R., *Over the Hills to Glory: Radicalism in Banburyshire, 1832-1945*, (Southend-on-sea: Clifton Press, 1978)

HODGSKIN, THOMAS, *Labour Defended against the Claims of Capital or the Unproductiveness of Capital proved with Reference to the Present Combinations of Journeymen*, (London: Steil, 1825)

HOLLIS, PATRICIA, *The Pauper Press: A Study in Working Class Radicalism of the 1830s*, (Oxford University Press, 1970)

HONE, J. ANN, *For the Cause of Truth: Radicalism in London, 1796-1821*, (Oxford: Clarendon Press, 1982)

HORRELL, SARA AND HUMPHRIES, JANE, 'Women's labour force participation and the transition to the male breadwinner family, 1790-1865', *Economic History Review*, 48/1, (1995)

HOUSTON, GEORGE, 'Labour relations in Scottish agriculture before 1870', *Agricultural History Review*, 6, (1958)

HOWARD, N. P., 'The strikes and lockouts in the iron industry and the formation of the ironworkers' unions, 1862-69', *International Review of Social History*, 18, (1973)

HOWE, ELLIC (ed.), *The London Compositor: Documents relating to Wages, Working Conditions and Customs of the London Printing Trade, 1785-1900*, (Oxford University Press, 1947)

HOWELL, GEORGE, *Conflicts of Capital and Labour, Historically and Economically considered. Being a History and Review of the Trade Unions of Great Britain*, (London: Chatto & Windus, 1878)

HUDSON, PAT, *The Industrial Revolution*, (London: Edward Arnold, 1992)

_____, 'Proto-industrialization in England', in S. C. O'Gilvie and M. Cerman (eds.), *European Proto-Industrialization*, (Cambridge University Press, 1996)

HUNT, E. H., *British Labour History 1815-1914*, (London: Weidenfeld & Nicolson, 1981)

JACOB, M. AND JACOB, J. (eds.), *The Origins of Anglo-American Radicalism*, (London: Allen and Unwin, 1984)

JAMES, M., 'Ritual, drama and the social body in the late medieval town', *Past and Present*, 98, (1983)

JEFFERYS, JAMES B., *The Story of the Engineers*, (London: Lawrence & Wishart, 1945)

JENKINS, MICK, *The General Strike of 1842*, (London: Lawrence & Wishart, 1980)

JOHN, ANGELA V., *Unequal Opportunities: Women's Employment in England 1800-1918*, (Oxford: Blackwell, 1986)

JOHNSON, PAUL, *Saving and Spending: the Working-Class Economy in Britain, 1870-1939*, (Oxford: Clarendon Press, 1985)

JONES, DAVID J. V., *Chartism and the Chartists*, (London: Allen Lane, 1975)

_____, *Crime in Nineteenth-Century Wales*, (Cardiff: University of Wales Press, 1992)

JOWITT, J. A., 'The retardation of trade unionism in the Yorkshire worsted textile industry', in Jowitt and McIvor, *Employers and Labour in the English Textile Industries, 1850-1939*.

_____, *Mechanization and Misery: the Bradford Woolcombers' Report of 1845*, (Halifax: Ryburn, 1991)

JOWITT, J.A. AND MCIVOR, A., *Employers and Labour in the English Textile Industries, 1850-1939*, (London: Routledge, 1988)

JOYCE, PATRICK, *Work, Society and Politics: the Culture of the Factory in Later Victorian England*, (Hassocks: Harvester, 1980)

_____, 'Labour, capital and compromise', *Social History*, 9/1, (1984)

_____ (ed.), *The Historical Meanings of Work*, (Cambridge University Press, 1987)

_____, 'Work', *The Cambridge Social History of Britain, 1750-1950*, vol. 2, (Cambridge University Press, 1990)

_____, *Visions of the People: Industrial England and the Question of Class, 1840-1914*, (Cambridge University Press, 1991)

KAIJAGE, F. J., 'The manifesto of the Barnsley Chartists', *BSSLH*, 33, (1976)

KELLETT, J. R., 'The breakdown of guild and corporation control over the handicraft and retail trade in London', *Economic History Review*, 10, (1958)

KIDD, ARCHIBALD T., *History of the Tin-Plate Workers and Sheet Metal Workers and Braziers Societies*, (London: National Union of Sheet Metal Workers and Braziers, 1949)

KIDDIER, WILLIAM, *The Old Trade Unions, From Unprinted Records of the Brushmakers*, (London: Allen & Unwin, 1930)

KIRBY, R. G. AND MUSSON, A. E., *The Voice of the People: John Doherty 1798-1854: Trade Unionist, Radical and Factory Reformer*, (Manchester University Press, 1975)

KIRK, NEVILLE, *The Growth of Working-class Reformism in Mid-Victorian England*, (London: Croom Helm, 1985)

_____, *Labour and Society in Britain and the United States, Vol. 1: Capitalism, Custom and Protest, 1780-1850*, (Aldershot: Ashgate, 1994)

_____, *Labour and Society in Britain and the United States, Vol. 2: Challenge and Accommodation, 1850-1939*, (Aldershot: Ashgate, 1994)

KNOOP, DOUGLAS AND JONES, G. P., *The Medieval Mason: an Economic History of English Stone Building in the Later Middle Ages and Early Modern Times*, (Manchester University Press, 1933)

_____, *The Genesis of Freemasonry: An Account of the Rise and Development of Freemasonry in its Operative, Accepted and Early Speculative Phases*, (Manchester University Press, 1947)

KOCKA, J., 'Problems of working-class formation in Germany: the early years, 1800-75', in I. Katznelson and A. R. Zolberg (eds.), *Working-Class Formation: Nineteenth-Century Patterns in Western Europe and the United States*, (Princeton: Princeton University Press, 1986)

KODITSCHEK, THEODORE, *Class Formation and Urban Industrial Society: Bradford 1750-1850*, (Cambridge University Press, 1990)

LAMOINE, GEORGES (ed.), *Charges to the Grand Jury 1689-1803*, (London: Royal Historical Society, Camden Society Fourth Series, vol. 43, 1992)

LANE, MARGARET, *Apprenticeship in England 1600-1914*, (London: UCL Press, 1996)

LAQUEUR, THOMAS, 'Bodies, death and pauper funerals', *Representations*, 1, (1983)

LATIMER, JOHN, *The Annals of Bristol in the Eighteenth Century*, (Bristol: privately printed, 1893)

LAWSON, JOSEPH, *Letters to the Young on Progress in Pudsey during the Last Sixty Years*, (Stanningley: Birdsall, 1887)

LAYBOURN, KEITH, *British Trade Unionism, c.1770-1990: A Reader in History*, (Stroud: Alan Sutton, 1991)

LAZONICK, WILLIAM, 'Industrial relations and technical change: the case of the self-acting mule', *Cambridge Journal of Economics*, 3, (1979)

LEESON, R. A., *Travelling Brothers: The Six Centuries' Road From Craft Fellowship to Trade Unionism*, (London: Granada, 1980)

_____, 'Business as usual: craft union developments, 1834-51', *BSSLH*, 49, (1984)

LEVINE, DAVID, *Family Formation in an Age of Nascent Capitalism*, (New York: Academic Press, 1977)

LEVINE, DAVID AND WRIGHTSON, KEITH, *The Making of an Industrial Society: Whickham, 1560-1765*, (Oxford: Clarendon Press, 1991)

LEWENHAK, SHEILA, *Women and Trade Unions: An Outline History of Women in the British Trade Union Movement*, (London: Ernest Benn, 1977)

_____, *Women and Work*, (London: Fontana, 1980)

LINDERT, PETER H., 'Unequal living standards', in Floud and McCloskey, *The Economic History of*

Britain Since 1700.

LINEBAUGH, PETER, *The London Hanged: Crime and Civil Society in the Eighteenth Century*, (London: Penguin, 1993)

LINEBAUGH, PETER AND REDIKER, MARCUS, 'The many-headed hydra: sailors, slaves and the Atlantic working class in the eighteenth century', *Journal of Historical Sociology*, 3/3 (September, 1990)

LIS, CATHARINA AND SOLY, HUGO, '"An irresistible phalanx": journeymen's associations in Western Europe, 1300-1800, in Lis, Lucassen and Solly, 'Before the Unions: Wage Earners and Collective Action in Europe, 1300-1850'.

LIS, CATHARINA, LUCASSEN, JAN AND SOLY, HUGO, 'Before the Unions: Wage Earners and Collective Action in Europe, 1300-1850', *International Review of Social History*, 39/2, (1994)

LITTLE, ALAN, 'Thomas Winters: Chartist and trade unionist', *BSSLH*, 49, 1984)

LLOYD, T. H., 'Chartism in Warwick and Leamington', *Warwickshire History*, 4/1 (Summer, 1978)

LOGUE, KENNETH, *Popular Disturbances in Scotland 1780-1815*, (Edinburgh: John Donald, 1979)

LOPATIN, NANCY, *Political Unions, Popular Politics and the Great Reform Act of 1832*, (Basingstoke: Macmillan, 1999)

LOVELESS, GEORGE, *The Victims of Whiggery; being a Statement of the Persecutions Experienced by the Dorchester Labourers...*, second edition, (London: Central Dorchester Committee, 1837)

LOVETT, WILLIAM, *Life and Struggles of William Lovett in His Pursuit of Bread Knowledge, and Freedom*, (London: Bell, 1920; first published 1876)

MACHIN, FRANK, *The Yorkshire Miners: A History*, (Barnsley: National Union of Mineworkers, 1958)

MALCOLMSON, ROBERT, *Life and Labour in England 1700-1800*, (London: Hutchinson, 1981)

_____, 'Workers' combinations in eighteenth-century England', in Jacob and Jacob (eds.), *The Origins of Anglo-American Radicalism*, (London: Allen & Unwin, 1984)

MARLOW, JOYCE, *The Tolpuddle Martyrs*, (London: Deutsch, 1971)

MARSH, ARTHUR AND RYAN, VICTORIA, *Historical Directory of Trade Unions. Volume 1: Non-Manual Unions* (Farnborough: Ashgate, 1980)

_____, *Historical Directory of Trade Unions. Volume 2: Engineering, Shipbuilding and Minor Metal Trades, Coal Mining and Iron and Steel, Agriculture, Fishing and Chemicals*, (Aldershot: Ashgate, 1984)

_____, *Historical Directory of Trade Unions. Volume 3: Building and Allied Trades, Transport, Woodworkers and Allied trades, Leather Workers, Enginemen and Tobacco Workers*, (Aldershot: Ashgate, 1987)

MASON, JOHN, 'Mule spinner societies and the early federations', in Fowler and T. Wyke, *The Barefoot Aristocrats*.

MATERNÉ, JAN, 'Chapel members in the workplace: tension and teamwork in the printing trades in the seventeenth and eighteenth centuries', in Lis, Lucassen and Solly, 'Before the Unions: Wage Earners and Collective Action in Europe, 1300-1850'.

MATHER, F. C., 'The General Strike of 1842: a study in leadership, organisation and the threat of revolution during the Plug Plot disturbances', in Quinault and Stevenson, *Popular Protest and Public Order*.

_____, *Chartism and Society: An Anthology of Documents*, (London: Bell & Hyman, 1980)

_____, *Public Order in the Age of the Chartists*, (1959; new edition 1984, Westport, CT: Greenwood Press)

MATHIAS, PETER, *The First Industrial Nation*, (London: Methuen, 1983)

MATSUMURA, TAKAO, *The Labour Aristocracy Revisited: The Victorian Flint Glass Makers*, (Manchester University Press, 1983)

MAYHEW, HENRY, *The Morning Chronicle Survey of Labour and the Poor: the Metropolitan Districts*, volumes 1-6 (vol. 1 1980, vols 2-4 1981, vols 5 and 6 1982, Horsham: Caliban)

MCCLELLAND, KEITH, 'Masculinity and the "representative artisan" in Britain, 1850-80', in Michael Roper and John Tosh (eds.), *Manful Assertions: Masculinities in Britain since 1800*, (London: Routledge, 1991)

MCIVOR, ARTHUR, 'Cotton employers' organisations and labour relations, 1890-1939', in Jowitt and McIvor, *Employers and Labour in the English Textile Industries, 1850-1939*

MCNULTY, DAVID, 'Bristol trade unions in the Chartist years', in Rule, *British Trade Unionism, 1750-1850*

MINCHINTON, W. E., 'The beginnings of trade unionism in the Gloucestershire woollen industry', *Transactions of the Bristol and Gloucestershire Archaeological Society*, 70, 1951

MOHER, JAMES, 'From suppression to containment: roots of trade union law to 1825', in Rule, *British Trade Unionism, 1750-1850*

MOORE, SIAN, 'Women, industrialization and protest in Bradford, 1780-1845', (University of Essex, D.Phil thesis, 1986)

MORE, CHARLES, *Skill and the English Working Class, 1870-1914*, (London: Croom Helm, 1980)

MORGAN, KENNETH (ed.), *An American Quaker in the British Isles: The Travel Journals of Jabez Maud Fisher 1775-79*, (Oxford: British Academy, 1992)

MORRIS, R. J., 'The rise of James Kitson: trades union and mechanics' institution, Leeds, 1826-51', *Thoresby Miscellany*, 15, (1973)

_____, *Class, Sect and Party: The Making of the British Middle Class, Leeds, 1820-1850*, (Manchester University Press, 1990)

MORRIS, R. H., *Chester in the Plantagenet and Tudor Reigns*, (Chester: n.p, (self-published), 1893)

MORTIMER, J. E., *History of the Boilermakers' Society: Volume 1, 1834-1906*, (London: Allen & Unwin, 1973)

MUSSON, A. E., *The Typographical Association: Origins and History up to 1949*, (London: Oxford University Press, 1954)

_____, *British Trade Unions, 1800-1875*, (London: Macmillan, 1972; reprinted in L. A. Clarkson, (ed.), *British Trade Union and Labour History: A Compendium*, (London: Macmillan, 1989), pp. 1-70

_____, 'Class struggle and the labour aristocracy, 1830-60', *Social History*, 3, (1976)

NASH, GARY B., 'Artisans and politics in eighteenth-century Philadelphia', in Jacob and Jacob, *The Origins of Anglo-American Radicalism*

NATIONAL ASSOCIATION FOR THE PROMOTION OF SOCIAL SCIENCE, *Trades' Societies and Strikes. Report of the Committee on Trade Societies, appointed by the National Association for the Promotion of Social Science, Presented to the Fourth Annual Meeting of the Association, at Glasgow September 1860*, (London: Parker, 1860)

NEALE, R. S., *Bath: A Social History or; A Valley of Pleasure, yet a Sink of Iniquity*, (London: RKP, 1981)

NEAVE, DAVID, *East Riding Friendly Societies*, (Beverley: East Yorkshire Local History Society, 1988)

NEFF, WANDA, *Victorian Working Women: An Historical and Literary Study of Women in British Industries and Professions, 1832-50*, (London: Allen & Unwin, 1929)

OBELKEVICH, JAMES, *Religion and Rural Society: South Lindsey 1825-1875*, (Oxford: Clarendon Press, 1976)

O'BRIEN, PATRICK, 'Central government and the economy, 1688-1815', in Floud and McCloskey, *The Economic History of Britain Since 1700*

———, 'Introduction: modern conceptions of the industrial revolution', in O'Brien and Quinault, *The Industrial Revolution and British Society* .

O'BRIEN, PATRICK AND QUINAULT, ROLAND, *The Industrial Revolution and British Society*, (Cambridge University Press, 1994)

O'CONNOR, EMMETT, 'A historiography of Irish labour', *LHR*, 60/1, (1995)

OLIVER, W. H., 'The Consolidated Trades' Union of 1834', *Economic History Review*, 17, (1964)

———, 'Tolpuddle Martyrs and trade union oaths', *Labour History*, 10, (May, 1966)

OLNEY, R. J., *Rural Society and County Government in Nineteenth Century Lincolnshire*, (Lincoln: History of Lincolnshire Committee, 1979)

ORTH, J. V., 'The legal status of English trade unions, 1799-1871', in A. Harding (ed.), *Law-Making and Law-Makers in British History*, (London: Royal Historical Society, 1980)

———, 'The Combination Laws reconsidered', in Francis Snyder and Douglas Hay (eds.), *Labour; Law and Crime: An Historical Perspective*, (London: Tavistock, 1987)

———, *Combination and Conspiracy: A Legal History of Trade Unionism, 1721-1906*, (Oxford: Clarendon Press, 1991)

OWEN, HAROLD, *The Staffordshire Potter*, (1901; new edition 1970, Bath: Kingsmead)

PALLISER, D. M., 'The trade gilds of Tudor York', in Peter Clark and Paul Slack (eds.), *Crisis and Order in English Towns, 1500-1700*, (London: RKP, 1972)

———, *Tudor York*, (Oxford University Press, 1979)

PALMER, STANLEY H., *Police and Protest in England and Ireland 1780-1850*, (Cambridge University Press, 1988)

PANKHURST, RICHARD, *William Thompson (1775-1833): Pioneer Socialist*, (London: Pluto, 1991; first published 1954)

PARSSINEN, T. M. AND PROTHERO, I. J., 'The London tailors' strike of 1834 and the collapse of the Grand National Consolidated Trades' Union: a police spy's report', *International Review of Social History*, 22/1, (1977)

PATTERSON, A. TEMPLE, *Radical Leicester: A History of Leicester; 1780-1850*, (Leicester University Press, 1975)

PEACOCK, A. J., *Bradford Chartism, 1838-1840*, (York: University of York, Borthwick Institute of Historical Research, 1969)

PELLING, HENRY, *A History of British Trade Unionism*, (London: Macmillan, 1963)

PHILIPS, DAVID, 'Riots and public order in the Black Country', in Quinault and Stevenson, *Popular Protest and Public Order*.

———, *Crime and Authority in Victorian England: The Black Country 1835-1860*, (London: Croom Helm, 1977)

PHILP, MARK (ed.), *The French Revolution and British Popular Politics*, (Cambridge University

Press, 1991)

Phythian-Adams, Charles, *Desolation of a City: Coventry and the Urban Crisis of the Late Middle Ages*, (Cambridge University Press, 1979)

Pickering, Paul, *Chartism and the Chartists in Manchester and Salford*, (London: Macmillan, 1995)

Pinchbeck, Ivy, *Women Workers and the Industrial Revolution, 1750-1850*, (1981; first published 1930)

Pollard, Sidney, *A History of Labour in Sheffield*, (Liverpool University Press, 1959)

Pollard, Sidney and Salt, John, *Robert Owen, Prophet of the Poor: Essays in Honour of the Two Hundredth Anniversary of his Birth*, (London: Macmillan, 1971)

Postgate, R. W., *The Builders' History*, (London: National Federation of Building Trade Operatives, 1923)

Price, Richard, *Masters, Unions and Men: Work Control in Building and the Rise of Labour 1830-1914*, (Cambridge University Press, 1980)

Prothero, Iorwerth J., 'London Chartism and the trades', *Economic History Review*, 24, (1971)

_____, 'William Benbow and the concept of the "general strike"', *Past and Present*, 63, (1974)

_____, *Artisans and Politics in Early Nineteenth-Century London: John Gast and His Times*, (Folkestone: Dawson, 1979)

_____, *Radical Artisans in England and France, 1830-1870*, (Cambridge University Press, 1997)

Quinault, R., 'The Warwickshire county magistracy and public order, *c*.1830-1870', in Quinault and Stevenson, *Popular Protest and Public Order*.

Quinault, R. and Stevenson, J. (eds.), *Popular Protest and Public Order: Six Studies in British History 1790-1920*, (London: Allen & Unwin, 1974)

Randall, Adrian, 'The shearmen and the Wiltshire outrages of 1802: trade unionism and industrial violence', *Social History*, vol. 7, no. 3, (1982)

_____, 'The industrial moral economy of the Gloucestershire Weavers in the eighteenth century', in Rule, *British Trade Unionism, 1750-1850*

_____, *Before the Luddites: Custom, Community and Machinery in the English Woollen Industry 1776-1809*, (Cambridge University Press, 1991)

Rappaport, Steve, *Worlds within Worlds: Structures of Life in Sixteenth Century London*, (Cambridge University Press, 1989)

Records of the Borough of Nottingham, being a Series of Extracts from the Archives of the Corporation of Nottingham, vol. 8, (Nottingham: Forman, 1952)

Reddaway, T. F. and Walker, L. E. M., *The Early History of the Goldsmiths' Company 1327-1509*, (London: Edward Arnold, 1975)

Redford, Arthur, *Labour Migration in England 1800-1850*, (Manchester University Press, second edition, revised and edited by W. H. Chaloner, 1964; first published 1926)

Rediker, Marcus, 'Good hands, stout heart and fast feet: the history and culture of working people in early America', in Geoff Eley and William Hunt (eds.), *Reviving the English Revolution: Reflections and Elaborations on the Work of Christopher Hill*, (London: Verso, 1988)

Reed, Mick and Wells, Roger A. E. (eds.), *Class, Conflict and Protest in the English Countryside, 1700-1880*, (London: Frank Cass, 1990)

Rees, Bryan, 'The lost years: Northumberland miners, 1844-62', *North East Labour History*, 19,

(1985)

REID, ALASTAIR J., *Social Classes and Social Relations in Britain, 1850-1914*, (London: Macmillan, 1992)

REID, DOUGLAS, 'The decline of Saint Monday', *Past and Present*, 71, (May, 1976)

REID, ROBERT, *The Land of Lost Content: the Luddite Revolt*, (London: Heinemann, 1986)

RENDALL, JANE, *Women in an Industrialising Society*, (Oxford: Blackwell, 1990)

RICHARDSON, RUTH, *Death, Dissection and the Destitute*, (London: RKP, 1987)

RICHMOND, ALEXANDER B., *Narrative of the Condition of the Manufacturing Population and the Proceedings of Government which Led to the State Trials in Scotland*, (London: John Miller, 1824)

ROBBINS, KEITH, *John Bright*, (London: Routledge, 1979)

ROBERTS, MARIE M., 'Pleasures engendered by gender: homosociality and the club', in Roy Porter and Marie M. Roberts (eds.), *Pleasure in the Eighteenth Century*, (Basingstoke: Macmillan, 1996)

ROBERTS, MICHAEL, 'Another letter from a far country: the prehistory of labour, or the history of work in pre-industrial Wales', *Llafur*, 5/2, (1989)

_____, 'The empty ladder: work and its meanings in early modern Cardiganshire', *Llafur*, 6/4, (1995)

RODGER, RICHARD, *Housing in Urban Britain, 1780-1914*, (Cambridge University Press, 1995)

ROLLISON, DAVID, *The Local Origins of Modern Society: Gloucestershire. 1500-1800*, (London: Routledge, 1992)

ROSE, ARTHUR G., 'Early cotton riots in Lancashire, 1769-79', *Transactions of the Lancashire and Cheshire Antiquarian Society*, vols 73 and 74, (1963-4)

ROSE, SONYA, *Limited Livelihoods: Gender and Class in Nineteenth-Century England*, (Berkeley: University of California Press, 1992)

ROSSER, GERVASE, 'Workers' associations in English medieval towns', in Pascale Lambrechts and Jean-Pierre Sosson (eds.), *Les métiers au moyen age: aspects économiques et sociaux*, (Louvain-la-neuve: Université Catholique de Louvain, 1994)

_____, 'Myth, image and social process in the English medieval town', *Urban History*, 23/1, (1996)

_____, 'Crafts, guilds and the negotiation of work in the medieval town', *Past and Present*, 154, (1997)

ROWE, D. J., 'Some aspects of Tyneside Chartism', *International Review of Social History*, 16, (1971)

_____, 'A trade union of north-east coast seamen in 1825', *Economic History Review*, 25, (1972)

ROWLANDS, MARIE B., *Masters and Men in the West Midland Metalware Trades before the Industrial Revolution*, (Manchester University Press, 1975)

ROYLE, EDWARD, *Chartism*, (Harlow: Longman, 1996)

RULE, JOHN, 'General introduction' to J. L. and Barbara Hammond, *The Skilled Labourer*; new edition, (London: Longman, 1979)

_____, *The Experience of Labour in Eighteenth Century Industry*, (London: Croom Helm, 1981)

_____, *The Labouring Classes in Early Industrial England 1750-1850*, (London: Longman, 1986)

_____, 'The property of skill in the period of manufacture', in Joyce, *The Historical Meanings of*

Work

_____ (ed.), *British Trade Unionism, 1750-1850: The Formative Years*, (London: Longman, 1988)

_____, 'Labour consciousness and industrial conflict in eighteenth-century Exeter', in Barry Stapleton (ed.), *Conflict and Community in Southern England: Essays in the Social History of Rural and Urban Labour From Medieval to Modern Times*, (Stroud: Sutton, 1992)

_____, 'Trade unions, the Government and the French Revolution, 1789-1802', in John Rule and Robert Malcolmson (eds.), *Protest and Survival: The Historical Experience — Essays for E. P. Thompson*, (London: Merlin, 1993)

_____, 'Against innovation? Custom and resistance in the workplace, 1700-1850', in Tim Harris (ed.), *Popular Culture in England c. 1500-1850*, (London: Macmillan, 1995)

_____, 'Review essay: proto-unions?', *Historical Studies in Industrial Relations*, 2, (1996)

_____, 'Employment and authority: masters and men in eighteenth-century manufacturing', in Paul Grifiths *et al.*, *The Experience of Authority in Early Modern England*, London: Macmillan, (1996)

RULE, JOHN AND WELLS, ROGER, *Crime, Protest and Popular Politics in Southern England 1750-1850*, (London: Hambledon Press, 1997)

SABEL, C. AND ZEITLIN, J., 'Historical alternatives to mass production', *Past & Present*, 108 (August, 1985)

SALZMAN, L. F., *English Industries in the Middle Ages*, (Oxford University Press, 1923)

SAMUEL, RAPHAEL, 'The workshop of the world: steam power and hand technology in mid-Victorian Britain', *History Workshop Journal*, 3 (Spring, 1977)

SANDERS, J. R., 'Working-class movements in the West Riding textile district, 1829 to 1839, with emphasis on local leadership and organisation', (University of Manchester D.Phil. thesis, 1984)

SAVAGE, MIKE AND MILES, ANDREW, *The Remaking of the British Working Class, 1840-1940*, (London: Routledge, 1994)

SAVILLE, JOHN, *Ernest Jones: Chartist*, (London: Lawrence & Wishart, 1952)

_____, 'J. E. Smith and the Owenite movement, 1833-1', in Sidney Pollard and John Salt (eds.), *Robert Owen, Prophet of the Poor*, (London: Macmillan, 1971)

_____, *1848: the British State and the Chartist Movement*, (Cambridge University Press, 1987)

_____, *The Consolidation of the Capitalist State, 1800-1850*, (London: Pluto, 1994)

_____, 'The "crisis" in labour history: a further comment', *LHR*, 61/3, (1996)

SCHWARZ, L. D., *London in the Age of Industrialisation: Entrepreneurs, Labour Force and Living Conditions, 1700-1850*, (Cambridge University Press, 1992)

SEWELL, WILLIAM H., *Work and Revolution in France: The Language of Labor from the Old Regime to 1848*, (New York: Cambridge University Press, 1980)

_____, 'Uneven development, the autonomy of politics and the radicalization of workers', in L. R. Berlanstein (ed.), *The Industrial Revolution and Work in Nineteenth-Century Europe*, (London: Routledge, 1992)

SHARPE, PAMELA, 'De-industrialization and re-industrialization: women's employment and the changing character of Colchester, 1700-1850', *Urban History*, 21/1 (April, 1994)

SHEPHERD, MICHAEL, 'The origins and incidence of the term "labour aristocracy"', *BSSLH*, 37, (1978)

SHOEMAKER, ROBERT B., *Gender in English Society 1650-1850*, (London: Longman, 1998)

SHORTHOUSE, R. W., 'Justices of the Peace in Northamptonshire, 1830-45', *Northamptonshire Past and Present*, 5/3, (1975)

'SHUTTLE, TIMOTHY', *The Worsted Small-Ware Weavers APOLOGY &c*, (Manchester: n.p., 1756?)

SIMON, CHRISTIAN, 'Labour relations at manufactures in the eighteenth-century: the calico printers of Europe', in Lis, Lucassen and Solly, 'Before the Unions: Wage Earners and Collective Action in Europe, 1300-1850'

SIMON, DAPHNE, 'Master and servant', in J. Saville (ed.), *Democracy and the Labour Movement: Essays in Honour of Dona Toor*, (London: Lawrence & Wishart, 1954)

SMITH, ADAM, *The Wealth of Nations, Books I-III*, edited by Andrew Skinner, (Harmondsworth: Penguin, 1970)

SMITH, JONATHAN, 'The strike of 1825', in D. G. Wright and J. A. Jowitt (eds.), *Victorian Bradford. Essays in Honour of Jack Reynolds*, (Bradford: City of Bradford Metropolitan Council, 1981)

SMITH, L. D., *Carpet Weavers and Carpet Masters: The Handloom Carpet Weavers of Kidderminster 1780-1850*, (Kidderminster: Kenneth Tomkinson, 1986)

SNELL, K. D. M., *Annals of the Labouring Poor: Social Change and Agrarian England 1660-1900*, (Cambridge University Press, 1985)

SOMERS, MARGARET R., 'The "misteries" of property: relationality, rural-industrialization, and community in Chartist narratives of political rights', in John Brewer and Susan Staves (eds.), *Early Modern Conceptions of Property*, (London: Routledge, 1995)

SOUTHALL, HUMPHREY, 'Towards a geography of unionization: the spatial organization and distribution of early British trade unions', *Transactions of the Institute of British Geographers*, new series 13, (1988)

_____, 'British artisan unions in the new world', *Journal of Historical Geography*, 15/2, (1989)

SOUTHALL, HUMPHREY, GILBERT, DAVID AND BRYCE, CAROL, *Nineteenth Century Trade Union Records: An Introduction and Select Guide*, (n.p., Historical Geography Research Series, 1994)

SPRY, JAMES, *The History of Oddfellowship*, (London: Pitman, 1867)

STACK, DAVID, *Nature and Artifices the Life and Thought of Thomas Hodgskin, 1787-1869*, (London: Royal Historical Society, 1998)

STEDMAN JONES, GARETH, 'Class struggle and the industrial revolution', *New Left Review*, 90 (1975), reprinted in Stedman Jones, *Languages of Class*

_____, 'The language of Chartism', in Epstein and Thompson, *The Chartist Experience*

_____, *Languages of Class: Studies in English Working-class History 1832-1982*, (Cambridge University Press, 1983)

_____, *Outcast London : A Study in the Relationship between Classes in Victorian Society*, (London: Penguin, 1984)

STERN, WALTER M., *The Porters of London*, (London: Longman, 1960)

STEVENSON, JOHN, 'Food riots in England, 1772-1818', in Quinault and Stevenson, *Popular Protest and Public Order*

_____, *Popular Disturbances in England 1700-1832*, second edition, (London: Longman, 1992)

_____, 'Social aspects of the industrial revolution', in P. K. O'Brien and R. Quinault (eds.), *The Industrial Revolution and British Society*, (Cambridge University Press, 1993)

STONE, JOHN, *The Practice of the Petty Sessions...*, (London: Baldock, 1841)

STORCH, ROBERT, *Popular Culture and Custom in Nineteenth Century England*, (London: Croom Helm, 1982)

SUTTON, PAUL, 'Soup and supervision: the metropolitan watch and clock trade, 1797-1817', *Journal of Historical Sociology*, 9/3 (September, 1996)

SWANSON, HEATHER, *Medieval Artisans: An Urban Class in Late Medieval England*, (Oxford: Blackwell, 1989)

SYKES, ROBERT, 'Popular politics and trade unions in south-east Lancashire, 1829-42', (University of Manchester D.Phil. thesis, 1982)

_____, 'Early Chartism and trade unionism in south-east Lancashire', in Epstein and Thompson, *The Chartist Experience*

_____, 'Physical-force Chartism: the cotton district and the Chartist crisis of 1839', *International Review of Social History*, 30/2, (1985)

_____, 'Trade unionism and class consciousness: the "revolutionary" period of general unionism, 1829-1834', in Rule, *British Trade Unionism, 1750-1850*

TAYLOR, BARBARA, *Eve and the New Jerusalem: Socialism and Feminism in the Nineteenth Century*, (London: Virago, 1983)

TAYLOR, PETER, *Popular Politics in Early Industrial Britain, Bolton, 1835-50*, (Keele University Press, 1995)

THALE, MARY (ed.), *The Autobiography of Francis Place (1771-1854)*, (Cambridge University Press, 1972)

THOLFSEN, TRYGVE, *Working-class Radicalism in Mid-Victorian England*, (London: Croom Helm, 1976)

THOMIS, MALCOLM, *The Luddites: Machine Breaking in Regency England*, (Newton Abbot: David & Charles, 1970)

THOMIS, MALCOLM AND GRIMMETT, JENNIFER, *Women in Protest, 1800-1850*, (London: Croom Helm, 1982)

THOMPSON, DOROTHY, *The Chartists: Popular Politics in the Industrial Revolution*, (London: Temple Smith, 1984)

THOMPSON, E. P., *The Making of the English Working Class*, (Harmondsworth: Penguin, 1968; first published 1963)

_____, 'English trade unionism and other labour movements before 1790', *BSSLH*, 17 (Autumn, 1968)

_____, 'The moral economy of the English crowd in the eighteenth century', *Past and Present*, 50, (1971; reprinted in Thompson, *Customs in Common*)

_____, 'The peculiarities of the English', in Thompson, *The Poverty of Theory and other Essays*

_____, *The Poverty of Theory and other Essays*, (London: Merlin, 1978; first published 1965)

_____, *Writing by Candlelight*, (London: Merlin, 1980)

_____, *Customs in Common: Studies in Traditional Popular Culture*, (London: Merlin, 1991)

THOMPSON, NOEL, *The People's Science: the Popular Political Economy of Exploitation and Crisis, 1816-34*, (Cambridge University Press, 1984)

THOMPSON, WILLIAM, *Labor Rewarded: The Claims of Labor and Capital Conciliated or How to Secure to Labor the Whole Products of its Exertions*, (London: Hunt & Clarke, 1827) (reprinted New York: Franklin, 1971)

THRUPP, SYLVIA, 'The gilds', in M. Postan, E. E. Rich and E. Miller (eds.), *The Cambridge*

Economic History of Europe, vol. 3, (Cambridge University Press, 1963)

TILLER, KATE, 'Late Chartism: Halifax, 1847-58', in Epstein and Thompson, *The Chartist Experience*

TILLY, CHARLES, *Popular Contention in Great Britain, 1758-1834*, (Cambridge MS: Harvard University Press, 1995)

TREBLE, J. H., 'The attitude of the Roman Catholic Church towards trade unionism in the north of England, 1833-42', *Northern History*, 5, (1970)

The Trial of Feargus O'Connor and Fifty-eight Others on a Charge of Sedition, Conspiracy, Tumult and Riot, (Manchester: Heywood, 1843)

TRINDER, BARRIE, *The Industrial Revolution in Shropshire*, (Chichester: Phillimore, 1973)

[TUFNELL, EDWARD CARLETON], *Character, Object, and Effects of Trades' Unions; With Some Remarks on the Law concerning them*, (London: Ridgway, 1834)

TURNER, H. A., *Trade Union Growth, Structure and Policy: A Comparative Study of the Cotton Unions*, (London: Allen & Unwin, 1962)

UNWIN, GEORGE, *Industrial Organization in the Sixteenth and Seventeenth Centuries*, (Oxford University Press, 1904)

_____, *The Guilds and Companies of London*, (London: Methuen, 1908)

VINCENT, DAVID, *Testaments of Radicalism: Memoirs of Six Working-class Politicians, 1790-1885*, (London: Europa, 1977)

_____, *The Culture of Secrecy: Britain, 1832-1998*, (Oxford University Press, 1998)

WADSWORTH, ALFRED P. AND MANN, JULIA, *The Cotton Trade and Industrial Lancashire*, (Manchester University Press, 1931)

WALKER, M. J., 'The extent of guild control of trades in England, *circa* 1660-1820: a study based on a sample of provincial towns and London companies', unpublished Ph.D thesis, (University of Cambridge, 1985)

WALLER, P. J., 'Democracy and dialect, speech and class', in P. J. Waller (ed.), *Politics and Social Change in Modern Britain: Essays Presented to A. E. Thompson*, (Brighton: Harvester, 1987)

WARD, JOSEPH P., *Metropolitan Communities: Trade Guilds, Identity and Change in Early Modern London*, (London: Stanford University Press, 1997)

WARD, J.T. AND FRASER, W. HAMISH (eds.), *Workers and Employers: Documents on Trade Unions and Industrial Relations in Britain since the Eighteenth Century*, (London: Macmillan, 1980)

WEAVER, STEWART ANGUS, *John Fielden and the Politics of Popular Radicalism, 1832-47*, (Oxford: Clarendon Press, 1987)

WEBB, SIDNEY AND WEBB, BEATRICE, *The History of Trade Unionism*, revised edition, (London: Longmans, 1920; first published 1894)

WEISNER, MERRY E., 'Guilds, male bonding and women's work in early modem Germany', *Gender and History*, 1/2 (Summer, 1989)

WELLS, ROGER A. E., 'The development of the English rural proletariat and social protest, 1700-1850', *Journal of Peasant Studies*, 6/2, (1979; reprinted in Reed and Wells, *Class, Conflict and Protest in the English Countryside, 1700-1880*)

_____, *Insurrection: The British Experience, 1795-1803*, (Gloucester: Alan Sutton, 1983)

_____, 'Rural rebels in southern England in the 1830s', in Clive Emsley and James Walvin, *Artisans, Peasants and Proletarians, 1760-1860*, (London: Croom Helm, 1985)

_____, *Wretched Faces: Famine in Wartime England 1793-1803*, (Gloucester: Alan Sutton,

1988; new edition: London: Breviary Stuff Publications, 2011)

_____, 'Tolpuddle in the context of English agrarian labour history, 1780-1850', in Rule, *British Trade Unionism, 1750-1850*

WHYTE, IAN D., *Scotland before the Industrial Revolution: An Economic and Social History c. 1050-1750*, (London: Longman, 1995)

WILENTZ, SEAN, *Chants Democratic: New York City and the Rise of the American Working Class, 1788-1850*, (New York: Oxford University Press, 1984)

WILLIAMS, GWYN A., 'Merthyr 1831: Lord Melbourne and the trade unions', *Llafur*, 1/1, (1972)

_____, *The Merthyr Rising*, (London: Croom Helm, 1978)

WILSON, ALEXANDER, *The Chartist Movement in Scotland*, (Manchester University Press, 1970)

WILSON, KEITH, 'Chartism and the north-east miners: a reappraisal', in R. W. Sturgess (ed.), *Pitmen, Viewers and Coalmasters: Essays on North-East Coalmining in the Nineteenth Century*, (Newcastle upon Tyne: North-East Labour History Society, 1986)

WINSTANLEY, MICHAEL, 'Oldham radicalism and the origins of popular liberalism', *Historical Journal*, 36/3, (1993)

WOOD, ANDY, 'Social conflict and change in the mining communities of north-west Derbyshire, c.1600-1700', *International Review of Social History*, 38/1, (1993)

_____, 'Custom, identity and resistance: English freeminers and their law, c.1550-1800', in Paul Griffiths *et al.*, *The Experience Of Authority in Early Modern England,* (London: Macmillan, 1996)

WOODS, D. C., 'The operation of the Master and Servants Act in the Black Country, 1858-75', *Midland History*, 7, (1982)

WOODWARD, DONALD, 'The background to the Statute of Artificers: the genesis of labour policy, 1558-63', *Economic History Review*, 33/1, (1980)

_____, *Men at Work: Labourers and Building Craftsmen in the Towns of Northern England 1450-1750*, (Cambridge University Press, 1995)

WRIGHT, LESLIE C., *Scottish Chartism*, (Edinburgh: Oliver & Boyd, 1953)

WRIGHTSON, KEITH, *English Society 1580-1680*, (London: Hutchinson, 1982)

WRIGLEY, CHRIS, 'The Webbs working on trade union history', *History Today*, (May, 1987)

WRIGLEY, E. A., 'Urban growth and agricultural change: England and the continent in the early modern period', in Peter Borsay (ed.), *The Eighteenth-century Town: A Reader in English Urban History*, (London: Longman, 1990)

WRIGLEY, E. A. AND SCHOFIELD, R. S., *The Population History of England, 1541-1871: A Reconstruction*, (Cambridge University Press, 1989; paperback edition with new introduction; first published 1981)

YEO, EILEEN JANES, 'Robert Owen and radical culture', in Pollard and Salt, *Robert Owen, Prophet of the Poor*

_____, *The Contest for Social Science: Relations and Representations of Gender and Class*, (London: Rivers Oram, 1996)

YEO, STEPHEN, 'Organisation and creativity: mere administration and mere theology', *Journal of Historical Sociology*, 9/2, (June, 1996)

YOUINGS, JOYCE, *Tuckers Hall, Exeter: The History of a Provincial City Company Through Five Centuries*, (University of Exeter, 1968)

Index

Aberdeen, 3, 14, 18, 27, 31, 38, 106, 189
   Female Operatives' Union, 121
   United Trades, 121
   trades and Chartism, 169
agrarianism, ix, 63, 100, 125-6, 135, 167-8, 175, 180-1
agricultural labourers, 1-2, 15, 41, 55-7, 97, 110, 132-3, 180, 194, 196
   see also Tolpuddle Martyrs
Agricultural Labourers' Conjunction Union Friendly Society, 135
Airdrie, 165
Alison, Archibald, 150, 202
Allan, William, 181, 183, 185, 191
Alnwick, 56
Alton, 19
Amalgamated Society of Carpenters and Joiners, 180, 196
Amalgamated Society of Engineers, 180-5, 187, 189-91, 193, 195, 197
American colonies, 8, 41, 92
Anti-Corn Law League, 165
Antrim, 120
apprenticeship, ix, x, 6, 7-9, 16, 17, 18, 20, 21-2, 25, 27, 32-6, 36-43, 45, 52, 63, 68, 75, 77-81, 85-6, 92-3, 103, 118, 171, 176, 184, 193-4
arbitration, 12, 67, 73, 76, 135, 176, 178-9, 191-93
Arch, Joseph, 180, 196
aristocracy of labour, see labour aristocracy
army, used against industrial action, 56, 84, 129, 157, 161, 162 n.98, 166
Artisans' General Committee, 79-80, 105
Ashley, W., 193
Ashover, 75
Ashton-under-Lyne, 119, 126, 129, 146, 173
Aslin, William, 68 n.58
Associated Ironmoulders of Scotland, 195
associationism, see co-operation (producer)
Austria, 3
Aylesham, 55
Ayrshire Colliers' Association, 91-2, 94-5

bakers, 10, 12, 13, 18, 48, 175
Banbury, 119
barbers, 15
Barnsley, 89, 97, 102, 119, 135
   Chartists, 154
   linen weavers' union, 133, 148
basket makers, 11, 179 n.68
Bath, 7, 15, 30, 49, 72, 78-9, 107, 171
Batley, 119
Beaumont, Augustus, 150-1
Bedfordshire, 136
Belfast, 73, 106, 115, 120, 121, 136, 194
Benbow, William, 112, 128-9, 140, 156
Berkshire, 56
Berwick upon Tweed, 71, 95
Betts, John, 118-19
Beverley, 7, 14, 18
Bible, use made in trade unionism, 92, 97, 116, 138-9
'binding', 61, 146-7
Bingley, 171
Birmingham, 26, 28, 29, 33, 39, 49, 84, 87, 97, 105, 109, 115, 127, 155, 160, 190
   Chartism and trades, 156, 158, 169-70
Blackburn, 80
Blackrod, 116
blacksmiths, 32, 33, 48, 61, 156, 196
Blaize, Bishop, 21
Bocking, 19
boilermakers, 15, 50, 139, 182, 195, 199
   and Chartism, 158, 176
Bolton, 50, 65, 69, 72, 76, 104, 116, 129-30, 147, 155, 157
bookbinders, 35, 49, 88, 126, 160, 173, 176, 183, 196
Bo'ness, 44
box clubs, see sick clubs
Bradford, 73, 103-4, 109, 115, 140, 141, 156, 199
   Trades' Union, 119
   Chartism and trades, 155, 168, 173
Braintree, 19
brassworkers, 126, 190
Breeches Makers' Benefit Society, 65
Breuilly, J., 200
Brewer, William, 44
brewsters, 18

bricklayers, 5, 11, 48, 88, 120, 158, 179 n.68
brickmakers, vii, 129, 195
Bridport, 133
Brief Institution, 45-6, 74, 103
Bright, John, 165, 181
Brighton, 134
Bristol, 1, 14, 30, 42, 45, 49, 58, 79, 81, 99, 111, 126
   Chartism and trades, 159, 169, 172
British Association for Promoting Co-operative Knowledge, 127
Bronte, Charlotte, 73
'brothering', 39, 94
Brown, Arthur, 180
brushmakers, 35, 50, 51, 71, 86, 106
Bufton, Joseph, 20 n.84, 21
building trades, vii, 11, 14, 126, 130, 136, 138, 148, 159, 190, 193-4, 198-9, 200, see also under individual trades
Bulwell, 74
Burgh-le-Marsh, 56
burial societies, ix, 6, 45, 87, 120, 188, 189, 196, see also funerals
Bury, 155, 157, 189
Bussey, Peter, 141, 155
butchers, 13, 31
button burnishers, 87

cabinetmakers, 29 n.28, 38, 51, 71, 88, 120-1, 148, 152, 172
Calhoun, C., 59
calico printers, 49, 115
Cambridge, 28, 99, 136
Campbell, Alan, 95
Campbell, Alexander, 121, 202
Campbell, John, 154, 163
capital, 100-1
Carlile, Richard, 97-8, 113
Carlisle, 38, 73, 78, 99, 115, 157
Caroline, Queen, 88, 97
carpenters, 8, 9, 10, 11, 17, 19, 30, 38, 41 45, 48, 50, 51, 84, 88, 106, 118, 120, 126, 180, 198, 195, 196, 201
   and Chartism, 154, 156, 158, 163
carpet weavers, 105, 126, 178, 181, 189
Carse of Gowrie, 136
Carter, John, 64, 70

225

Cato Street conspiracy, 83
Central Association of London Trades, 148, 176
chandlers, 8 n.21
Cheshire, *vii*, 29, 46, 49, 102, 115, 155, 157, 161-62, 163
   coalfield, 160, 170
Chester, 13
chainmakers, 33
chairmakers, 188
Chartism, *vii*, *x*, 5, 102, 103, 111-13, 122, 132, 143-86
   and 1848, 165-6, 167
   'The Charter and something more', 180
   Conventions, 156-7
   criticism of trade unions, 168, 180, 184
   decline, 145, 187, 181, 185, 187, 198
   and general strike, 156-8, 161-2, 167
   and general unionism, 147, 170
   Land Plan, 125, 143, 167-8, 169, 175, 179-80
   and liberalism, 180
   and miners, 170-2
   National Charter League, 180
   Scottish, 150, 155, 158, 164-5, 180-1
   trade unionism as a factor in rise, 148, 153-6
   trade unionists active in, 149, 155, 160-1, 168-70, 173, 175-6, 181-2, 183
   trades' affiliation to, 155, 158-9, 168-9, 172, 174, 175, 181
   trades critical of, 159-60, 168, 173
   trials 159, 161, 163
   see also National Association of United Trades
child labour, 27, 81 n.117, 85
China and Earthenware Turners' Society, 146
Christian Socialism, 175, 185
Christie, I., 60, 70
civic life and ritual, 4, 30, 36, 49
civil servants, 196
Clackmannanshire, 165
Clarion movement, 5
Clark, Anna, 18, 132
class, ideas of, 58, 59, 61, 100, 111, 114, 124, 140, 181
Cleave, John, 176 n.58
clothdressers, *see* croppers
coachmakers, 17, 27, 48, 49, 63, 83, 88, 121, 156, 160, 189, 195
coal industry, 24, 52, *see also* miners
Coal Miners' Association (Sheffield), 93, 116
coalporters, 11, 28
Coatbridge, 165
Cobbett, William, 64, 101, 123
Cockburn, Henry, 57 n.9
Coggeshall, 19, 20-2, 31, 34, 44
Colchester, 20, 21, 22, 32, 35, 44, 64
   trades and Chartism,169
Cole, G. D. H., 116, 119, 123
collective bargaining, 13, 14, 64, 70-1, 78, 88, 105, 191-3
collegia, 6
Combination Acts, *see under* parliamentary legislation
communitarianism, 92, 114, 123
community (concepts of), *ix*, 3, 15-16, 22, 36, 41, 51, 59-60
compositors, *see* printers
Compositors' Union Society, 71
Conservative Party, 178
conspiracy, law of, *see* law
Convention, 127-8, 156-7, 166
Cooper, Thomas, 163, 167
co-operation (retail), 112, 123, 143, 145, 174, 187
co-operation (producer), 99, 103, 125-6, 146, 175, 184-5
coopers, 27, 50, 71, 92-5, 160, 188
Cork, 19, 27, 30, 49, 99, 120, 194
cordwainers, *see* shoemakers
Cordwainers' General Mutual Assistance Association, 169, 175
Cornwall, 16, 51, 71, 147
corresponding societies, 57, 63, 65, 67, 77, 125
Cotton Famine, 186
cotton industry, 20, 24, 25, 29, 34, 35, 37, 39-40, 42, 46, 58, 62, 68, 69, 72-3, 74, 80, 92, 97, 98, 104, 106, 130, 149, 160, 165, 186, 189, 191, 195, 196, 199
cotton spinners, 35, 61, 67, 84-5, 87, 92, 93 97, 98, 102, 105, 106, 109, 115, 117, 126, 129-30, 131, 119, 149-52, 160, 173, 191-2, 193
   and Chartism, 154, 156, 175
cotton weavers, 40, 41, 46, 65-6, 72, 73, 80, 84, 89, 93, 97, 104, 109, 115, 129, 148, 168, 175, 189, 195, 196
Coventry, 8, 9, 17, 36, 48, 63, 80, 85-6, 88, 89, 97, 103, 139
covins, 9-10
Crawford, William, 81, 85
Crisis, 114, 124, 31-2, 135
Cromford, 29
croppers, 43, 45-6, 61, 74, 76, 115, *see also* shearmen
Crowley, Ambrose, 25, 26
Cumberland coalfield, 80, 171 n.28
Cupar, 65
cutlery trades, 3, 19, 61, 76, 80, 97, 179 n.68

Davenport, Allan, 78, 79, 105, 126, 127
Defoe, Daniel, 28, 29
d'Eichthal, Gustave, 109
Denbighshire, 116
Dengie, 56
Deptford, 94
Derby, 111, 115, 121, 130
Derbyshire, 2, 16, 29, 75
Derry, 120, 121
Devon, *viii*, 8, 19-20, 27, 45, 49, 65, 136
Devonport, 103
Dewsbury, 73, 115, 119, 155
Dicey, A. V., 178
division of labour, 81, 85
Dixon, William, 175
Dobson, C. R. 39, 58-9
dockworkers, 188, 201
'document', the, 115, 130, 135, 169, 175, 184
Doherty, John, 105, 116, 117, 118, 119, 128-9, 140
Dolphinholme, 119
domestic service, 28
domestic system, 25, 41-2
domesticity, 86-7, 131-2
Dorset, 134, 136, *see also* Tolpuddle
drinking, 36, 38, 50-3, 193, *see also* public houses
drovers, 188
Dublin, 19, 27, 40, 49, 64, 67, 99, 102, 106, 120, 152, 194
   Company of Hosiers, 76
   Trades' Political Union, 151
Dumbarton, 149
Duncombe, Thomas Slingsby, 196, 174-5, 178, 181

Dundee, 99, 136, 158, 160
  Trades Democratic Universal Suffrage Association, 158
Dunfermline, 165
Dunning, Thomas, 155
Duntocher, 149
Durham, 25, 80, 91, 188
  coalfield, 27, 53, 157, 171, 172
dyers, 17, 40, 84, 97, 102, 104, 115, 126, 130

edgetool trades, 179 n.68, *see also* cutlery trades
Edinburgh, 17, 44, 61, 121, 148
Eisenberg, C., 200
Elizabeth I, 21, 36, 40, 76, 77
Ellis, William, 155, 161
employers
  attitudes to trade unionism, 69, 103, 110, 120-1, 130, 176, 185, 191, 197, 199
  combination and federation of, 67, 98, 118, 185-6, 191, 194
  prosecuted by workers, 11-13, 32, 40-1, 45, 67, 78, 87
engineers, 50, 78, 115, 123, 129, 147, 182-5, 194, 200
  and Chartism, 147, 156, 159, 168-9, 175, 180-1
  and NAUT, 174
  see also Amalgamated Society of Engineers, smiths, steam enginemakers, tenters
engravers, 89
Epstein, S., 6-7
Essex, 19-22, 27, 31-2, 36, 40-1, 45, 49, 56, 70, 136, 137
Evans, Thomas, 77
Exeter, *x*, 8, 49, 65

Fabianism, 5
factories, 29, 43, 61, 189
factory reform, 111, 117, 123, 148, 150
Fairburn, John, 97, 98
Farnley Tyas, 136
Farsley, 119
feltmakers, 80, *see also* hatters
Fife, 165
flaxdressers, 134, 136
Fleming, George, 174
Flintshire, 116
Foresters, Ancient Order of, 50

Foster, J., 113, 138
Fox, A., 70
framework knitters, *see* knitters
Framework Knitters' Company, 35, 74
France, 15, 17, 57, 62, 63, 69, 77, 83, 175, 177, 201
Franklin, Benjamin, 51
Fraser, W. H., 12, 59, 73, 121, 130, 150
fraternity, *viii*, 4, 9-10, 15-20, 86, 92, 94, 133, *see also* masculinity
freemasonry, 18, 20, 31, 48, 52, 95, 137
French Revolution (1789), *xii*, 3, 55, 57-8, 59, 62, 63-4, 66, 86, 110
  (1830), 110, 201
  (1848), 175, 185, 201
Friendly and Protective Agricultural Association, 135
Friendly Associated Cotton Spinners, 87
Friendly Associated Coal Miners' Union Society, 116
Friendly Institution of Boot and Shoemakers, 156
friendly societies, *xvii-ix*, 30, 43-5, 47-9, 50, 56, 57-8, 77, 80, 84, 86, 95-6, 98, 105, 123, 131, 137, 168, 188-9, 201, *see also* burial and sick clubs
Friendly Society of Coal Miners, 116
Friendly Society of Cordwainers, 49
Friendly Society of Fustian Shearers, 156
Friendly Society of Ironfounders, 106, 195, 197
Friendly Society of Operative Iron Moulders, 182
Friendly Society of Operative House Carpenters and Joiners, 106 n.99
Friendly Society of Operative Spinners, 156
Friendly Union of Mechanics, 146
Friends of Humanity, 92, 94-5
Frome, 29
fullers, 9, 17, 20-22
funerals, 16, 74, 87, 93, 132-3, 182, 189
fustian cutters, 129, 148, 156, 158
Fyson, R., 146, 160, 166

Galloway, Alexander, 63, 77-8, 81
Gardeners, Order of Free, 50
Gast, John, 65, 84, 96, 99, 103, 105, 112, 147, 155
gender, *x*, 18-19, 32-6, 131, *see also* masculinity
General Association of Operative Weavers, 73, 80, 91
General Builders' Association, 194
General Smiths' Association, 182
general strike, 124, 127-8, 140, 155-7, 158-66, 167, 171
General Goldbeaters' Protection Society, 176
General Trade Union, 121
General Union of Carpenters, 106, 118, 120, 195
general unionism, *x*, 84-5, 96, 99, 104-7, 111-41, 146, 147, 170-1, 174
General United Tailors' Trade Protection Society, 169
Gent, Thomas, 39, 49
George, D., 67
Germany, 3, 18, 44, 200
Glasgow, 12, 102, 106, 136, 171, 180, 202
  labour exchange, 127
  trades' committees, 112, 121, 148
  bakers, 12
  building trades, 130
  cabinetmakers, 130
  Chartism and trades, 155, 159
  printers, 38
  spinners, 149-52, 154, 160, 176, 190, 192, 202
  Trades' Council, 178
  weavers, 73, 149
Glasgow and West of Scotland Association for the Protection of Labour, 121
glass cutters, 131
glass makers, *ix*, 50, 84, 183, 190, 193, 195, 196, 197
Gloucestershire, 46, 61, 62, 74
glovers, 131, 167-8, 176
goldsmiths, 9, 88, 176
Gorgon, 38, 89, 97-9, 101
Gott, Benjamin, 61
Grand General Union of Cotton Spinners, 106, 120
Grand Lodge of United Operative

Tailors, 126
Grand National Consolidated Trades' Union, 111, 114, 115, 120, 121-3, 124, 125, 126, 127, 130, 140, 147, 172-3, 174, 194
Grand Union of England, 105, 112
Gravesend, 49
Great Yarmouth, 99, 180
Green, Frederic, 176
Grimsby, 7
Guild Socialism, 5
guilds, 3-22, 25, 27, 30-4, 37, 39, 41, 42, 45, 47-9, 87, 132, 200-1
gunmakers, 28, 39

Habermas, J., 29
Halifax, 29, 119, 163, 165, 170, 173, 181
hammermen, 15, 25, 154, 158
Hammond, J. L. and Barbara, 66, 67, 73
Hampshire, 19, 56, 134
handloom weavers, *see* particular trades
Hanley, 160-1, 170
Harney, George, 216-17
Harrison, J. F. C., 111-12, 123, 125
Hatcher, J., x
hatters, 11-12, 17, 31, 32, 40, 49, 50, 61, 80, 88, 118, 120, 129, 130, 201
Hawick, 102
Haynes, M., 122
Henson, Gravener, 74, 76, 89-90, 104, 182
Hertfordshire, 56, 165
Hobsbawm, E. J., 4, 48, 55
Hobson, Joshua, 154
Hoddesdon, 56
Hodgskin, Thomas, 100-2, 114-15
Holmfirth, 119
Holmfray, Samuel 64
home, *see* domesticity
homosociality, 31, 34
Hone, William, 52
Hopkins, William, 191
hosiery workers, *see* knitters
hotpressers, 61
houses of call, 47-50, 70, 126, 170, 188, 193
Howell, George, 5
Huddersfield, 43, 76, 127, 129, 136, 140
Political Union, 128
1842 strikes, 162
and NAUT, 173
Hull, 7, 14, 61
Hume, Joseph, 89, 98
Hunt, Henry, 83-4, 123, 163
Hutchinson, Alexander, 147, 155, 164
Hutton, William, 33
Hyde, 102

iconography, 92, 138-9
industrial disputes, 27-8, 59, 61, 102-7, 129, *see also* strikes
industrialization, 2, 4, 23-7, 55, 57, 109, 114
insurance, 145, 168, 189
Ireland, *xii*, 1, 2, 19, 27, 30, 36, 49, 58, 64, 66, 67, 71, 73, 76, 77, 99, 102, 106, 115, 120, 136-7, 139, 151-2, 171 n.28, 183, 194
Irish migrant workers, 103, 137, 149, 196
Irish Suffrage Union, 171 n.28
iron industry, 97, 174, 191, 192
ironfounders, 25, 50, 84, 106, 132, 147, 182, 195, 197
ironstone miners, 180
ironworkers, 64, 110, 191-2, 199

Jacobinism, 58, 60, 62, 64-5, 72
Jacobs, Sam, 172-3, 175, 179
Jefferys, J., 185
Jones, Ernest, 180-5, 187
Journeymen Steam-Engine and Machine Makers' Society, 147, 156, 168, 176, 182-3, 185
jubilee, 128
Jude, Martin, 171, 180

keelmen, 7
Keighley, 80
Kent, 2, 49, 56, 133, 137
Kerr, George, 121
Kershaw, Thomas, 72 n.74
Kidderminster, 105, 178, 180
Carpet Weavers' Co-operative Association, 126, 189
Kiddier, William, 86
Kilmarnock, 95
King's Lynn, 98

Kirkheaton, 155
Knaresborough, 115, 119
Knights of Labour, 122
knitters, 2, 25, 35, 40, 61, 70, 74-7, 88, 120, 126, 131, 168, 191, 186, 195-6

labour aristocracy, 181-2, 184-5, 187
labour exchange, 124, 154-5, 171
labour history, 4-5, 21, 26, 43, 46, 55, 58
labour, property in, *see* skill
labour supply, 1-2, 4, 18, 23-4, 25, 33-4, 40, 47, 48, 60, 197-8, *see also* tramping
labour, theories of, 97, 100-1, 118-19, 154-5, 156, 167, 175-6, 190, *see also* skill
labourers, 2, 6-7, 9, 13-15, 16, 47, 168, 188, 196, *see also* agricultural labourers
lacemakers, 126, 131
Lambeth Co-operative Trading Union, 127
Lanarkshire, 162, 164, 170, 171, 202
Lancashire, 2, 28, 60, 61-2, 65, 72, 73, 74, 76, 80, 102, 104, 106-7, 116-17, 139, 147, 148, 150, 177
Chartism and trades, 143, 155, 156, 157, 169, 175
coalfield, 160, 175
cotton industry, 34, 73-4, 191-3, 195, 199
engineering trade, 176, 182, 184, 185
1818 strike wave, 84-5, 88, 98
1842 strike wave, 161-6, *see also* specific towns
Lancaster, 46, 119
land, 2, 16, 36, 145, *see also* agrarianism
Large, Thomas, 88 n.26
laundresses, 131
Law, Daniel, 132
law,
in relation to trade combinations and unions, 28, 32, 36-7, 39, 45, 48, 56, 62, 64, 66, 68, 80, 88-9, 102, 120-1, 129-30, 136-7, 153, 154, 173, 176-8, 198-9
use made of by labour, 12, 32, 40-1, 45, 67, 78-9, 88
see also legal decisions and parliamentary legislation

Lawson, Joseph, 166
Le Chapelier Law, 62
Leamington, 130
leather trades 11, 27, 32, 45, 47-8, 49, 50, 65, 88, 174, 176, 188
Leeds, 7, 29, 61, 74, 126, 129, 148, 153, 172, 175, 189, 196
   Clothiers' Union, 119, 129-30, 134-6, 155
   Linen Trades' Union, 119, 120
   Union, 119, 126
   1842 strikes, 162
legal decisions
   1721 Cambridge tailors, 28
   1813 Scottish crime of combination, 68
   1832 *R v Bykerdyke*, 129
   1851 Wolverhampton tin-plate workers, 177
   1866 *Hornby* v *Close*, 199
   1867 *R v Druitt*, 199
   1868 *Springhead Spinning Co* v *Riley*, 199
Leicester, 35, 120, 126, 136, 165
   Union, 119-20, 130
Leicestershire, 115,168
leisure, 38-9, 50, 109, *see also* Saint Monday
Lewis, Richard, 116
Liberal Party, 178, 180
Lincolnshire, 56
linen industry, 89, 97, 119, 120-1, 133-4, 136, 148
linen weavers, 89, 133
Linney, Joseph, 181
Lisburn, 120
Little Bolton, 157
Liverpool, 45, 49, 72, 99,106
Llanidloes, 156
London, *vii, ix*, 1, 3, 6, 7, 9-12, 13, 26, 28, 31, 38, 40, 44, 47, 48, 58, 60, 65, 84, 88, 97, 99, 102, 104, 106, 118, 123, 127-9, 135, 136, 140, 153
   bakers, 10, 48
   basket makers, 11
   blacksmiths, 27, 32
   bookbinders, 35, 81 n.117, 88, 126
   brassworkers, 126
   bricklayers, 48, 88
   brushmakers, 51, 71
   building trades, *vii*, 126, 130, 162 n.98, 198
   cabinetmakers, 51, 88
   carpenters, 9, 11, 17, 48, 51, 88, 126, 188
   chairmakers, 188
   Chartism in, 143, 152-3, 156, 158, 168-9, 173-6, 180
   coachmakers, 17, 27, 47-8, 49, 63, 83, 88
   coal porters, 11, 28, 162 n.98, 196
   coopers, 93-5, 188
   drovers, 188
   dyers, 104
   engineers, 78, 147, 175-6, 182
   goldsmiths, 9, 88
   hatters, 12, 17, 27, 31, 32, 88, 193 n.40
   ironfounders, 106
   labourers, 14
   lace weavers, 126
   leather trades, 11, 27, 32, 38, 47, 188
   painters, 32
   paviours, 11
   pipemakers, 126
   porters, 14, 196
   printers, 11, 32, 48, 71, 88, 112, 192
   saddlemakers, 10
   sailmakers, 27
   sawyers, 11
   seamen, 28
   shearmen, 9
   shipwrights, 11, 19, 33-4, 84, 91, 93, 99 103, 126, 155, 188
   shoemakers, 49, 69, 72, 78, 83, 88, 104, 126, 159, 168, 175-6, 187-8
   silk weavers, 35, 40, 86, 88-9, 96, 103-4, 174
   smiths, 9, 27, 48
   stevedores, 196
   stonemasons, *vii*, 17, 32, 40, 88, 162 n.98
   strikes, 162, 173, 179
   tailors, 27, 28, 47, 49, 70, 83, 88, 127, 169-70, 175, 188
   tin-plate workers, 88, 176
   trade union headquarters in, 182
   trades committees, 77-9, 85, 88, 99, 147-8, 152, 176
   typefounders, 83, 148
   watermen, 7
   wheelwrights, 32
   wigmakers, 48
   wireworkers, 32
   woollen industry, 10, 12, 20
London Coachmakers' Society, 63
London Mechanics' Institute, 100
London Operative Tin-plate Workers Society, 176
London Philanthropic Society of Coopers, 71
London Society of Cabinetmakers, 152
London Society of Compositors, 123, 195
London Working Men's Association, 143, 152-3
Londonderry, 120, 121
Londonderry, Lord, 172
Longson, William, 104-5
Loveless, George, 134-8
Lovett, William, 51, 52, 152, 153, 156
Loyal Albion Lodge (button burnishers), 87
Loyal Vulcan Society, 107
Luddenden, 163
Luddism, 43, 58, 72, 73-7, 80, 81, 104
Ludlow, 15
Lyon, 121

Macclesfield, *vii*, 29, 45, 102, 157
McDouall, Peter, 158, 164, 167
McFadyen, Allan, 180
machine makers, 115, 156, 168
machinery 12, 24, 28, 34, 42, 43-4, 73-7, 84, 103-5, 126, 131, 149, 160, 165, 176, 184, 190, 193, 197, *see also* Luddism
magistrates, 12, 21, 30, 40, 68, 73, 76, 78, 80, 84, 89, 90, 134, 136, 171
Maidenhead, 49
Maidstone, 87
Manchester, *vii*, 29, 38, 40, 46, 49, 61, 72, 76, 80, 83, 84-5, 87, 88, 96, 97, 99, 105, 109, 110, 115, 117-8, 119-20, 122, 127, 128, 129, 140, 148
   1848 and, 173
   boilermakers, 158
   brickmakers, 129
   bricklayers, 84
   carpenters, 84, 154, 158, 163
   Chartism, 147, 156-7, 158, 163
   engineering trades, 129, 147, 154, 156, 158
   fustian cutters, 129, 148, 156, 158
   painters, 158
   shoemakers, 156
   silk weavers, 40
   stonemasons, 150, 179
   tailors, 132, 156

Trades' Congress (1842), 159, 166
Trades' Council, 178
United Suffrage Association, 156
United Trades' Association, 147, 182
weavers, 31, 34, 37, 40, 45, 84, 104
spinners, 84, 87, 96, 98, 106, 129, 156
strikes, 129, 159, 165
'Manchester School', 178
Mandeville, Bernard, 27 n.13
Mansfield, 157
Marseille, 201
Marshall, James, 162
Martineau, H., 194, 196
Marx, Karl, 100, 101
masculinity, 18, 22, 36, 38-9, 70, 86, 91, 130-2, 185, 195, *see also* fraternity, gender, homosociality and patriarchy
Mason, John, 169
master and servant legislation, 68, 89-90, 174, 199
Mather, F. C., 159, 162
Mayhew, Henry, 188, 194
Mayo, William, 85
Mechanics' Friendly Union Institution, 147
Mechanics' Protective Society, 169, 182
Melbourne, Lord, 135-6
Merthyr Tydfil, 64, 110, 116, 129, 136, 166
metal trades, 15, 25, 28, 29, 33-4, 39, 50, 64, 97, 169, 194, *see also* blacksmiths, cutlery trades and smiths
Metropolitan Trades' Union, 112, 118
middle ages, *viii*, *x*, 1-17
Middlesbrough, 189, 200
'middling son', 9-10, 17, 29, 31, 86-7
migration, 30, 103, 137, 139, 149, 196, *see also* tramping
Milfordhaven, 49
millenarianism, 123-4, 133
milliners, 131
millwrights, 8, 77, 1747, 168, 182
Mills, James, 155
miners, *ix*, 2, 16, 25, 27, 39, 41, 52-3, 61, 62, 84, 91-2, 94, 96, 102, 110, 116, 127, 146, 170-2, 192, 196, 199-200
and Chartism, 160, 164-5, 171, 175, 181

1842 strikes, 160-2, 164
1844 strike, 172
Miners' Association of Great Britain, 170-2
monarchy, attitudes to, 63, 93
Moore, Peter, 89, 104
moral economy, 42-3, 63
More, C., 193
Morley, 119
Morrison, David, 159
Morrison, James, 113, 114, 133
'Mother Shorney', 51
Murray, Charles, 187
Musson, A. E., 112, 117, 122, 144, 146, 173

nailmakers, 33
National Agricultural Labourers' Union, 180, 196
National Association of Ironworkers, 192, 199
National Association of Organized Trades, 179-81
National Association of United Trades, *ix*, 169, 172-9, 181, 183, 185, 192
National Association for the Promotion of Social Science, 191, 201-2
National Association for the Protection of Labour, 114, 115-21 123-4, 146, 147, 173
National Charter Association, 122, 143, 154, 155, 158, 159, 160, 163-4, 170, 180-1
National Charter League, 180
National Equitable Labour Exchange, 124, 127, 128, 131
National Typographical Association, 176, 195, 197
National Union of Operative Potters, 146-7, 155
National Union of the Working Classes, 102, 112, 118, 122, 129, 134
naval mutinies, 63, 74, 136
needlemakers, 28
needlework trades, 34, *see also* tailors
New Lanark, 29, 109
new model unionism, 182-4

New York, 201
Newcastle upon Tyne, 7, 15, 17, 30, 36, 61, 84, 106, 125, 190
and Chartism, 148, 150, 155-6, 157, 160
Newport, 116, 157
Newton, William, 181, 183, 185
Newton-le-Willows, 176, 182, 184, 185
Norfolk, 55-6, 98, 99, 102
'Norman Yoke', 5, 176 n.58
North (Chartist), 166
North Shields, 91-2, 93, 95
Northampton, 122-3, 146, 159, 190
Northern Star, 143, 153, 154, 155, 162, 167, 169, 171, 174
Northern Trade Union, 121
Northumberland, 56, 80, 92, 171, 199, *see also* Newcastle
Norwich, 15, 55, 61, 62, 102, 155, 162
Nottingham, 38, 49, 61, 69, 74, 76, 84, 105, 109, 111, 155, 157, 159, 190, 195
Hosiery Board, 192
Nottinghamshire, 62, 73, 115

oath-taking, 38, 90, 95, 121, 136-40
O'Brien, J. Bronterre, 102, 114-15, 180
O'Connell, Daniel, 115, 151-3
O'Connor, Feargus, 102, 123, 140, 148, 150-1, 152, 153, 155, 157, 159, 164, 167, 168, 169, 171, 147, 179, 180
Oddfellows, 50, 170, 189
Old Body of Bricklayers, 120
'Old Mechanics', *see* Journeymen Steam-Engine and Machine Makers
Oldham, 46, 99, 113, 129-30, 136, 140, 155, 165
Oliver, W. H., 122
Operative, 183
Operative Brickmakers' Society, 195
Operative Cordwainers' Society, 120
Operative Society of Builders, 116, 126, 130, 135, 138, 157, 174
Operative Stonemasons' Society, 138, 147, 159, 168, 177, 179, 195
Operative Typefounders' Association,

176
Orth, J. V., 88, 178
Oswestry, 46
Otley, Richard, 162-3
overtime, 184
Owen, Robert, 109, 111, 112, 114-15, 116, 122-5, 127, 135, 146
Owenism, 111, 112, 114-15, 117, 123-5, 126, 131, 133, 135, 144, 163, 174, 202
Oxford, 31, 49, 87
Oxfordshire, 119

Paine, Thomas, 58, 62, 63, 97
painters, 32, 158
Paisley, 148, 159
Palmerston, Lord, 177
papermakers, 61, 68, 71, 87, 93-4, 106
Parker, John, 175
Parliament, 81, 86, 89, 148, 153, 156, 163, 175, 177-8, 198-9
parliamentary legislation
　on combinations generally, *viii*, 45, 66 n.48, 67, 88, 99, 104
　1361 against covins in building trades 10
　1563 Statute of Artificers, 2, 7, 20, 21, 32, 36, 40-1, 42, 53, 67, 76, 77-81, 89-90
　1721 Tailors' Combination Act, 28
　1766 re combinations, 90
　1773 Spitalfields Act, 40-1
　1777 re apprenticeship, 40
　1779 re framework knitters, 40
　1793 Friendly Societies' Act, 19, 45
　1797 Unlawful Oaths Act, 136
　1799 Combination Act, 43, 55, 57, 58, 60, 64, 65, 66-70, 77, 78, 88, 94
　1800 Combination Act, 55, 57, 60, 64, 66-70, 72-3, 76, 79, 85, 87-91, 97
　1800 Cotton Arbitration Act, 67
　1809 re woollen industry, 74
　1813 wage-fixing repeal, 79
　1814 apprenticeship repeal, 20, 25, 39, 77-81, 86, 89
　1815 Corn Laws, 81, 83, 105
　1823 Master and Servant Act, 89-90, 174, 199-200
　1824 Combination Laws Repeal Act, *x*, 19 n.77, 68, 88-91, 94, 96, 102-3, 109, 113, 199
　1825 Combination Laws Repeal Act, 89-91, 102-3, 176-7, 198
　1832 Anatomy Act, 133
　1832 Reform Act, 111, 144, 146
　1833 Irish Coercion Act, 111
　1834 New Poor Law, 111
　1835 Municipal Corporations Act, 15
　1848 Summary Jurisdiction [Jervis's] Act, 199
　1855 Friendly Societies Act, *vii*, 190, 198-9
　1859 Molestation of Workmen Act, 176 n.58, 178, 198-9
　1867 Arbitration and Conciliation Act, 178
　1867 Master and Servant Act, 200
　1871 Criminal Law Amendment Act, 198
　1871 Trade Union Act, 178, 198
　1875 Employers and Workmen Act, 200
parliamentary commissions and committees
　1817 on Coventry Watchmakers' Petition, 85-6
　1824 S.C. Artizans and Machinery, 71, 76 n.92, 89, 96, 98, 120
　1825 S.C. Combination Law, 91-6, 103, 106
　1838 S.C. Combinations of Workmen, 151-2
　1843 R.C. Children's Employment, 81 n.117
　1844-5 R.C. Condition of Framework Knitters, 168 n.9
　1854 S.C. Stoppages of Wages in Hosiery Manufacture, 168 n.9
　1856 S.C. Settlement of Disputes between Masters and Operatives, 178, 183, 197 n.65
　1860 S.C. Settlement of Disputes between Masters and Operatives, 168 n.9, 178
　1867-8 R.C. Trade Unions, 191
parliamentary reform, 110-11, 112, 118-19, 128, *see also* Chartism and radical politics
patriarchy, *ix*, 18, *see also* masculinity
Peel, Robert, 145, 148, 169
Peel, William, 176
pensions, 189
Perceval, Spencer, 43, 69
Perth, 136
Peterloo, 83-4, 122, 163
petitioning, 76, 81, 83, 102, 121, 144, 146, 156, 163, 173, 174, 177
Petrie, George, 114, 125

Philadelphia, 41
Philanthropic Hercules, 84-5, 86, 105, 112
Philanthropic Society, 84-5, 106
Philanthropic Society of Boot and Shoemakers, 169
Phoenix Society of Compositors, 71
picketing, 68, 149, 150, 159, 160, 165, 178, 199
piece-work, 11, 71, 184-5, 192
Pilling, Richard, 155, 164
Pioneer 113, 114, 131, 135, 139
pipemakers, 126
Pitt, William, 68-9
Place, Francis, 38, 65, 76 n.92, 89-90, 98-100, 101-2, 104, 129, 152
'Plug Plot', 160-6
plush weavers, 46
Poole, S., 58-9
Poor Laws, 33, 37, 38, 104, 110, 111, 133, 147-8, 150, 161, 174
Poor Man's Guardian 18 n.69, 102, 123, 136, 140
population growth, 1, 23, 25, 29, 33-4, 39, 109
porters, 3, 11, 13-14, 15, 17, 18
Portland, Duke of, 65, 94-5
Portsmouth, 94, 103
Post Office workers, 196
potters, 105, 119, 130, 146, 147, 160-2, 178, 189, 192, 199
Potteries, *see* Staffordshire
powerloom weavers, 84, 115, 165, 176
'Powlett, John', 119, 155, *see also* Leeds Clothiers' Union
Prentice, Archibald, 110-11
Preston, 130, 176, 186, 189-90
Preston, Thomas, 49, 120
printers, 11, 32, 38-9, 48, 49, 50, 52, 71, 88, 112, 120, 121, 123, 173, 178, 183, 192, 194, 196, 199, 201
　and Chartism, 160, 172
production, workers' control of, 99, 101, 160, 187, 197
Prothero, I., 52, 103, 104, 144, 159, 175, 201
proto-industrialization, 2, 15, 25-6, 32
Prussia, 200
public houses, *x*, 11, 38, 44-50, 65,

155, 160, 170, 177, 188-190, 193, 195
'public sphere', 29, 32
Pudsey, 166
Pynours Society, 3, 14

Queensferry, 44
quittance papers, 182

radicalism, ix, x, 49, 57-8, 63, 84-5, 96, 99-100, 101-2, 106, 112-13, 118, 119, 128, 159, 165, 197, *see also* Chartism, Jacobinism, parliamentary reform
Railway Spring Makers' Society, 193
railway workers, 184, 188-9, 196
Rainbow Society (Salisbury), 49
Randall, A., 43, 62
Rappaport, S., 6
Raven, Robert, 94
Reform League, 183
Registrar of Friendly Societies, *vii*, 50
Reid, R., 73
religion, 3, 6, 8, 9, 10, 41, 138-40, 199, *see also* Bible, millenarianism
residential patterns, *ix*
'respectability', 4, 16, 85-6, 94, 107, 130
retail trades, 15
revolution, threat of, 83, 96, 125, 128-9, 134, 137, 156-8, 167
ribbon weavers, *vii*
Ribbonism, 139, 196
Ricardo, David, 97, 101
Richards, John, 160-1
Richardson, R., 133
riots, 42-3, 60, 64-5, 83, 137
    Colchester weavers (1675), 20
    London weavers (1675), 20
    Wiltshire textile workers (1726-7), 27
    Lancashire machinery (1768, 1779), 28
    Leicestershire machinery (1780), 35
    Merthyr ironworkers (1800), 64
    Wiltshire shearmen (1802), 43
    Manchester (1812), 72
    Spa Fields (1816), 77, 83
    Staffordshire (1842), 161-2
    see also Luddism
ritual, 16-17, 18, 38, 50, 51-2, 60, 68, 84, 87, 133, 138-40, *see also* funerals

Roberts, William Prowting, 169-70, 171, 176, 181, 188
Robertson, Duncan, 180
Rochdale, 104, 105, 115, 1129, 130, 165, 181
    Association of Journeymen Weavers etc., 91-3
Roman Britain, 1, 6
Roman Catholic Church, 110, 139, 196
Rose, George, 79
Ross, David, 175
Rosser, G., 4, 10
Rowntree, S., 189
Royal Dockyards, 19, 94, 103
Rule, J., 41, 59, 63, 74, 147, 170, 194
Rushton, Ben, 165 n.114
Ruthin, 17

saddle-makers, 10
sailmakers, 27, 48
Saint Helena Society, 19, 45
'Saint Monday', 50
Salford, *vii*, 130, 148
Salisbury, 49, 134
saltworkers, 174
Samaritan Society, 71
Sanders, J., 126-7
Saville, John, 102
sawyers, 11, 99, 126, 129, 130, 176
scale of firms, 24-5, 199
Scotland, x, 1, 2, 6, 12, 13, 18, 27, 28, 29, 39, 42, 44, 48, 49, 50, 58-9, 61, 65, 66, 68, 71-2, 80, 92, 95, 103, 125, 137, 148, 180, 189, 190, 194, 202
    agricultural workers, 136
    apprenticeship in, 78
    Chartism and the trades, 155, 158, 164-5, 180
    cotton industry, 73, 80, 149-51, *see also* Glasgow
    engineers, 195
    legal position of labour organizations, 89, 149
    and Luddism, 73
    miners, 91-2, 95, 139, 162, 165, 170-2, 180, 196
    NAUT in, 172
    petitions against Combination Act, 102
    strikes, 73, 130, 149-51, 162, 164-5, 171
    trades' committees, 121, 148, 178

weavers, 89, 91, 148
women trade unionists, 121
Scottish Radical Association, 148
seamen, 28, 44, 91, 92, 93, 94, 180
Seamen's Loyal Standard Association, 91, 94, 95
'searchers', 7, 76
secrecy, 18, 38, 68, 71, 75, 95, 107, 151
Seer, Isaac, 56
Selsby, Henry, 176, 185
shearmen, 8, 9, 29, 43, 45, 74, *see also* croppers
Sheffield, 3, 19, 29, 42, 45, 49, 61, 64, 76, 80, 93, 102, 105, 186, 197
    Trades' General Union. 119
    and Chartism, 155, 163, 169, 175
Shepherds (friendly society), 139 n.141
shipbuilding, 33, 178, 192, 194
shipwrights, 11, 19, 33, 34, 45, 84, 91, 92-3, 94, 96, 103, 155
    and Chartism, 160
shoemakers, 2, 9, 15, 40, 45, 49, 50, 61, 69, 72, 78-9, 83, 87, 88, 102, 104, 105, 120, 122, 123, 126-8, 130-1, 146, 190, 201
    and Chartism, 155-6, 159-60, 168, 169-70, 175, 188
Shropshire, 15, 46, 160, 164, 170
sick clubs and benefits, *vii*, 22, 32, 43-8, 50, 52, 71, 87, 93, 133, 135, 182, 190, 196, 197
silk industry, 35, 40, 48, 86, 178, 192
Skelton, John, 175
skill, ix, x, 4, 16, 26, 37-43, 63, 76, 79, 84, 86, 91, 97, 113, 124-5, 130, 137, 154, 184-5, 187, 193, 195, 197, *see also* apprenticeship
skinners, *see* leather trades
Slaithwaite, 119
smallware weavers, 19-20, 31, 34, 115
Smith, Adam, 37, 50, 74
Smith, James Elishma, 113, 114
Smith, Sydney, 185
smiths, 9, 15, 48, 49, 97, 147, 182, 189
    and Chartism, 158, 164
Society for the Diffusion of Useful Knowledge, 1 n.1
Society of Journeymen Brushmakers,

51, 71, 89, 106
Somerset, 19, 27, 29, 37, 45, 58, 61, 84, 134
South Shields, 91, 92, 93, 95, 99, 126
Shipwrights' Union Society, 91, 94, 95
Southampton, 18, 99
Southcott, Joanna, 97
Southwark, *vii*
Spa Fields, 77, 83
Spence, Thomas, 63, 65, 77, 78, 84-5, 105, 112, 125, 126, 128
Spitalfields, 35, 40, 86, 104
Stack, D., 101
Staffordshire, 90, 97, 105, 116, 127, 130, 136, 146-7, 155, 159-62, 170, 181, 199
  coalfield, 160-1, 164
Stalybridge, 96, 163
State, attitudes to trade unionism, 63, 113, 198, *see also* law and parliamentary legislation
Steam Engine Makers' Society, 50, 106, 182, 195
Steam Enginemen's and Firemens' Society, 189, 196
Stocking Makers' Association for Mutual Protection, 74
stockingers, *see* knitters
Stockport, 35, 61, 76, 92, 93, 106, 129, 154, 155
Stockport Cotton Jenny Spinners' Society, 92-3
Stockton-on-Tees, 188, 196
Stoke, 161
stonemasons, *vii*, 10, 16, 17, 32, 48, 50, 88, 119, 138, 147, 150, 177, 183, 201
  and Chartism, 153, 159, 168
Storrington, 61
Straddling, Alexander, 181
straw hatmakers, 131
strike-breaking, 95, 119, 137, 149, 171-2, 176, 177, 190-1, 199
strikes and lockouts, *viii*, 11, 55-6, 59, 64, 90-1, 98, 117, 183-4
  1552 York, 13
  1577-8 Chester bakers and butchers 13
  1654 and 1659, Tyne keelmen, 13
  1682 London hatters, 11-12
  1720-50 London trades, 13
  1731 Durham coalfield, 27

  1768 London seamen and coalheavers, 28
  1790 Norfolk farm workers, 55
  1792 Merthyr ironworkers, 65
  1792/3 Cork shoemakers, 49
  1793 Essex farmworkers, 56
  1795 farmworkers, 56
  1800 farmworkers, 56
  1800 Merthyr ironworkers, 64
  1801 Kent farmworkers, 56
  1801 Leeds spinners 61
  1810 Lancashire spinners, 106
  1812 Bath shoemakers, 78-9
  1813 Scottish weavers, 73
  1818 Lancashire strike wave, 84, 88, 96, 98, 106, 107
  1821 stockingers, 69
  1824 Bradford woollen industry, 103-4
  1824 Thames shipwrights, 103
  1825-6 London trades, 104
  1826 Lancashire weavers, 104
  1827 Bradford woollen industry, 104
  1828 Kidderminster weavers, 126, 189
  1829 Lancashire textiles, 129
  1830 Lancashire textiles, 129
  1831 Merthyr, 110
  1831 Leeds textiles, 129
  1833 north Lancashire, Leeds, Leicestershire, 130
  1834 strike wave, 121, 129-32, 136, 146
  1834 Derby spinners, 115, 121, 130
  1834 Oldham, 113, 130, 140-1
  1834-5 Potteries, 147
  1836 Thornaby potters, 147
  1836 Essex farmworkers, 137
  1836 London engineers, 147
  1836-7 Potteries, 146
  1836-7 Glasgow cotton, 149-51
  1839 'general strike', 156-8
  1842 'general strike', *x*, 158-66, 167, 170, 172, 175, 181
  1844 North-east miners 171
  1847 Newton-le-Willows engineers, 176, 184
  1851-2 Wolverhampton tin-plate workers, 176
  1852 engineering trades, 184-5, 197
  1853 London, 129
  1853-4 Preston cotton, 176, 196
  1859-60 London builders, *vii*, 190, 199
  1864 Middlesbrough iron trade, 199-200
  1865 London, 129
  1866 iron trade, 192
  see also industrial disputes
Sunderland, 93, 95, 105, 126

Associated Trades, 105
Sussex, 2, 56, 61, 106, 134-5, 136, 137
Swansea, 116
sweating, 34
'Swing', 57, 110, 134, 136
Sykes, Robert, 116-8, 140, 144, 148
syndicalism, 125

tailors, 9, 11, 15, 17, 18, 27, 28, 31, 36, 44, 45, 47, 48, 49, 61, 64, 70, 83, 88, 89, 98, 114, 125, 127, 129-31, 188, 201
  and Chartism, 146, 158-9, 170, 173, 175
Taunton, 19, 29, 37, 45
Taylor, John, 149
Teesside, 146, 172, 181, 191, 199
tenters, 121
Tewkesbury, 74, 102
Thames Shipwrights' Provident Union, 103
Thaxted, 56
Thelwall, John, 63, 64, 101
Thomis, M., 59
Thompson, E. P., 20, 22, 39, 57-60, 62, 73, 76, 98-9, 101, 113, 144, 188
Thompson, D., 145
Thompson, William, 106, 107, 114, 115
Thornaby, 146, 147
The Times, 56, 88, 98, 185
tin-plate workers, 50, 88-9, 97, 144, 169, 176, 182, 185, 190
Tiverton, *viii*, 29, 45, 49
Todmorden, 84, 130
Tolpuddle Martyrs, 110, 111, 121, 122, 125, 134-41, 146, 149, 154, 155, 176
Tower Hamlets, 183
trade unionism
  defined, *vii*, 20, 52-3, 106-7
  governance, 41-2, 48-9, 95, 106, 159, 161, 182-3, 193
  legal status of, 66-7, 177-8, 198-202, *see also* specific parliamentary legislation
  numerical strength, 194-6, 201
  and regulation of quality, 75, 197
  and the press 79, 97-100, 112-13, 117, 122, 147, 148, 153, 171, 174, 179, 183

233

supported by non-trade unionists, 96
and workplace discipline, 70, 93, 197
trades' councils, 178
Trades' Newspaper 99-100, 102, 104, 105, 118
Trades' Union, *see* Yorkshire Trades' Union
tramping, 30, 47-50, 60, 80, 104, 106-7, 120, 134, 197
transportation, 120, 137, 150-2, 154, 166
Trowbridge, 44
Tucker, James, 135
tuckers, 8
Tufnell, Edward, 139
Tunbridge, 133
Twiss, William, 116
Tyneside, 2, 13, 83, 156, *see also* Newcastle
typefounders, 83, 148, 176
typographers, *see* printers

Ulster, 2, 73, 120
unemployment and unemployment benefits, 105, 135, 149, 154, 182, 189, 197
Union Exchange Society, 112, 127
United Brothers of Industry, 135, 136
United Committee of Framework Knitters, 74-5
United Feltmakers of Manchester, 80
United Irishmen, 77
United Journeyman Shoemakers Society, 61
United Societies of Woolcombers, 103
United Society of Boilermakers, 139 n.140, 195
United States of America, 122, 186, 201
United Trades' Association (Bristol), 169, 172
United Trades' Association (London), 127
United Trades' Association (Manchester) 147, 169, 182
urban growth, 2, 23, 30, 109

Victoria, 148

violence, 42-3, 89, 93, 95, 102, 103, 143, 149-52, 157, 160-2, *see also* riots

Wade, John (journalist), 97, 98
Wade, John (GNCTU chaplain), 137
wages, *viii*, 1-2, 9-10, 11, 13, 27, 30, 31, 37, 47-8, 56, 62, 64, 68, 72-3, 104, 107, 109, 117, 154, 60, 163, 175, 187, 195
Waithman, Robert, 72
Wakefield, 29, 89, 171
Wales, *x*, 1, 17, 49, 58, 94, 110, 116, 156, 157, 160, 166, 194
 ironworkers, 64, 110
 miners, 110, 116, 160, 166, 171, 189
 NAPL in, 116
Walpole, Horace, 28
Walsall, 33
Warrington, 29, 49
Warwick, 137
watchmakers, 63, 85-6
watermen, 7
weavers, *see individual specialisms*
Webb, S. and B., 4-5, 22, 47, 57, 67, 101, 113, 118, 122, 144, 146, 147, 162, 179, 183, 195
Wells, R., 60-2, 134
West Riding Fancy Union, 93, 96
Western Union Exchange, 127
Westmorland, 80
wheelwrights, 8, 32, 40, 61, 156
White, George, 169
Whitehaven, 80
whitesmiths, *see* tin-plate workers
Wigan, 116
wigmakers, 48
William IV, 111
Williams, G. A., 116
Wilson, K., 164
Wiltshire, 27, 43, 44, 45, 49, 58, 74
Winlaton, 25, 83, 156
Winters, Thomas, 168, 174, 176, 178, 180, 197
wireworkers, 32
Wolverhampton, 169, 176-7, 181, 185
women, 32-6, 50, 86, 125, 172, 174

and Chartism, 143
and guilds, 14, 18
in industrial disputes, 95
as industrial workers, 12, 18, 26, 32- 6, 109, 130-2, 147, 194-5
trade unionists, 34, 119, 121, 130-2, 146-7, 169, 194-5
trade unionist attitudes to, *vii*, 33-6, 52, 130-1
see also masculinity
woolcombers, *viii*, 19-20, 21-2, 27, 31, 36, 37, 48, 49, 80, 103-4, 138, 189
 and Chartism, 168-9
woollen and worsted industry, 1, 2, 10-11, 12, 17, 19, 20-2, 26, 27, 31-2, 33-4, 37, 41, 43-4, 48, 58, 61, 62, 74, 76, 78, 91, 103-5, 115, 119, 126, 129, 160, 186
woollen/worsted weavers, 8, 11, 17, 19, 35, 40, 45, 49, 91, 93, 96, 97, 103, 105, 155, 162, 168-9, 173, 181
woolpackers, 18
woolsorters, 97
woolspinners, 35, 91
woolstaplers, *viii*
Worcestershire, 105
work, attitudes to, *ix*, 6, 159-60, 197-8, *see also* skill
work, hours of, 10, 27, 32, 45, 49, 147, 182
Wormingford, 137
Wycliffe, John, 10
Wymondham, 102

Yeovil, 134
York, 1, 6, 9, 13, 49, 119, 189
Yorkshire, 2, 26, 29, 41, 43, 45, 60-1, 74, 76, 80, 84, 93, 102, 104, 115, 116, 117, 119, 123, 127, 140, 144, 146, 147, 155, 157, 186, 190, 196
 1842 strike wave, 162-3, 165-6, 173, 181
 miners, 61, 171, 190
 see also Teesside and specific towns and cities
Yorkshire Trades' Union, 119, 121, 123, 124, 138, *see also* Leeds Clothiers' Union

Also available from
Breviary Stuff Publications

Ralph Anstis, Warren James and the Dean Forest Riots, *The Disturbances of 1831*
£14.00 • 242pp *paperback* • 191x235mm • ISBN 978-0-9564827-7-8

The full story of the riots in the Forest of Dean in 1831, and how they were suppressed, is told here for the first time. Dominating the story is the enigmatic character of Warren James, the self-educated free miner who led the foresters in their attempt to stave off their increasing poverty and unemployment, and to protect their traditional way life from the threats of advancing industrial change.

John E. Archer, 'By a Flash and a Scare', *Arson, Animal Maiming, and Poaching in East Anglia 1815-1870*
£12.00 • 208pp *paperback* • 191x235mm • ISBN 978-0-9564827-1-6

'By a Flash and a Scare' illuminates the darker side of rural life in the nineteenth century. Flashpoints such as the Swing riots, Tolpuddle, and the New Poor Law riots have long attracted the attention of historians, but here John E. Archer focuses on the persistent war waged in the countryside during the 1800s, analysing the prevailing climate of unrest, discontent, and desperation.

Bob Bushaway, By Rite, *Custom, Ceremony and Community in England 1700-1880*
£14.00 • 206pp *paperback* • 191x235mm • ISBN 978-0-9564827-6-1

Bringing together a wealth of research, this book explores the view that rural folk practices were a mechanism of social cohesion, and social disruption. Through them the interdependence of the rural working-class and the gentry was affirmed, and infringements of the rights of the poor resisted, sometimes aggressively.

Malcolm Chase, The People's Farm, *English Radical Agrarianism 1775-1840*
£12.00 • 212pp *paperback* • 152x229mm • ISBN 978-0-9564827-5-4

This book traces the development of agrarian ideas from the 1770s through to Chartism, and seeks to explain why, in an era of industrialization and urban growth, land remained one of the major issues in popular politics. Malcolm Chase considers the relationship between 'land consciousness' and early socialism; attempts to create alternative communities; and contemporary perceptions of nature and the environment. *The People's Farm* also provides the most extensive study to date of Thomas Spence, and his followers the Spenceans.

Nigel Costley, West Country Rebels
£35.00 • 220pp *full colour illustrated paperback* • 216x216mm • ISBN 978-0-9570005-4-4

The West Country was famous for its wool and cloth but the battles by textile workers is less well known. For generations communities around the South West organised and engaged in riot and uprising, for food, for access, for fair tax and to be heard in a society that denied most people the vote. Women were at the centre of many of these disputes and their battle with poverty and inequality is featured along with West Country women who challenged those that kept them out and held them back.
Trade unionism has many a West Country story to tell, from the Tolpuddle Martyrs in Dorset, the longest strike in Plymouth, the great china clay strike of 1913, 'Black Friday' in Bristol and the battle for rights at GCHQ in Cheltenham.
This book features these struggles along with the characters who defied convention and helped organise around dangerous ideas of freedom, equality and justice.

Barry Reay, The Last Rising of the Agricultural Labourers, *Rural Life and Protest in Nineteenth-Century England*
£12.00 • 192pp *paperback* • 191x235mm • ISBN 978-0-9564827-2-3

The Hernhill Rising of 1838 was the last battle fought on English soil, the last revolt against the New Poor Law, and England's last millenarian rising. The bloody 'Battle of Bosenden Wood', fought in a corner of rural Kent, was the culmination of a revolt led by the self-styled 'Sir William Courtenay'. It was also, despite the greater fame of the 1830 Swing Riots, the last rising of the agricultural labourers.

Buchanan Sharp, In Contempt of All Authority, *Rural Artisans and Riot in the West of England, 1586-1660*
£12.00 • 204pp *paperback* • 191x235mm • ISBN 978-0-9564827-0-9

Two of the most common types of popular disorders in late Tudor and early Stuart England were the food riots and the anti-enclosure riots in royal forests. Of particular interest are the forest riots known collectively as the Western Rising of 1626-1632, and the lesser known disorders in the Western forests which took place during the English Civil War. The central aims of this volume are to establish the social status of the people who engaged in those riots and to determine the social and economic conditions which produced the disorders.

Also available from
Breviary Stuff Publications

Dorothy Thompson, The Chartists, *Popular Politics in the Industrial Revolution*
paperback • 191x235mm • ISBN 978-0-9570005-3-7

The Chartists is a major contribution to our understanding not just of Chartism but of the whole experience of working-class people in mid-nineteenth century Britain. The book looks at who the Chartists were, what they hoped for from the political power they strove to gain, and why so many of them felt driven toward the use of physical force. It also studies the reactions of the middle and upper classes and the ways in which the two sides — radical and establishment — influenced each other's positions.

E. P. Thompson, Whigs and Hunters, *The Origin of the Black Act*
paperback • 191x235mm • ISBN 978-0-9570005-2-0

With *Whigs and Hunters*, the author of *The Making of the English Working Class*, E. P. Thompson plunged into the murky waters of the early eighteenth century to chart the violently conflicting currents that boiled beneath the apparent calm of the time. The subject is the Black Act, a law of unprecedented savagery passed by Parliament in 1723 to deal with 'wicked and evil-disposed men going armed in disguise'. These men were pillaging the royal forest of deer, conducting a running battle against the forest officers with blackmail, threats and violence.

David Walsh, Making Angels in Marble, *The Conservatives, the Early Industrial Working Class and Attempts at Political Incorporation*
£15.00 • 268pp *paperback* • 191x235mm • ISBN 978-0-9570005-0-6

In the first elections called under the terms of the 1832 Reform Act the Tory party appeared doomed. They had recorded their worst set of results in living memory and were organizationally in disarray as well, importantly, seemingly completely out of touch with the current political mood. During the intense pressure brought to bear by the supporters of political reform was the use of "pressure from without" and in this tactic the industrial working class were highly visible. Calls for political reform had been growing since the 1760s and given fresh impetus with the revolutions in America and France respectively. The old Tory party had been resistant to all but the most glaring corruption and abuse under the pre-Reform system, not least to the idea of extending the electoral franchise to the 'swineish multitude', as Edmund Burke notoriously described the working class. Yet within five years after the passing of reform the Conservatives — the natural heirs to the old Tory party — were attempting to politically incorporate sections of the working class into their ranks. This book examines how this process of making these 'Angels in Marble', to use Disraeli's phrase from a later era, took shape in the 1830s. It focuses on how a section of the industrial working class became the target of organizational inclusion into Peelite Conservatism and ultimately into the British party political system.

Roger Wells, Insurrection, *The British Experience 1795-1803*
£17.50 • 364pp *paperback* • 191x235mm • ISBN 978-0-9564827-3-0

On the 16 November 1802 a posse of Bow Street Runners raided the Oakley Arms, a working class pub in Lambeth, on the orders of the Home Office. Over thirty men were arrested, among them, and the only one of any social rank, Colonel Edward Marcus Despard. Despard and twelve of his associates were subsequently tried for high treason before a Special Commission, and Despard and six others were executed on 21 February 1803. It was alleged that they had planned to kill the King, seize London and overturn the government and constitution.

Roger Wells, Wretched Faces, *Famine in Wartime England 1793-1801*
£18.00 • 412pp *paperback* • 191x235mm • ISBN 978-0-9564827-4-7

"The history of riots reaches its full maturity when riots break out of monographic case studies to be incorporated into full histories. Roger Wells includes riot as one dimension of his rich attempt to comprehend the whole range of responses of British society to the famines of 1794-96 and 1799-1801. These famines *dramatically revealed the fragile equilibrium underpinning national subsistence*, and its propensity to collapse. Wells explains how and why the archaic structure of state and society in Britain did just manage not to collapse."

www.ingramcontent.com/pod-product-compliance
Lightning Source LLC
Chambersburg PA
CBHW080223170426
43192CB00015B/2733